the Hypersexuality *of* Race

celine parreñas shimizu

DUKE UNIVERSITY PRESS   Durham and London   2007

the Hypersexuality *of* Race

performing Asian/American women on screen and scene

Library of Congress Cataloging-in-Publication Data

Shimizu, Celine Parreñas.

The hypersexuality of race : performing Asian/American
women on screen and scene / Celine Parreñas Shimizu.

p. cm.

Includes bibliographical references and index.

ISBN 978-0-8223-4012-6 (cloth : alk. paper)

ISBN 978-0-8223-4033-1 (pbk. : alk. paper)

1. Asians in motion pictures. 2. Women in motion
pictures. 3. Asian American women in motion pictures.
4. Erotic films—History and criticism.

I. Title.

PN1995.9.A78S55 2007

791.43′6522—dc22   2006102426

for DAN PARREÑAS SHIMIZU *with passion*

CONTENTS

ACKNOWLEDGMENTS

This book attempts to honor the work of many women of color whose experiences of race, gender, and sexual subjection led to the stories, images, and analyses that sustain and fuel me. Thank you to the filmmakers, actors, and writers for crafting your voices in order to reach others. You provide myriad ways of better understanding each of us and the world in which we wrestle with power, pain, pleasure, and the struggles of everyday life. I am grateful to Helen Lee, Grace Lee, Machiko Saito, Veena Cabreros-Sud, Margaret Cho, Tracy Quan, Evelyn Lau, Hyun Mi Oh, Asia Carrera, Annabel Chong, and others whose presence makes possible this work.

Profound thanks to Jerry Miller, who read the manuscript closely over the years and pushed me to imagine the possibilities, and to Rhacel Parreñas, who continually offered important responses, suggestions, and support. Very special thanks to Helen Lee, Bakirathi Mani, and Viet Nguyen for responding to the entire manuscript with great insight. For reading parts of the manuscript and offering advice, I most appreciate Sucheng Chan, Juliana Chang, Kelly Coogan, Jon Cruz, Nicole Fleetwood, Estelle Freedman, Shelley Lee, Kathleen McHugh, Chon Noriega, Eve Oishi, Louisa Schein, and Lok Siu.

My advisors, colleagues, and the staff members at Stanford University's Program in Modern Thought and Literature really helped me and worked with me when I first conceptualized this project. Members of my dissertation committee provided great mentorship. Harry Elam encouraged me to imagine this work and helped me to navigate the literatures I needed to mobilize, from performance theory to psychoanalysis. Purnima Mankekar grounded my race and sexuality research in the method of ethnography and the discourse of transnational popular culture, and always reminded me of the stakes, especially during my most difficult chapters. Linda Williams helped me to think through sexuality and subjection in cinema and to practice the serious and careful study of pornography. David Palumbo-Liu paid attention to the development of my scholarship as a filmmaker entering the academy. He guided me as I crafted the central ideas organizing my study. His unflagging confidence truly enabled me to bring together discourses that may seem unmatched in order to generate productive and unexpected findings. I am also indebted to other faculty members with whom I worked, including Judith Butler, Estelle Freedman, Janet Halley, Claire Fox, Valentin Mudimbe, Michael Thompson, Anthony Antonio, Rudy Busto, Yvonne Yarbrough Bejarano, Dina Al-Kassim, Gordon Chang, Elaine H. Kim, Trinh T. Minh-ha, and Sylvia Yanagisako. They shared an incredible wealth of ideas in ways that truly benefited me. The Stanford Humanities Center's Race and Sexualities Workshop and the Asian Americas Workshop provided good intellectual communities for thinking about vexing issues. Cindy Ng, Rick Yuen, Monica Moore, and Jan Hafner provided a great deal of support. A strong intellectual community sustained me in graduate school: Lisa Arellano, Falu Bakrania, Magdalena Barrera, Yael Ben-Zvi, Raul Coronado, Manishita Dass, Nicole Fleetwood, Vida Mia Garcia, Mishuana Goeman, Shona Jackson, Rachael Joo, Pauline Lee, Shelley Lee, Bakirathi Mani, Patricia Pender, Miriam Ticktin, Jennifer Chan Tiberghien, and Jacqueline Wigfall.

I thank my colleagues, students, and the staff members in the Department of Asian American Studies as well as the Department of Film and the Program in Women's Studies at the University of California, Santa Barbara. For providing the space to enable the completion of this manuscript, I thank my colleagues Jon Cruz, Douglas Daniels, Diane Fujino, James K. Lee, erin Ninh, John S. W. Park, Hung Thai, and Xiaojian Zhao in the Department of Asian American Studies at UCSB. For intellectual camaraderie, thanks to my colleagues at UCSB including Paul Amar, Kum-Kum Bhavnani, Jacqueline Bobo, Eileen Boris, Sucheng Chan, Anna Everett, Sarah Fenstermaker, Michael Gurven, Carlos Gutierrez Jones, Barbara Herr Harthorn, Shirley Lim, Maria Herrera Sobek, Mireille Miller-Young, Claudine Michel, Melvin Oliver, Lisa Parks, Constance Penley, Horacio Roque Ramirez, Leila Rupp, Beth Schneider, Chela Sandoval, and Janet Walker. Arlene Phillips, Venus Nasri, Elizabeth Guerrero, Blanca Nuila, as well as Kathryn Carnahan, Lou Anne Lockwood, Sharon Hoshida, Judy Guillermo-Newton, Teja Ream, George Michaels, Ray Tracy, Anita David, Robin McCloud, Todd Gillespie, and Shirley Ronkowski extended their support.

For their conversation, I thank Gilberto Blasini, Dawn Suggs, Anne Keala Kelly, Russell Leong, Pablo Mitchell, L. Katherine Frank, L. S. Kim, Yeidy Rivero, Peter X. Feng, Diane Tober, and the members of the Queer Theory Workshop at UCSB. I appreciate Stephen Hong Sohn, Sharon Doetsh-Kidder, and other graduate students with whom I enjoy good conversation. I am immensely thankful to the women with whom I grow old in this profession: Tania Israel, Stephanie LeMenager, Miriam Metzger, and Laury Oaks.

My research assistants, Christian Reyes, Chrissy Lau, Deborah Gin, and Sharon Lee Bocalig, helped me to complete all the different aspects of production required by this book.

This work would not be possible without the support of the following institutions and the very important people there. The Social Science Research Council Sexuality Research Program, with funds from the Ford Foundation, provided generous research funding. I am grateful to its visionary director, Dr. Diane Di Mauro. The Institute for Research on Women and Gender at Stanford provided space and a wonderful community. The Race and Independent Media Group convened by Chon Noriega and Eve Oishi at the University of California, Los Angeles, links me to a great intellectual community. The Asian American Activities Center at Stanford awarded and affirmed this work. The University of California, Santa Barbara Regents' Humanities and the Regents' Junior Faculty Fellowships, the Academic Senate Committee on Research, the Interdisciplinary Humanities Center, and the Institute for Social, Behavioral, and Economic Research provided much needed funding.

Immense thanks go to Martha Harsanyi, Helen Lee, Grace Lee, Luzviminda Lor, J. Elaine Marcos, Edmund Nalzaro, and Machiko Saito for their interviews. Accolades go to the staff at the Kinsey Institute for Sex Research, especially Liana Zhou and Shawn Wilson; to the librarian Gary Colemenar at UCSB; and to the librarian Josie L. Walters-Johnson of the Motion Picture Collection at the Library of Congress; you deserve a long and strong thanks.

Theatre Journal and *Yale Journal of Law and Feminism* previously published different versions of chapters 2 and 5. Thank you to the editors and readers, and especially to Monica Bell and Sarah Bishop for their editorial efforts.

I enjoyed presenting parts of this work at Arizona State University, Cornell University, Dartmouth College, Emory University, Indiana University, the Johns Hopkins University, Pitzer College, the University of California, Berkeley, UCLA, UCSB, the University of California, Santa Cruz, the University of Maryland, the University of Texas, Austin, Wheaton College, Rutgers University, Stanford University, and Yale University Law School. Thank you to the audiences at these sessions, as well as those at *Screen*, the American Anthropology Association, the American Literature Association, the Association for Asian American Studies, Crossroads in Cultural Studies, LatCrit IV, the Society for Cinema and Media Studies, and the World Congress on Sexology for their responses. Thank you very much to the various organizers for inviting me to share my ideas, especially Alex Juhasz, Elsa Barkley Brown, Suzanna Walters, Oi Ying Pang and the East Asian Studies Journal at JHU, Rudy Busto, Mia Carter, David Palumbo-Liu, Kum-Kum Bhavnani, Anthony Ocampo, Eve Oishi, Chon Noriega, Linda Williams, Constance Penley, John W. I. Lee, the Yale Journal of Law and Feminism, and the Women's Sexuality course at UC-Berkeley.

As an editor, Ken Wissoker held my hand throughout the process, and I am honored by his commitment to making this book find its best shape. The anonymous readers helped me to make this book better. Anitra Grisales and Katharine Baker very graciously helped with the production process. Sharlette Visaya carefully proofread earlier versions and the talented writer-filmmaker Cynthia Liu copyedited earlier versions of this manuscript.

I am deeply appreciative of my family. Love for my sisters Rhacel, Rhanee, Cerissa, Juno, Aari, and Mahal, and for my nieces Bea and Zoe inspires these pages. My parents and brother Rolf mark these pages too. The entire Shimizu family, the Risks and McCobbs, genuinely expressed their interest in my work. Paula Foscarini and Ster Vogel helped my family care for our sons when this work called me away.

My sons, Bayan and Lakas Parreñas Shimizu, my home and my strength, form the main addictions of my life. I look forward to our conversations about the issues I explore in this book. Across the golden hills of the Bay Area, from Berkeley, San Francisco, and Silicon Valley to the trails and beaches of our home in Santa Barbara, I whispered these pages to my husband, Dan Parreñas Shimizu, at all hours of our shared lives. I wholeheartedly dedicate this book to him, all the years of its making, tied together with ropes made of my hopes, heart, and spirit.

1 ❖

THE HYPERSEXUALITY OF

ASIAN/AMERICAN WOMEN ❖ Toward a Politically

Productive Perversity on Screen and Scene

I am seventeen and riding the bus home alone at night. At first in whispers, the man across from me insists that we have met in Manila, then
more brazenly, in Angeles or Olongapo, where he presumed that I had
shot ping-pong balls from my vagina. The very public hailing bewilders,
shocks, freezes, confuses, and confounds me. Foremost was my response:
that is not me! From that visceral moment of misrecognition came my
desire to understand what had transpired in that encounter. Years later,
the ability to name this stranger's interpellation of both Asian and Asian
American women as hypersexual beings was not enough. I now seek to
retool the stranger's lens of perverse sexuality so that it can be a more
productive optic, acknowledging how Asian/American women are seen by
others and allowing them to see themselves anew—especially when desiring sexual perversity and shamelessly owning the pleasure and pain that
comes from sexual representations of race.

I love sexy Asian women gyrating in bikinis on stage in *Miss Saigon*
(1989), prancing across ornate Oriental sets in *The Thief of Bagdad* (1924),
and singing about forsaken love in the melodrama *Madame Butterfly*
(1904). Encountering the gorgeous Nancy Kwan late at night on cable TV,

I am immediately dancing on the sofa, hungrily consuming the sight of her as she sashays and commands the gaze of all kinds of men in popular movies dismissed for their racism and sexism.[1] I lick my smiling lips while watching Lucy Liu kicking white male ass in films such as *Payback* (1999). As the dominatrix Pearl in leather ass-less chaps, she thrills to beating up her white male lover, who slaps her back with equal opportunity force. Clad in black in *Charlie's Angels* (2000), she wields chains and twists in mid-air to kick Crispin Glover. In a short cheong-sam and with chopsticks in her hair, she is a masseuse walking on Tim Curry's back before "knocking him unconscious" with a small foot on his neck. I love Asian women porn stars delivering silly lines in broken English while performing in dragon lady fingernails, long black wigs, and garish yellowface makeup that exaggerates slanted eyes. The Southeast Asian women prostitutes talking about transactions with their johns in *The Good Woman of Bangkok* (1991) preoccupy me. From between the fingers covering my eyes, I keep looking at the prostitutes performing orgasms in the pornographic tapes *101 Asian Debutantes* (1995–98). When watching films by other Asian American women filmmakers, I embrace the whorish, the bad, and the dangerous. I love the urban Asian/American woman wearing short shorts, combat boots, and red lipstick strutting the brown streets of Los Angeles, fucking around on rooftops with an illegal immigrant, and fleeing her proper marriage in Hyun Mi Oh's *La Señorita Lee* (1995), the sexually available Asian women who have easy sex (for big and small reasons) with men of color they just meet in Helen Lee's numerous films, and gender/race-ambiguous women in fetish wear who masturbate and perform with dildos in Machiko Saito's experimental movies. In my own short films, I am obsessed with fucking and other sex acts to illustrate the dynamics of power, desire, and colonial history regarding Asian/American women. With intense pleasure, I direct a character to offer herself up like dessert in *Mahal Means Love and Expensive* (1993), name my characters various versions of the Tagalog word for vagina in *Her Uprooting Plants Her* (1995), and shoot numerous vigorous interracial sex scenes in *Super Flip* (1997).

My enjoyment in consuming and composing representations of Asian/American women's sexuality and power may seem inappropriate and improper to good racial and feminist politics. Complicated questions arise regarding the political nature of such pleasure: What is the relationship between history and representation? What is the role of fantasy and the psychic life of images in formulating our understanding of their power?

How do images of the suffering, suicidal Asian woman complement colonial projects in the encounter between Europe, the United States, and Asia across the twentieth century? How do hypersexual women's representations as dragon lady, prostitute with a heart of gold, and dominatrix unify differing eras of the yellow peril in the first half of the twentieth century and the model minority in the last half? How does the production of the desirable and desiring Asian woman mesh with campaigns to sell East Asian and Southeast Asian prostitution to white male sex tourists in the case of *The World of Suzie Wong* (1960) and contemporary professional-amateur pornography shot in the Philippines, Thailand, and Korea today? Does *Flower Drum Song* (1961) ultimately present Asian Americans, with Asian women as traditional gender objects, within a model minority framework that counters the emergence of a militant black power movement? Doesn't Lucy Liu's contemporary image ultimately belong to a tradition of imperialist images that commodify, objectify, and fetishize the bodies of Asian women? Are performances of Asian/American women porn stars as well as the production of sexually explicit images by Asian American women filmmakers dangerous products of false consciousness? Why am I obsessed with the sexualities of Asian/American women on screen and in their relationship to the scenes of everyday life?

My intense pleasures coexist with a terrible pain regarding racialized hypersexuality. Are we to relegate to the margins bodily pleasures generated from race, sex, and representation—such as my embrace of images of the dragon lady, the prostitute with a heart of gold, the dominatrix, the slut, the whore, and easy Asian girls? Similarly, do we repress the pain of sexual interpellation that we encounter on the streets when misrecognized as a fantasy image—slut, whore, easy Asian girl? How come I feel comfortable only in porn shops run by Asians? Because I am an Asian American woman, are the Asian owners truly more able to disconnect me from the material I buy? How do we reconcile the guilt that haunts our enjoyment of sexual performances with our admiration of the celebration of sexuality in the performances of, say, Nancy Kwan and Lucy Liu, as well as in the dazzling technical and narrative innovations in the work of such independent Asian/American filmmakers as Veena Cabreros-Sud, Grace Lee, Helen Lee, Hyun Mi Oh, and Machiko Saito? Can porn about Asian/American women produce political knowledge or can visual pleasures, especially from "bad object" representations such as whorish Asian women, truly contribute to anti-racist politics?

To consider my pleasurable reaction as excessive to good politics would ultimately be an insufficient response to the power of representation and the rich experiences of racialized sexuality. When encountering the litany of dragon lady, the lotus blossom, the prostitute with a heart of gold, the little brown fucking machine powered by rice, the dominatrix, and the whore, a powerful misrecognition transpires for Asian women off screen. Asian/American women in the scene of viewing are subjected to the simultaneous elation, seduction, and horror of "Is that me/not me? I adore it but it tortures me. Stop looking, oh no, keep looking! Give me more! How do I describe feeling pain/hate and pleasure/love at the very same time?" It is an extremely painful and intensely pleasurable contradictory experience of viewing, producing, and criticism. To insist on pleasure comes into confrontation with the painful aspects of such representations. As such, these experiences of viewing dramatize the political and economic inequalities not only of representation but of the social experiences of Asian/American women.

So *The Hypersexuality of Race* ultimately emerges from my own "bad subjectivity": as a viewer drawing pleasure from sexualized images of Asian women while juggling its injuries, harms, and injustices, and as an Asian American feminist filmmaker dramatizing, narrating, and experimenting with the role of sexuality and eroticism in the race and cinema experience, especially as that sexuality and eroticism enable a more autonomous subject formation for Asian women.[2] For example, in my latest video work, *The Fact of Asian Women* (2002/2004), I interrogate how perverse sexuality unifies the representations of Asian American femme fatales in Hollywood from the 1920s to the present. Anna May Wong, Nancy Kwan, and Lucy Liu each represent various modes of excessive sexuality as the dragon lady, the prostitute with a heart of gold, and the dominatrix. The perversity unifying their representations, which are palpably different from normal sexuality usually embodied by a white woman, can be interpreted variously: as strength, diversity, or pathology. By examining the sexual lighting, male gaze, and their racialized performances, I locate their performances historically—somewhere between the wound of sexual racialization and the remedy of pleasure in visual and sexual representations of race.

Almost twenty years since the kernel of this project was planted on that Berkeley bus, what is clear like never before is the ease with which we can resort to striving for a kind of normativity in the face of hypersexual ascription. To panic about being identified within perversity can too easily lead us to strive toward self-restricting sexual normalcy or the impossible constraints of sexual purity. If we limit understanding of racial sexuality within good or bad, abnormal and normal, or right and wrong we may also limit how to enjoy, appreciate, and more fully understand our own sexuality as Asian/American women. We can too easily confine the vast sea of experience between the polarities of bad/painful and good/pleasurable that frame racialized sexuality.

The fear of sexual perversity, pleasure, and badness can choke the voicing of complex experiences of sexuality and curb the beauty emergent from the chronicles of our sexual histories and the survival of sexual subjection.[3] Sexuality—thrilling, compelling, and mysterious—organizes my expression as a film and performance scholar and producer. The voices and visions of Asian American women performers, writers, and critics representing themselves as hypersexual beings—as overdetermined by sex and speaking through sex—show that I am not alone in my obsession with the bottomless pit of wonder that is sexuality. They insist upon the ambiguity and ultimate unknowability of race, sexuality, and representation, especially in reinscribing the perverse sexuality traditionally ascribed to Asian/American women, and they do so using tremendously beautiful and innovative forms. I aim to keep open the complexity of images as well as the experience of their production and consumption in order to formulate a theory of race-positive sexuality that takes seriously the challenge of engaging issues of power in defining race, sexuality, and representation in terms of Asian/American feminist women's practices, politics, and priorities.

The Hypersexuality of Race takes up the challenge offered by the work of Asian/American actresses, filmmakers, performers, and critics at the site of industry blockbusters and independent stage and screen, including Broadway, Hollywood, and a hundred years of pornography and video art. Within these sites, Asian/American actresses, spectators, performers, filmmakers, and critics present complex, rich, and nuanced representations of sexual desire, pleasure, and pain. In paying attention to the desire for identities that centrally pivot on sexuality, I aim to show how hypersexuality, performed and consumed pleasurably as well as painfully, expresses yearning for better representations and realities for those marginalized by race and gender. Instances of hypersexuality alert us to limited definitions of sexuality, race, and representation and therefore are crucibles for the creative formations of subjectivity. Thus, representations of racialized sexuality offer a tremendously political critique in rewriting the utility of "moving image" cultures to race and sex politics.

This first chapter provides the theoretical underpinnings of the book. I begin with the work of Asian American actresses, filmmakers, writers, and performance artists, as well as critics, who powerfully claim the perversity attributed to their sexuality as feminist, anti-racist, and sex-positive critique. They provide new priorities of race, sex, and representation as told with new grammar and vocabularies. By developing critical concepts that account for the ultimately paradoxical experiences of race, sex, and representation, I question the limited deployments of interpretive tools that do not do justice to the engagements of power and resistance within the production and consumption of representations of racialized sexuality. My description of the conundrum of race/sex/representation leads to my introduction of terms centrally important to my project—Asian/American, the bind of representation, the bondage of hypersexuality, insisting on the unknowable quality of social experience and the unreliability of representation, performing politically productive perversity, and race-positive sexuality.

Through my study of Asian/American women's authorship, spectatorship, and interpretation, I define hypersexuality in representation as a form of bondage that ties the subjectivity of Asian/American women. The legacy of hypersexuality is a vibrant combination of fantasy and reality charging the fashioning of the self that moralism, or the power of puritanical discourse, and scopophilia, or the love of looking, cannot accommodate, opening the door to my argument that pleasure and fantasy from the sexualization of race must be part of race politics. When we evaluate the embrace of hypersexuality, what I call productive perversity or the critique of the power of normalcy, especially in limiting definitions of sexuality, we find efforts to make sense of one's punishment and disciplining as Asian American women hypersexualized in representation. By recasting sexuality and visuality in Asian American women's terms, or race-positive sexuality, the work aims to center the social experiences not only of Asian/American women but sexual minorities in history, culture, and representation. Descriptions of each chapter begin to show how the work of Asian/American feminist cultural producers redefine not only the relationship between race, sexuality, and representation, but our very notions of power, pleasure, pain, and the political.

I never saw Asian people on television or in movies, so my dreams were some-what limited. I would dream [voice changing to a high-pitched girly squeal] "Maybe someday I can be an extra on *MASH*." "Maybe someday I could play Arnold's girlfriend on *Happy Days*." "Maybe I could play a hooker in some-thing." I'd be looking in the mirror, "Sucky fucky two dolla! Me love you long time!"—Margaret Cho, "My Dreams Were Limited," *Notorious C.H.O.* (2002)

In *Revolution* (2004), the popular comedian Margaret Cho lists roles typi-cally available for Asian/American women on screen: manicurist, geisha, opium smoker, chicken-wielding peasant, Korean store owner, and Bond girl. In her one-woman concert film, *Notorious C.H.O.* (2002), Cho delivers the punch line "Sucky fucky two dolla! Me love you long time!"—deriding the popular expletives describing Asian women, and distorting the line with contortions of her face, body, and voice. In this "mirror" scene sever-ing fantasies of Asian women with "real" Asian women, she identifies the perils of identification with popular cultural representations. To aspire to such derivative roles is a dead-end deal Cho not only refuses but defies in contemporary performances that assert a more complex world of poly-morphous perversity—critical of normative race, gender, sexual, and class identity. That is, she defies the phantasmic screen of Asian female sexuality, a tradition long established in the late nineteenth century and preceding her on stage from the ghostly presence of *Madame Chrysanthemum* (1887), to *Madame Butterfly*, to the contemporary presence of Lucy Liu's domi-natrix.[4] In the face of such a legacy, Cho demands a redefinition of ra-cialized sexuality in representation entirely, *refusing to settle for merely any visibility*. She banishes the specter of the small, silent, servile heterosexual Asian femininity ascribed as "natural" for Asian women with a large, brash, and shameless embrace of hypersexuality—as irrepressibly perverse, car-nal, pleasure-seeking, traumatized, different, and uncontainably queer.[5] Margaret Cho's performance resonates loudly in the "living images" al-luded to by the screenwriter Veena Cabreros-Sud, who describes the pro-cess as engaging Asian/American women both on scene and screen.

I am an animal who eats, sleeps, fucks, and fights voraciously—I assume a "good" woman does it gently and in missionary position only. To deny our instinct for self-protection is to slam the door on all desires, to create a lustless, cookie-baking, June Cleaver in drag. A combo Stepford Wife/Virgin Mary. The polite, "good" woman who goes *eek* at the mousies. In reality, we seem more like exhausted, overworked, protective, hungry women and mothers who cling to our children longer than they would like and would willingly, even eagerly, protect them and ourselves with a sledgehammer.[6]

Sud describes a relationship of bondage to "moving images" in U.S. popular culture that organizes the scenes of her everyday life. Expanding notions of femininity to include aggression and strength, she blurs boundaries of sex and gender. In fact, her award-winning short film *Stretchmark* (1996) dramatizes the disciplining gaze upon her brown female single mother's body. As she rides the train and plays with her son, we are made aware of the persistence of the collective disapproval she imagines surrounds her. She describes the assault she feels in intensely physical terms. The film creates an equally physical vocabulary of self-affirmation as she bathes her naked body in dark rose petals and plays energetically with her young son among a cascading flock of birds. Sud is among many Asian/American feminist performers who speak in sexual terms in order to dissect and deliver a more complex picture of Asian/American female hypersexuality. They present spirited critiques of popular scripts for Asian American women through sexual self-authorships in literature, performance, and film that do not shy away from belligerence and aggression that are simultaneously gorgeous and loving.

This highly charged relationship with sexuality is presented in the work of the writer, prostitutes' rights activist, and ex-prostitute Tracy Quan, who emphasizes a non-moralistic framing of Asian/American female sexuality. In *Diary of a Manhattan Call Girl* (2001), she demystifies the sexuality of girlhood: "By the time I started baby-sitting, I was also planning to be a hooker," says the character Nancy Chan. With this frank admission, Quan poses a deliberate response to what she considers a conservative feminist truism that girls do not aspire to be prostitutes.[7] In an essay introducing glamorous photos of Asian sex workers by the Asian American photographer Reagan Louie in *Orientalia* (2003), Quan describes the pleasures of feminine sexuality and beauty as part of the business of prostitution. Refusing to accept the diagnoses that Asian women are pre-feminist havens for western men, she criticizes white feminists for their xenophobia in depriving Asian women prostitutes of complexity, agency, and pleasure. Quan's voice uniquely indicts what she characterizes as the self-centeredness of white feminists in framing the lives of third world women. She does so with a brashness that rejects any minority positioning.[8] Quan's perspectives regarding prostitution and racialized sexuality echo the perspectives of sex work articulated by third world feminist women who critique the lack of agency in frameworks such as sexual slavery.[9]

The same de-privileging of moralistic judgment demonstrated by Tracy Quan allows the former prostitute Evelyn Lau to describe the tremendous humanity found within her intimate relations with johns. In the television movie *The Diary of Evelyn Lau* (1994), Sandra Oh plays a young Asian female model minority gone awry. As a fourteen-year-old, the character Evelyn Lau runs away from a mother who obsesses about her daughter's body. She quickly unravels upon fleeing home, enduring rape by the man who provides a "safe-house" for her. She looks for safety, love, and companionship and instead meets an endless slew of men who hail her sexually. One requires sex after providing her with pizza; he pleads with her gently, offers her drugs, and, as soon as he gets sex, hurries her out and closes the door in her face. Confused and puzzled, she makes sense of her life by writing wherever she may be: huddled in dirty blankets under tunnels, hunched over her bed in group homes, or walking the city streets. With a controlling lover, a drug-dealer, she becomes addicted to drugs and emerges in public barely dressed. One day, barely able to walk in tattered short shorts, she encounters her mother and initiates a senseless and inarticulate confrontation. When meeting her court-appointed therapist, she simply forgets to wear anything over her fishnet stockings. In the face of her trials, the character ultimately accepts sexual transactions as a young prostitute as part of her self-formation. She describes coming to this perspective through a hitchhiking encounter with an older man, a former runaway street kid as well, who picks her up after a series of men and women take advantage of her. The hitchhiking scene is pivotal in her understanding of paid sex as a commodity to exchange rather than a vessel invested with one's self-worth. Like Michel Foucault, Lau argues that one's truth is not necessarily located in sex.[10] The former prostitute and heroin addict she encounters encapsulates the protocol for surviving on the street for teen runaways like herself: "Sex is only part of life. I never hated any of the johns who screwed me when I was a kid; they helped me get where I am now. After a while a few of them kept coming back. And then I found that we were spending more time rapping than we were screwing. Then they became people. But they had to be objects first—you can't have it the other way around."[11]

Here, Lau comes to understand sex premised not on the accepted equation that sex is bad or that marginal people are entirely powerless. Rather, they are situated within structural locations that must be accounted for in all of their unwieldy ugliness. The key act is her writing not only to record details of her encounters but to make sense of her experiences. To write about these experiences gives worth to a marginalized subject position frequently dismissed as one without value. To write about sex work, trauma, and sexual consciousness with an accounting of their race and gender implications is to centralize the way in which they organize the experiences of women of color who live in the margins and under the umbrella of the perverse. Furthermore, such an act demystifies "lower" worlds frequently dismissed as unworthy of narration—runaway, prostitute, drug addict. Through incisive, attentive, and detailed analyses of the power dynamics in Lau's relationships, the experiences of people in the margins emerge.

Through their work as Asian American feminist cultural producers, Cho, Cabreros-Sud, Quan, and Lau give voice to a sexualized, racialized, gendered, and classed subject that—no matter how unreliable and unraveled—*1) should occupy a central place in racial discourses, and 2) is deserving of richly nuanced and complex representation.* Simply put, the complex intersections of sexuality in terms of race, gender, class, and diaspora comprising Asian American women's lives warrant full, abundant, and intense representations as argued well in different contexts by Stuart Hall, Michele Wallace, and Isaac Julien.[12] These Asian/American women writers, performers, and filmmakers insist on a corporeal understanding of female subjectivity as historically and structurally situated carnalities, finding voice while innovating filmic, literary, and performance genres. They re-identify sexuality as crucial to their social legibility and self-recognition in terms of forging their freedoms from the bonds of racial, gendered, sexual, and classed classifications.[13] They move beyond self-exotification or diagnoses of damage in performing the hard work of self-acceptance and self-recognition in the face of and through hypersexual representation. Moreover, they imagine new worlds where their lives are central enough to witness and to be recognized as worthy of consideration.

The powerful, explicitly sexual self-representations of Asian American women cultural producers, critics, and spectators is a puzzling formation in Asian American and women of color feminist studies. An outrageous embrace of "bad" or improper womanhood by Asian American cultural producers, critics, and spectators *co-exists with an assessment of injury regarding race and sexuality in representation.* For many, it is extremely difficult to think about embracing explicit representations of racialized hypersexuality beyond repugnance and fear. Asian American feminists Renee Tajima, Lynn Lu, Jessica Hagedorn, and Laura Kang offer various readings of representations of Asian/American women, and in different ways each establishes an understanding of representation as injuriously constitutive. Renee Tajima demands more ordinary representations of Asian women, Lu and Hagedorn advocate for the importance of creative viewing practices in the face of industry inequalities, and Kang suggests that Asian American feminists take care not to reinscribe the powerful way Asian/American women are rendered as Other in spatiotemporal terms and vis-à-vis the power of images to flatten subjectivity.[14] Can injury lead to power?

Various contests constitute our understanding of the intermingling of race, sex, and representation from the danger versus pleasure debates in feminist scholarship and politics to the victim versus agent tensions in African American and ethnic studies scholarship to the efforts to acknowledge women's sexual power, such as histories of prostitution that avoid dichotomous readings.[15] Acknowledging intra-ethnic sexual "transgressions" has been problematic for scholars in these fields. The interpretations of racial and sexual images that deny the ambiguities of representation and sexuality further discipline, police, and demand that Asian/American women become docile subjects who must abhor their own sexual racial carnalities and subjectivities as racial traitorship and false consciousness.

In Grace Lee's *The Grace Lee Project* (2005), interviews with passers-by capture the public expectation for Asian women to be small, petite, quiet, and attractive. Lee's documentary speaks of a social demand placed upon Asian/American women to be docile subjects. Correspondingly, David Marriott's argument in *On Black Men* is a powerful indictment of the role of popular representation and national fantasy in making "demands" upon black men. Marriott's understanding of imagists making demands on viewers registers as a violence black men must live under, similar to the case of Asian/American women who must negotiate such familiarly forceful images. He argues that "there is a demand that black men perform a script—become interchangeable with the uncanny, deeply unsettling, projections of culture. The legacy of that demand on black male identity not only works to sustain a repertoire of relationships between black men, imago and cultural fantasy, but continues to have a distorting, and necessarily violent, effect on how black men learn to see themselves and one another."[16]

Marriott's assessment that images set the expectations for one's subjectivity and one's relations with others resonates with Asian/American women who must confront the hypersexuality organizing their popular representation—whether it is Lucy Liu's character on the popular television show *Ally McBeal*, who causes public turbulence by the very act of saying the word "sex," or the numerous characters of Asian female prostitutes and sex slaves we see in popular media today.[17] As subjects, Asian American women are born into a world where a representational tradition of hypersexuality forms and shapes general consciousness. To be clear, the popular for Asian/American women is infused with a particularly powerful and perverse sexuality in U.S cinema and performance in the twentieth century.[18] Indeed, Asian American women encounter their imagined others as figures central to their self-formations in limiting terms, as described by Tajima, Lu, Hagedorn, and Kang. They and I build upon Marriott to acknowledge how these encounters with imagined others also enable exciting new inscriptions of race, sexuality, and representation.

My discussion of resistance at the site of sexuality, race, and representation raises different concerns, especially regarding how sex works differently in queer and straight scenes of representation and self-formation.[19] What do women lose in valorizing sex that others do not? For example, what does it mean to claim promiscuity in gay contexts versus straight female contexts? How do different gendered and racialized contexts shape sexual acts, behaviors, and choices? I believe that a particular bondage persists for women to live under demands of chastity, demureness, and moralism so that their embrace of sex produces a different force than the valorization of sex for queer publics. While queer sexuality and both queer and heterosexual pornography may occupy a more visible place in society today, we need to pay attention to the multiplicities of sexuality and representation, particularly in terms of patriarchy, heteronormativity, and their work alongside racism.[20] Sex and representation continue to be feared forces in the United States, ever present in cultural approvals and disapprovals of sexual behavior, practices, acts, and identities in the screens of cultural representation and scenes of everyday life.[21] In movies and in life, the racial, gendered, and sexual identities of those you sleep with and love and who become your family continue to be culturally contested, questioned, and challenged. We see this in up-to-the-minute debates about the "proper" gender constitution of marital love in the United States as only between men and women.[22] The link between this debate and the hypersexuality of Asian women presented here is the limited definition of "proper" sexual identities and acts in relation to ideas of belonging not only in the nation but within communities. The stakes are indeed high—the bodies of women, people of color, and sexual minorities signify reproductive futures and new morphologies of the family and American national identity.[23]

This project ultimately queers heterosexual frameworks of race. That is, in centering the notion of perversity as well as what I will describe as the unknowability of social experience and the unreliability of representation, I insist upon a more vulnerable understanding of the process of representing racialized sexuality. In other words, the importance of expanding the normal to include the perverse makes the unknown not only acceptable but human. I now introduce key terms and concepts that ultimately explain why Asian American women who traffic in explicit sexuality practice feminist theories of racialized sexuality and visual culture in the sites of authorship, spectatorship, and criticism. Along the way, I establish the grounds that lead to their use of sexuality as a force that binds and ultimately unleashes their powerful social critique.

ASIAN/AMERICAN WOMEN

Following feminist film criticism, we must remember that Asian women as fantasy figures on screen do not simply correspond to Asian American female viewers, even as they certainly shape perceptions of Asian and Asian American women.[24] A particular conflation of Asian and Asian American women occurs in Hollywood and film industry images wherein Asian American ethnicities stand in for one another. It is a violent homogenization of Asian American women who are lumped together in representation where cultural and other specificities are obscured and eclipsed by hypersexuality.[25] David Palumbo-Liu inserts the slash between Asian and American in order to question how Asian American people persistently occupy questionable status in the United States as Asian or American—and particularly their failure to meet the racial standards of true citizenship as part of a "dynamic, unsettled" process.[26] Laura Hyun Yi Kang introduces the formulation of Asian/American women to account for the distinctions and linkages between Asian and Asian American women in her book *Compositional Subjects* (2002). She identifies the varying groups who are grossly generalized under the reference. Kang uses the term in order to "stress what the contradictory claims made about, by and for Asian/American women might suggest about the instability and inadequacy of those generic delineations of individuality and collectivity."[27] So I use the term Asian/American in order to comment on the frequent conflation of Asian and Asian American at work within representation. Thus, the "intervening slash" in Asian/American identifies the tensions within the unwieldy reference. I aim to use the terms Asian/American, Asian, or American precisely in order to capture how particular representations, fantasies, material conditions, and actual beings amalgamate and divide. Following Palumbo-Liu and Kang, I identify the power of representation to establish knowledge, create vocabularies, and deploy fantasies regarding the identities of Asian American women at different and equally important sites.

To keep the different sexual racializations of Asian/American women at the forefront of our analysis acknowledges how they have different histories and genealogies even as they are bonded by perverse sexuality. Each occurrence of hypersexuality is a different manifestation of power so that each evaluation requires attention to the specificity of the problem's dynamics. In persistently accounting for the diverse racial, sexual, cultural, and historical experiences among Asian American women, such as East Asian versus Southeast Asian versus South Asian, we acknowledge how these trends in representation shift over time but vary across skin color difference, regional context, and other factors. In this project, I insist on this ambiguity of difference not only in the larger deployment of the concepts of race, sex, and representation but throughout each close reading and the experiences of these representations through the methods of ethnography and interview. I do so in order to keep open the possibilities of different representations in the face of homogenized sexuality bonding various Asian/American women. What I find is that while Asian/

American women are not free from interpellation as sexualized and racialized subjects in representation, there are opportunities to redefine our sexuality every time.

Is a particular essentialism required to this project of identifying moral panic and reclaiming the repugnant? Or in other words, does it require an Asian/American woman to make these arguments so as to avoid accusations of racism and sexism? The risk of reinscribing precisely what needs to be contested indeed exists. The demand to pay attention to Asian women's discussion of sexuality is rendered within a kind of traitorship not only to the race but to one's racialized gender. Such a policing and disciplining of Asian/American women's sexual expressions echoes early debates between feminism and nationalism outlined by Elaine H. Kim and King-kok Cheung in Asian American studies discourse as what is precisely at stake in the Frank Chin and Maxine Hong Kingston debates of the 1980s.[28] I emerge from a converse formulation of the problem. I problematize what it means to author, view, and critique as an Asian/American woman in the various sites of my study. My location certainly plays a role in what I see and what I make. The articulation of this viewing and speaking position contributes to what we know about these various objects and subjects. Ultimately, the project of politicizing the perverse argues for the importance of the experience of discomfort in its power to transform our notions of what is normal and what an acceptable form of sexuality is for racialized and gendered subjects. The project defends those in the sexual margins from further stifling their experiences and expressions. It aims to make space for the formation of alternative sexualities, races, genders, and classes. My studies of the social experience of representation aim to contribute to other studies that enable this project, such as political economic analyses not only of industries of expression but of race, class, gender, and sexual subjectivities.

THE BONDAGE OF ASIAN/AMERICAN WOMEN TO HYPERSEXUALITY IN REPRESENTATION

I now introduce the framework of bondage so as to show how Asian/ American women are tied to a tradition of excessive and perverse hypersexuality in representation. While this bondage indicates a particular tie to perverse sexualization in representation, Asian/American women can use it in other self-enabling ways. That is, bondage, or what I term the "bind of representation," describes the experience of viewing, performing, and criticizing hypersexuality as both punitive and pleasurable, as well as political, for Asian/American women. Or, love her or leave her, the hypersexual Asian woman in representation haunts the experiences and perceptions of Asian women across different contexts.

To rework and redefine this bondage of hypersexuality as inseparable from Asian/American women in representation and in history, I build upon the work of Laura Kang, who describes how an epistemic violence occurs against Asian/American women when we collapse images with reality. My argument goes further by asserting that any Asian/American woman who must understand her identity and her possibilities must engage hypersexuality in representation. That is, sexuality imbricates them so that Asian women must always engage it as a force for understanding the self and their relations with others who project hypersexuality upon them. Thus, I argue for how the bondage of hypersexuality and the bind of representation both must be put in service of making the pleasures and traumas of racialized sexuality relevant in our understanding of race, sex, and representation.

In reframing the Asian female as bottom (occupying the traditional role of the passive position in a sexual relation), I reveal a site of possibility in power relations and the veneer of perverse sexuality indicated by that bondage. I prioritize the subjection of Asian/American women and deliver a critique regarding their marginalization as subjects of knowledge. That is, if we were to accept sexuality as unavoidable to discourses of Asian women in representation, then let us blow the doors wide open in terms of recasting how to make that sexuality political. These include making alternative sexualities more available as well as opening up the possibilities for how Asian/American women are constructed through sexuality as a disciplining and objectifying force—as well as its affirming power when put in service of Asian American women.

I return to Margaret Cho, who exemplifies the act of resistance and self-definition in sexual and representational agency. She illustrates how being caught in the throes of pleasure and pain in performing, viewing, and criticizing hypersexual images offers potential for charting viable new subjectivities for raced and gendered subjects. Her intensely sexual performances—the discussion and suggestive performances of lewd acts—including the scatological experience in the car to kissing Anna Nicole Smith to fisting—compel the acceptance of perverse and polymorphous sexuality.

Margaret Cho shows that Asian/American women cannot but live through their racial sexualization; it hails them. Unable to flee easily from race-gender-sex interpellation, she contests the meaning of that hypersexuality and leads us to the possibility of forming a critical new subjectivity and a new aesthetic that is humorous and powerful in its creative counter-racial-sexualization. The framework of bondage and the bind aims to capture the restrictions and constraints limiting Asian/American women's choices, made within aggravated situations in order to open the possibilities of redefining sex, race, and representation in an open-ended fashion, rather than shutting them down. The demand for Asian American women to perform a script can too easily blind us to a more inclusive definition of sexuality and representation that Asian/American women deploy through representations of desire for sexual pleasure and sex work, like the work of Tracy Quan, through sexual trauma and alternative existence, like that of Evelyn Lau, through sexual power and violence, like that of Veena Cabreros-Sud, and through raunchy political lewdness, like that of Margaret Cho. I draw inspiration from prominent Asian American women performers, filmmakers, and actresses for they embody the bind of representation. Hypersexuality for Asian American women is a network of social forces that ground their legibility in culture, as terms for self-recognition and as condition of social marginalization that leads to opportunities for creative self-invention.

THE UNKNOWABILITY OF RACE, SEX, AND REPRESENTATION: MORAL PANIC AND SCOPOPHILIA

Our sexuality is embedded in history; our history is embedded in the sexuality we see on screen. It is important to recall the historical context of sexuality that inscribed the immigration of Asian women into the United States as it significantly informs my exploration of alternative responses to sexuality in Asian American discourses of representation. Figures of Chinese women prostitutes occupied a prominent place in popular culture to the extent that this imagined threat shaped immigration, resulting in the Page Law in 1870, which curbed their population.[29] At the turn of the century, Chinese women prostitutes were routinely harassed on the streets. Japanese women entered the United States as "picture brides" at the beginning of the twentieth century and as "war brides" after World War II.[30] In Filipino American history, a woman was stoned to death for her adultery, which was considered a gender and racial traitorship.[31] Korean women "war brides" arrived in the United States with their American G.I. husbands after the Korean War. Mail-order or pen pal brides from the Philippines are introduced through catalogues today.[32] Mail-order brides are especially vulnerable because their legal status is conditional upon their marriage to a U.S. citizen or permanent resident, regardless of domestic violence.[33] Asian sex workers travel to the United States to become transnational sex workers.[34] The process of racialization includes the sexuality of Asian women as a central subjugating force in ways that can be better reflected in our approaches to representation.

Because of the strong establishment of perverse interiority associated with particular racial visibility, Asian Americanist feminist approaches to the study of hypersexual representation can unconsciously get caught up in an agenda of moralism and propriety if sexuality is not defined more precisely. The repudiation of sexuality in stereotype critique as fueled by moral panic, or the irrational fear regarding how sexual issues challenge the basic moral fiber of societies,[35] is apparent in the binary between the lotus blossom and the dragon lady that exists as the predominant framework in assessing Asian/American women in Western cinema. Such an approach exemplifies how representations of subservience and nonnormative sexuality in representation are continually framed as bad, negative, and ultimately injurious. Such a limited framework of bad versus good applied to a more ambivalent process of representation often leads to the sight of sex as simply resulting from systemic racism that does not capture the dynamic and ever complicated specificity of history.[36]

The attendant moralism galvanized in response to racialized sexuality in representation marginalizes Asian/American women. To panic about sexual, visual, or gendered images reifying Asian/American women is to ignore the importance of questioning how racialized sexuality constitutes subjects and identities. The existing approaches to the study of Asian/American women in representation include defining racialized sexuality within heteronormative standards and repudiating visuality through the method of classifying and thus calcifying images in a form of moralistic-scopophilia or visual paranoia. When these approaches are theorized as injurious in representation, our understanding of the political utility of these images is aggravated by moral panic responses that shut the door down on different kinds of viewing as well as alternative sexual forms and relations that emerge from the experience of both sex and representation.

As such, the lotus blossom and dragon lady dichotomy, as applied to

Asian women in American scenes or on screen, does not capture what we actually see when watching moving or living images, nor the incredible contradictions of pain and pleasure within the images of Asian women on screen, nor the experiences of Asian women off screen in consuming, criticizing, and producing these images. What if we study Asian/American women's representations by centering sexuality as their own, even if that sexuality looks different from what is considered normal and acceptable? What can we draw from pornography in the Southeast Asian sex tourism scene, for example, when the prostitutes writhe in pleasure and directly announce their desires for pleasure in professional-amateur videotapes? What about lesbian sadomasochistic practices in movies created by Asian American feminists?[37]

How do we assess what pleasure and pain look like? How do we register how trauma shapes perception? How do we explain pleasure in watching one's annihilation on stage or screen? Within racialized communities, sexual abuse, rape, and trauma must be accounted for in the gendered experience of race as well as perverse pleasures and enjoyment in sex and in representation.[38] At the same time, the experience of pleasure or ambivalence in representation must remain part of our analyses. For example, to reinsert sexual pleasure in discourses of racial pain *would not only recast hypersexual images of race as unstable figures rather than knowable entities but would also acknowledge how moralism stealthily creeps in to discipline Asian/American women.* Inserting what Michel Foucault has said may help: that sex forms identity and thus expresses new horizons of being that need to be mined for their political possibilities.[39] When moral panic continues to inform our understanding of racialized sexuality in representation, informing theories that privilege ordinary normalcy, we lose the opportunity to reimagine what is missing, unaccounted for, and excluded in the normal—such as perverse practices that criticize the disciplining of women by sexuality.[40]

When we dismiss Asian American women's embrace of sexuality in representation as simply dangerous and immoral we deprive ourselves of the profoundly interesting ways race, sex, performance, and visual culture work together to convey creativity, pleasure, power, and trauma simultaneously. The discussion of sexuality in all of its challenging complexity undoes the secondary and supplementary status of Asian American women. Sexuality, as punishment, discipline, pleasure, and possibility, comprises Asian American women, so its discussion acknowledges them as truly viable subjects of study especially as they introduce alternative realities from the norm. Furthermore, when we tend to run and hide from sex, we do not solve the problem of how the pathology of hypersexual images will haunt and return publicly, privately, and intimately—invading our self-perceptions, defining our most important relations, and our very movements in the world. If the Asian/American woman cannot be imaged outside of sex, her self-formation must occur in terms of redefining sex.

Looking at sex in terms of the quality of unknowability, rather than as a containable entity, is a process of enlarging the imagination, enabling entry into the dialogue of pleasure in our own terms and in our own language. I use the term unknowability to capture the limits of moving image media to represent social experience adequately and to remind us of how media are capable of presenting alternative realities. Let us remember that representations are historically situated attempts to comment on social experience and do not perfectly capture anyone or anything. Moreover, any representational facts are up for debate—while there are indeed certainties in what may occur on screen or stage, the concept of unknowability insists on the ultimate unreliability of representation as a creative process involving living subjects who contribute variously to meaning making as they undergo ever changing understandings of subjectivity, memory, and history-organizing interpretation. In her study of the materiality of film itself, Laura U. Marks describes how video can bring to being what is lost and unsaid, while also failing to do justice to the densities of experience at the level of the senses.[41] She describes filmmaking as the attempt to capture what is gained and lost in social experience. Similarly, Catherine Russell describes the element of unknowability in representations of the Other to comment on what Martin Jay terms "ocular centric discourse in western culture" and Kent Ono has called "ocularcentrism."[42] They describe the dominance of visuality in understanding the world when seeing does not necessarily mean knowing. Similarly, I insist upon keeping open the possibilities raised in works too easily condemned as knowable. I move forward the discourse by acknowledging how Asian American feminist cultural producers engage the taboo or subjects like the whore and druggie who embrace the non-normative perverse. How can we deploy representation so as to imagine new worlds and possibilities for Asian/American women?

To move debates about racialized sexuality in representation away from moralistic scopophilia that sees sexuality, perverse or otherwise, as the demise of racialized women is to complicate the process of viewing as simply an act of violence upon the viewer. We can acknowledge images of Asian women as perversely and pathologically sexual in Western cinema and from there argue that the condemnation of non-normative sexuality and the simplification of the process of viewing a film do not sufficiently capture the political possibilities raised in watching race and sex on screen. The space between bondage and freedom in defining racialized sexuality is vast, ambiguous, and complex in ways we need to sustain as unknowable, or ever mysterious and surprising. To know oneself as unknowable is to remain open to change and the process of self-transformation in both social experience and our engagements with representations.

PERFORMANCE AND POLITICALLY PRODUCTIVE PERVERSITY

Because minority communities can acquiesce to the power and prevalence of dominant perceptions and representations, Richard Fung argues that efforts must be made to truly prioritize one's different experience of representation, especially as it relates to understanding the self.[43] I extend his argument to formulate the notion of performing race and sex against the punishment of Asian American women in representation, as part of a kind of productive perversity. Productive perversity involves identifying with "bad" images, or working to establish a different identity along with established sexual images so as to expand racial agendas beyond the need to establish normalcy and standardization.[44] To engage hypersexuality as a politically productive perversity pays attention to the formulations of sexual and racial identity that critique normative scripts for sexually and racially marginalized subjects.

Ultimately, an important assumption I aim to undermine is that sex and visuality are inherently transgressive in a project that aims to recognize simultaneously the power of disobeying categorical scripts in the performance of identities and the importance of acknowledging the situation of racial sexualization described by Abdul JanMohamad. In his essay on the racial borders of sexuality, JanMohamad describes how Michel Foucault's discussion of the pervasiveness of sexual knowledge does not capture the amplified silences surrounding the sexualities of people of color as exemplified in the case of black sexual slavery in the United States, where the brutal rape of black women was culturally ignored and accepted as a natural part of the system.[45] As such, to render racial critique grim in championing play is too simplistic. But if sex is so bad, how can we talk about both the lives and the representations of girls and women who are shaped by it? Specifically, how do we not discount those within sexually oppressive situations or disregard marginalized lives such as those of prostitutes or third world women sex workers, who are immediately assumed as victimized and powerless or too unwieldy to consider in shaping good racial politics? While acknowledging that sex is not simply good, what if we assume that sex is not entirely bad either and that poor third world women are not powerless in order to expand our knowledge about race, sex, and representation in ways that account for the lives of women? In other words, what if sex can be good and third world women can have power? Such questions can expand and extend our understanding of power and ethics as each specific scene demands.

A key element of understanding politically productive perversity is performance and its role in constructing race, gender, sex, and representation. When we wrestle with images of hypersexual Asian/American women, the possibilities of performance are ever present in the process of what it means to act and to respond to being bound as an object and a subject of such sexual projection. Rather than resist projections of hypersexuality, I am interested in accepting how hypersexual ascription is part of what forms our very self-recognition every day and every minute. That is, to reject the hypersexuality of Asian women is to reject how we are shaped by and wrestle with these images. Rejecting hypersexuality as external to Asian/American women, something imposed entirely by others, seems as equally insufficient as accepting it as entirely essential and internal to us.[46] A more promising solution is to develop critical literacy regarding not only how visuality but also sexuality and race secure meaning and organize reality, history, fantasy, and ideology today. Performance, or the ability to work against and with these images, is part of the dynamic process of representation itself—especially as it binds the racial, sexual, and gendered experiences of Asian/American women.

Like Dorinne Kondo, Josephine Lee, and Karen Shimakawa, I aim to address performance pointedly—in order to capture the experience of authorship and viewing as a deeply private and simultaneously public act of sieving and sifting through the fleeting nature of living and moving images with critical attention and energetic inquiry.[47] I am committed to making my way in the darkness of the theater where images conjoin very powerfully with the scenes of everyday life. Immersed in everyday representations of sexuality, one may formulate who one is and is not. One also engages who one is said to be and who one may be through sexual representation.

Asian and Asian American women's sexualities within visual culture produce both damaging and productive perversions as the critical element in the definition and recognition of Asian women in the popular imagination. The reception of the popular images of Asian women's sexuality abounds in ways that describe a wide range of expressions and experiences that include pleasure at the production of sexuality and desire as well as the pain and violence in the experience of being hailed as hypersexual sex machines. Hypersexual representations of Asian women actually express various experiences of trauma, terror, and pain as well as joy, self-recognition, and alliance for those who produce, consume, and criticize these images.[48] *By engaging them through critical interpretation, or screening—in the sense of seeing them and making sure to study them—we may put these powerful images into the service of articulating how Asian/ American women, as subjects and objects, are enabled as well as limited by sexual and scopic regimes.*

The embrace of hypersexuality as politically productive perversity by viewers, producers, and critics attests to the dynamic life of race, sex, and visuality—as experiences that need to be told, represented, and reclaimed as part of Asian American women's lives in the twenty-first century. Aiming to open up new discourses regarding the controversial representations of sex, I argue for embracing perversity as political. The Asian American feminist filmmakers and actresses and the Asian prostitutes and performers in the films and performances I study embrace perverse sexuality in their self-representations as a political critique of the normal.[49] They contradict the classification of sexual acts, identities, and pleasures as simply technologies of racism and sexism demanding us to go beyond stereotype analyses and the ease of political and moral judgments into open territory that can evaluate the seductive power of images and sexuality in representation.[50]

Rather than fear the forces of excessive sexuality and flee the power of representation, I study and dissect these images that comprise Asian women on screen, with a keen eye on how sexuality is being deployed and defined, especially in relation to race and representation. That is, to accept where perversity—in the sense of not normal, not normative, not the same old tired race, gender, and sexual scripts—may lead, beyond the equation of Asian women's sexual pleasure as problematic, is to reject the persistent marginalization of Asian American women as subjects of inquiry and to open up new possibilities of Asian women within knowledge, representation, public fantasy, and history.

THE TRIANGULATION OF DESIRE FOR SEXUALITY, OR
AUTHORSHIP, CONSUMPTION, AND CRITICISM:
TOWARD A RACE-POSITIVE SEXUALITY

In my study of screen and stage images, I refer to scenes of spectatorship, authorship, and criticism as a triangulation. It helps to understand one with the others. My use of the term "on scene" in describing engagements with sex at the site of production and consumption refers to Linda Williams's formation of "onscenity"—a reworking of "obscenity" as a way to capture the pervasiveness of sex in contemporary life.[51] I use her term "on scene" to point to the moment of encounter between the sexual image, the spectator, and the performer as a living exchange of fraught meaning. I extend the act of authorship or representing the self in performance, writing, and film to the act of viewing—for both practices critically offer redefinitions of hypersexuality and representation for Asian/American women.

The scene of consuming Asian/American women's hypersexual self-representations mirrors the bondage of pleasure and pain found in engaging sexuality as authors. For Asian/American women spectators who recognize the tradition of representing Asian women as objects of white male fantasy in representation, to reconcile the intense emphasis on sexuality as a being-for-others with sexuality that comprises our intimate self-recognition and our public everyday life remains a challenge. If engaging sexuality on scene and screen "perverts" Asian women, it may be a productive perversion worthy of exploration for what subjectivities emerge from this location of cultural formation and transformation.

Ultimately, the hypersexuality of Asian women occurs at the sites of production, consumption, and criticism. This hypersexuality persists in popularity, recruits Asian American female fans, and somehow leads to the explicitly sexual self-authorships of Asian American feminist filmmakers and cultural workers. As such, the positing of Asian women as desiring subjects, as sexual objects, as polymorphously perverse, easy, and promiscuous, as sluts, whores, call girls, and prostitutes—who re-enact sexual abuse and fashion themselves in fetish gear—describes a particular understanding of race, sex, and representation that acknowledges their subjugating power but also the possibilities of their equally intense pleasures or what I will call race-positive sexuality.[52] In these practices between race and sexuality in representation is truly a redefinition—for it describes how sexuality is part of Asian American women's everyday identities and subject formation.

My analysis finds that the trauma, pain, and violence within our intimate relationships, with each other on scene or on screen, and the most improper desires found in our deepest fantasies and experiences, should find a place in defining racial formation and politics. What if we embrace sexual perversity ascribed to race as an opening to what Robert Lee calls the third sex, which he defines as "an alternative of imagined sexuality that was potentially subversive and disruptive to the emergent heterosexual orthodoxy,"[53] or what David Eng calls "race as a queer formation" in understanding the marginality of race as so centrally sexual (and vice versa)?[54] Moreover, what if we completely go against the instinct of averting our eyes and disciplining our bodily response to seeing sex and instead look at it head on for what sexual visualization may say about race and its complicated desires and unexpected affinities?

Moving beyond reverence or abhorrence, to make the figures of Asian female hypersexuality available for other productive forms of anti-racist, feminist and sex-positive dissemination does not necessarily mean drawing pleasure from one's own demise. Instead, it illustrates a commitment to deciphering one's subjection for the purposes of crafting new self-formations—and utilizing how sexuality may open other possible subject positions beyond subjugation. As such, it is through the representation of sex within a context of power relations that experiences of racism, colonialism, and their many contradictory legacies for Asian/American women can be recast in a form of race-positive sexuality. Race-positive sexuality emerges from the cultural production of Asian/American feminists who present pleasure, pain, and trauma simultaneously in ways that embrace the liberating possibilities of sexuality while also acknowledging the risks of reifying perversity and pathology traditionally ascribed to women of color in popular culture. Through this lens, racialized sexual scenes on screen are represented as acts, events, and relationships where Asian women may shift into more viable subject positions within fantasy and ideology. That is, we cannot have an accurate picture of Asian women's subject positions within U.S. representation, sociality, and history that does not account for the productive force of sexuality as something not just imposed upon us, but as something we own.

The Hypersexuality of Race tours through instances in the visual culture of moving images. Moving from popular musicals such as *Miss Saigon,* to Hollywood Asian American femme fatales from the 1920s to the present, to stag films, to the Golden Age of pornography, to contemporary gonzo pornography and independent films and videos by Asian American women, this book grapples with the simultaneously powerful social forces of race, sex, and representation on cinema and stage.

Within the context of moral panics about racialized sexuality, chapter 2, "The Bind of Representation: Performing and Consuming Hypersexuality in *Miss Saigon,*" more fully establishes the theory of the bind of representation, which aims to capture how Asian women cannot be imaged outside of perverse sexuality or non-normative sexuality ascribed to racial identity. Therefore, they must use that sexuality in order to create new morphologies in representation and in history. The theme of productive perversity is established at the sites of spectatorship, authorship, and criticism. While it focuses almost entirely on the stage production of *Miss Saigon* along with the video documentary *The Making of Miss Saigon* (1991), it features in-depth interviews with Broadway theater actresses. My interviews with the actresses emphasize the process of refunctioning the legacy of hypersexuality through performance and performativity. I begin with the stage for it is unlike film, a medium we receive long after production and post-production. The immediacy of the theater enables discussion with actresses about the process of making these images from their perspectives soon after the moment of their production and consumption. I study the site of theater with an understanding of the stage and the scene of reception as the forming of community bound by experience, the fleeting nature of memory, and a shared focus within a particular historical moment.

The bondage of hypersexuality is useful in framing the three Hollywood Asian American femme fatales (1920s to the present) in chapter 3, "The Sexual Bonds of Racial Stardom: Asian American Femme Fatales in Hollywood." Perverse authorships by Anna May Wong in films such as *Toll of the*

Sea (1922), *The Thief of Bagdad* (1924), and *Shanghai Express* (1932) leave an ancestral legacy for Asian American actresses today. Today, Wong's legacy haunts the ability of Nancy Kwan and Lucy Liu to negotiate the sexual bonds of racial stardom, fandom, and the cinema apparatus within changed industry and social contexts in films such as *The World of Suzie Wong* (1960), *Flower Drum Song* (1961), *Payback* (1999), *Charlie's Angels* (2000), and *Kill Bill: Vol. 1* (2003). By comparing the interviews conducted with Anna May Wong, Nancy Kwan, and Lucy Liu, we see that their subjectivities are in process and in progress within their differing historical contexts as "subjects-in-struggle." Such a subject formation for actresses and spectators is helpful in order for us to understand how culture is a site of bondage and to achieve viable legibilities in the larger society while also acknowledging the political risks and ethical problems in playing the game of performing hypersexuality for the sake of visibility in Hollywood.

Chapters 4, 5, and 6 focus on pornography from three different eras (the 1920s to the present) in order to show how sexuality is a process, not just a position of racial formation. Only by evaluating the sexual role of Asian/American women in transnational popular culture throughout the twentieth century and seeing Asian/American women performing sex acts through close readings of pornography can we more fully understand the bondage of hypersexuality. The pornography chapters read the explicit sex acts comprising the hypersexual production of yellowface Asian women, Asian/American porn stars, and Southeast Asian prostitutes. By identifying how race, sex, gender, and nation operate in these scenes, I articulate more clearly the conundrum of race and sexuality expressed in the visual problematization of racialized sexuality common in these texts.

As such, I explore how sex speaks of race such as in chapter 4, "Racial Threat or Racial Treat? Performing Yellowface Sex Acts in Stag Films, 1920–34" wherein the Asian face replaces genitalia as the site of sexual perversity through the production of racial difference. The stag films *Chinese Love Life* (1921), *Menage Moderne du Madame Butterfly* (1921–1930), and *China* (1934) bring to light the relationship of history to representation and the ancestry of Asian women in porn through the presence of white women in yellowface. How does race function in the sexual fantasy life of the nation in a time of yellow peril fears? Asian women as representation in early pornography performed a particular role in national fantasy that crucially racialized their sexual attributes. These films show how sexuality defines racial difference centrally in the popular imagination and as such must contribute to our analysis and understanding of Asian/American women.

Chapter 5, "Queens of Anal, Double, Triple, and the Gangbang: Producing Asian/American Feminism in Pornography, 1940s–1990s," studies the particular historical subjection of and performances of sex acts by Asian American female porn stars from the 1940s to the present in order to assess the racialization of sex and the sexualization of race—to see sex acts is to see how sex and race bind Asian women forcefully and productively. Continuing from the stag film's racial pornotopia, race functions as an important bind, a central determinant and contributor to the sexual thrill offered in pornography. In stag films from the 1940s through the 1990s, such as *Geisha Girl* (1948–55), *Geisha* (1958), and *Oriental Girlfriend* (1961), and the work of the porn stars Linda Wong, Mai Lin, Kristara Barrington, Asia Carrera, and Annabel Chong from the 1970s through the 1990s, race is the primary identity for Asian women in porn. Racialization constitutes their perversity so that Asian women must perform yellowface in order to be legible in pornography. In demonstrating the conundrum of race, sexuality, and representation, I show the political power of productive perversity in the work of Asian/American porn stars who negotiate sexuality and stardom in order to redefine hypersexuality and resistance differently. Specifically, I discuss how golden age porn stars play the stereotype in order to exceed it, how Asia Carrera uses the Internet to redefine hypersexuality and in the process works to own her commodification, and finally, how Annabel Chong's performance of feminist monstrosity helps us to approach the problems of race, sex, and representation as ultimately unknowable and unreliable processes. More than any other subject, Chong embraces the messy morass of race, sex, and representation. She relinquishes the traditional understanding of resistance in owning one's own commodification in order to articulate the unknowability of social experience and the quality of unreliability in representation as a critique of the agency/slavery divide framing discussions of race and pornography. Instead, she offers a diagnosis of the rich, complex, difficult, and harsh commingling of race, sexuality, and representation.

Chapter 6, "Little Brown Fucking Machines Powered by Rice or Sex Tourists with Movie Cameras and Prostitutes without Movie Cameras: Politicizing the Bottom in Southeast Asian Sex Tourist Movies," studies two forms of representation featuring Southeast Asian women prostitutes: documentary fiction and gonzo pornography where white male filmmakers purport to center Asian women's subjectivity through film and video. How do these women usurp the camera and their bondage within hypersexual representations of their racialized sexualities in order to speak across the mediation of transcendental love? The chapter studies performance within a particularly popular genre of pornography, redefines what constitutes acceptable representation, and argues for the currency of representing sex acts in order to focus on the failure of hermeneutic projects that purport to locate authentic Asian women and hail in them particular sexualities or resistances. Toward substantiating my argument about performance and politically productive perversity, I visit two different sites articulating Asian/American women's sexual difference and find unexpected results regarding critique within pornography and the consuming of explicit sex acts. I argue for seeing the sex act in order to show the unknowability of the relation of power, as something hard to pin down and impossible to interpret in a monolithic fashion. Rather, I formulate how perversity is not limitless in the need to account for how power works in each scene.

Chapter 7, "The Political Power of Hypersexuality in Asian American Feminist Films," focuses on how the Asian American feminist filmmakers Helen Lee, Grace Lee, and Machiko Saito answer the haunting of Asian women's hypersexuality in representation. Through their cinematic and performance languages, they articulate a passionate attachment to hypersexuality and its particular ability to critique fetishism. Hypersexuality in public culture is not necessarily bad—but to bolster hypersexuality as constitutive and self-formative beyond the repressive captures the contradictions of race, sexuality, and representation. This chapter looks at how images by Asian American feminist filmmakers test the limits of bondage: race to sex, fantasy to reality, pleasure to pain, and top to bottom. They provide a hopeful conclusion by redefining race and gender identity through visuality and sexuality. Centrally, these filmmakers shift our understanding of desire, fantasy, and subjectivity while innovating cinematic and performance forms. They demand a recognition of alternative sexualities and reclaim the perverse as political, painful, and pleasurable.

Lastly, in chapter 8, "New Horizons in Race-Positive Sexuality," I assess what it means to reclaim the perverse in an era of intense conservatism wherein civil rights struggles entail fighting for the right to be normal.[55] To acknowledge Asian women's hypersexuality in representation as political in feminist, anti-racist, and sex-positive terms is to open the doors to Asian American women's self-fashioning in all of its various forms: good woman, bad woman, and every formation in between.

2 ❖

THE BIND OF REPRESENTATION ❖ Performing and
Consuming Hypersexuality in *Miss Saigon*

All the Vietnamese women in *Miss Saigon* are prostitutes, either hypersexualized Dragon Ladies in string bikinis or Kim, the single Lotus Blossom—shy,
passive, virginal in an ersatz Vietnamese wedding gown. Boasting of her exotic
attributes, Yvonne (one of the other prostitutes) promises, "I'll show you/My
special trophy of war," thrusting her hips . . . and the GIs roar with approval.
In contrast, Kim is portrayed as unwilling and unpracticed ("I'm seventeen
and I'm new here today . . . I've not done this before").—ĸaren shimakawa,
National Abjection

The persistence of stereotypes is evident in the *Miss Saigon* text. All the featured
female Asian roles in *Miss Saigon* (i.e., roles that stand out from the ensemble)
are prostitutes. One should not assume that prostitution connotes immorality.
In *Miss Saigon* however, the prostitutes, while allowed to display something of an
emotional life, clearly signal desperation and squalor. Paradoxically, *Miss Saigon*
also romanticizes the prostitutes' plight: by highlighting Kim's virginity and the
vulnerability of the other women, *Miss Saigon's* text employs the "hooker with a
heart of gold" scenario that erases the actual circumstances endured by particular women in the sex industry with an image of the "triumph of the human
spirit."—David schlossman, *Actors and Activists*

A fiction of hypersexuality composes the roles of Vietnamese female prostitutes in the stage musical *Miss Saigon* (1989). Hypersexuality is the inscription of pathologic or non-normative sexuality as if it were a natural characteristic, one that is directly linked to a particular raced and gendered ontology.[1] A Western fantasy of a perverse subject position for racial and gendered subjects in popular representations, the production of hypersexuality directly contrasts with normal or standard white male sexuality. While this specific notion arises through my study of Asian/American women, this phenomenon powerfully ascribes the sexuality of nonwhite others as aberrant.[2] While hypersexuality is a "fiction" that ultimately fails to capture the sexual subjectivities of raced and gendered subjects as a "factual" or coherent group, the differences between normal and abnormal classifications have values: right versus wrong, knowable versus unknowable, acceptable versus unacceptable, and familiar versus different.

The normal versus abnormal framing of sexuality has important implications for the interpretation of racialized images. The assumption that sexuality gives bad impressions of racial subjects keeps us from looking at the images in order to see other meanings and other engagements. Through an exploration of Asian/American female sexuality in *Miss Saigon*, this chapter revisits and reevaluates discourses of sexual promiscuity, deviancy, and pathology in order to move beyond a one dimensional understanding of sexual representation as always already injurious, dangerous, and damaging. Asian women's performance and consumption of racialized hypersexuality provides the terms for resistant authorial and spectatorial relations in the theater.[3] By utilizing the analytic lens of sexuality toward anti-racist ends, we see how the framework of the "bind of representation" identifies the ways in which racial subjects undergo hypersexual interpellation, on both sides of the stage, as a productive and formative social and political experience. That is, the bind of representation posits that hypersexual representation is an experience of bondage for minoritized spectators and actors. Situated in marginalized histories within the theater, minority actors and spectators are bound subjects who nonetheless invest in representational forms as contingent and ambivalent and engage hypersexual terms as re-directable and changeable.

The blockbuster musical hit *Miss Saigon* rehearses a ritual representation of the "Butterfly" defined by David Henry Hwang in his own play *M. Butterfly* (1994) as the performance of the ultimate femininity exemplified by the self-sacrificing Asian woman. *Miss Saigon* reenacts on stage the warring encounter between Vietnam and the United States through a narrative of interracial bodies enmeshed in sexual relations. A distraught American soldier, Chris, meets an innocent Vietnamese prostitute, Kim, in a bar. They have sex and immediately fall in love. She then arranges to marry him in an impromptu ceremony attended by other prostitutes. The couple stays in bed together for days during the fall of Saigon and then Chris is abruptly called to the military base. Considering herself his wife, Kim tries to flee Vietnam but fails as Chris reluctantly leaves on the last helicopter. For three years, Kim waits for his return while working as a prostitute in Bangkok and taking care of their child. Upon the discovery of his son, Chris ultimately comes back with his American wife. The appearance of the more "legitimate" wife leads Kim to recognize her "fate" and kill herself in order to give up her child to the American couple.

While the musical mainly follows the life of the virginal prostitute (in other words, perversely innocent) Kim, the minor female actresses play prostitutes who more tacitly accept their hypersexuality in military rest and recreation sites in Vietnam or the commercial sex tourism scene in Bangkok.[4] Whether innocent or lascivious, the Asian women signify extreme perversity against the white female norm or what Lauren Berlant frames as the innocent symbol of reproductive sexuality for white women in American national fantasy.[5] Throughout the musical and in its conclusion, the American wife is a pillar of motherhood, family, and nation.[6] I extend Berlant's argument to posit that Asian women signify perverse sexuality in American national fantasy as exemplified by *Miss Saigon.*

From the beginning, the musical itself is organized by hypersexuality. Kim enters the scene in a white dress, a signal of her virginity that only emphasizes her exceptional status amid the women in the brothel. The excessive sexuality of the Asian women prostitutes in the show is soon established as they exhort Kim "to put the virgin act to rest." The first musical number explodes with glaring lights exposing expanses of naked brown skin, as Asian/American female performers sing, dance, squat side-

In the opening scene of *Miss Saigon*, fully clad American men mingle in the bar. Mimi dances vigorously in her bikini while Kim provides contrast in her white, full-length dress. Yvonne grabs her crotch while singing "I'll show you my special trophy of war." From *The Making of Miss Saigon*.

ways in spread eagles, and grab their own crotches with vigor, gusto, and power. Downstage, a gang of roaring American GIs approaches this line-up of bikini-clad Asian women whose backs face the audience. Bottoms bared, breasts minimally covered, backs bending, hips shaking, and bodies exceeding the scanty coverings, the women are surrounded by the fully clad men before they rub together while singing, simulate fellatio with long eyelashes fluttering, and fake stand-up intercourse with long hair cascading. The documentary *The Making of Miss Saigon* (1991) features the various women performers in rehearsal. The soft-spoken French actress who performs the crotch grab in the London performance of the musical and the youthful demureness of Monique Wilson, the lead Lea Salonga's childhood friend who plays Mimi, register as significantly different from the performances of the opening scene. The disjuncture between the ac-tors, roles, and characters are ripe for analyses regarding the political power of their authorship and performance.

In her oft-cited article on the musical's 1991 debut in New York, spectator-protestor-critic Yoko Yoshikawa provides a highly ambivalent, contradictory, and complicated response to the opening scene. She at-tempts to repress the powerful seduction of the Asian female bodies sing-ing and dancing with sexual fervor. She describes her intense viewing experience as a denial of pleasure.

> The opening number was dazzling—and loud. The musical opens in a brothel in Saigon, where prostitutes vie for the title, *Miss Saigon.* U.S. soldiers buy raffle tickets; Miss Saigon will be the prize. But I was not following the songs—this lusty dance of glistening legs and dark breasts, of ogling eyes and lathered lips in uniform mesmerized me. It pulled me in, as soft porn will. But I also felt sickened and alienated. The show was designed to seduce, flooding the senses with a 3-D fantasy—specifically targeted at a heterosexual man's pleasure center.[7]

In this scene, hypersexuality leads to a traumatic viewing experience. In denying one's own pleasure from the sight of pathologic sexuality, the spectator is made perverse. That is, Yoko Yoshikawa's intensely self-aware analysis reveals confusing feelings of political impropriety for receiving pleasure from images "targeted at a heterosexual man" when she herself is an Asian female spectator. At an intellectual level, she understands that enjoyment of this image is a deviant act and feels guilty at being "pulled in." The framing of sexual performance on stage as a negative force that dominates and determines racial and gendered beings cannot adequately confront Yoshikawa's experience. Her very thoughtful description evidences the need to further develop a more profound appreciation for the seduction of sexual representation. Occupying a masochistic position in receiving pleasure from hypersexuality—or the excessive sexuality that must turn in on itself in the form of suicide—should not be punished but should remind us that there are never any clear choices or easy responses to difficult images. Conditioned to repudiate sexuality as repulsive and negative, we need to shift our understanding of sexuality in relation to racial representations.

The responses to *Miss Saigon* range from political analyses that privilege protest and performance studies that achieve powerful close readings of the musical but overlook sexuality as its own analytic vector. The protests against *Miss Saigon* and racial discrimination practices in the theater, including large and small acts of intervention such as televised protests, blocking ticket-holders' passage into the theater, and staged walk-outs, constituted an important historical moment for Asian American activism in the 1990s.[8] While I strongly support direct action platforms in expressing existent inequalities and the lack of control in regimes of representation, all-or-nothing stances simply dismiss actors as complicit and ultimately advocate closure of such cultural production or a kind of race panic, to appropriate Gayle Rubin's concept of sex panic, in fixing representation as a "bad object" and prioritizing moralism at the expense of critical inquiry.[9] What is lost in such an all-or-nothing framework is the bondage that Yoko Yoshikawa's position illuminates: the coexistence of pleasure and pain strapping the critical Asian female viewer.

While the critiques of Asian Americanist scholars of performance enable my work, sexuality as an analytic remains peripheral within the important contributions made by these scholars. Focusing on the contentious nature of pleasure in "the seduction of the stereotype," Josephine Lee's work describes the tense nature of the stereotype as both factual and phantasmatic for the Asian American actor and spectator. She describes the stereotype in terms of an "erotics," that is the felt pleasure garnered in watching Asian American actors occupying stereotypic roles flawlessly.[10] "Erotics" refers to the enticing power of performance and does not directly engage Asian American feminine sexual being on and off stage. Dorinne Kondo's critique of *Miss Saigon*'s content can be summarized as the "familiar paternalistic narrative White Man saves Asian Woman from the Asian Man and the Asian Woman dies for White Man." Critiquing the "changing same" from *Madame Butterfly* to *Miss Saigon,* I agree with her problem of identifying with the colonized content of the work, her address of the psychic operation of the musical, and the stress she places on the painful contradiction of employing a significant number of Asian actors in terrible roles.[11] Similarly, Angela Pao illuminates the cross-racial casting politics of the musical in order to describe unequal practices within the industry.[12] These works enable my study on the role of hypersexuality in framing Asian female presence in the theater.

In terms of the most recent scholarship, David Schlossman offers important critiques of racism in describing as classic the "Orientalist formulation" at work in the process of consultation used in creating the musical.[13] According to Schlossman, the creators consulted professional, presumably paid experts on American culture. But when it came to representing Vietnamese culture, the lyricist Alain Boublil surveyed Vietnamese waitresses for cultural information, and when he was unable to collect a consensus, he simply chose the "best sound(ing)" one. Schlossman asserts that "where relations among Westerners must be conducted with care, 'Oriental' voices may be obtained as informally (and, perhaps as inexpensively) as possible and may be deployed in order to achieve an ambiance that may have little to do with the particularity of Asians' lives."[14] The marginalization of Asians within the creative process extends to the text itself in Schlossman's analysis of the derogatory language used in the representation.[15] Indeed, racist logic seemingly informs the producers' specific requirements for "real" Asian women in their show. As Angela Pao argues, the establishment of natural Asian female beauty made illogical the performance of Kim in yellowface. The producers themselves essentialize Asian women when they describe how "the physical demands made on performers in *Miss Saigon* required an authentic (Asian female) litheness and grace."[16] Schlossman and Pao demonstrate an incisive critique of the power dynamics of the production here in ways that effectively evidence racial and sexual inequality.

In terms of content analysis, David Schlossman rightly reminds us that the representation of prostitution does not "immediately signify immorality"[17] as part of a critique of the process by which the Asian female actress stands in for an actual prostitute, whose life experiences are commodified in the production. For Schlossman, in the quote opening this essay, there is an important disjuncture between the actress (a speaking subject) and the character of the real prostitute (a subaltern subject erased by the narrative). However, we must make sure that our definitions of sexuality do not create blanket categorizations of actresses and prostitutes. That is, the production of *Miss Saigon* may actually represent other "particular women in the sex industry" beyond those enmeshed within conditions of sexual slavery. While sexual slavery indeed exists for Asian female prostitutes, other situations coexist simultaneously in ways that should not be removed. According to the speculations of the Asian American feminist novelist, critic, and ex-prostitute Tracy Quan, some Asian women prostitutes enjoy the beauty, glamour, and seduction required in their jobs. They also endure its boredom.[18] This analysis counters the prevalence of victimization discourses regarding Asian female sex work. In her commitment to humanizing prostitutes in the West and the East, Quan asserts that sexuality does not simply victimize "real" prostitutes, in an argument that challenges the coherence and stability of such groups and descriptions of their experiences.[19] Accordingly, the analysis of the roles and characters of Asian women in scenes such as Southeast Asian military or commercial prostitution should reflect the complexity of the situation.

Similarly, the bodies and psyches of Asian American actresses in *Miss Saigon* are frequently collapsed with the hypersexuality of the fictional role. The raced grouping of prostitutes under the umbrella of victimization is manifested in the grouping of actresses as hypersexual. Described as an innocent virgin, both on and off stage, Lea Salonga played the lead role of Kim, winning both a Tony and an Olivier acting award. Her virginal star persona and role offered a direct contrast or an exception to the rest of the Asian actresses, whom we know nothing about except for their roles as prostitutes. The collapse of the fictional characters and the living performers as sexual beings informs the international casting search for an innocent, young Asian female with "lungs of steel." The documentary *The Making of Miss Saigon* (1991) details how the producers deem it impossible to find a young Asian woman who is both *innocent* and has lungs of steel. Innocence is the quality emphasized in the difficulty of the search for Kim so that the Vietnamese "boatperson" auditioning is evaluated not for her voice but for her looks: as being "too much like a model" who has "come a long way" because of her revealing dress and heavy makeup. Later, the same producers hover excitedly over the cherubic and chubby-cheeked Lea Salonga, whose voice comes closest to the description "lungs of steel" and whom the media frames as a virgin who had "never been kissed" until the actual show. The media portrayal supports the impression that Lea Salonga's "innocence" is exceptional to the Asian female presence in the musical and among the others in the open call.

Framing sexuality within a non-normative/normative framework, Karen Shimakawa identifies the perverted sexualities of Asian men and women in the musical as directly related to Asian American abjection in the theater. Shimakawa describes the collapse of nation, race, ethnicity, and bodily identity that occurs for Asian Americans as constitutive of a normative experience of abjection, or what she defines as a positioning of alien status, otherness, foreignness that creates a productive tension or friction Asian Americans are able to "expose and exploit" in life and performance.[20] Karen Shimakawa's analytic of national abjection brilliantly provides a framework for understanding the conflation of role and actress for Asian women and the tradition of Asian female exclusion and marginality within the performance industry. She argues well that both conditions are directly related to histories of Asian female conquest and colonization. That is, abjection defines Asian women as racially and sexually perverse, deviant and non-normative.

In the convincing analyses above, Schlossman and Shimakawa use sexuality to evidence the concrete practices of racism in the musical. In the quotes that open this chapter, the eagerness to perform crotch-grabbing by the character Yvonne is mentioned by Shimakawa and the erasure of victimized conditions for their "real" counterparts in the sex industry is forwarded by Schlossman. In these illuminating critiques, I am concerned that positing white male sex as normative may mistakenly condemn Asian female hypersexuality. If Asian women are perverse against a white male white supremacist, patriarchal, and heterosexual standard, political critique possible at that site of performing hypersexuality is ignored. Simultaneously, Yoshikawa's fraught enjoyment of hypersexual perversity would not be deemed a political viewing position.

When Asian women themselves perform and enjoy viewing the hypersexual roles representing white male versions of "aberrant" or improper Asian female sexualities, they should not be relegated to the realm of the inappropriate and improper. We should not stand in fear of the reinscription of white male fantasy; rather, we need to mine the performances' potential to undermine racial, gender, and sexual interpellation. When we flee the complex power of sexual seduction in representation, or identify the deviant and pathologic sexualities of Asians as an endpoint, or identify the disconnection between representation and reality rigidly, we must not lose sight of using sexuality to pervert the logics of racism, patriarchy, and heteronormativity.

Almost ten years after its debut, an ethnically heterogenous group of Asian and Asian American girlfriends and I finally saw *Miss Saigon* in San Francisco. I say *finally* because I did not want, for so long, to see or endure the trauma of seeing the Asian woman's death on stage for pay. As a first-time spectator of *Miss Saigon,* my experience of a simultaneous recognition and a deep laughter at different moments of the show took me aback. The Asian woman as the ultimate feminine—crying, coy, melodramatic—registered for me differently in a misrecognition or "that is not me" identification.[21] She emerged as a representational construct, more precisely a repository of racial and sexual anxiety in the post-Vietnam era. I could see she was someone else's invention, a fantastic figure linked to ideologies precisely diagnosed by David Schlossman as "imperialism and sexism"[22] on stage. The juxtaposition of my laughter and the melodramatic figures on stage looked and felt ridiculous. Despite this disconnection, I knew there existed a strong bond between the image and me. It was a relationship that I accepted, then and in my everyday life—as the possibility of my being misidentified for her. Her constructed character told me, an Asian female spectator, and others unlike me, who I am. But in watching *Miss Saigon,* I was not there to listen or to see. Instead, I not only refused her but I remade her myself as she was presented to me. As I watched the self-sacrificing, waiting, and dying Asian woman, I instead recognized in myself a life and body responding against the image that hailed me.

At the end of the night, our group descended to the lobby, arms interlocked, walking and chatting with the older white folks who had laughed with and sat behind us in the balcony. In the crowded stairwell, a Filipina American woman who had been sitting in front of us suddenly burst forward and accused us of ruining the show. Startlingly vehement for someone who chose to say nothing during the show or the break, she yelled, calling us obnoxious, loud, and the worst people she had ever encountered in the theater. My friends yelled back. I was mostly shocked. The ongoing confrontation of barbs and retorts interjecting the movement of the exiting crowds attracted the attention of the other mainly white middle-class patrons all the way down the stairs, through the long hallway, across the lobby, and into the street. Coincidentally, our cars were parked next to each other in a dark alley of the city's Civic Center so that the confrontation from deep inside the Orpheum Theatre continued for blocks and blocks as my girlfriends yelled back to her. All the while she walked with her strangely silent and unmoved group, primarily composed of Asian American women paired with Asian American men. It ended with a frightening spat at the doors of the cars until we all drove off without resolution.

What a huge spectacle of Asian women fighting on the street—loud, crazy, and powerful! My companions, primarily middle-class Asian American female academics, speculated upon her rage. Did she want so much to enjoy the romance of the self-immolating Asian woman? Was her experience that radically different from ours? In the deferred moments of expletives and taunts, all I could finally do was to say to her, at the end, something about how we viewed the thing differently and the problem of policing others' responses. It was really too late for me to do anything more productive except write here. The fight was not about talking to each other as a community of spectators (much less Asian/American women) but her need to express rage because we curtailed her enjoyment.[23]

Later, my friends and I were more genuinely bewildered. We ruined a melodrama of a desperate Asian woman spurned by a white man who wrote her off as mad. Was it not a show that was already an assault on women like her and me? But Asian and Asian American women spectators do not constitute a coherent viewing bloc. It would be futile to speak for the "Asian American woman spectator" as there is no single desire, projection, identification, or coping mechanism that can be declared for any "us."[24] A more precise question emerges about the relations that form, not only among Asian and Asian American women, but also among larger audiences who perceive Asian woman against a sexy, suffering, and suicidal representation. Like Stacy Wolf, who asks about the visibility of femmes within a visual field saturated with heterosexual women, I ask about the specter of hypersexuality infusing Asian women in representation.[25]

Since my first show in San Francisco, I have attended the Broadway production six more times in near capacity-filled houses from November 1999 to October 2000. After one viewing of the musical, I met some of the main female actresses who play the Asian woman prostitutes. When waiting for them backstage at the Broadway Theater, I found myself standing in front of a large group of Filipina American teenage girls. In my brief introduction to one Filipina American actress, she told me immediately that she was rethinking the crotch grab she performs at one point in the musical. She was going to stop doing it. I responded, "No, I love it, it works." I tried to remember which crotch grab she performed: the one at the top of the opening act or another performed when encircled by men. The moment was awkward. I do not know what compelled her so suddenly to talk to someone she had only just met about the raunchy gesture she performed on stage. Maybe she assumed I was acting as a chaperone to the young Filipina fans behind me. It was as if she knew that the power of this image confirming the lewdness ascribed to Asian women was something that tied us together: the multitude of teenage Filipina fans, her, and me. She seemed to speak from guilt or discomfort.[26]

This, however, is an act that the actress performs every night when she embodies the role of the prostitute. I believe that it gives a sense of her agency as an actress on stage creating her own image. What I realized upon meeting her is that what confirms the Asian woman as lewd is actually, at least partly, an Asian American woman's own creation. How does this stunning act of creation by an Asian actress counter the fictional Asian woman's own masochistic self-annihilation? The act of creation is stunning because it illuminates the fact that actresses are actually working within the constraints of their craft, roles, and jobs rather than simply working in a job. That is, while the act may simply reaffirm the role of the prostitute, it is nonetheless not possible without this woman who works within her assigned space where some kind of limited authorship occurs. How do we make sense of the Asian American woman I fought with and the Asian American woman here, who plays the prostitute on stage and expresses a kind of disdain and resentment of her role? I bring up these women together, along with myself as a theorist and a critic, in order to help me formulate the creative process of spectatorship, criticism, and production as situated relationships essential to the study of racialized sexual images.

AUTHORING ASIAN/AMERICAN FEMALE HYPERSEXUALITY

My reading of *Miss Saigon* and *The Making of Miss Saigon* focuses on the minor roles of Filipina actresses in the musical and gives special attention to hypersexuality—perverse sexuality—manifested as the large number of sex acts they perform onstage in relation to the size of their roles.[27] My analysis centers on the sexualized masses of the Asian female prostitutes.[28] Indeed, few sex scenes are represented between the main characters in *Miss Saigon*. Lights go down on the sex scenes between Chris and Kim and Chris and Ellen, his American wife, also played by a biracial (hapa) woman on Broadway. We know sexual liaisons occurred by the disheveled appearance of Chris and Kim when the lights come up, the content of the songs, and, finally, the interracial son they produce. The minor character Gigi and others perform raunchy sex acts on stage to titillate the audience, standing in to establish the normalcy of perversity for Asian women and underscoring the heroine's anomalous and singular innocence. While sex is crucial for the main characters, the minor characters perpetually engage sex in the peep show and other acts. The large presence of women of the chorus as vehicles of hypersexuality establishes the norm of perverse sexuality through the performance of sex acts. Accordingly, the minor roles burst with potentiality for recasting the hypersexual Asian woman in popular culture.

The site of performance by Asian American actors is too easily dismissed as complicity with the white men who write the productions. Interviews with women actors of *Miss Saigon* recast the terms of the debate and insert the power of acting as creative and political work. The actors demonstrate awareness of their self-authorship on stage as a form of struggle for self-fashioning. Drawing from the literature on acting by Constantin Stanislavsky, Lee Strasberg, and Michael Chekhov in order to describe the authorial process of performance even within a script that requires one's racially and gendered visible body to be authentic or believable, these works closely cohere with the processes of embodiment and performance described by the actresses in the interviews. That is, the actresses describe the processes and procedures of acting within the craft and language of these theater scholars.

The actresses I interview understand authorial agency to be quite limited within their situations. Constantin Stanislavsky describes the work of actors as a creative production of collaboration with the director, composer, and other authors. The creative work actors bear is unique: they are responsible for using their "bod[ies], voice[s], speech, walking, movement" in order to "create an image . . . convey an inner, living spirit."[29] This inner life is drawn from the very life experiences of the actors themselves. When on stage, however, the building of the character requires that the actor not lose the self. Instead, the actor occupies the self, the work, and the character in what Chekhov defines as "divided consciousness," or the fourth stage of the creative process of acting. In his book *On the Technique of Acting*, Chekhov cites Rudolph Steiner, who says, "The actor must not be possessed by his role . . . he must stand facing it so that his part becomes his objective. He experiences it as his own creation with his ego; he stands beside his creation. . . ."[30] The theorists and practitioners of representational theater above all describe the process of embodiment that actors attempt to achieve in each performance. Embodiment, as defined by Stanislavsky, is the "creative work of emotionally expressing a part then putting it into physical form. . . . At first, you experience your role mentally, and then it is embodied. . . ."[31] Each actress works on making sense of, inhabiting, and bringing to physical life her role. In *Miss Saigon,* the process of embodiment does not necessarily come to mean collaboration in light of the racial and gender differentials in the casting and the demographics of the production as a whole.

In the video *The Making of Miss Saigon,* the director, producer, playwrights, composer, choreographer, lighting and graphic designers, white men all, produce a particular version of the Asian woman in their production. They comb the world looking for actresses to embody the characters available in the musical. Hordes of enthusiastic "unknown" Asian women audition—mirroring sex tourism in which a few white men judge and select from numerous Asian women. Stanislavsky describes the relationships in theater as follows. "Every worker in the theatre, from the doorman . . . and finally the actors themselves, they are all co-creators with the playwrights, the composer . . . for the sake of whose plays the audience assembles."[32] In light of the racial and gendered disparities in the theater, when the words, costumes, movements, and songs of the above authors become the words, costumes, movements, and songs of the actresses in their work, these women do not achieve the role of collaborators in the sense of equal "co-authorship." This is not quite possible, especially so in a scene of racial inequity within commercial theater. However, the industry cannot be said to simply use these Asian actresses to authenticate white male authorships of Asian women, especially when we investigate the creative process required in acting.

Lee Strasberg's essay "The Actor and the Director" points to the role of the director in "conducting" the work of the actor so that their convergence constitutes the "totality of the art."[33] Although the director must explain and interpret the role for the actress, the actress must still make sense of the role in her own terms. Actresses have a life and power of their own in terms of fulfilling their work on stage for the audience. The question of central importance to me is the nature of these specific actresses' power in light of their performance of roles that are Western male-authored fantasies of Asian female sexuality. In my interviews with the actresses of *Miss Saigon,* I asked them how they came to embody their roles in the context of their lives as Asian Americans in the profession. The specificity of Filipina/o American culture also arises in terms of the experience and performance of sexuality by the actresses, who as a group are predominantly Filipina American.[34]

Within the theoretical context provided above, my interviewees analyze why their creative choices as Asian/American actresses are not seen as direct engagements with power. They index the tense relationship between the fictional role of the Asian woman and their own more "factual" subjectivities in order to provide a larger theory of sexuality and representation. The performance of sexuality is framed as transformative to their own subjectivities as actresses and also within the narrative itself. They render how Asians are, too frequently, merely the objects of the sexual story. Through objectification, however, they become subjects. That is, even within the constraints of playing into fantasy, small acts defy, contest, and reshape hypersexual scripts.

The opening act, a display of carnality in the context of the Vietnam War and military rest and recreation culture, powerfully captures the actresses' creative processes. The actresses describe the scene of carnal energy as true to the situation of sex tourism in Asia. Within this representation, J. Elaine Marcos, who plays two prostitutes on Broadway, one named Yvette and another named Yvonne, describes her famous crotch-grabbing act (as Yvonne) during the lyrics "my special trophy of war" as a gesture that requires "strength of character."[35] It is a gesture that speaks both of the specificity of her character as a person and the kinds of roles prescribed to Asian women. I isolate her emphatic use of the word "strength" in order to capture the tensions between the agenda of the role and of the performer. At the same time, I am very cautious about what we can extract from various definitions of strength in terms of diagnosing any form of viable power. More precisely, I wonder if her personal declaration of strength reaches others across the stage.

While the crotch-grabbing act seems to submit to the myth of the hypersexual Asian woman, it also authorizes a certain kind of sexuality deployed by the specific actress in her role. If the crotch-grabbing act indexes the "truth" of the fantastic figure of the Asian woman, it is only a representation of reality according to the narrative in place. But J. Elaine Marcos chooses to occupy that role with a different embodiment and a different understanding of sexuality. She plays, or uses her body to perform, the prostitute as refusing to be left behind. She explains this act as part of her character's goal to will or dupe men into saving her. Her own subjectivity as a racialized actress is also captured in her creative choice to play sexuality with "strength." That is, her choices say something about her as an actress and a performer. The actress Sandra Oh describes a similiar situation: "If you're going to have to be the whore to the left, are you going to be the whore to the left with a good fuckin' story? And if you are, then you tell that story the way you want to do it."[36] It is at these instances that the Asian/American woman can be seen as a triangulation of actress, woman, and role, which refutes the idea of simply re-presenting original identities in the performance of such roles. The occupation of hypersexuality, while severely delimited by the industry, is creative and particular to the actress within each performance. Acting is contextual and contingent on performance, as well as reception, for the audience may not even recognize the actress's critique of the text.

According to Luzviminda Lor, who plays a bargirl in the Broadway and Toronto productions, choosing sex also indicates strength in a larger cultural sense.[37] Sex, for the character Kim, and for actresses like Lor who joined the production as teenagers ten years ago, means an unexpected transformation of the self. She highlights a different relationship to sexuality when she describes her reading of the plot. "Kim kills herself in the face of a love she does not want and the man she wants who marries someone else. Her suicide is an act that takes a strong person." She discusses the lack of choices available for women such as Kim, a prostitute in Bangkok. As such, suicide is an indictment of the lack of choices available for third world women. She asks, was this the same for *Madame Butterfly?* Lor's reading of strength in the contradictory act of self-immolation continues the postfeminist analyses by Tracy Quan as well as postcolonial feminist readings of the sati by Lata Mani and Rajeswari Sunder Rajan. Mani and Sunder Rajan locate the sati or widow burning, and the women's expressions of pain and suffering, as an index of their lack of freedom.[38] The fantastic production, in a sense, functions like a historical documentation and critical diagnosis of the "strength" of Asian actresses within particularly severe constraints, namely, the bondage of hypersexuality in their profession.

To understand acting as simply re-presentation of corresponding phenotypes and national identities is to say that actors and actresses play roles as non-creating beings. The way they occupy their roles and fill them with specific choices help to determine the roles they play and capture the tension of forging resistances to white male authorial intentions for the roles. If they simply play themselves or absently fulfill the directions of the producers, the work of cultural production is understood as absolute. Acting requires filling the role with parts of themselves: their specific bodies and histories.[39] Such an embodiment allows us to see the ways in which actresses such as Luzviminda Lor and J. Elaine Marcos choose to bring themselves into the production. In the process, they articulate a different relationship to sexuality than the one offered by the producers and the one expected by the audiences. They also present an understanding of their work as a political critique that enables them to engage with powerful producers on Broadway as well as paying audiences. While this explanation can be seen as nothing more than self-assuring, it also captures how they are caught within such great constriction between those who pay them—the producers—and the audience. In the face of these limits, the actresses work hard to establish their authorship as grounded in a situated, historical subjectivity continually fighting for representation as a worthwhile struggle for recognition.

Both Lor and Marcos identify in the audience a trend of refusing to attribute anger to their performances. That is, they encounter audiences who find anger to be an incongruent emotion for Asian women. Lor describes how the bargirls play the opening scene with an enormous amount of power and anger, so much so that they must look incredibly large on stage. But because the women are petite and Asian, the actresses feel that the audience refuses to accept what it sees. That is, the expression of power is seemingly incompatible with behavior deemed proper to Asian women: servility and passivity. "Why do people miss that it takes a strong person? Is it the way our faces are arranged as Asian women? Or because we are petite? You are so little, so dainty, you cannot be strong."[40] The visual efficacy of Asian women's smallness seems incompatible with the popular cultural expectation so that their rage and largeness on stage are refused. Conceptions of their bodies precede and seem to stay fixed regardless of performance. Even if actresses are visible, the audience does not see them. They are rejected. The actresses understand this as part of their work and seek to fight such preconceptions at every single performance of strength, every night.

Marcos describes the capacity of actresses to author and produce themselves through the concrete bodily processes of acting on stage. "Whoever originates the role sets up the tradition [of the movements performed]— the actions on the stage." As a later actress, performing ten years after the first shows, she asks herself, "Why do I walk there to give that guy a beer? I just have to follow the same traffic patterns on the stage. We have freedom within the practices of the play."[41] That is, the actresses have to make choices every time they perform and they get criticism in the form of notes from the producers, who consider whether or not their choices make sense. The actresses decide at every performance if they want to walk fast or slow or how they should hand over the beer: with a bad attitude or with something else. "It's up to me how I move in the traffic setup. For example, the crotch grab: I do it vigorously because I am saying to myself, in a sense, 'I got balls! I want to show everyone else up!' "[42] But even they, in making the choice, do not control its meaning. Marcos, however, expresses complete awareness that her agenda is different from what the narrative says: "But for me, the story is not what the narrative says." She explains her performances, as a very raunchy prostitute, as a more powerful production: "I am good enough to work at a bar and not a pathetic whore waiting to be saved. I am a strong woman and men cannot take advantage of me! The opening uses both a sad and happy tone—it is a bad life but a party too! Hey, I might actually meet a GI; I am higher than the menial people. I got a 'get myself out of here' attitude."[43]

Marcos's description of "it is a bad life but a party too" captures an important process that must not be lost in our interpretation of the actresses' performances of hypersexuality. The actress makes a particular interpretation of the role based on the specific emotional and physical life of the scene. In approaching the scene of sex tourism, she must ask how she would actualize the scene in terms of concrete gestures and feelings. To judge the scene in terms of morality would prevent her creative work of making sense of the role. While the previous actress in the role could not grab her crotch with conviction, Marcos herself does so with "strength." She describes the previous actress who did not want to touch her crotch as wimpy, "barely gesturing down there. It takes strength to go there [perform that action]—you gotta have guts in real life. To do a choreography move like that takes a tough person."[44] From the video *The Making of Miss Saigon,* in which we see the choreographer direct the dancers in particular affects as well as movements, we can see that the crotch grab may indeed be choreographed. I watch the crotch grab after the interview and I squirm. It is certainly a powerful gesture that requires a conscious decision by the performer for it to work. It shows the tension between the Asian American actress and the Asian woman's limited role. The act is an important measure for understanding agency in recording a particular subjectivity for the actress as well as the character. The actresses create a record of their personal subjectivities and struggles within the roles. Such small acts of resistance should be accounted for in the analyses and understanding of the production.

Luz Lor understands the limited roles actresses play when the producers, director, costume designers, choreographer, composer, and others already delimit what they can do with the material. She describes the depth of the actresses' involvement in creating and shaping the show: "For us, where power comes in, is in performance. It is your story to tell. When you are on stage, no one can tell you what to do. True, that there are parameters set by the writer and decided by the director. But we do and see something else! We are involved with the show long enough that we turn it inside out. We rehearsed for two months in Toronto and talked and worked through every part of the show with the actors and producers."[45]

The actresses show a sophisticated understanding of their work that differs from the "re-presentation" as understood and offered by the producers, especially in terms of their roles' corresponding to some Asian woman "out there." Yet, the actresses also acknowledge an awareness of their very constrained resources. Luz Lor continues:

> We ourselves don't know how to dissect the underlying story so much since we are in it. We see the trees not the forest. We do not have the privilege of the director or the freedom of the director. The message is determined by the director anyway—there is only so much you can do to change the story. The big picture is the industry. Look at our littlest sets, so small unlike other Broadway shows. The hotel scenes—there's lots of space in the back of the stage. Like the production uses only a small stage, we only have small powers.[46]

In their small role within the industry, they work with what they have in giving life to the characters: gestures, bodies, movements, voices within limited space, pace, and "traffic" as performers.

The question raised by the actresses' articulation of their work and power is to what extent the audience can read the actresses' authorship of the roles. While the answer would be difficult to measure, what we do know is that the roles emanate in ways that contribute to the multiple viewing positions occupied by audience members who leave the theater with different meanings, including my friends and I and the angry woman we fought with in San Francisco. The actresses actively and significantly contribute specific emotions and specific contexts. Their contributions are not vague and general. Even if their audiences do not get their redeployments of sexuality, their interactions with sex are telling of a different engagement with their work. They emphasize their critical redeployment of sexuality as a technology for authoring themselves, not only in the production but also in writing themselves into history. It is a personal act whose power and resistance is hard to quantify even in light of the actresses' descriptions of their life-changing implications. While the degree of their success may be difficult to ascertain, the ambiguity of the value of their performance introduces the complexity of meanings produced in the show. Its dismissal as a racist and sexist production misses such an important theory of representation. By understanding the unreliability and unknowability of sexual representation, we can see how these women's performances allow them to assert more powerful Asian female subjectivities.

The scene of spectatorship and performance is a dialectical encounter in that audiences actively participate in producing meaning through performance. The actresses describe how the audiences of *Miss Saigon* help to shape their performances on stage. And the actresses demonstrate their awareness of community with the audience in the sense of meaning shared and produced between them. Lor describes how she sees audiences' active resistance to change:

> There are couples I see determined not to clap. Either they don't like the language or the sex. Clapping is a gauging meter. The show has a rhythmic body to it—set up jokes so audiences get it—and the audience is not responding to it; how I have to fix the part . . . how tight the show is—and do[ing] a good job. Sometimes the audience does not respond at all. It affects people on stage. Emotionally, *Miss Saigon* is draining for the performers. The audience participates, not only in applause . . . , but also in affirming our craft.[47]

Lor shows that the audience sees her but once again relegates her to a place that refutes her performance. In a sense, they refuse to be changed by her or to learn from her. She is not granted the power she claims when she acts. Luz continues, "Clapping is all you have at times—to see if they take away what you are trying to say. . . . You have the power to shape perception."[48] Actresses and audience are in a creative and productive relationship, so that every performance is a unique and interactive discussion between fantasies, real lives, and subjectivities. More than this, what is at stake exceeds these relationships in creating knowledge and culture.

The stage itself is a microcosm of such knowledge and culture. Lor asserts that actresses produce roles, not only with their own imaginations, bodies, and minds, but also through their relationships with each other. Acting is creative, relational, and contingent on specific relations with other actors. Marcos explains:

> It's different every time. I try to get the feeling—a rush! I try to get that feeling every night when I go on. Sometimes I focus on different body parts to do something new. It's as basic as using my right foot tonight—to re-create energy that would otherwise be the same. The new action re-energizes you. I am doing this everyday for years like any other job—boring for you if not different. When understudies go on, there is a change. I adapt a new character on stage with me. It's like, hey, what's going on here! Sometimes when [Anthony] Foronda plays the engineer, Whoa! He is scary! Luoyang Wang plays the engineer differently; he is a more compassionate man who is nice to Kim.[49]

Marcos reminds us that the craft of acting requires the constant negotiation and restructuring of reality, which cannot be performed monotonously but must be continuously nurtured and reinvented. Her description of the two different engineers clearly captures the emotional and psychic life of their relations on stage. Lor adds, "There's another actress who says, 'Tonight I will be a drugged out whore.' Her energy means a subtle change in the ensemble that we can all feel. In long-running shows like *Miss Saigon*, I feed from fantasy, imagination, or my real life in acting. You cannot play a part without understanding it."[50] As transformation of the self through acting occurs for actresses, whether in individual performances or in terms of their own lives, viewing can also transform audiences. Because the specifics of each night are dynamic, audiences can also be seen to occupy their spectatorship as a role to be embodied differently, depending on which actors and actresses they encounter in a particular performance. Thus, the performers also limit the audience in a mutual dependency. That is, they respond to each performance differently as well. The site between the stage and the seats is a dialectical confrontation and a struggle for mutual recognition every night.

In *Miss Saigon,* the audience and the performers meet and encounter each other through issues and images of hypersexuality. The actresses describe how involvement with a highly sexualized production transforms their self-understanding in terms of their families and traditional Filipino backgrounds. According to Lor,

> You feel embarrassed, not so much because we're portraying something real— the opening number is a different reality represented on Broadway. Very different from Broadway typically: it is a powerful, sad, happy scene. But I was raised Filipino: I could not sleep over [at] anyone's house, I had to be demure, no dating. Then, suddenly playing this opposite character on stage. When my mom first saw me she said "*Ay, naku! Anak ko, grabe, kawawa, pinapakita ang singit!*" [Oh no, my child, how awful, pitiful, showing her snatch on stage][51]

Both Lor and Marcos discuss how the show opens the door for "safe" discussion of sexuality and "figuring myself out too." Luz describes how sex opens up the self—like Kim in the narrative. Exposed to sex, she decides to pursue a different life—"and goes for it!" The actresses all comment on the novelty of the experience for us as Filipinas to talk about sex so openly upon meeting each other for the first time. These narratives are testaments to how involvement with sexuality does not necessarily damage or destroy you; rather it opens up further definition of particular cultural experiences.

For Asians and Asian Americans organized by hypersexuality in representation, sexuality allows for both pleasure and pain and for new, local understandings of the self that might seem narcissistic if it were not for the fact that they tell more about minority positions in cultures of performance. When the actresses redeploy sexuality as a technology of personal strength and self-authoring, sex is both the technology that condemns the musical and redeems it. Their discussions of power in sexual performance show the political role of Asian actresses within the center of culture industries. Within critiques of *Miss Saigon* as a neocolonial technology in globalization, the actresses describe their work as an everyday encounter with audiences regarding myths about Asian women and sexuality. And to understand the political power of acting is to allow for a theory of sexual representation to emerge from hypersexuality as a dialectical encounter among multiple subjects, or what I call the bind of representation.

Stacy Wolf describes women's relationships to the mythic figure of Cinderella as follows: "Love her, hate her, or ignore her . . . desire to be her or desire to have her, most women recognize her."[52] Similarly, Asian/American women live under the sign of the prostitute in U.S. popular representations from *Shanghai Express* (1932), *The World of Suzie Wong* (1960), and *The Deer Hunter* (1978), to the lawyer Ling Woo (Lucy Liu), who owns an escort service in *Ally McBeal* (1997–2002), to contemporary Southeast Asian sex tourist pornography (1990s to the present). The bind of representation is a term I formulate to describe how actresses caught within the performance of hypersexuality insert themselves within the limited terms of legibility available to them. Similarly, spectators are bound by hypersexual representation, which they complete in order to secure the meaning of the production, whether toward normative aims or alternative readings.

The bind of representation is a theory regarding the ways in which to engage popular culture. What is to be gained by being a part of a discursive conversation where one is a less than equal conversant? To understand cultural production within a bind of representation is to commit to staying in the conversation, to engage with the industry on all fronts: producing, acting, viewing, and definitely protest and critique, whether in mainstream or independent production. Rather than call for a complete stop to the conversation, the bind of representation understands the contingency of the battle and the multivalency of spectatorial, authorial, and critical positions. The bind of representation does not invest much in the end of certain conditions that deny full entry of minority subjects in the most mainstream of discourse. Rather, it recognizes the engagement with persistent exclusions and inclusions in cultural industries as an ongoing struggle.

The actresses found on the streets of Toronto, New York, Los Angeles, Manila, and Honolulu capture the minority position of Asian/American performers without access to representation in the traditional venue of casting agencies. As spectators and critics, we are situated beings informed by our historical and social locations. We enter the theater with our own desires and goals of protest, enjoyment, and the like. In this way, I understand the performance form as unique, that through live performance and the suspension of judgment we all await the possibility of transformation in the theater.

Spectatorship also identifies a specific space for experiencing and examining our relations with each other in the world. A psychic analysis emphasizes the larger cultural landscape in which the viewing and production experience is situated. Psychic analysis of production and consumption can help us understand the power of cultural production, what logic it installs, and how it generates pleasure. Toward extending the definition of "living image" production of racialized sexuality as a set of relationships or as a bind of representation, the Asian American woman in the audience whose pleasure I interrupted returns here. She presumably wanted to identify with the Asian woman on stage through the enjoyment of what may be seen as a "universal" love story. Identification, in the Lacanian sense of "the transformation that takes place in the subject when (assuming) an image,"[53] occurs as a multivalent and unpredictable one in the sense discussed by cultural theorists such as Stuart Hall and Kobena Mercer.[54] The woman may have wanted to be subsumed in the fantasy of the Asian woman as a forgotten love object in an enjoyment of the suturing pleasure of the text (even if the Asian woman eventually dies). Or she may have enjoyed identification with the white wife who represented American women in civilization. Or she may have shared my interpretation.

Regardless of whether or not her true enjoyment can be found in any racial or sexual terms, my presumptions about her protest help me to define the position of identification as a resistant subject position. The wish to be enveloped in romance and pleasure in the Asian woman's death is an act of active spectatorship and even this masochistic position cannot simply be rendered as passive acceptance. In this viewing position, a reading against the grain occurs so that even Asian women themselves find seemingly contradictory pleasure in their own paradoxical subjection. Identification is a particular positioning situated within a context. The woman's position of identification is valid, whether or not she truly occupies this role. It raises the crucial question of how pleasure can be drawn from watching or performing one's own symbolic self-annihilation. Such enjoyment is meaningful and critical, even if it may not necessarily signify political critique.

The second position is the political platform of privileging boycott, protest, and strike that must not necessarily occlude pleasure or poorly render any participation within the musical as simply complicit. Protest, direct action, and organizing against racist representation and institutional exclusion have an important role in culture. It is an articulation of the need for recognition and an assertion of injustice and inequality that must be heard. Protest should not be dismissed as simple or uncritical. However, there must remain an opening for the work of actors and actresses as authors, critics, and agents.

The response of the Asian American activist Yoko Yoshikawa, who earlier described her reaction to the opening scene, should not be a traumatic site of refusing her arousal. Succumbing to the seduction should not simply be seen as complicity with the misrepresentation that must be disavowed (in a different form of sublimation). Such a platform does not account for the work performed by all subjects involved in performance— as contextualized within an interdependent relationship. To refuse and disavow one's responses to the process and experience of viewing can marginalize the protest of actresses on stage asserting selves excluded from the white and male authors of *Miss Saigon*. The political voice, understood in a binary way outside of the stage, should not be privileged in order to stifle the particular struggles for recognition engaged by performers. Political possibility occurs inside and outside the theater.

Even as we remain invested in naming a viewing practice committed to the inclusion of multiple and contradictory interpretations that accounts for the position of the protestors, performers, spectators, and critics—all as creative subjects—remembering the creativity of the production should not be disconnected from analyses of representation and politics. I do not necessarily identify with the intended pleasures or disidentify radically at the occlusion of pleasure. Rather, I understand that any representation is always a misrepresentation and that recognitions or identifications in cultural production are creative practices that always have the potential to dislodge established tropes. Whether it is the black sidekick in the character John or the perversely innocent Asian female sexual being in Kim, representation can never adequately capture those represented as minority —nor as majority for that matter. Representation cannot capture real people, but it can construct versions of people that change depending on who produces, consumes, and criticizes the image.

Within the bind of representation, representation is understood as misrecognition, especially for marginal subjects. The conceptualization of the bind of representation, thus, highlights the limitations of demands for positive images in identification and redress in protest.[55] The looking-for-myself approach to popular images is a kind of doomed narcissism—for one cannot find oneself wholly and directly in representation so that the ideology of "I want to become that" or "I refuse to become that unless it looks like me" stands insufficiently. Relationality reminds us that popular representation is an exchange of power; it is a site for the powerful to speak through the industries of popular culture and for performers and audiences to insert critical revisions and similarly claim power. As such, representation is a conversation from which lessons about power can be extracted and within which small freedoms of the spectator-individual can be exercised even if within constraints.

The bind of representation accounts for perception as a political practice. In my case, I did not expect to be moved into a different self-recognition by a production aimed at seducing me into identification with any of its constructions: whether it is the regretful American GI or the suicidal Asian woman whose death the audiences applaud. The problem with investing representation with politics is that the meaning of representation should not be simplified as totalizing. I do not want to conflate protest with simplicity and celebrate representation as complex. It is not as if representation is removed from politics (and vice versa). But we must remember the *instability of representational forms,* in that to speak for anyone will always be a misspeaking. One person cannot stand for a whole, as there will always be exceptions. The only certainty is the importance of intervening inventively—which also includes strategic deployments of boycott, when necessary—in the work of culture, whether as authors, critics, or spectators.

Through the bodily performance of actors and actresses and the viewing experience of spectators, representation constitutes a form of bondage among audiences, performers, and producers. Relationality is the interaction and communication between individuals and groups based on shared cognition. The production of *Miss Saigon* is itself tied to how we relate to each other as nations, civilizations, and citizens as well as spectators, actresses, and theater makers within the historical moment of its appearance. The bodily and psychic experiences in the consumption and production of culture generate meanings. Actresses and spectators, required to help complete the meaning of the production through their bodily expressions, shape and alter intended meanings of film and theater, at times in unintended and insurgent ways. When we pay attention to the bodies of actresses and audiences in production and spectatorship, the power relations within the production of meaning in culture become more apparent. To acknowledge the processes of acting and viewing as contextual, contingent, and dependent on specific situations is to open up an understanding of the self as engaged by popular cultures of race and sexuality. The self is an actress, a racialized woman, and a fantasy figure of an Asian woman simultaneously—and such a figure is a complex formation that recasts existing understandings of the possibilities of resistance at the site of sexualized images.

By framing the stage production as a site of power relations—director/performer, director/audience, audience/performer, performer/performer, and audience/audience—a set of historically situated relations is made evident, notably, in the typically propagandistic making-of video. Since these relationships consist of subjects who are products of their time, their encounter on stage and in the scene of spectatorship can help us know about more ostensibly material relations such as the tension between the roles prescribed for Asian women and the persons of Asian American actresses. Meaning is contested and created within the body of the actress. The versions of meaning produced and interpreted vary therein, onstage, backstage, and in the scene of spectatorship inside and outside the theater. Theaters are sites for the study of sociality itself, or how we come together as communities in psychic and bodily ways through culture. To acknowledge the bind of representation is to practice creative engagement and interpretation that engages the politics of cultural production as changeable.

CONCLUSION: PRODUCTIVE PERVERSITY

Through an examination of the scene of spectatorship, interviews with actresses in *Miss Saigon,* and an analyses of stage corporeality, we can see how the production and performance of sex by actresses and their consumption by audiences deploy competing subjectivities. The redeployment of the hypersexual Asian woman in *Miss Saigon* by actresses and audiences recasts the political significance of hypersexuality in representation. When the subjectivities of the actresses are emphasized, such as the context of Filipina American sexualities as well as the radically competing identifications for Asian American spectators and critics, sexuality is redeployed within racially conscious contexts. Rather than the less productive strategy of flight from images of sexuality or a negative understanding of sexuality, to open up the possibilities for representing sexuality in all of its explicit engagements with differing subjectivities and experiences as sites of study is to make them of service to anti-racist and anti-colonial platforms.

When consuming perverse images, representation must be remembered as a lively encounter and a situated experience full of multiple desires and identifications. Perversity in viewing is produced at various sites: the creation of non-normative sexualities in representation as well as perverse identifications with the themes and characters. Perverse authorships and spectatorships need to be accounted for in analyses of racialized sexual representation because of their critique of normative subjectivities. That is, sexual proclivities attributed to Asian actresses and their fictional roles in popular culture provide the terrain for asserting productively perverse Asian American female subjectivities. The position of perversity is productive not only if it creates standards of measurement beyond the acceptable and the normal but also if it offers alternative forms of being in terms of race, sexuality, and representation.

Asian American actresses and audiences creatively deploy sexuality in order to counter the perception of the stability of hypersexuality. To close off the possibilities of power garnered through the performance and consumption of perversity would stifle the highly contradictory portrayals by the actresses of the prostitutes' sex work as both enjoyed and resented, simultaneously fueled by resignation and boredom as well as vitality. It would also punish spectators who occupy the masochistic position of enjoying hypersexuality. Hypersexuality can be redefined beyond racist injury toward presenting the contradictory ways Asian women have been overdetermined by representation. No matter how minute, Asian American female agency in living image representational processes matters—for Asian women cannot simply be measured by standard definitions of normativity, in terms either of their sexual being or their varied and active participation in the production of culture. The bondage of hypersexuality in representation need not be reviled, because if normalcy signifies the rigidity of the status quo, perversity may be the opportunity to critique normative scripts of race and sexuality in representation.

3 ❖

THE SEXUAL BONDS OF

RACIAL STARDOM ❖ Asian American Femme

Fatales in Hollywood

I was tired of the parts I had to play. Why is it that on the screen the Chinese are nearly always the villain of the piece, and so cruel a villain—murderous, treacherous, a snake in the grass? We are not like that. How could we be, with a civilization so many times older than that of the West? We have our rigid codes of behaviour, of honour. Why do they never show those on the screen? Why should we always scream, rob and kill? I got so weary of it all—of the scenarists' conceptions of the Chinese character. You remember Fu Man Chu? *Daughter of the Dragon?* So wicked!—Anna May Wong

An Asian lady was talking to me . . . and all of a sudden she said to me: "Do you know that because of Suzie Wong you made a bad impression for a lot of Asian American women?" I said, "What are you trying to say?" So she said, "You know, because Suzie Wong was a prostitute a lot of Americans got the wrong idea and they thought that all Asian women were prostitutes." I said, "I don't have any problems with the movie and I don't know why you bring this up because I think it's up to you and how you feel about yourself. It's only a role and it happened to be a very successful film and I'm sure that you feel that way." —Nancy Kwan

It's not just Asian groups. A lot of groups have gotten so limiting and politically correct. Ling is just a person with this personality. If you do an immigrant with an accent, that's no good. If you do something that's a strong woman, that's no good either. . . . I love this role (of Ling Woo on *Ally McBeal*) and I defend this role, but people forget: Sometimes you take roles because you've got bills to pay or you've got kids. Sometimes you have no choice. It's about making a living.
—Lucy Liu

How do we evaluate the political possibilities of performances by Asian/American actresses in Hollywood who are caught in a specific bind of hypersexual representation at different moments in history? Within two years in the early twentieth century, two separate films featuring Anna May Wong inaugurated what have since become the defining poles organizing Asian/American womanhood on screen and scene: the lotus flower and dragon lady archetypes. Even the lotus blossom is a femme fatale figure in killing herself and threatening to overwhelm the white man with her devotion and loyalty. *Toll of the Sea* (1922) presents Anna May Wong in her first starring role as a pathologically devoted Chinese "wife" of an American husband who disavows her love. The film established Anna May Wong's talent in Hollywood with the introduction of an Asian American woman playing the character of "Lotus Flower," the self-sacrificing, servile, and suicidal Asian woman, a role so compelling it continues to bind contemporary Asian/American women on screen and scene.[1] On the other end of the spectrum, opposing the abject, self-abnegating Asian woman is the dragon lady—also embodied by Anna May Wong in the classic film *The Thief of Bagdad* (1924). There, Wong plays a Mongol slave girl, a minor role that initiates a major trope of the Asian woman: the dragon lady whose excessively dangerous sexuality is a major emblem of her race and gender visibility. The dragon lady uses her "Oriental" femininity, associated with seduction and danger, to trap white men on behalf of conniving Asian males. The publicity materials for the film show her in an elaborate headdress that creates the effect of a large dragon shadowing her. Her contorted body mimics the dragon's shadow and her revealing ensemble of net-like silver threads shows off most of her skin. Sexuality, animality, and eroticism come together in selling this body. Linking the elements of primitivism in the early-twentieth-century *Madame Butterfly* (1904) to the late-twentieth-century *Miss Saigon* (1989), the image of Anna May Wong shows the Asian-woman-as-dragon-lady as a sublime object of beauty hiding a grotesque interior.[2]

Coinciding with the transfer of military rest and recreation to commercial sex tourism, *The World of Suzie Wong* (1960), an elaborate big-budget Hollywood film, organizes its elaborate production around an Asian female lead, considering hers a life worthy of narration as both desiring subject and object of desire. Signifying the "prostitute with a heart of gold," she embodies immoral practices while projecting an innate innocence. In this role, Nancy Kwan captured stardom through a girlish and wholesome performance of hypersexuality. Since her breakthrough role, Nancy Kwan has offered a particularly controversial model for negotiating her roles, her stardom, and the industry. Even today, she will reject stereotype analysis and racial critique of her work in order to prioritize the importance of visibility and presence in Hollywood. In the context of the civil rights movement that emerged in the national scene as she established her stardom, she holds on to a particular understanding of her acting as separate from racial critique in order to emphasize her craft, technique, and artistic intentions.[3]

Forty years after Nancy Kwan's performance as Suzie Wong, another Asian American femme fatale reigns on screen. Lucy Liu is one of the most recognizable celebrities in popular culture today, this status cinched by her securance of a highly coveted lead role in the hit remake of *Charlie's Angels* (2000) and its sequel (2003), in which her character took on campy disguises (among them a bikini waxer, a masseuse, and a whip-wielding, leather-clad workplace dominatrix), and her performance as O-Ren Ishii in Quentin Tarantino's *Kill Bill: Vol. 1* and *Kill Bill: Vol. 2* (2003 and 2004). In *The New York Times* article "The Perks and Pitfalls Of a Ruthless-Killer Role," Lola Ogunnaike writes,

> In the decade or so she has been in the business, Lucy Liu has fashioned a lucrative career out of playing the icy vixen—first as emotionally barren Ling Woo . . . coldblooded dominatrix in *Payback* . . . frosty princess in Jackie Chan's *Shanghai Noon*, a federal agent in . . . *Ballistic* . . . and . . . bikini waxer by day, private investigator by night in . . . *Charlie's Angels*. . . . But it is her role as O-Ren Ishii, a kimono-clad femme fatale in Quentin Tarantino's blood-drenched, slice-em-up *Kill Bill: Vol. 1* . . . that has elevated Liu, 34, to an entirely new level of ruthlessness and secured the actress' position as one of America's leading action heroines at the risk of being typecast as a dragon lady.[4]

As Ogunnaike writes, Liu's roles thus far significantly harbor characteristics of ruthlessness and callousness. The emotional range of her performances is limited in favor of an extreme and identifiable sexual persona so that in Lucy Liu's career thus far the trajectory of hypersexuality for Asian American females persists.

From Anna May Wong to Nancy Kwan to Lucy Liu, how have Asian American actresses coped with this restriction of sexual subjectivity? How do we account for the differences among Anna May Wong's anger, Nancy Kwan's rejection of political accountability to racial critique, and Lucy Liu's balancing act as she carves roles in Hollywood today? What of their powerful, wide-reaching work leaves a hopeful legacy for Asian/American women? What if we reclaim the hypersexuality of Asian women on screen as both enslaving and empowering? The performance of work exceedingly problematic precisely for its hypersexuality seems to involve both a re-inscription and redefinition of racialized sexuality. Or in other words, to understand what is political about the work of Asian American femme fatales in Hollywood in the last one hundred years may specifically require us to perform a balancing act between appreciating individual resistance and recognizing the structural ramifications of engaging hypersexuality and representation.

Representations in the U.S. film industry since the early twentieth century have invariably presented Asian women as sexualized and vampish. The figure of the Asian American femme fatale signifies a particular deathly seduction. She attracts with her soft, unthreatening, and servile femininity while concealing her hard, dangerous, and domineering nature. Early images, particularly the performances of Anna May Wong, continue to this day to haunt the production and reception of Asian women on screen, such as in the star-making roles of Nancy Kwan in the 1960s and Lucy Liu in the present. If Asian/American women's subjection is fundamentally dependent on sex, creating the parameters for Asian women's presences in popular film and in history, racialized sexuality on screen must then be sites where the bondage of representation is itself reimagined, recast, and criticized at the very moment of performance.

Recently, at least three book-length studies have focused on Anna May Wong's situation as a racialized and gendered figure who achieved a great deal of representational power while caught within history, ideology, and community. The most notable work is Karen Leong's *The China Mystique*, wherein Anna May Wong "believed that her portrayal of highly exoticized and sexualized roles—directly associated with perceptions of her as Chinese—actually evidenced her increasingly American perspective."[5] Unlike these projects, however, I focus on a sexual and racial bondage that recasts sexuality in Wong's and other Asian American femme fatales' rendering of race and representation in Hollywood, especially through close readings of sexual performance and narrative in order to posit a way of reading their politically productive perversity.

That is, in identifying the sexuality of Asian/American women in Hollywood across three generations, my close readings of performances by Anna May Wong, Nancy Kwan, and Lucy Liu show how these actresses' particular deployment of sexuality illuminates the persistent sexual bondage of Asian female stardom. In assessing their performance, I note two important matters essential to their being: hypersexuality is essentialized to their race and gender ontology and it is constructed in direct relation to the innocence and moral superiority of white women. I then read the actresses' off-screen interviews and biographies in fan culture magazines to describe a bind of representation specific to subjects of color becoming perverse authors and spectators—as a way of very creatively redeploying the power of race, sex, and cinema.

Diane Negra argues that rather than uncritically celebrate the presence of ethnic female stars such as Dorothy Dandridge and Anna May Wong in Hollywood, their particular types varying among exotic, sexual, pure, and evil, we need to assess their larger role in national identity formations through the cinema.[6] As such, the framework of bondage aims to recognize the limited value of gaining access to Hollywood deal-making for racialized women. Like the actresses in *Miss Saigon,* one step forward in redefining representation can feel like two steps backward in terms of reinscribing stereotypes. Nonetheless, actresses of color situated within industry practice have the opportunity to make a difference and provide material to forge resistant practices.

My ultimate aim is to complicate the received understanding of Asian American femme fatales whose works are too rich simply to be cast as complicitous with the agenda of the racially exclusive industry. It may be more precise to characterize them as subjects-in-struggle within it. They are particularly important for they represent the face and the future of Asian/American women in popular culture. The key question I address is how to understand the situations of Asian/American women who play a part in the Hollywood game of shaping our popular culture and imaginaries. The contributions of the three major Hollywood Asian femme fatales certify the constraints and potentialities of engaging the industry as

part of a larger struggle for recognition by racialized and gendered subjects in the U.S. film industry. Their work also shows a particular sexual
bondage to their racial stardom—which I will argue is a politically important phenomenon for it illuminates their engagement with the instability
of representational forms. They work as subjects-in-struggle, operating
within representation that requires the triangulation of their selves, roles,
and work. I describe this process as "passionate attachment" or what I
will define as a phenomenological approach of inserting the body in our
understanding of these women's resistances and power.

THE BIND OF BEING AN ASIAN
AMERICAN ACTRESS IN HOLLYWOOD

The sexuality characterizing the racial stardom of Anna May Wong, Nancy
Kwan, and Lucy Liu can be too easily vilified as sources of terrible pain,
irritation, or racial traitorship. Such an approach does not capture what
Homi Bhabha calls the "ambivalence" of the stereotype in producing the
colonial Other as insidious process.[7] His definition of how the stereotype
must repeat itself "in changing historical and discursive conjunctures . . .
and convince as real the improbable" captures a more complicated relationship between history, fantasy, and image production. By formulating a
facile relationship between history and representation, describing a passive spectatorship equation, and positing a list of images as always already
damaging, the typical stereotype framework constitutes a crisis in racial
discourses of representation, particularly in terms of sex and gender as
discussed by Kobena Mercer and others.[8] That is, if sexual representations
not only represent trauma but also acts as sites for wrestling with power,
resistance, and redemption, such an avenue must be explored for Asian/
American women.

The stereotype is not logical or simply contained by the historical situation of Asian American women, who supposedly correspond to the image.
In order to move away from paranoia about the visualizing of sexuality for
racial Others, I offer an alternative reading of the images of the lotus blossom versus the dragon lady and the murderous vamp, embodied by Anna
May Wong, which can be extended to the prostitute/whore with a heart of
gold embodied by Nancy Kwan's roles and the dominatrix/sex queen con-
veyed by Lucy Liu's characters. The purpose of my alternative reading is to
extract a more productive relationship among race, sex, and visuality as

they appear within the acting, spectatorship, and other creative acts found within Hollywood's productions about Asian/American women.

Understanding any moving image media as simply a stereotype-generating machine, in the sense of totalizing and homogenizing meaning, allows for solutions that simply list images that *always* dehumanize and delimit more complex subjectivities. Such taxonomy ignores the complexity of authorial, spectatorial, and critical experiences. The experience of engaging with images is enormously complicated. While stereotypes as "arrested representations"[9] rightly tie them to the particular historical moment of their construction,[10] they do not capture the racial-sexual complexity in representation instantiated from production to reception. Such analysis also fails to describe the performances of Asian American feminist actresses such as Sandra Oh and feminist performers such as Margaret Cho and Denise Uyehara[11] who deploy stereotypes in order to articulate a critique of racial and sexual representation as argued by critics such as Sheng Mei Ma.[12] Considerations of the dialectic relationship between makers and viewers in reflecting and shaping each others' desires enrich our understanding of stereotypes as living images and not simply frozen ones.[13] In particular, the intersubjectivity of the film experience in film phenomenology argues for the power of film as a subject in its own right, coming to life at the moment of production and in conversation with spectators, validating Homi Bhabha's theory that stereotypes require reiteration in order to secure their power.[14]

In the quotes opening this chapter, the actresses regard their hypersexual roles as a triangulation that challenges our two-dimensional understandings of cinematic roles for Asian women. The figures of hypersexuality are not simply found on screen but are widely intertextual and multidimensional within the characters, actresses, and women who, in playing them, belong to particular historical, social, and cultural contexts. To see the triangulation—the multidimensional figures—is to see the site of collision between concrete conditions and fantasies, created within a relationship of production or what I called in my discussion of *Miss Saigon* the "bind of representation" in the process of production itself. These figures of fantasy rely on the visible facticity of the Asian actresses so that they themselves must engage (as we see in their interviews) the popular definition of racialized sexuality as perverse. They do so in differing but resistant ways—for their varying resistances characterize the ultimately unknowable and vastly rich quality of hypersexual representations.

The Asian/American woman in Hollywood cinema is bound to sexuality as essential to any imaginings about her as well as her actual appearances in popular culture. From the general Orientalized roles played by Anna May Wong to the detailed specificity of the "Half Chinese, half Japanese" O-Ren Ishii played by Lucy Liu in Quentin Tarantino's popular *Kill Bill* series, hypersexuality is the primary legibility of Asian/American women in Hollywood. The particular sexual subjection for the Asian woman occurs at two levels. First, the Asian femme fatale's sexual subjection in film involves an inherently different sexuality essentialized to race and culture. That is, her sexuality is ascribed as natural to her particular raced and gendered ontology. Second, the Asian femme fatale's sexuality is framed in a rivalry with a white woman, in terms of competing for idealized heterosexual femininity.[15] The Asian woman's racial visibility works against the white woman's domestic or tameable gender and sexuality. Furthermore, it is a racialized sexuality linked in its perversity to other women of color in representation such as the African American mammy/Jezebel, the Native American squaw/princess, and the Chicana/Latina virgin/whore.[16] They each present contradictory sexualities that persist across time, hailing women of color variously and widely.

For example, sexuality in Anna May Wong's roles is marked by racial perversion and racial visibility as secured through cartoon-like gestures in her most emblematic or star-making roles in *The Thief of Bagdad* (1924) and *Shanghai Express* (1932). In each of these films, Anna May Wong's roles are perverse as constructed against white women. Similarly, for Nancy Kwan's character in *The World of Suzie Wong* and *Flower Drum Song* (1961), a discourse of sexual morality prevails as a narrative she must disprove. She also contends with the racialized construction of gender and sexuality. For Lucy Liu, her "frigidity" inspires her breakthrough television role as Ling Woo, a character so sexual that her articulation of the word "sex" causes havoc in the world—rendering with terrible certainty that the truth of the Asian woman lies in her uncontrollable sexuality. Compared to more normative yet nonetheless modern women, she plays the role of dominatrix in films such as *Payback* (1999), *Play It to the Bone* (2000), and *Charlie's Angels* (2000), and reprises her role as a bixini waxer cum detective in *Charlie's Angels: Full Throttle* (2003).

Close readings of the locations, sets, actions, dialogue, and narrative structures of the most popular representations of the Asian woman in Hollywood bring to physical manifestation the dreaded convergence of race and sexuality in the loaded terms of innate sexual capabilities and immoral sex acts, as well as threats to reproductive and social relations. I argue that the films specifically indicate the rise of Asian/American women as agents of pleasure and power carved in their own right, as racial stars bound by sex within representation.[17] Alternative readings of their negotiations with fandom are also significant when we consider how they charted their gender and race conundrums through interviews.

The silent film *The Thief of Bagdad* is a morality tale based on "an Arabian Nights fantasy." A thief, played by Douglas Fairbanks, transforms into a prince eligible to win the princess and the kingdom, an enchanted land populated by exotic racialized characters, spectacular sets, and grand beasts. Like the chimps and leopards that guard the castle, the presence of racial others establishes the exotic setting of the film.[18] The sly and unscrupulous Mongol prince embodies "Far East Asia" as a greedy, rapacious, and evil force; he aims to conquer Baghdad and lustfully possess the princess. Unlike the transformation of the thief into a prince, the Mongol slave girl and Mongols from Far East Asia are hopelessly immoral. In cahoots with these men, the Asian woman supposedly projects Oriental treachery in a new gendered form.

The film begins with an excerpt attributed to the literary *Arabian Nights:* "Verily the works of those gone before us have become instances and examples to men of our modern day, that folk may view what admonishing chances befell other folk and may there from take warning." How does this beginning lead toward figuring a legacy for the Asian woman in representation, as well as those who live under her sign? What if we take heed from Anna May Wong's own critical reading of the limited nature of her roles and read her Mongol slave girl as a multilayered construct? Can we see alternative readings of her animalistic bodily gestures and the sexual physicality of her appearances as redeployments of racist sexuality? What do we make of her framing, in parallel relation to the princess, as a formation of an aggressive sexuality that widens the subjectivities available to women? Can we reclaim the agency of her characterization within the spectacle of this silent film, in which she is dismissed as a fixed problem?[19] What if we analyze her role within the narrative context of this film? In her performance, Anna May Wong's manipulation of racial sexuality into a more compelling sexual subject position for Asian women or gendered female racial others is too easily ignored or underappreciated for its political possibilities. Anna May Wong's own words regarding her limited roles invite us to interpret powerful political possibility in her work.

In the film, the Mongol slave girl's perversity is a necessary contrast to the princess's innocence. We first encounter the two together. The princess is enshrouded in whiteness while Anna May Wong's Mongol slave girl is dressed in the skimpiest of bandeau tops and very tight briefs. The figure of Anna May Wong reveals the most skin, which is barely interrupted by the solid black attention-grabbing color of her coverings. She stands out distinctly from the white cotton softness of the bed and the murky mass of the other slave girls. Because she fans the princess to sleep, her movements are the grandest, leading spectators toward her as the visual target in the wide shot. Then a medium wide shot on Anna May Wong gives detail to her ensemble. Even more titillating, we see that her costume is barely held up by an apron with strings that hang in a fragile way from her necklace. Within this medium wide shot, we see her solemn expression as she peers in on the sleeping princess. It is a shot showing her inscrutability as a mysterious Oriental figure. Soon after this shot, she poisons the princess, whom we see in a medium close-up, a confection of sleeping softness. These types of shots, white figure and dark figure, asleep and awake, at rest and at work—directly contrast the two. The contest between the two women ensues. While the slave girls all direct their attention to the center of the room and within the narrative, the Mongol slave girl will initiate her own centrality, in terms of choreography and action, within the spectacular narrative. Her small presence will constitute a threat to the kingdom, and she will become the target of desire and visual pleasure within the film.

When the thief invades the private chambers enclosing the languid luxuriating princess, Anna May Wong moves swiftly like a small animal, hovering and kneeling in a way that delineates a cramped space around her. As she encounters the thief, who puts a knife to the flesh of her back and then to her throat, she is constructed as an object of desire, quite different from the chaste princess. The knife draws us to her naked skin and when the thief leads her to a side room, his action suggests the possibility of sexual threat. He leans the knife on a pillow so it stays put on her back. With fluttering hands and eyes open extra wide, she begs him not to kill her. But he is already gone to the one he truly desires. Realizing that the phallus on her back is the false one (not an extension of him), she

Anna May Wong in her solemn and conniving pose as
the inscrutable and actional Mongol slave girl in *The
Thief of Bagdad* (1924).

turns to scream. The thief flees by jumping from the balcony. And why
does she scream? Is it an expression of her anger or fear? Does she resent
his misdirected sexual attention toward the princess? Or does she desire to
protect the princess she will eventually poison and give up to the Mongol
prince? The performance raises other possibilities if she is seen as a subject
in her own right. The specific possibilities raised if we were to center her
subjectivity are the critique of dead-end lives for Asian female protago-
nists and the functioning of those dead-end lives as an allegory for Anna
May Wong's own life.

I reread her actions to recognize her as an actional subject with self-
interests that contradict her role as slave. While she performs the role of
devoted slave, a divergent agenda of sexual and racial anarchy motivates
her presence. She is an intriguing force within the scene, as well as in the
film. In "Asian Women in Film: No Joy, No Luck," Jessica Hagedorn
celebrates the resistances of Asian American female spectators who align
themselves with "bad" Asian females in film. Refusing more fetid definitions of femininity embodied in white women, identification with the
"bad" Asian female, the fierce, bold, aggressive, and actional Jade Cobra
girls in the Michael Cimino film *Year of the Dragon* (1985), is a political
practice of misidentification.[20] Anna May Wong, as the minor character,

actually moves the narrative of the film as much as the film's protagonist. And she moves in terms of her physicality just as she moves in ways that further the story.[21] Thus, the Mongol slave girl's agenda and actions take us to the film's conclusions. In a sense, she performs an active role that is significant to the world of the film in two meaningful ways: her behavior asserts subjectivity with intentions and aims contrary to the heroes, and she occupies a substantial position within the film's narrative economy. In her next appearance, the blocking within the wide shot introduces her as the demonic presence within the domain of the "good" princess.

On the balcony, the princess lounges in white-colored drapery as a white-clad, veiled slave girl tells her fortune. The Mongol slave girl stands between them, a figure still dressed in the same revealing black ensemble as before. Visually central, the movements of her fan bring together the other figures in the frame. The visual treatment of the white princess contrasts directly with the Mongol slave girl. The princess moves slowly and languidly, her shots intercut with those of the Mongol slave girl, who gesticulates and squints, her manner distracted and her eyes wild. Her frenzy registers in her uneven hair ornaments, her swift and short gasps of breath, and the fast, furtive movements of her eyes. While the film's scenes are entirely shot within palatial spaces, the Mongol slave girl seems constrained inside the frame as she moves frantically in the confined space. The scenes between the princess, the Mongol slave girl, and other better behaved slaves are easily read as the representation of the slave girl as suspect, but her acts can also be read more favorably as the dynamic deeds of a character aligned with the maligned East. That is, the Mongol slave girl performs this way deliberately so as to distract the others from her plot. In either case, her final exit remains ambiguous. She flees the palace after causing great havoc. Unlike the Mongol prince, who is left hanging by his neck, the Mongol slave girl scurries off to plot some more.

Thus, the Mongol slave girl occupies a viable subject position from which the story can be told beyond this film. Her character's destiny remains open-ended. So while the role she performs represents the perversity of Asian femininity, it offers an alternative to static white femininity. Moreover, this gender alternative comes with a racial critique when she aligns herself racially against her masters. Diane Negra describes this feminist disloyalty as a possible reason why ethnic female stars are not addressed in feminist film criticism while Karen Leong offers a more critical reading of women of color's racial agendas in film as "characteristics of a primitive, aggressive and uncivilized female."[22] Building from these theorists, I recast Anna May Wong as a subject-in-struggle through close readings of her performances.

The Mongol slave girl is loyal to her race to no fault. Simultaneously, she is a gateway to perverse sexuality. She engineers the Mongol prince's viewing of the princess in her private chambers, providing access to hidden sexuality so as to arouse his desire. Given a back view of Anna May Wong guiding the prince, we see her whole back exposed except for thin straps of black cloth across her back and buttocks. Within the film, nakedness signals perversity in the sense that one becomes more moral when putting on more clothes (like the thief) and less moral when wearing fewer clothes (like the Mongol slave girl).[23] And in this shot, she is the most naked. The figures most similarly naked are the black guards, racialized as figures to be feared, and the thief himself, who comes to be civilized by the film's end.

The Mongol slave girl relishes her nudity and her access to the privacy of the princess's sexuality. When she opens the compartment that leads to the princess's chambers, the Mongol prince hides his face behind his fan, as if to mediate the openness of the scene before him. She does not retreat from the privacy she reveals. Stripped to reveal her own sexuality, she delights in denuding her chaste foe. I point to these tensions between her two contrasting roles—one as a kind of progressive racial agent and the other as a regressive sexual agent—in order to identify her as a subject-in-struggle, rather than a fixity. Another question about her character also arises—is she truly a femme fatale? Is she simply self-serving in her treachery?

While her treachery may seemingly affirm the reading of the Asian woman as dragon lady, it is also a redeployment of sexuality toward freedom from slavery. For example, the rivalry between the Mongol slave girl and the white princess comes to closure when the Mongol slave girl finally poisons the princess and engineers her capture. As the white-cloud of a princess fantasizes about the thief-turned-prince, a cut to the black bandeau-clad slave girl reveals her plans to curtail the princess's pleasure. She adds drugs to the incense, filling the room with poisoned smoke. At this juncture, the parallel close-ups end and the two are joined in a wider medium shot. Bending over the fully clad, white confection of a princess, the gloriously bare Mongol slave girl spreads her palm brazenly over the prized royal mouth. Upon this act of assault, executed with an expression of determination, the Mongol slave girl releases herself from the servile bond to her mistress so that she no longer supplements her in the rest of

The Mongol slave girl poisons the princess in
The Thief of Bagdad.

the narrative. To be sure, the act of drugging the princess is a sexualized one. After making contact and caressing her hand over the princess's mouth, the slave girl understand the volatility of her actions and looks around to make sure no one sees her. This highly charged act transforms the Mongol slave girl into the subject position of vixen, now with a more viable future that competes directly with the princess's position.

The Mongol slave girl's physicality and presence change when she is released from the princess. Later, as the princess lays down in near death, the Mongol slave girl stands apart as a solitary and serious presence among the crowd of men. The other slave girls bend over the mistress. When the princess is revived, the parallel medium close-up shots begin again and the contest between the Mongol slave girl and the princess is renewed. The princess looks up, hoping to see her thief-turned-prince return. The Mongol slave girl stands upright, observes the scene, and then runs off to plot again. She runs back to save the Mongol prince and, as before, scurries around like an animal. Although Wong's character is indeed caught within the bonds of slavery, the stereotype diagnosis that calls the character a dragon lady does not appreciate her as a subject who devises her own transformation, under severe constraints, from docile servant to daring vixen. She is not so much cartoonish or evil; rather, she possesses a serious determination and engages in sexual anarchy. And it is this determination that she evinces within her gendered, racial, and sexual situation that clarifies her as a subject-in-struggle.

What happens to the Asian woman at the end of *The Thief of Bagdad?* She simply disappears after saving the Mongol prince. The entry of the Oriental female sex symbol on screen in *The Thief of Bagdad* initiates a subject-in-struggle who continues in *Shanghai Express.*[24] The film features the star Marlene Dietrich as Shanghai Lily, the notorious "white flower of China," who reforms for her ex-lover, the staid British military doctor Donald Harvey. The crisis of the film centers on the sexuality of the white woman corrupted by China and its incongruity as a place, not only within the specific moment of civil war but as a racially marked sexual economy. The film centers its action on the train called the Shanghai Express, which is hijacked by fiendish Chinese revolutionaries. The passengers undergo a "test of faith" when terrorized by the evil Chang, the revolutionary who takes Harvey as a hostage. Chang also preys on Shanghai Lily and the native prostitute, Hui Fei, the character played by Anna May Wong. The sexual liaisons between these three figures challenge the rigid morals of the passengers, especially Harvey, who must choose to wager his love on a sexually suspect Shanghai Lily.

No other figure embodies the (sexual) strangeness of China than Hui Fei in *Shanghai Express.* She commits murder as revenge for her rape, provides no background regarding her character, and, in a puzzling act at the end, saves the white woman. The open-ended rivalry and homoeroticism played out between the white woman and the Asian woman in *The Thief of Bagdad* is once again taken up here by Marlene Dietrich and Anna May Wong. However, this contest places Hui Fei in a supplementary position to Shanghai Lily's transformation. While both are prostitutes, the fantasy figure in the film is Shanghai Lily, whose importance relegates the Asian woman into a status of marginality, the one who must be raped. The diagnosis of Hui Fei as a murderous vamp stereotype is insufficient because she performs acts that generate a spectral presence. She kills her rapist not only to extract revenge, but also to redeem herself. It is an act that indicates a complex story as performed by Anna May Wong.[25]

Sex and violence punctuate the relationship between two individually perverse entities, the villain Chang and Hui Fei, both of whom are Chinese. When dressing to sleep, Chang approaches Hui Fei, speaking Chinese. She opens her compartment window to reveal herself, informally dressed in a cheong-sam and her long hair let loose. The framing, along with the production design and the acting, reveals the expectation of the Asian woman's sexual compliance. When he closes the blinds and she turns toward him, she seems acquiescent to his advances but quite suddenly kicks him out. The Asian woman's sexuality is ambiguous here—not aligned with the Chinese man and not acquiescent to his oblique advances as a potential john. What sort of female sexuality does she represent? Regarding this last question, we might surmise that Hui Fei's sexuality is one central to the constitution of the white woman's definition as the heroine who must be saved not only from China but from the Asian woman whose sexuality remains ambiguous.

The Asian woman and the white woman visually allure. Their arrivals at the train station establish their shared and differing status as women. Distinct from the masses milling around the train platform, Hui Fei arrives in a carriage, while Shanghai Lily shows up in a car. Hui Fei demonstrates awareness of her surroundings, looking around with caution. Upon embarking the train, she stops and surveys the scene behind her as if to see if she is being followed. Unlike Hui Fei, Shanghai Lily moves and dresses as if the world centers on her body. Feathers and finery emanate from her as the core attraction of the scene. Hui Fei blends into the stark environs with stick-shaped dresses and subdued colors. They speak similar snappy lines in low tones and move gracefully in the otherwise bouncing train, all the while striking cool postures here and there framed in light. However, Shanghai Lily's intonation reveals a certain self-satisfaction and smugness. Hui Fei's speech lacks enjoyment and sounds more like resignation or bitterness. To see the never smiling Hui Fei is to anticipate the looming threat of Shanghai Lily's fall from grace and civilization. Shanghai Lily could become entirely part of China as indicated by Hui Fei, an entirely fallen woman in a savage and primitive place.

The Asian woman represents the terrible future of the white woman if the latter is not diverted from the path of sex—in a film where sexuality is the measure of a woman's worth. Although they are both degraded women, Hui Fei is not protected by the myths of white upright womanhood that ultimately save Shanghai Lily. Harvey comes to Lily's rescue when Chang makes forceful advances toward her. But when Chang is unsuccessful in his approaches toward Lily, he calls for Hui Fei, whose subsequent rape is ignored by the rest of the passengers. The Asian woman as receptacle for the sexual aggression that the white woman escapes is forgotten and goes unacknowledged.

When sexually threatened, Hui Fei does not warrant protection from either the men or the respectable community of white people. Eventually, even the white woman she saves will not advocate for her. Earlier, for example, Shanghai Lily makes sure to tell Harvey that Hui Fei is not her friend and that she is "only trying to be decent" when introducing her. While the biracial man rapes Hue Fei, she receives no protection from the Chinese men. And when she emerges from Chang's compartment after the rape, we see his head guard eyeing and touching her against her will. Afterward, Shanghai Lily herself will not comment on the Asian woman's rape as she negotiates with Chang, who now plans to blind Harvey. Lily refuses to protect Hui Fei but gives herself up for Harvey. At this juncture of Shanghai Lily's self-sacrifice, Hui Fei saves herself proudly. This is an important conclusion in the film for someone deemed so Other. Her act of murder is a saving of the self that her assignation as simply a "murderous vamp" evades.

Hui Fei kills for herself. In fact, she makes it quite clear that she kills solely for herself. For example, when she emerges from the chambers of the rapist, she actually goes to her room and pulls out a knife. Shanghai Lily thinks Hui Fei will kill herself. But she will not commit suicide; she will not efface herself. This is precisely the kind of reading Anna May Wong invites in her own critique of her limited roles. That is, she makes sure to place in the record her protest in ways that authorize such interpretation. In the dark of Chang's chambers, Hui Fei waits. As he bends over the table to sign papers, she moves deliberately to stab him twice in the back. Her arm movements are large and wide and he falls before her. She scurries away, looking around to make sure she can escape, moving like she did in *The Thief of Bagdad:* purposeful, upright, and extremely tense. Captured in a wide shot, these scurrying movements and gestures, along with her smallness, again raise the issue of whether these acts fulfill expectations of the Asian woman as a racialized sexual entity defined by her physicality. These gestures and movements—affirming as they do her primitivized sexuality—must be understood within the context of the narrative and by the ways in which her recognizability as a racial and sexual Other may be redeployed toward unexpected or contradictory ends. In *Shanghai Express,* the avenging Asian woman kills an Asian man in service of herself and her country, as well as for the white passengers. The Asian man is actually a hybrid, whose allegiances to race and nation are muddled. As such, he is constructed as a monstrosity of confusion deemed dangerous to both entities. The Asian woman kills him yet remains outside the community of the film; she cannot be the hero.

In *Shanghai Express*, a similar doubleness of meaning occurs in certain scenes. The murder the Asian woman commits enables the white couple's reform. While the Asian woman is not the central character in this film, her role is pivotal. Hui Fei instructs Harvey, "You better get her out of there. I have just killed Chang." When Shanghai Lily returns to their compartment, she says: "I don't know if I ought to be grateful to you or not." The following response is enigmatic: "It's of no consequence. I didn't do it for you. Death cancels debt to me." The Asian woman remains a puzzling figure, for Hui Fei saves herself from the rapist and along the way saves the white woman. Because the white woman chooses to be a receptacle for the savagery of Asian men for the sake of saving the white man, the Asian woman who chooses instead a different and more vengeful, aggressive femininity is the one who saves her. That is, the white woman gives her body to service male pleasure and male survival. But the Asian woman refuses both in an alternative form of gender and sexuality. She kills a man and saves the woman in a more liberatory and woman-centered equation. This is a significant saving of the white woman who gives in to Chang, the racial Other, while giving up Harvey, the white man. This act is an ultimate sexual self-sacrifice, a deeper falling. The white woman begins to lose her composure and begins to become disheveled and destroyed. The Asian woman carves a new heroism that enables the film's closure and the white woman's salvation. Thus, her heroism is an alternative formation of gender and sexuality produced within the confines of her smaller role and from within the heteronormative confines of the film.

At the end of the film, when the Asian woman is surrounded by reporters and given the opportunity to speak of herself to the cameras, she instead steps away. In a complex cinematic moment not captured by stereotype analysis, she refuses to speak after she kills a man. Frenzied reporters surround her as she gets off the train. Newspaper headlines celebrate her act, "Chinese Girl Kills. . . ." They gather around in a crowd and shout over her: "Did you kill him with a knife?" and "Say something!" Her refusal to speak here may be seen as a testament to the constraints of the Asian woman in film. Barely seen in celluloid, the unfinished product of her role opens up possibilities for how she is understood. There may be space provided for her on screen, but in no way can she be understood

In *Shanghai Express*, Chang unsuccessfully propositions Hui Fei. Later, she stabs him with slow, tense, and deliberate movements before scurrying away.

within the existing terms. But what can she say—earlier she declares that she saved herself and did it for no one else: "Death cancels debt to me." What is the debt to which she refers? She kills Chang so as to make space for herself, to pass on a different legacy, and to refuse a death-in-life existence as raped and silenced. She mutters something in Chinese, holds up her hand in a halting command, then walks away.

It is exactly this ambiguity that I isolate in her performances and presence on screen. The Asian woman is an absent/present, dead/living subject on screen upon whose body race, sex, and gender in colonial narratives are kept open with possibilities for various interpretations. Moreover, the Asian woman functions as a haunting presence within this scene, for in the historical moment she cannot occupy a viable role. It seems, in the end, that she must remain unintelligible within the film. It is a legacy present in the work of the major Asian American actresses who follow her. By presenting the ambiguity of the Asian American femme fatale in Hollywood, we may better recognize the political possibilities present in their limited roles.

THE HAUNTING OF ANNA MAY WONG IN NANCY KWAN AND LUCY LIU

The platforms and performances of Nancy Kwan in *The World of Suzie Wong* and *Flower Drum Song* and Lucy Liu today in *Payback, Play It to the Bone, Charlie's Angels,* and *Kill Bill* are haunted by the performances and presences of Anna May Wong. The life and work of Anna May Wong exemplifies the ethical "burden of representation" actors and actresses of color continue to contend with in their work. Nancy Kwan and Lucy Liu demonstrate how Anna May Wong's legacy does not continue in a progressively linear fashion of development. Instead, Kwan exemplifies a resistance to political responsibility that raises the question of how to assess the meaning of sexual pleasure exploding from her star persona, performances, and roles. Does her sexual representation introduce progressive politics if reclaimed outside of a moralistic framework? And then there is Lucy Liu, whose interviews advocate a critical post-racist logic, or an explicit disavowal of racial responsibility in choosing her roles while demonstrating an awareness of how racial critique can limit her opportunities. How do we asses such a move, apart from how she may secure roles that benefit her career individually? In order to understand these different approaches to the question of ethical and racial responsibility for Asian American actresses in Hollywood, I now briefly outline how hypersexuality connects three generations of Asian American femme fatale roles in major Hollywood films. In so doing, I begin to break open the hold of stereotype analysis that is delimiting our understanding of the Asian American femme fatale's bondage and to open up more productive discussion regarding the range of resistances in these women's work.

The film *The World of Suzie Wong* (1960) features Nancy Kwan, in her breakthrough role, as a prostitute "with a heart of gold." Despite incredible hardship as an illiterate prostitute with an illegitimate son, she maintains her goodness, beauty, and innocence. The film tells the story of an interracial romance between Suzie Wong, a wholesome prostitute and single mother, and an American businessman attempting to become an artist in Hong Kong. By the film's conclusion, her son dies and the couple intends to marry and live in the United States in the face of his community's disapproval. Peter Feng describes *The World of Suzie Wong* as a "classic racist and sexist text" that is easy to love and which formulates a theory of spectatorship that offers a contextualized understanding of the limits facing actors and actresses who have to take on stereotypical roles in order to survive financially as well as to cultivate their talent and craft.[26] A binary that understands good people and bad roles persists in approaches to films such as *The World of Suzie Wong,* which are incredibly pleasurable to watch for a multitude of reasons: their grand Hollywood production values; Technicolor and seductive production design; and the articulation of fantasies about the racial Other, at a time when its "real counterpart" circulates in popular culture as well. That is, the tastiness of the taboo of interracial white-Asian sex is exploited in this romantic narrative.

While Nancy Kwan's roles are pre-feminist icons in both *The World of Suzie Wong* and *Flower Drum Song,* both films offer combinations of sweetness and vampiness that characterize the Hollywood Asian American femme fatale. It is essentially the "good woman" caught in a "bad role" that presents a different form of pleasure in the performances of Nancy Kwan. That is, her roles show how Asian/American women fulfill normative standards of beauty and racialized gender as argued by Anne Anlin Cheng.[27] It is a pleasure much more ambivalent than the brazen embrace of "bad" womanhood in Anna May Wong's roles.

In *The World of Suzie Wong,* the theme of morality as organized by racialized sexuality embraces the Asian woman. Essays in the anthology

Before and after Suzie read the construction of interracial romance dynamically in *The World of Suzie Wong*. "Lomax," for example, "has become a part of Suzie's world-crossing borders of race and gender. Racially he has rejected Kaye and the colonial world of wealth, secure 9 to 5 jobs and men who may deplore relationships with the Chinese and yet have Chinese mistresses whom they never marry."[28] Meanwhile,

> the most interesting and unique feature of the character of Suzie Wong is that she is not a common whore, lacking in self-respect. She is pragmatic but also a dreamer, a person with her own principles and character. For example, she does not sleep around. She is the classic embodiment of the person with a heart of gold. She gives birth to a child whose father has abandoned her. Rather than give up the child to the father, she hides it. In the film, her character is even more beautified. She is hardly regarded with jaundiced eyes. It does not appear that she has been degraded and that she has suffered. On the contrary, she appears a most lively and energetic creature.[29]

The interracial romance is idealized: the lovers transform each other and join together across racial difference. As a prostitute, Suzie is also idealized as girlish, naive, and innocent. Difference is not transcended in a love intensely racialized, gendered, and sexualized. Using David Henry Hwang's *M. Butterfly*, Ford and Chanda describe the narcissism of Lomax, seeing the kind of man he wants to be in her eyes. Law describes Lomax's love as a colonial attitude of transcendent love within the historical context of Hong Kong.[30] I add to these dynamic readings that reject binarisms of bad racist films (for engaging the taboo) by highlighting the particular femininity of the Asian woman in contrast to the dull and less desirable white woman's sexuality.

In *The World of Suzie Wong*, the prostitute Suzie Wong's sexuality is described within her race and gender ontology. She is also described in contrast to the white woman in presenting competing womanhoods attractive to white men. For example, Suzie is disenfranchised from the bourgeois social circles of the white community in Hong Kong. A dinner party conversation centers on the different sexual morality attributed to the Chinese so that the romantic lead Robert Lomax must cross social boundaries for the love of the Chinese woman as a sign of social progress. Marchetti reads this as an indictment of British colonialism in favor of American rescue of the racial Other.[31] Unlike the British, the American presumably comes to recognize her humanity. However, Suzie is also posited as a more ideal version of femininity compared to the aggressive white woman. She is submissive and prioritizes her man's desires. Throughout the movie, a white woman manipulates her rich father into bankrolling Lomax's career choice as an artist and as a potential husband. While Suzie attempts to support him with her earnings, she returns to a more traditional role at the end of the film when she declares, "I will follow you until you say, 'Suzie, go away.'" Her ideal femininity is also anti-modern. According to Gina Marchetti, Lomax finds Suzie undesirable in Western clothing and finds her most desirable in traditional Chinese clothing.[32] Her appeal is also secured with lines exemplifying anti-feminism in an era when the civil rights movement involved women's rights activism. For example, Suzie rushes downstairs to show off bruises she collected from a beating supposedly given by Lomax in a jealous rage.

While we can understand Nancy Kwan's role within the film as a performance of good womanhood that critiques white femininity and Asian masculinity, the role also aims for recognition across difference and inequality with the white man. That is, the man is required to recognize her situation and transform when reflecting upon what he would do in her situation. He occupies the role of the Other in order to learn and to change. Her closing line of "I will follow you until you say 'Suzie, go away'" is met by his confirmation of mutual desire, "That long?" The pleasure in identifying with Suzie Wong expresses desire for normalcy that typically excludes Asian/American women.[33] Even today, for example, we still do not generally see Asian/American women as leads in romantic comedies, such as Sandra Oh's role in the Canadian feature film *Double Happiness*. Such a character fulfills normative definitions of good womanhood in privileging how she may serve her man or she may fulfill the position of a legitimate wife despite her racial lack. Her role ultimately aspires to normative womanhood across a racial divide. Nancy Kwan's platform, politically viable in its own right, echoes the spectator of *Miss Saigon* who wanted to be engulfed in roles that may seem to advocate self-annihilation. Nonetheless, political critique occurs at the site of her resistance to racialization and racial critique. In a reversal of the butterfly trope, the Asian woman partners up with the white man who chooses her over the white woman.

The first major Hollywood movie featuring an all-Asian cast, *Flower Drum Song* presents similar ambiguities regarding the political possibilities of performing a seemingly sexually liberated character. The story centers on Mei Li, an illegal Chinese immigrant who comes to the United States as part of an arranged marriage to a Chinese American man named Sammy Fong. The Chinese American community idealizes the immigrant's "Old World" femininity as the ideal reproductive partner for an increasingly established ethnic minority community. Mei Li falls in love with Wang Ta, a good-looking young Chinese American man for whom his family also seeks a proper wife. Competing for Wang Ta's affections are Linda Low and Helen. In *Flower Drum Song*, Nancy Kwan plays Linda Low, a character whose beauty, as insightfully argued by Anne Anlin Cheng, represents a sexually liberated American woman against the Asian Mei Li and the Asian American Helen.[34] While Nancy Kwan performs roles that may seem to critique moralistic approaches to women's sexual subjection, the ultimate goal for her character is to achieve normalcy in terms of good woman-hood. In both the Suzie Wong and Linda Low role, she demonstrates a particular kind of masochism when she must be publicly punished or continually humiliated for manipulating Wang Ta or Robert Lomax.

The enjoyment, at the site of performance and spectatorship, quite apparent in moments throughout the film poses a political dilemma to my questions about liberating possibilities in sexual performance. Kwan famously performs the Rodgers and Hammerstein hit song "I Enjoy Being a Girl" while wrapped in a white towel dress in front of mirrors within a big luxurious bathroom: "I'm strictly a female female. And my future I hope/ will be/in the home of a/brave and he male who/enjoys being a guy/having a girl just like me." She presents a seductive role within the film in this dance number and others such as "Grant Avenue" and "Fan Tan Fanny." Linda Low offers a racial occupation of traditional white femininity. She seduces and manipulates in order to serve her needs and to formulate a performative definition of gender. She accesses traditional gender roles in order to manipulate men to meet her needs. The mirror scene precedes her seduction of Wang Ta in a car overlooking San Francisco. In this scene, she articulates her mission to succeed in her performance of gender. She executes this performance as she faces the mirror to sing a declaration of self-love and to celebrate female beauty in terms of attracting men. We see Nancy Kwan's character, wearing a towel dress, from multiple angles. She is undeniably beautiful. The presentation of numerous images of Linda Low shows the Asian/American woman's achievement of normative standards of beauty for women. The mirror scene enables us to see Linda Low in triplicate as she models a gown, a cocktail dress, a bikini, and a towel.

While she identifies her character as an agent of seduction, her discussion as an actress highlights the importance of representing an Asian woman as an object of beauty and as a subject of desire.

In the film, however, she is punished and humiliated as an unreliable and untrustworthy figure. A deceptive femme fatale, she uses her feminine sexuality in order to seduce Wang Ta into a marriage proposal, which is a ploy to catch her true love, Sammy, who in comparison to Wang Ta represents an alternative male sexuality. Rather than being dependent on his father, Sammy is well known as an entrepreneur who finds traditional Chinese women boring. In a later scene, he and Linda Low sing a song about redefining monogamy and marriage. They are, in a sense, offering a critique of heteronormativity in their coupling as American: she as a white woman in Anne Anlin Cheng's argument and he as a hipster in an alternative form of masculinity.

Sammy Fong and Linda Low are a perfect match as an unconventional couple, who love each other, as they formulate nontraditional roles as men and women. They call for a new envisioning of gender roles within the Asian American community in the film. Linda Low's role is particularly illuminating in demanding a broader definition of gender and power. While Linda Low pretends to be a "good" woman, she cannot but help answer the call of wild music, and she dances inappropriately with Ta's brother at a family party. Her lies are exposed when she is ultimately humiliated on stage when Ta's family discovers her "true identity" as an untrustworthy entertainer who derives pleasure from revealing and manipulating her body for public display, barely dressed and wearing a ridiculous hat. The "Fan Tan Fanny" dance features Linda Low snapping her butt and flicking her head to the beat. Upon seeing Wang Ta's father, the patriarch, she is truly denuded. With an alarmed expression on her face, she stops dancing. She stops the rhythm of her life as a seductress who critiques the traditional bounds of gender. Her eyes bulge out of her face. She covers herself with her pink fans in a moment of shame.

Linda Low is a character caught within racialized and gendered constraints so that she must resort to ruses in the context of gender and racial inequality.[35] Happy to center her subjectivity in terms of fulfilling good woman roles to male partners, she aspires for normalcy usually accorded to white women. Quite unlike Anna May Wong's roles in which we can imagine the possibilities of fleeing the limited avenues for women's lives, Nancy Kwan's roles are about manipulating the world in order for "bad

Linda Low sings about performing
gender, freezes upon seeing the
patriarch, and unsuccessfully
hides, humiliated, in *Flower
Drum Song*.

women" such as sex workers to become engulfed in gendered normalcy from which they were previously excluded. The roles are both about disciplining and rewarding bad women into good womanhood.[36] Ultimately, there is a political critique in aspiring to normalcy if such an aspiration provides a critique of exclusion for minoritized raced and gendered subjects.

Lucy Liu's roles offer a different challenge to assessing a viable representational politics. *Play It to the Bone* (2000) presents one of Liu's many roles of flagrantly excessive sexuality. The film's previews feature a sassy Lucy Liu on the receiving end of violence: she gets hit on the face by the white female lead.[37] Cynthia Fuchs describes as disturbing Lucy Liu's character as an object of violence: "*Play It to the Bone* treats Liu-as-Lia in a particularly asinine way" by wreaking havoc between the three leads in all the worst ways. This is apparent " . . . in the movie's trailer: Grace (the white woman) punches Liu full in the jaw and sniffs, 'I don't like you either!' Apparently someone thinks this is a joke that will draw audiences, the sturdy white woman belting the hell out of the young, lithe interloper."[38]

In the contemporary movie *Charlie's Angels* (2000), Lucy Liu performs what may seem to be a racially unmarked character as one of three highly accomplished professional female spies whose jobs involve masquerading in various racial and gendered forms. As a masseuse at an Oriental establishment, she performs a massage with her feet in order to spy on a suspect. Costumed in a tube top mini-dress using the same thick, silky fabric as the cheong-sam and with chopsticks holding up her hair bun, she walks on Tim Curry's back before "knocking (him) unconscious" with her small foot on his neck. As a postmodern heroine, she is a dynamic playful figure, donning various costumes and characters. In her masseuse disguise, her movements are reminiscent of Anna May Wong's in *The Thief of Bagdad* and *Shanghai Express;* after Liu's character Alex incapacitates the bad man, she scurries on the floor and looks around in case she gets caught. The performance of tension, mysterious plotting, and escape evokes Anna May Wong's performance in *The Thief of Bagdad*. The lighting, however, is different. Unlike the starkness and high-contrast ration exposing Anna May Wong in *Shanghai Express,* the lighting in *Charlie's Angels* is sexual in making her skin delectable and golden. While Marlene Dietrich's close-ups framed by Josef Von Sternberg are famous, Anna May Wong did not enjoy a similar fetishistic gaze. While the Asian woman is now a heroine of the Hollywood film, in the sense of her framing as a

The framing and lighting make Lucy Liu look golden and delectable in a close-up during the masseuse scene in *Charlie's Angels*.

In *Charlie's Angels*, Lucy Liu's pose evokes Anna May Wong's figure in *The Thief of Bagdad*.

sexual object, she recasts the disturbing sexual gestures in order to comment on the role.[39] Alex's eye-rolling derision and knowing smile as the masseuse character enable resistant readings while simultaneously reinstalling the sexual trope of the Asian/American woman masseuse in popular culture. Her smile is also notable in an otherwise jarring repertoire of unsmiling dominatrix roles for which she is most known. In the close-up of the smile, we notice the accoutrements in her coiffure and costume that establish the Orientalism evoked in the scene. Indeed, Liu's role displays a certain kind of postmodern play of the stereotype. Is there political progress in such expression?

Read as postmodern play, Lucy Liu's performance offers a form of political critique. Generally speaking, if stereotypes are imprints carrying ambivalence, then tropes are the basic structure upon which the meanings hang. Such tropes include the masseuse, the slave girl, and other roles that can be donned in the service of the potentially rupturous meanings they produce. Specifically, Lucy Liu is simply presented as just one of three other masquerading women who can perform various races and genders. Her racial identity is not mentioned except that her character's fake job is as a bikini waxer, which draws upon the stereotype of Asian/American women service workers in the United States. Even her father is played by the famed white British actor John Cleese. All three women indeed play with gendered representations of race: they don kimonos and a sexy variation on the Swedish national costume. Unlike the roles played by Cameron Diaz and Drew Barrymore, Lucy Liu's main scripted roles build on established hypersexual images of Asian women such as the masseuse and the whip-wielding leather-clad dominatrix. Thus, the assertion of post-racist logic in the play of various races and genders does not account for the historical continuity in stereotype deployment for the Asian/American figure.[40] As I argue, however, her performances offer productive commentary.

If political pleasure in the performance and consumption of stereotypes entails a non-normative embrace of perverse sexual politics, Lucy Liu's roles question the efficacy of such a strategy. Playing Pearl, Lucy Liu embraces perversity wholeheartedly in *Payback,* a film about a spy who comes back to wreak vengeance against the villains who presumed him dead. Her wholehearted embrace of perversity demonstrates awareness of the limited role and relays a kind of campiness in her performance. In the film, Mel Gibson's character fights a gang of Chinese thugs lead by the dominatrix Pearl. Introduced in an extreme close-up of her long red nails and feathered sleeves, she turns to face the audience with a smile on her very red lips, as the elevator closes with a special effects sound of a ferocious roar. The white male sadomasochist villain opens the door and she immediately smacks him in the face while commanding: "On your knees, bitch, I want satisfaction." She punches him in the stomach as she tilts her head back with pleasure. He slumps his body on to her as she supports his weight with no problem. Lucy Liu plays the dominatrix very well—she looks polished, with her hair perfectly coiffed and the feathers on her outfit intact. She does not break a sweat. He hits her back on the face with no holds barred. Dressed in leather fetish wear, long red nails, and furs,

As Pearl in *Payback*, Lucy Liu smiles after punching her white male lover in the stomach.

she yields a whip and relentlessly returns all of his jibes with the great conviction that Lucy Liu became famous for as the cold and ferocious Ling Woo in *Ally McBeal*.

Lucy Liu skillfully performs the dominatrix role in *Payback,* and it is her performances in such roles that teeter on the edge of affirming and breaking the Hollywood tradition of representing Asian/American women within hypersexuality. While it is quite pleasurable to see Liu "kick ass," especially as she delivers a performance full of enjoyment of its physicality and violence, the mainstream nature of the role questions how the embrace of perversity and power expands our imagination of Asian/American women's lives. In the movie, she gets hit in the face several times by different men and derives pleasure from it, in direct contrast to the white women who fear violence and are almost paralyzed by it. Like Anna May Wong's character in *The Thief of Bagdad*, Liu's character is also a formation of alternative femininity. She works in cahoots with criminal Asian men. When the white men confront each other across the bed where she sleeps with her villainous lover, Lucy Liu's Pearl is aroused by the power of Mel Gibson's hero so that she beats up her lover with great energy. She narrates her kicking and beating of his limp body with the lines, "Me love you baby . . . me love you long time." Like Margaret Cho's performance of similar lines, rewriting the lines ascribed to prostitute Asian women, Pearl wields great sexual power, racialized by the stereotype she hails in her speech. The scene is punctuated firmly as she turns around to reveal her chaps or assless leather pants. At the end of this scene, however, she is marginalized as so perverse that she is undesirable to the white male lead. The dominatrix is unlike Nancy Kwan's roles that aspire to good woman-hood. While there is pleasure in seeing Lucy Liu hit powerful white men and embrace violence, the larger picture poses a problem for she is rendered inhuman, a sex machine.[41] It is her embrace of hypersexuality in such roles—in terms of her deriving sexual enjoyment from giving and receiving pain—that makes Lucy Liu's roles hover on the edge of defying or reinscribing stereotypes of Asian women as hypersexual. It is her play with race, gender, and sexuality as a subject-in-struggle that allows us to see how her performance pushes us toward an understanding of the vast possibilities of political resistance in representation.

TRIANGULATIONS OF ACTRESS, WOMAN, AND ROLE: INTERVIEWS WITH ANNA MAY WONG, NANCY KWAN, AND LUCY LIU, 1920S TO THE PRESENT

The roles played by Anna May Wong, Nancy Kwan, and Lucy Liu are commonly placed within the stereotype framework popular in racial discourses of representation as a manifestation of racist ideology in contemporaneous life. Anna May Wong herself very clearly and consistently expressed disdain for the racially limited nature of her roles in her many interviews and in the works by contemporary Asian American novelists, poets, filmmakers, and critics who revive her legacy.[42] How do Nancy Kwan's and Lucy Liu's interviews and commentary on their authorships contribute to our reception of their roles? In their interviews, Nancy Kwan and Lucy Liu cannot avoid engaging racial and sexual thematics in discussing their work. However, they take different approaches. In their performances, Nancy Kwan strives for normalcy and inclusion and Lucy Liu ultimately presents a post-racist logic. Both help me to define and insist upon the importance of the factor of unknowability, or the instability of representational forms, within the politically powerful nature of sexual pleasure in Hollywood productions of the hypersexual Asian/American women. The three different platforms of Wong, Kwan, and Liu remind us of the changing historical contexts and cultural demands shaping the possibilities and interpretations of performance.

What the three share is a response to the coexisting desire for Asian women's hypersexual visual representation to involve the possibility of verifying real Asian women—and the fear that it already does. Commenting on the publicity around her movies, Anna May Wong "speaks" about the attribution of exotic background to provide grounds for verifying her fictional roles. "After *The Thief of Bagdad*, the press begins to call me the 'celestial maiden.' They call me 'sloe-eyed.' They call me 'exotic.' They call me the 'Oriental Siren,' the 'China Doll,' the 'Lotus Girl,' the 'Chinese Flapper.' They call me the 'Queen of the B-films.' They say I've never cut my hair, never worn eyeglasses, never worn wool underwear, never curled my hair, never eaten lobster, never been on a bicycle, never owned a radio. They say I have the longest nails in Hollywood."[43] In the passage above, Anna May Wong captures the projection of group racial characteristics on her individual body. She is placed within a freakish subjectivity—outside modernity as one untouched by technology or unaffected by cosmopolitanism. She is constructed instead as primarily racially different—that is, race organizes what subjectivity and what roles/characters are available for her.

Anna May Wong herself attempted to deal with the complex scenes she performed on screen. She also occupies an iconic position within Asian American cultural production in which many speak on her behalf or attempt to understand her situation, such as in Elizabeth Wong's play *China Doll* or in Asian American poetry as discussed by Cynthia Liu.[44] Through creative production by others, she steps off the frame to speak "in real life." And in her life off screen, Anna May Wong also walked away. At first, after *The Thief of Bagdad*, she fled to Europe, then to China, and then back to Santa Monica as an exile of Hollywood. What could she say about the limited roles she was made to play? As a partial response to this sort of inquiry, the writer Lisa See reconstructs the subject position from which Anna May Wong speaks: "When I left Hollywood, I vowed I would never act for film again. I was so tired of the parts I had to play."[45]

What does it mean to view the body of her work with the knowledge of Anna May Wong's early death at the age of fifty-six and of her futile attempts at recovery from the traumas of Hollywood, stardom and miscegenation, community and a kind of homelessness?[46] In her body of work at the Library of Congress, Wong features prominently in the starring credits of numerous films even though the parts she played in these films were often minor roles as domestics and mysterious dragon ladies.[47] Nevertheless, she performed them with powerful dignity apparent whenever she walked into the scene. It is as if her earlier roles as Hui Fei and the Mongol slave girl, as well as her starring roles in European productions such as *Piccadilly* (1929), inform these minor roles with immense star power.

There is something about representation and its relationship to the reality it entangles that should be accounted for in our understanding of spectatorship and production. The relationship between representation and reality is a very different one captured in the frameworks of linear effects or bad stereotypes. Anna May Wong, Hollywood's first Oriental female sex symbol, left us with evidence of her rage and frustration through so many intense glances and facial expressions that convey what she did not or could not say within the films.[48] Whether directed, self-authored, or projected by the spectator, her looks show the possible convergence of a racialized woman's life with her acting roles. In my readings of her roles, it is clear that Anna May Wong left a haunting in her performances relevant to the Asian/American actresses following her lead. As Hui Fei and the Mongol slave girl, she played her roles with an attitude that came to be her identifiable signature. She was not merely a "Chinese woman" but Anna May Wong, a disenfranchised and enraged woman as well as an exceptional and extraordinary working actress within an intensely racially segregated era. She became Anna May Wong by playing these roles, rather than the other way around. Her version of a self-effacing bowed-head character typical of racial representations of her time allowed for her to be a recognizable star. She kept open the possibility of interpreting her presence on film, as authored within the constraints placed on an Oriental actress. And in salvaging her self within the narrative, she produces Anna May Wong as an open-ended figure who brings together an enraged life on and off screen that lives beyond her death.

In her research, Karen Leong unearths Wong's own dynamic theorization of the significance of her many deaths on screen. Wong maintains a critique of gender and racial norms for women of "any ethnicity" and offers an understanding of the need to discipline women who exceed such norms.[49] According to Wong, "On the screen it is very necessary to do something conclusive with any personality that's glamorous or exotic. One cannot just leave them floating around. They are too definite. . . ." In Leong's analysis, they "had to be eliminated."[50] As such, Anna May Wong's presence on the celluloid record describes great power produced from a critical life on the frontlines of engaging issues of representation in history and society. As an Asian American actress, she had to negotiate problematic roles and find ways to comment on their limits. She established a different voice to accompany her important celluloid legacy.

Forty years later, Nancy Kwan described the dilemma of racialized representation as an unfair demand for her to represent all Asian women as an actress. Unlike Anna May Wong, who worked primarily in the 1920s, Nancy Kwan worked in the 1960s and her protests primarily involved a critique of those who placed demands on her as a racial actress, typically Asian American viewers shaped by civil rights activism organizing around and recommending particular approaches to representation, purportedly without an understanding of the craft of performance. She explained in an interview: "I guess they blamed me for that image, yes of being a prostitute. The first time I heard it I thought well, if she had been a nun it would have been a whole different thing, but because she was a prostitute they thought that every Asian woman was a Suzie Wong. I've never seen myself as an icon for Asian American women. I'm an actor and I play these roles; one happens to be a prostitute, next it's another role. But I never thought of myself as a role model."[51] Indeed, she identifies the bind constraining Asian actresses while refusing to acknowledge how representations can stand in for racial others marginalized by such images and roles. While Kwan ultimately argues for the role of artists to address the details of life that are not captured in other ways, she does not account for the possibility that these images may hurt others. She does not acknowledge the social impact of such problematic images, in contrast to Anna May Wong, whose own acknowledgment of the impact resonates loudly in her interviews. Kwan simply expresses her resentment at how her performance comes to stand in for an entire group. As an actress whose constraints involve negotiating an entire industry, Kwan expresses her bondage. That is, she must become a representative, a burden impossible to shoulder. She rejects the validity of the racial critique regarding her roles in favor of prioritizing the impact of her films in terms of visibility.

Nancy Kwan describes the heated racial reception of the film as somewhat incomprehensible to her as an actress. Kwan identifies the stakes projected upon popular culture images for Asian female spectators who invest a great deal of meaning in representation in the name of how they concretely affect their lives. In response, Kwan critiques the assessment while opening the door to her own experience of creative production. It is a role, not real life, she insists. She also begins to deconstruct the production of sex for Asian women in popular culture from the position of the actress as an active, thoughtful, and creative contributor to "gendered" and "racialized" hypersexual roles. The production of hypersexual Asian women engages the "imago"—or fantasies about Asian women and their links and disjunctures to biological bodies situated in particular historical, political, and social contexts as authors and spectators. Ultimately, Nancy Kwan's platform resists this linkage. While not all performances of bad sexuality or bad womanhood are politically useful, it is important to achieve the widest range of representations possible, including Kwan's struggling for access to heteronormative femininity by way of her performances and commentaries—precisely because the romantic female lead is still not available to Asian/American women today.

In a great range of international media presence, the bona fide superstar Lucy Liu is today discussed in full-length articles in the *New York Times* and USA Today, as well as online entertainment articles such as CBS Entertainment and Women.com. In addition, she graces the covers of popular men's magazines, such as *Maxim* (twice) and the U.K.-based *Arena,* and top-of-the-line women's magazines, such as *Allure, Jane, Mademoiselle,* and *Marie Claire.* She describes an indefatigable pressure that comes from living under the shadow of a powerful character whose face and body are hers. "I'm like the anti-Ling," she says of her breakthrough character Ling Woo on *Ally McBeal.* "It's so much fun playing her but I have this fear that people are going to run away from me in terror on the streets. They think I'm going to bite their heads off or something."[52] In her statement, Liu demonstrates an awareness of the power of representation and her specific role. Richard Dyer observes how stars come to embody social categories.[53] According to patterns in the interviews of these three generations of Asian femme fatales in Hollywood, racial stars represent entire constituencies as if they are simply representing untranslated and unmediated versions of themselves.

Race-based queries frame her stardom persistently, especially in terms of the sexual, a legacy Liu acknowledges: "I think there's definitely a kind of the fetish of the Asian woman being kind of like a flower, like a lotus flower, or that she's just like this powerful bad girl, nasty girl. I think the stereotypes definitely exist."[54] In an interview with Lucy Liu, *Playboy* magazine is most direct: "Asian sex secrets; myth, hype or just plain good sense?"[55] In a response that captures a particular dance she performs with the media so that she offers racial critique indirectly, Liu claims to bear no secrets and dodges the question by shifting her focus to dating patterns. She refuses to date men who have dated other Asian women. In a strategy widely different from Anna May Wong, who delivered her critique of racism and sexism directly, or Nancy Kwan, who refused it, Lucy Liu maneuvers the race questions of exotification toward a smoothly delivered critique of a recognizable cultural practice of "yellow fever"—the chronic preference for Asian women dating partners in contemporary practice. Liu displaces racial sexualization to offer a critique, albeit indirectly.

In her quote opening this chapter, a double-pronged approach can be identified in her handling of the media. While Liu seems to refute racial protest regarding the limited demands of positive and negative images articulated by audiences of color, she subsequently makes sure to insert a more complicated critique of Hollywood that typecasts racialized actors and actresses into limited roles. Her politics prioritize her individual agenda, however political, and reject the burden of representing the race. Liu's recent interview in a popular British daily reveals a political agenda that strives for popularity and power in Hollywood, specifically as an author. She states that she must take on stereotypical roles to prove box office power in order to afford more opportunities for herself.[56] Is her political agenda limited to self-interest or is it futile to flee group identification or politics futile within any investment in the industry? In the U.K. interview, she responds to a question about racial stereotypes by describing the bondage of her stardom in the clear voice of someone fighting in the forefront of the industry.

> INTERVIEWER: [In *Kill Bill*] aren't you perpetuating the stereotype of Asians doing martial arts in the movies?
> LUCY LIU: It's like this—I get a few opportunities, and I try to make them as full and as three-dimensional as possible. Once those movies succeed, the studio sees that I am a viable person, who can bring in money. I still work on a couple of movies which perhaps wouldn't be my first choice, but as I build on momentum and audience, then I start doing my own projects. I already have two in development at my production company. *You don't have a choice when you don't have options. So you have to create options that will ultimately create new opportunities* (my emphasis).

Lucy Liu explains her racialized position within struggles for opportunity. In playing roles that may be limited not only for Asian women but women in general, she creates viability and the means to make different kinds of images. While Liu is empowered to make inroads, her position is quite exceptional so that the possibility of making new roles and new stories really needs to be framed accurately as a great struggle that her presence also delimits.

How do we understand the stardom of Asian American femme fatales in Hollywood today within the transnational nature of stardom as well as the development of racially aware audiences? Does the singular super stardom of Wong, Kwan, and Liu within particular historical moments delimit more direct indictment of their roles? How much of a political critique comes to be possible in the site of Hollywood? What significantly constitutes Wong's, Kwan's, and Liu's presences is the tension among representation, its social function, and the person of the actress performing the role. The roles of actresses must be understood as complex triangulations within themselves or a kind of sexual bondage for racial stars. Peter Feng writes, "I'd like to suggest that when an actor continues to accept derogatory roles, we tell ourselves the star has a family to support, or that the exaggerated way in which the star conforms to the stereotype is actually a parody of that stereotype."[57] Such a proposal lacks power in its intervention because of its limited definition of the stakes in stardom. Actors and actresses should not be let off the hook for doing a job that represents and affects the lives of many others.

As Foucault diagnoses quite well, "Where there is power, there is resistance."[58] In the case of Asian femme fatales wrestling with sexual bondage in Hollywood, their performances and other acts are redeployments of problematic entanglements. Anna May Wong makes use of fan magazines to rewrite her actions in film, and Nancy Kwan indeed frames her performances with various commentaries on the political aims of Asian American presence in Hollywood.[59] And I dissect Lucy Liu's strategy in popular culture as a kind of racial and sexual compromised dance. In the previous chapter, I illustrate this tension through the creative choices of "strength" performed by actresses in the Broadway production of *Miss Saigon*. These women discussed their performances as active redeployments of Filipina American sexuality from within their limited powers on stage. While these are hard to gauge in terms of political efficacy, they should be accounted for in analyses of racialized sexuality in popular performance on screen as well.

Similarly, Anna May Wong's performances index a particular creative occupation of the pressured site of race and sexuality. Women of color did not occupy roles as women, much less as heroines. She wrote herself into history both through her performances and her popular interviews in which she decried the industry and complained about her roles. Whereas Nancy Kwan's responses to racial critique are limited to her own career and a limited definition of success, and Lucy Liu's resistance is more constrained, the pioneer actress Anna May Wong significantly engaged the industry in contrast to later actresses in supposedly more racially progressive eras. She left a fierce legacy on and off screen that truly provides an important ancestry for Asian American actresses today. I look back at her legacy as an important struggle of recognition that must be continued and honored. Her image not only accounts for the wavering and anxious visual cues of ghosts in the narrative, but also the internal struggle in the Asian/American woman's dialogue and performance as it mobilizes history and its anxieties. The notion of Asian/American women as always racial and sexual in the overdetermination of their characters releases complex, eternally unfinished characters within the narratives and also as triangulated figures imaged in U.S. history. Thus, readings of the Asian/American woman as such show that all representations are unfinished parts standing in for undetermined and complex wholes.

To understand images as re-presentation of prior normative identities ignores their creative construction in the production and consumption of media. What we should look for instead is a Foucauldian "regime" of truth, and not so much "real" Asian women existing before representation. As I outline in the previous chapter, what we see in film and on stage are performances of sexuality that actresses redeploy and re-create through their unique bodily occupation of roles deemed proper or essential to the Asian woman character. No prior, essential, and natural Asian woman precedes image, but a particular subject of sex and a tradition of hypersexuality do emerge in her appearances in film. To understand the filmic image of the Asian woman as a production is to frame her presence as a site of action that allows us to explore how the grotesque and the sublime can be a place for the Asian/American woman to speak, as well as to discover what the production of sexuality in film produces in culture beyond frozen images.

The phenomenon of Asian femme fatales standing in for the heterogenous group of Asian American women is hard to grasp when the images themselves are so constructed and so fantastic. If they were to be placed in collision with real bodies on the streets, their construction would encounter laughter or just come apart at the seams.[60] While the Douglas Fairbanks character in *The Thief of Bagdad* moves like a clown, he does not come to exemplify a whole group. Anna May Wong's exaggerated movements have a significant impact in the context of the dearth of Asian female images. They amplify the power of the actress, the role, and the woman who is a subject-in-struggle.

What is graspable is that there is always some form of sexuality in the presence of Asian women in the U.S. cinema industry. The consistency of sex for Asian women is addressed inadequately in traditional stereotype analyses of representation, sexuality, and race. In my exploration of race and sexuality in visuality, I show Asian femme fatales as "subjects-in-struggle" within a phenomenological approach to the medium of film, for they are caught within a complex triangulation as self, actress, and role. I understand the film role to be a subject, conflicting and collaborating with the actress and the female subject. When Anna May Wong plays the slave girl or concubine, then decries it in public culture discourses such as fan magazines and interviews, she redeploys her roles as a woman and as an actress.[61] Because the meanings extracted from film are many times multivalent, the Asian/American woman emerges in different ways. The unities required in the diagnosis of the media as a misrepresenting stereotyping mechanism disserve the frenzy that gender and sex make of the racial experience. The sex and gender experiences of the Asian woman show the limits of representational analyses told in an exclusively racial and patriarchal lens. Such a reading aims to contribute to the ways in which representation functions in the subject formation of racial and sexual subjects on and off screen. To be clear, my approach argues that we cannot get a full picture of these women's performances unless we also study their own narrative commentary, for the intentions of the authors can themselves cloud the political power of pleasure in their performance. From Anna May Wong's various protests to Nancy Kwan's refusal of racial critique to Lucy Liu's campy play in performance, these Asian American actresses provide a wide-ranging set of responses to the hypersexuality of Asian women across different historical eras.

By revising the diagnosis that the Asian woman in Hollywood works as no more than a symbol complicit with racist sexuality, hers is a predicament that expresses both agency and subordination. Important is the interrogation of how sexuality occurs and how pleasure is defined in the way we assess political critique in performance. What is the relationship between power and sexuality? And how do each define an ethics of representation and resistance? What we can know is the sexuality tied to productions of Asian/American women in Hollywood. I borrow Judith Butler's notion of "passionate attachment" to describe the popular perception of the Asian/American woman as fundamentally dependent on hypersexuality, and I use it as the basis for the redeployment of this perception in visual culture.[62] Passionate attachment describes a particular theory of subjection in which one must desire one's own subordination in order to persist as a subject. I use the concept to describe the ways in which certain acts, gestures, and movements by the Asian woman on screen simultaneously reinstall/reaffirm or recast/reimagine a racialized sexuality that is deemed proper to certain subjects. The doubleness of meaning regarding certain acts—the massage, the scurrying, the killing—hinges on her signification, which many times fluctuates between murderess vamp and feminist avenger and whose meaning depends on the context of the film's production and reception.

The desire located in passionate attachment is defined in terms of the subject's ambivalent relationship to power and how that subject deflects it through varied forms of resistance. The paradox of subjection in passionate attachment is the process by which one's need for social recognition powerfully motivates a desire for a classification that ultimately constrains.[63] *Because the Asian woman cannot be imagined outside of sex, her resistance is also found in sex.* As such, I am advocating for an understanding of the role of hypersexuality in those Hollywood parts that call for an Asian American femme fatale as a dynamic and creative production that attests to the confounding unknowability of race, sex, and representation. To counter the bind of hypersexuality, we may need to expose the varying degrees of its embrace and to create narratives that directly engage the experience of bondage by racialized sexuality.

Following Butler, the subject of the Asian woman is not a person or an individual, but a placeholder of ideology. She is a linguistic category that references sexuality, especially in terms of visuality, in which her presence alone signifies exoticism.[64] This power of visuality is apparent through an understanding of representation as an apparatus of subjection that secures its own power through the viewer's psychic cognition of the Asian woman, a perception of her that is mobilized as sexualized over and over again. Sexuality ascribes Asian women into a ghostly status through the repetition and reinscription of sex in her representation. When bound by hypersexuality, how do actresses and audiences cope?

There is a lack of understanding of the practice of producing culture. Against stereotype analyses of racial representation, I revisit the most targeted emblems of the Asian woman as sexual and as opportunities for offering alternative readings. By reading bodily movements, performances, and acting, I show how stereotypes are as multilayered and complex as the production processes by which they are made. The meaning of the Asian/American woman as sex in representation must thus be situated not only within history, but also within the concrete acts, gestures, speeches, and movements in her specific performances. We need to evidence what it is that we are seeing that secures meaning in order to avoid the traps of prematurely fixing complicated images into established tropes.

Creative acts of self-formation in the scene of perceiving Asian woman's sexual subjection are too often ignored. History does not adequately account for the power of Asian women's bodies and the objects and places that verify an "authenticity" that is required in their commodification. From the relationship between the materiality of Asian women's bodies and the immateriality of the Asian woman's fantasy projections emerges the representation of the Asian woman as a "naturalized" sexual subject.

The hypersexual Asian/American woman in representation lives through different generations, providing vocabulary for the social cognition of Asian women. She lives as a historical subject that affects different politics and struggles in a relationship between the real and the represented as interdependent: somewhere between life and death, present and absent. There is an immense political power to this ambiguity of representation in history. Only by an admission of the Asian/American woman as Oriental sexual phantasm can her status as sexual be rewritten as politically significant. Her subject position in representation is a diagnosis of the repression of possibilities for the Asian woman. Revisiting her sexual emblematic is required so as to make dents in the problem of race, sexuality, and representation within the silences of history.

The mechanisms of representation may be ephemeral performances in one moment of time, but they are informed by conditions of production, including the history of objects in film and the simultaneous agency and subordination of Asian American actresses. These images last beyond the different times and spaces of their reception. I understand representation as an apparatus that creates social figures that are both alive and dead, object and subject, and certainly players in social relations. Film and theater, specifically, are forms of communication and culture that rely on the power of spectators to meet the producers and actors in the process of making meaning. The psyche of the spectator is the site where meaning is completed in an understanding of representation and viewing as an active act of making sense of the world. Representation itself functions as a scapegoat, mediating between worlds. The dialectical operation of images has political potential because images unsettle the phantasmagoria, momentarily allowing new possibilities to emerge.[65] As Avery Gordon argues, visual culture is where we can stage fantasies and see ghosts as a phenomenological reality.[66] The figures of Asian femme fatales are phenomenological in the sense that they bring together the film and the viewer in mutually constitutive ways; the film itself is a subject interacting with the film spectator. This formulation of mutual constitution coheres with the study of the Asian woman as a cinematic subject. As such, she exists as a kind of separate subject in film.[67] As I showed in my intertextual analyses, the actress, role, and woman complete each other in the processes of production and consumption of film.

Critics attempt to conjure away the sex embodied in the Asian/American woman—as if they could! We need to confront ideas of the hypersexual Asian woman with the knowledge that representation can foretell what has not yet happened: the reclamation of sexuality as both subordination and resistance for the Asian/American women hailed by it as well as for those who confront such an interpellation. To understand representations of hypersexuality as a powerful and present legacy is to acknowledge the unresolved in us as spectators. Representations attempt to make visible what reside in the psyche. Representation reenacts these scenes as a kind of return of the repressed. The unresolved requires revisiting. The central thing that the theory of the sexual bondage of racial stardom untangles is the need to read not only the interior life of sexual subjection and racism, but also the way in which representation mediates such matters. The fantasy being sold and its audience are simultaneously challenged in spectatorship and production. Such reading, seeing, and hearing entail careful practice and affirm the need for spectators to learn the language, grammar, and vocabulary of production and performance that actresses wrestle with and under. It requires a re-education of seeing and perception so that the mythologies and representations of Asian women, as they produce psychic and physical scars, can be identified. The questions of how image hurts and how image pleases are equally important. Interpreting desire and pleasure at moments of domination in ways that do not ensure the project of racism and colonialism (where will and choice are otherwise contentious and dubious) is an exciting exploration. Through the sexual bondage of racial stardom, I am trying to capture how actresses, as well as viewers, cope with the complexity of the experience of screening culture.

Sex and the Asian/American woman in film, especially when the pleasure is based on a political critique of normative identities, reanimate the past. To say that what is seen as frozen is alive diagnoses the anxieties produced by race and sexuality in our histories. Representation itself, as living subject/object, full of contradiction and emotion, demands that resignification and refiguration of sex and race be made possible. To hide from sexual critique is to hide from the subject of Asian/American woman. As viewers of American popular culture, we are all inheritors. To refuse our inheritance of the hypersexual Asian woman will only instill her ghostliness as the viable subject position for Asian women in material relations. As such, characters that exude normalcy, such as Mei Li in *Flower Drum Song*, or good womanhood in their asexuality, or hypersexuality, such as Suzie Wong and the vampish Asian American femme fatales, push us to interrogate the role of sexuality, race, and representation in wide-ranging ways.

To rename the narratives of Asian/American women is to identify worlds behind the production indicated by their performances. Let us call back the dragon lady and the murderous vamp so as to initiate different conversations with the Asian/American woman's image: to retell the stories in which she appears; to see how these stories come to speak of the excesses of the historical, the logical, and improbable. To call back the ambivalent parts of the stereotype is to make other parts of its appearance more visible and to call for a different future from its legacy. To call on the past so as to carve a different future, we need to advocate for framing film as an ancestral legacy: to ask how Asian/American actresses are sexual heirs who rewrite hypersexuality in various ways. The Asian woman's hypersexuality needs to be reclaimed, for she is fetishized in the sense that her presence as sexual would never be allowed to actually disappear. She is kept hovering, causing anxiety and dread on the edge of absence and presence.

The next chapter explores further how the Asian/American woman's race functions as her sexual visibility in pornographic film. That is, the racial authenticity of her body relies on the visible evidence of sexual difference as it is evoked by skin and by acts. Through the study of stag films or early pornography from 1910 to 1934, we see that the performance of sex supposedly certifies visible evidence of racial difference. As such, for the racial other, sex is always visible, for sexual difference can be occupied and retold by racialized narrative, accoutrements, and other technologies of film. Through my discussion of Anna May Wong, Nancy Kwan, and Lucy Liu in this chapter, race is always a sexual production in Hollywood cinema, one that is bursting with conscious fantasy and unconscious phantasy, and therefore highly powerful because the seen seems just as probable as the bodies moving before us with substance. To see race is to see sex and vice versa, and nowhere is this agenda more apparent than in early pornography that claims to take Hollywood film "all the way."

On the edge of absence/presence, visibility/invisibility, power/powerless-
ness, I am looking for legacy in the dark theaters of the movies. In digging, I
find myself in archives attributing lineage to white women in yellowface
stag pornography. Queer men have looked at stag films and found some
ancestry for themselves in the historical documents of sexual representation.[1] Does it make sense for Asian/American women to look at past sexual
images in order to find and make sense of contemporary marginality?
What I find in these bodies of white women is the collision of fantasy and
ideology in an irrational relationship. A particular sexuality is produced
for Asian women in hard-core stag films from 1920–34 that are archived
at the Kinsey Institute for Research on Sex, Gender, and Reproduction.
In these films, white women perform racialized sexuality with various
makeup techniques that supposedly achieve Asian/American women's racially visible difference. By looking at the earliest pornographic representation of Asian/American women, I aim to illuminate how pornography
problematizes the visibility of race through sexual genitalia, acts, and relations in a peculiar bondage of race, sexuality, and representation.

Stag films show the production of Asian female hypersexuality in sex acts meant for white male viewing, in ways that also reveal how these productions occur at a disjuncture from popular history and the lives of Asian women in America. As such, yellowface porn seems to offer important yet unexpected legacies for Asian American women. Through stag films we can know about the fantasy circulating about hypersexual Asian women. The films isolate what is defined as desirable about racial difference in sex—the face, Orientalist objects, the racialization of certain sexual acts themselves, and the specific fantasy about Asian women's bodies that disturbs the stag film's usual eroto-visual economy.

Stag films—short, illegally made 8mm and 16mm pornographic films in circulation during the first half of the twentieth century in America and Europe—addressed a specifically white male private viewership. The major texts that focus on understanding stag films frame them within illegality, sex education, and male socialization but not so much in terms of their focus on white sex.[2] Stag films focus principally on white spectators in ways that these scholars do not directly acknowledge. In my discussion of these stag films, I describe systemic patterns of hypersexuality attributed to racialized gender in representation, while scrutinizing what can be claimed for Asian/American women in looking at the inheritance of these images. The chapter explores why, in contradiction to the times, the insistence of the truth of race in sexuality, and vice versa, leads to an equation of racial utopia rather than racial panic in stag pornography. The production of race through the use of "yellowface" to signify Asian women in stag films describes a fantasy of universal sex in a way that captures the conundrum of race and sexuality in history. The early American tradition of representing Asian women's hypersexual interiority through racially visible bodily evidence presents a commodification of the threat of race into a sexual treat. The chapter ultimately reevaluates the rendering of Asian women as threatening in terms of reproduction and miscegenation in the historical national and popular cultural record by focusing on the production of identities and the redefinitions of social categories of experience found in stag representations. While the previous two chapters prioritize cultural production as a battleground for Asian American actresses, spectators, and critics in terms of the role of sexuality as experience and expression, the focus of the next three chapters on pornography allows me to build upon this criticism and further interrogate the polarized analyses of sexual liberation versus racial subordination confounding moving image representations of racialized sexuality. Furthermore, my study of pornography asserts that racial formation is a process of sexualization and vice versa.

We must look at pornography in our effort to understand race and sexuality in the United States. In an era of porn studies that remains essentially white, as acknowledged by the leading scholars Constance Penley and Linda Williams,[3] a delicate balancing act characterizes racial studies of porn. That is, even though porn is not so damaging as to kill the racialized viewer, it still has the capacity to harm. How can we acknowledge the oppressive uses of pornography toward racial subjects, such as the unfair payment of wages according to race as frequently cited by porn stars of Asian descent and other minority actors?[4] An example of the possible exclusions that can occur is the forwarding of a monolithic understanding of incredibly rich pornographic representations, simply operating under a victimizing and moralistic scopophilia and universalizing the work of sex in various race and class contexts.[5] However, if pornography is an "expressive form," as Laura Kipnis argues, which "has attained popularity because it finds ways of articulating what its audiences care about," and "speaks to the audience because it's thoroughly astute about who we are underneath the social veneer, astute about the costs of cultural conformity and the discontent at the core of routinized lives and normative sexuality," it can also afford for Asian/American women the experience apart from the bondage of hypersexuality.[6] Pornography can tell us about cultural fantasies about Asian/American women that may be different from what is contained in the historical record. That is, through pornography, we see which acts and what identities constitute the sexual fantasy of Asian/American women for the American male audiences of stag pornography. To put it another way, what is the role of Asian/American women in what Teresa de Lauretis calls "public fantasy"?[7]

Because the women performing are not Asian but white women in yellowface makeup, the performances of race are more keenly in view. Yellowface stag films specifically arrest not just the role of Asian women in arousing pleasure and desire but also fears of interracial sex and perceptions of racial difference that dominated the era. I mention these basic premises because the question of the utility of porn in racial studies remains a very important one, which I mean to delineate carefully. While viewing porn will not necessarily kill the viewer, in the sense of infecting the viewer with a deathly and morally corrupting disease, engaging with porn confronts the racial legacy of representational issues as a whole.[8] Considering the excluded and segregated status of people of color in terms of participating in social scenes of movie spectatorship and authorship historically, we can now know about the construction of race and use it as a different occasion for finding recognition in the projection of Asian femaleness through white bodies.

Rather than subscribe to the typical stance of knowing what porn is without seeing it, or arguing against porn without evidence, I see the project of looking at porn closely and historically as a way to evaluate sex and its contributions to fantasies, ideologies, and knowledge about race. Studying porn may also lead to an understanding of sex as political and, as Gayle Rubin argues, an analytic vector in its own right.[9] Moreover, my conclusion aims to explain how sex as something self-conscious and politicized provides a way out of the bind of liberation versus domination that characterizes discourses of racialized sexuality. Stag pornography featuring yellowface versions of Asian women needs to be studied precisely because racialized desires and fantasies can be arrested in productions that see white women masquerade and perform racialized sexual difference.

RACE AND THE STAG FILM: PERFORMING YELLOWFACE SEX ACTS

Primarily one-reel films, stags featured "meat" shots—the explicit visible evidence of genitals engaged in the act of penetration.[10] Furthering what is available in the strip tease, the stag film gives a rare look at the genitals, an aim enough for the viewer earlier in the twentieth century when the sex act was a shocking sight in popular life. The contemporary porn film releases the constraints of the stag by making regular the climax of the "money shot" or the "come shot," which allows for the bodily confessional of ejaculate by the male audience. The stag films made sex acts, deemed deeply private at the time, available for quasi-public viewing in all-male venues such as brothels and gentlemen's clubs. I provide this history in order to differentiate the stag film from contemporary pornography and at the same time point to the limits of reading stag films transhistorically.

The display of genitalia for public consumption distinguishes the stag film from contemporary pornography practices of the money shot, which provides evidence of male pleasure on the female face in heterosexual porn. The specific display of racialized genitalia in the representation of interracial sex shows how racial difference is marked primarily in the "meat" or genital shot. If we re-evaluate the context of miscegenation and the fears and anxieties surrounding the migration and presence of Asians in the United States, how can we make better sense of the thrill of literal transgressions to popular culture and law in stag representation? In a glass-enclosed room visible to the library staff, I screened the racialized stag films archived at the Kinsey Institute for Research in Sex, Gender, and Re-production during one to two week long trips in September 1999, March 2000, May/June 2000, August 2000, and September 2001. I screened over two hundred stag films and viewed related photographs as well as materi-als on censorship and the distribution and acquisition of stag films. I also screened approximately fifty films involving figurations of the Asian woman from the institute's massive collection of American pornography from the 1960s to the present. I viewed a vast sampling, over one hundred on video and 16mm or 8mm film, of non-racialized stag films in order to draw comparisons and to get a sense of the genre's conventions. Searching a database of over twelve hundred stag films is a difficult task for a re-searcher interested in viewing sex involving racial others from the United States and colonial others from Latin America and Asia. That is, the classification system was not conducive to research on race except through titles and catalogue listings that explicitly mention race. Of the films I viewed, fifty-five involved racial and colonial others identified in the titles of the films. Films I viewed included classics discussed in previous scholar-ship, such as *A Grass Sandwich, Casting Couch, College Coed 1, College Coed 2,* and so on. Through the catalogued descriptions of the films, I also identified materials featuring miscegenation, cross-racial liaisons, and the racial identities of the participants when noted within the film itself. In light of the above categories, the films I discuss do not represent all the stag material "out there," but the form of identification I chose traces the particular role of race used to market these films as representing racialized sexuality.

The stag films in this chapter featuring the Asian woman were made in the same period as *The Thief of Bagdad* (1924) and *Shanghai Express* (1932).[11] These stag films used a grammar of skin color contrast in their representations of the meat shots. This was especially apparent in interracial black and white sex. In other words, a penis in a vagina is not racial unless marked by extreme differences in color. In the stag films featuring Asian women from the 1920s to the 1930s, such skin color difference did apply, but it appeared in conjunction with "Oriental" ornaments. The primary practice in these earlier stag films involved white women who donned "yellowface" accoutrements or attire such as chopsticks in the hair and kimonos in order to register themselves as visibly Asian.[12]

Early stag films featuring the act of miscegenation between yellowface Asians and whites offered double controversy and double titillation in an era of intense racial and sexual anxiety.[13] Privately consumed in brothels, bachelor parties, and men's clubs, they were an early form of sex education, entertainment, and an integral part of the sex industry. Serving as an aide to prostitutes, they accelerated the clients' arousal and lessened the women's work time. Surreptitiously produced by "purveyors" of sex, they were made in motels, homes, and then burlesque stages. Many of the women in the films were prostitutes themselves. According to Frank Hoffman, "Earlier production appears to have been primarily the work of what we might call professional purveyors of sex. That is, houses of prostitution, independent prostitutes, pimps, and the like. Many of the women are obviously prostitutes, either known as such or identified by their names to be in all probability members of that ancient profession."[14] According to Walter Kendrick, the link between pornography and prostitution is age-old, dating back to the inception of the word pornography itself.[15] The actors were not professional, but they were not necessarily amateur in terms of sex performance as they were frequently involved in the sex industry as dancers, prostitutes, or paid companions to men. While the films I study feature some of the same black and white women performing the same dances and sharing the same identities as prostitutes, none seem to be racially Asian. I may speculate that the lack of Asian women stems from their limited number in the United States during the time. While many were prostitutes who worked primarily in California, others were part of enclosed communities performing cheap labor. White women in yellowface drag fulfilled fantasies of Asian female sexual difference as informed by increasing East-West encounters.

Nation and geography act as central markers in the identification of Asians and Latinos in stag film, whereas the presence of black actors is indicated through words that signal a fetish regarding skin color, words such as "black," "night," or "dark." Asian stag film titles focus on the body's racial and ethnic cultural difference: *Geisha Girl* (1948–55), *Oriental Girl-friend* (1965), *China* (1930), *Chinese Love Life* (1921), *Philippino* [*sic*] *Couple* (1970–71), *Salt of the Earth* (1950s), *Korean Couple* (1967),[16] *Japanese Rape* (1970–71), *Indian Giver* (1958–62), and more such titles. The dates attributed to these films are questionable, as they were produced illegally and donated under strict conditions of privacy. Other racialized titles include: *Scherezade* [*sic*] *and the Sultan* (1936), *Mexican Honeymoon* (1937), *Cuban Dream* (1950–55), *Night in a Turkish Harem* (1931), *Negroes at Play* (1948), and so on. Apparent from both these lists is that race must be identifiable through the titles in order to solicit purchase of the sexual product. The film marketers offer the classifications both to create and fulfill specific desires for viewers who need to know if they are getting what they want—the difference that race fulfills. Furthermore, the distribution materials indicate a conscious marking of racial difference.

A kind of racial drag is performed in stag films purportedly featuring Asian women when white women who don "yellowface" makeup, costume, and even genital performance perform the roles. Tom Waugh discusses the role of gender drag as "arbitrary" and excessive in bearing no distinctions between partners, generically indicating perversion for the primarily heterosexual scene of reception.[17] He argues that Orientalism in stag films works as a device to "heighten an exoticism of difference."[18] As an example, he points to the lack of importance placed on cultural or racial authenticity, as the priority lies in the erotic meaning of difference for the consumer. "Whether the fez and turban came from the costume trunk or the casbah . . . is of no importance; once again the European consumer is aroused at signs of empire."[19] The placement of excessive Orientalist signs indicates the importance of communicating the Otherness of the locale and the people performing on screen so as to arouse pleasure in the stag film's male viewers.

The stag film's showing of meat—or the genital show of racialized bodies —serves a specific function. While visible evidence of ejaculate or orgasm is deferred in the stag by its emphasis on meat, seeing racial difference offers satisfaction in itself within the context of providing exoticism. Tom Waugh indicates that the saturation of objects without logic "signal[s] perversity" for the sake of creating "appeal."[20] Accordingly, such a ritualized sense of sexual practice arises in pornography featuring Asian women. We might surmise various reasons for this. For one, in the genital show, the Asian women's skin color difference may not be visible in black and white representation of racialized bodies. Thus, accoutrements act as visible evidence of race for the Asian women in stag films. This is the particular difference between films featuring Asian women versus other women of color. For black women in films such as *Two Nights and a Day*, skin color functions as certification of racial difference. In contrast to the marked ritualizations employed in stag films with Asian women, the makers did not blacken up the women in the films archived at the Kinsey. In the case of Mexican and Latina women in *La Señora y la Criada* (1938), location or place and decorations certify their difference, rather than objects on and of the body. Thus, it would seem that the Mexican and Latina bodies are rendered through space, an observation that of course requires further study. The specific furniture and architecture prominently mark the scene as racially different in Latino stags, while bodily objects make women recognizably Asian.

Through analyses of *Chinese Love Life* (1921), *Menage Moderne du Madame Butterfly* (1921–30), and *China* (1930), I discover that the racial essence of people is found in their sexual exterior in pornography, something secured not only in the performances of white women in yellowface but also in the racialization of the narrative and the visual representation of the Other. Moreover, I recognize that race is problematized through the production of visibility for race in the sex act itself. Because racial visibility is unreliable for Asian women, stag films establish what I call "the seeing of race as the seeing of sex." Specifically, they aim to show us the sexuality of the Asian woman, even though she is a white woman in yellowface, to say something about her race and gender interiority as a being-for-others, specifically for the white male author and spectator.[21]

THE PROBLEM OF RACIAL (IN)VISIBILITY:
CHINESE LOVE LIFE (1921)

The stag film *Chinese Love Life* (1921) begins with an ornate title card in the form of a stylized photograph. Appearing much larger than the other figures, the generously round rump and large thighs of a female nude occupy the center of the frame. On each side, halves of two other bodies in profile flank her. Featured from the shoulders down to the thighs, the female on the left wears a bathing suit with thin horizontal black and white stripes and ruffles on the bottom. The figure on the right has her arm bent at the waist and laid against her black bandeau-style bathing suit with a white border at the breast. Over this image is the title of the film, CHINESE LOVE LIFE. Then comes a bold declaration: "The Sex Life of all races of People are THE same" is printed over the same image. Formatted boldly, the word "THE" is emphasized. While the film begins with this sweeping racialized announcement, the racial identities of the black and white figures in the graphic remain unclear.

The actors and actresses involved in the film do not "look" Chinese; moreover, they appear racially ambiguous so that who is Asian, one or all, is unclear. Out of boredom, two women in a boarding house entertain each other sexually. One of their boyfriends interrupts the scene and ends up having sex with both women. Although the Kinsey Institute card catalogue file describes the younger woman in the film to be "Oriental," the card also lists the older woman's hair to be "an Oriental bun." The racial identification is both about the person and the ornament. Yet, it is hard to determine how race functions within the narrative and the visual narration apart from making sure that the audiences accept the imposition by the titles. Frank Hoffman describes how *Chinese Love Life* is a "meaningless title, one of the girls could be part Oriental, but the title bears no other relationship to the story line."[22] Since the difference is not visible or reliable, the text must make it readable and noticeable in order to construct difference within the stag.

The opening titles of *Chinese Love Life* racialize content that is seemingly not visible. The first narrative intertitle for *Chinese Love Life* announces that "Two boarding school girls sweet, charming and bright, had gone to their room to retire for the night." These titles do not racialize the women who are, in fact, established better through the visual language—in other words, through body choreography and actions. The two women occupy the first frame, composed of a direct shot of a single bed against a wall featuring a college pennant hanging in a diagonal direction, as well as two picture frames. The older and bigger woman, with her hair up in a bun, with ample breasts in a dark dress, sits on the single bed while the younger woman sits on the floor. We see most of the older woman's upper body, from her head to her knees. Only the head and shoulders of the younger woman are visible. Hoffman attributes the second woman to be part Asian, her dark hair arranged with buns above each ear—a style that is conventionally labeled in these films as "Oriental." Apart from the opening titles and the Kinsey card catalogue files about this film, nothing in the plot structure or the rest of the intertitles mark her as such. I will discuss,

The title card establishes a discourse of race in *Chinese Love Life*.

Nellie, the presumably Asian woman, shows her face as she looks directly at the camera in *Chinese Love Life*.

however, the ways in which racial difference is secured in the shooting style and choreography. Before doing so, I evaluate the texts framing the film's racial representation.

The Kinsey Procedure for Stag Film Analysis offers the following instructions: "Males are numbered 1, 2, 3. . . . Females are numbered A, B, C. . . . Describe each person as fully as possible. It is especially valuable to note such permanent features such as scars, tattoos, and dental anomalies." According to Martha Harsanyi, the former Kinsey film curator, the cataloguing process for the stag films actually occurred in the 1970s. Such a large historical disjuncture seems to show the unreliability of studying these films, while also placing into question the certainty of racial visible difference.[23] With the help of an external grant, Harsanyi organized the previously disorganized film material and watched all the films. She followed Alfred Kinsey's methodical manner of classifying sexual activity with precise details. Notes in the catalogue indicate conviction that these women are of different races. Does this racial identification depend entirely on the opening titles of *Chinese Love Life*, titles that require the people in the film to be composed of different races? Is their racial visibility also informed by the racial politics of the 1970s, ones that are very different from the 1920s and 1930s? Perhaps also contributing to the reading of race is the method of description, which is shaped by the viewer's structural location. Acknowledging her viewing position as a white woman in the Midwest during the 1970s, Harsanyi the librarian had to make judgments about racial identities, plots, and representations of sex acts, as decisions informed by her meticulous viewing. If in the 1970s, she was confident of Asian visibility in the films, enough to mark them in the catalogue, the audience of the 1920s may have noticed them as Asian too. Likewise, I incorporate methodologically a phenomenological description in my viewing of stag film, describing in detail what I see, knowing that these descriptions capture what I prioritize as a viewer in the details I gather from my present perspective.

Stag films are texts haphazardly produced, reproduced, and archived in ways that make it difficult to discern the function of race. The debate about who looks Asian is emblematic of the problem. In terms of production, to what extent is the Asian woman's performance like any other role-playing? The white woman plays "Asian" like she does a housewife, a dancer, or a maid. Can men and women only be Asian if announced or marked as such in the titles, set, or narrative? For them not to be marked in the title is to risk losing possible distribution. What can be learned here is that race cannot be visibly determined in the content; it only shows up fetishized and noted in the titles, production design, and the narrative. As the film degenerates, it is difficult to determine who is Asian, and further racial disintegration occurs. White women in yellowface begin to look Asian underneath. Or to me, everyone starts looking Asian—or at least racially ambiguous—in early porn.

When the cataloguer Martha Harsanyi classifies the women in *Chinese Love Life* as Oriental, there is an interesting slippage in her description. As I point out earlier, she labels as "Oriental" the hairstyle and the makeup of the woman, as well as the woman herself. To understand this curious classification, I reviewed the detailed notes taken by the film curators and the librarians who catalogued the films' contents and information based on the system organized by Kinsey and his devotion to the scientific exploration of sexual behavior. The system assigned each sex act a code and required cataloguers to note everything: the quality of the print and the shooting, the plot, the characters' appearances, and the specific actions and details of the set design. Through the narrative within the intertitles, the genre used race specifically as titillation. Without the racial narrativization, the content would not sufficiently identify the racial difference of Asian women. In the catalogue description of the women, they are listed as such:

WOMAN A: [who seems to be the white woman with "Asian" hair]
Dark Hair in bun (Oriental). Dark Dress. Taller. Large Breasts Large Belly. Heavy.

Is this demarcation of "Oriental" inferred from hairstyle, or the woman herself? And if the hair is Oriental, the woman who does not look Asian also helps to justify the title of a film that does not really seem to include any "real" Chinese people. The fetishization of race in the title must include the erotics of her hair arrangement.

WOMAN B: [who seems to be the small woman who is racially Asian]
Short, Dark Hair, (ear buns), slim, small, flat breasts.

In a different set of forms, the Kinsey cataloguer identifies the racial identity of each woman differently. The card descriptions contradict each other. The second woman—Woman B—is now the Oriental one, an assessment similar to my own observation. She identifies the first woman's race to be "White," while her makeup is "Chinese."

WOMAN A: [In the notes, the white woman has Asian makeup.]
Race: White. Dark Hair Pulled into Bun. Dark Dress. Female Make-up: Chinese.

What is meant by this classification of makeup? Is it acknowledgment of yellowface? The slippage in both these descriptions is interesting, one detectable not only between race and appearance, but also in the question of whether the woman is "made up" Oriental as a fashion of the time, or to convince the audience that she is Asian.

WOMAN B: [whom I note as the smaller Asian woman]
Race Oriental. Dark hair. Bun Over each ear. Dark Dress . . .

What is the basis for the racial identification? The actions described include "embraces between races without genitalia showing" and "interracial very graphic sex." So the catalogue identifies one woman as Oriental and the other as white in what it classified as a lesbian miscegenation scene. While there seems to be some ambiguity in the identification of these women, the visual treatment of the Asian woman is very different from the white woman, especially in the sex act. So analyzing what makes her Asian through formal analysis of the film may confirm her status and help determine how her race functions in the stag film.

The narrative role of the Asian woman, Nellie or Woman B, becomes more apparent when we see the sex acts. Now naked, the wide shot first features her torso as she lifts her arms high and expresses her loneliness in the intertitle:

> I wish at this moment my Johnnie was here
> For he is a darling little duck
> And I am half dying for a fuck.

The medium wide shot of her torso turning side to side, as if showing off her body to science, also becomes a medium wide shot of her bottom half. Her body is the center of the frame and the shot focuses on one half of her body; it is a thin body as well, unlike the body featured in the next shot. Despite wide-ranging body types for Asian and white women, how does thinness or tiny-ness indicate an Asian woman versus the heaviness of the white woman in the visual register? Out of sync with the narrative, we now see the older woman's lower body as the focus of the next frame. Kate or Woman A, the heavyset white woman, displays her bigger body in a similar manner, in a side-to-side sway, before pushing into her vagina something that looks like a long, thin light bulb. The bigger woman's lower body occupies the frame entirely. And she gyrates her hips so as to push the object into herself more deeply. After this short fantastic sequence, we return to the shot of the bed as the two women face each other. The intertitles read:

> Says Kate I will play that I am a man
> And give you a fucking the best that I can
> Says Nellie I am with you
> But where is the prick?
> Says Kate this candle will do the trick

Still standing apart, the two laugh with each other. Then the younger Nellie agrees and lies down with her eyes blindfolded as Kate leaves her to grab the candle. The use of the blindfold may be an attempt to work around the presumed slant of the Asian eye. While Nellie seems to have smaller Asian eyes, would their presence compete against the slanty genitalia, especially as we see the different treatment of genitalia across race?

So lay on the bed and close both your eyes
And open widely your beautiful thighs

Kate walks off to get the candle as a shot of Nellie focuses on her vagina. This shot is similar to other films that focus on the Asian woman's genitals as "different." The white woman, in contrast, does not receive such "coverage." The focus is on the vagina itself, which is framed by her open thighs. In any case, the young woman lies down silently as we watch her genitals. As stated earlier, the meat shot is defined as the sight of genitals in the moment of penetration. While there is no such action in the framing of the Asian woman here, her vagina occupies a starring role. In the stag film, which focuses on the meat shot in general, this is the only time we shall see Asian female genitalia in close-up without penetration. The sight of her racialized genitals seems to offer enough titillation as an object.

Furthermore, the upcoming sex act between the yellowface Asian woman and the white man is not told through the meat shot, but is seen instead in a wide shot and in a close-up of their faces. Suddenly, the blindfolded girl's boyfriend appears from below the bed, lays on top of her, undoes his pants, and penetrates her—all the while with a strange, humorous look on his face that articulates awareness of the camera. And he remains fully clothed. The Asian Nellie seems oblivious to the man's presence and expresses surprise at how much she enjoys the "candlestick." The titles narrate her pleasure; without the following words, her enjoyment may not be captured:

Her bosom swelled up like the wave
of the ocean, and her arse moved up
with a graceful motion

After these titles, the close-up shot focuses on her face in profile as framed by his bent arm. She smiles as his face hovers above her, with only his mouth and chin visible. Even though he is lying on top of her, she mistakes his slender body for Kate's. She says:

Oh Kate, was it a candle
That I felt
It seemed in my belly to
Tickle and melt.

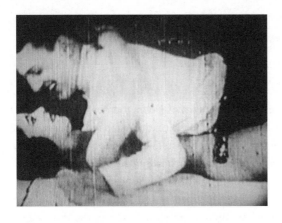

In a face-to-face encounter, the white male reveals himself to the "Asian woman" in *Chinese Love Life*.

The rhyming convention in pornography brings a humorous, lighthearted approach to racial difference here. Her human, and male, partner is revealed with a playfulness notable in an era of anxiety about interracial encounters. The man undoes her blindfold as if to say, "Aha! It's me." When Nellie is surprised, is she playing a coy Asian woman like the fantasy of the demure yet highly sexual Asian woman that is one of the Asian woman's most popular manifestations across time?

Interracial sex, told by way of the face-face shot of the Asian woman and the white man, indicates the special function of the face in the film grammar of early Asian-white porn. Racial difference of the Asian is told through the visible features of the face. The facial features function as proof of the body's manifestation of a psychic and spiritual content. David Palumbo-Liu's argument about the Asian face proves useful in explaining the prominent presence of the face in interracial stag films: "The display of the Asian face suggests a particular zone of contact, which in turn implies the contact of certain contents and elements."[24] In public culture, the grotesque face of the Asian indicated the myth of the Asian's interior savagery. In the stag film, the racial difference of the Asian is not so much captured in skin color difference or in the convention of the meat shot, but rather in the features of the Asian face, in its size, shape, and hair. Moreover, although portrayed by a white lady in yellowface, the Asian face functions like the skin, a racialized exterior supposedly indicating the threatening interior, as Frantz Fanon and Homi Bhabha also theorize in their work describing later scenarios.[25] In *Chinese Love Life,* explicit representation of genital engagement, typical only of stag films, happens only after the white woman enters the scene. Previously, the sex act between the white man and the Asian woman did not feature any meat shots as is the convention in stag films; the face stands in for the genitals. The contest for occupying the film frame ensues, as Nellie and the white man hug each other in the left side of the frame while the white woman grabs his crotch from the right of the frame. Laughing and looking off camera, the white woman talks to someone off screen. The three are entwined together facing the camera. Nellie and Johnnie hug and cuddle as Kate begins to look irritated. Johnnie soon turns his attention to Kate as Nellie leaves the scene. It is here that the first genital shot happens between the white woman and the white man, focusing on his butt in the center of the frame as he penetrates her. Her legs are open and her knees exceed the boundaries of the frame. The next shot is a close up of their bodies on top of each other in profile. Thus, what we see is skin against skin, almost indistinguishable from each other except for the line across the screen, indicating where the bodies end and rub against each other.

Unlike the Asian-white sex that focused on their faces, the white sex shot focuses on bodily and genital contact. The Asian-white sex necessitated a close-up of their faces so as to include her hair and features against his hair and features. Because there is no visible skin color difference registered in black and white film, her racial difference must be secured in some other way. While the lesbian scene featured genital shots of the Asian woman, the perversity of the girl-girl action in the stag convention seemingly sufficed to meet the criteria of difference for the goals of arousal. The Asian woman's face, as the site of the visible identification of her racial difference in this heterosexual interracial scene, becomes the sign of her genitalia. That is, her hair and face become the genitalia usually featured in meat shots of the stag film.

When we see the wide shot of the white man's fully clothed body arranging their bodies for his penetration, it is followed by the close-up of the face-to-face shot. The face-to-face shot replaces the genital-to-genital, or meat, shot. Although he is fully clothed, the white man's placement on top of her naked body in a wide shot is satisfactory proof of miscegenation!

To be clear, I reiterate that no explicit genital shots represent the sex act between the Asian woman and the white man in this film. The yellowface Asian-white sex is an entirely separate event that looks different from the rest of the sex acts in the film. Only when the white woman enters do we see the genitals in the traditional penetration shot. What this says about

Asian women and sex in representation is that their faces, not their genitals, signify their racial difference. The racialized body in stags must be told in a different way than the conventional meat shot in order to make sure the exotic difference is notable. It is difficult to assess the consistency of this aesthetic feature across other stag films. Among the hundreds of films, I chose this film to read closely along with the handful I found that explicitly feature Asians.

In the interracial ménage-à-trois, the meat shots interchange between yellowface Nellie and white Kate in two distinct ways. First, while they are each separately penetrated by Johnnie, the visualization of their sex acts is different. While the man looks the same in both scenes, the women are portrayed differently. Not all of the women's faces are shown in the sex sequences; the differences in their body sizes are what indicate that they are differently racialized women. Two fragmented body shots signify Kate: one is of a buxom bottom on top of Johnnie and the other is of her big breasts and very large nipples bouncing vigorously while riding him. Nellie, in contrast, is represented by one shot: we see her full body sitting on top of Johnnie, who is indicated partially by his legs framing her. The Asian woman is represented with her full body, especially with her long black hair now draped over her shoulders so as to remind us of her difference. In the meat shot interchange, the white man and woman are represented only as parts. Their difference is secured by way of their genitals. But since the Asian woman's genitals look the "same" as the white woman's, her difference must be told in another way.

The racial Otherness of the Asian woman is visualized differently in the sex act. Her genital difference specifically needs to be indicated by features supposedly more recognizable, namely her hair and, presumably, her body size. Unlike the white woman in the film, the Asian woman's body must be shown in its entirety for the viewer to remember her difference, which would otherwise not be apparent in the genitalia. Never seeing a close-up of her genitals engaged in penetration with the man is significant for this is usually a staple shot in regular stag films. Instead, we must see the Asian woman's whole body to know her difference. It will not be enough to see her genitals—we come to know that he is fucking an Asian woman whose body is different. And her body is as whole as possible, almost totally included in the shot. The only close-ups during the Asian-white penetration focus on her face, where her racial difference is considered to be most apparent.

Yet, without the narrative provided by the earlier titles, the racial agenda of the shots are not so easily secured. If we recall the title "The Sex Life of all races of People are THE same," we can see that the film's racial agenda has to be told through the shooting style as well. The proof of miscegenation is told through racial facial features as sufficient evidence of interracial sex. The sex act in the first half of the film suffices as proof of miscegenation. In the second half of the film, this shooting style comes to be subsumed in a larger narrativization of sex between the races.

When the sex acts become traditional, as in the case of the interracial ménage-à-trois, the film aims to illustrate its point that sex across the races is the same. It intercuts between scenes of the two women taking turns as the sexual partners of the man. Such an economy shows how sex universalizes racial difference for women. The Asian is just another kind of woman to engage with sexually. Her difference is fetishized in the visualization. But because the Asian woman is so ambiguous in her racial visibility, do we need the title in order to read the racial difference in the shooting style that I describe above? To be sure, the titles function in a central way so that race can be seen in porn. If the titles were not there, we would not see race at all. Such is the visual problematization of race in the stag film.

The Kinsey Institute records further complicate the actresses' racial legibility in the sex act. Upon my further research, the Kinsey Institute card catalogue credits the opening graphic image of *Chinese Love Life* (1921) as "Bathing Beauties," circa the 1940s. What does this disjuncture mean? What does it mean that the title that racializes the film seems to have been dropped twenty years after the film was made? With this discovery, we realize that *Chinese Love Life* may be another film entirely as well. The Oriental-looking woman is no longer Oriental in the repackaging of the film in the 1940s. Such confusion is very characteristic of stag films, as they are often composed of recycled footage from multiple films, often twenty years apart in age. In this case, the film may have been rereleased with a more modern and less racialized title. So the title *Chinese Love Life* may have nothing to do with the current content of the film or the original film itself. Considering the changes in perceptions of Asians over time, films may have been recut and recycled in order to arouse within changed contexts, further testifying to the unknowability of race, sex, and representation. That is, we do not have a complete picture regarding Asian/American female hypersexuality in popular culture. The following questions ensue: If the film was rereleased twenty years after its production, why would the theme "The Sex Life of all races of People are THE same" no longer sell to audiences in the 1940s? And how does this film contribute to the question of where the racial difference in the stag film hard-core sequence is? Was it even a racialized stag? And how do we authenticate authorship, production, and consumption of these illegal films? I now look at other films from 1920 to 1930 that employ the same narrative techniques as *Chinese Love Life* in order to ask how white women in yellowface perform Asianness. Sharing the same era as *Chinese Love Life,* the films *Menage Moderne du Madame Butterfly* (1921–30) and *China* (1930) use different techniques to visualize racial difference and sexual pleasure.

MENAGE MODERNE DU MADAME BUTTERFLY (1921-30)

In a sexually explicit way, *Menage Moderne du Madame Butterfly* visualizes the opera *Madame Butterfly* (1904) and its legend of the suicidal and devoted Asian woman. What I mean by explicit is that it shows the sex acts undergirding the narrative of the original opera—which does not show them. For example, a child is produced in both *Miss Saigon* (1989) and *Madame Butterfly,* in sex acts that occur in the dark or offstage. The use of the word "moderne" takes on significance within the context of the film's rewriting of the sexual relationships. In a sense, it calls up anxieties about Asian sexuality in the interracial encounter that inspired numerous productions of *Madame Butterfly*—one in 1904, its modern resurgence in the 1920s stag film, and the most recent upsurge at the end of the twentieth century in *Indochine* (1992), *M. Butterfly* (1993), and *Miss Saigon*.[26] Not only does the stag film modernize the opera by making sex acts explicit, it also visualizes homosexual relations that were possible in the scenario of the opera. Not only do we see Madame Butterfly have sex with Pinkerton, we also see lesbian relations with the handmaid, as well as Pinkerton's homosexual relations with the houseboy. According to Tom Waugh, the French-made film featured the director Bernard Natan, who often cast himself as the performer of gay sex acts in his movies, specifically as the giver of oral sex and the recipient of anal sex.[27]

The origin of this film is French, but the intertitles are bilingual. Inserted English translations of the otherwise French intertitles, and additional English intertitles during the sex acts, particularly the homosexual ones, indicate a narrativization that caters to a transnational cultural audience. As Tom Waugh indicates, the English translations do not resemble the more elegantly phrased French titles. In the scenes where the hand-maid Soosooky services Madame Butterfly with cunnilingus, the English title inserts commentary with a different sensibility from the French nar-rativization: "While she can't forget her male lover's kisses" is thus inserted before the title explaining the lesbian love acts. In French, the titles say, "The tears had dried up and Butterfly, cherished by Soussouki, didn't forget the caresses of his/her missing loved one." These intertitles describe gentleness in the sex scene but become more crude in tone when in English. Perhaps the crudeness anticipates a different attitude toward les-bian scenes in different contexts.

The more crudely phrased intertitle that is not in the original French is inserted during the reciprocal oral sex act on the women's purportedly slanted vaginas. The film inserts a title card that makes sure to identify the racial genitalia at this moment. Visually, in the particular reversal print I screened at the Kinsey Institute, the genitalia appear shockingly white, while the surrounding skin is black. Whatever the reason for finding and screening this film in reversal form, puzzling and bizarre as it may seem, the format indeed allows for interesting findings that would otherwise be less apparent, especially when compared to its non-reversal form. In terms of her dress, Soosooky is a combination of white and black patterns, evidenced by her kimono and her black hairpins on white hair. At the conclusion of the lesbian sex act, the intertitle card appears to say "Now let's watch the ships coming in." Without this transition card, the French would not explain the sex act between the women or isolate it from the next scene. The English transition seems to need an ending for the non-heterosexual act in order to justify its presence. A different framing of the lesbian scene and the racialization show that a seemingly original French production undergoes a cultural transformation so that it becomes a dif-ferent American product with different racial and sexual sensibilities.

The sex scene between Pinkerton and the coolie also includes new En-glish title cards that do not correspond with the French. The commentary makes fun of the coolie's effeminized homosexuality in title cards such as "Enter the coolie boy, an all around lad as you will discover." A series of short English title cards interrupt the sex act itself, making fun of the coolie's position with the particular narrative address: "The flavor lasts . . ." and "Good to the last drop." There are no original French titles in this scene. Title cards also provide motivation for the anal sex. When the coolie lifts his long shirt, turning around and bending over, the following appears: "He tells his master he'd like to show him the mole on his hip." Such narration seems to attempt explanation for the sex act between men. Without the English subtitles, the sex act would not be explained at all. It would simply be one of the acts among the four sex scenes represented in the film. The English title card describes the coolie's initiation and invitation for sex, makes an exception of him, and mocks him as "just a Japanese handman," rather than the masterful Pinkerton who has sex with two women.

Returning to my analyses of what we see in the film, especially the production of racial difference through Orientalist accoutrements, the intertitles create a narrative about the sex acts within the libretto as well. The film begins with an explicit graphic that makes use of emblems signifying the Orient. The first card reads "MENAGE MODERNE DU" and features a naked male slave on the right. A white figure in the black screen wears a loincloth. Directly underneath his figure is a cherub. On the left, a large hand gives a blessing, a kind of benevolent gesture that finalizes the situation of power somehow depicted. The mosaic of excessive Orientalist emblems that both fit and do not fit with the cherub and other Western architectural objects supposedly lend a splendorous authenticity to the image of the East meeting the West.

The next title is "MADAME BUTTERFLY," which is written on the right upper corner in the same Orientalist script. Over the shoulder of a man, we see that he is naked, penetrating from behind a woman on all fours. On the top left of the title card within the title card are a white butterfly and a parasol. A naked Asian woman, marked by her Geisha-styled hair, holds up the card. Above her, some sort of pillar-sized lion or cat-like statue floats between the other images. To emphasize the mosaic of incongruous but somehow related objects, a miniature Mount Fuji rises on the top left corner. The negative photography lends a book-like quality to the unraveling of the narrative in this particular print. The choice of caricature symbols also lends the quality of children's book to the film. White scratches on the black screen look similar to a book of illustrations. As such, the materiality of the film and its relationship to a literary original are more emphasized.

The editing of the stag film also evokes a book, unfolding in its telling. The cuts from shot to shot resemble the turning of pages. The effect produces a direct link between the film and the text of the opera. It emphasizes how the film shows us the hard-core version of this classic imaging and imagining of the Asian woman. But the visual representation does not necessarily fit with the opera in an accurate way. For example, the shot sequence to follow includes text and illustration intercut with moving bodies in negative. A light white penis over a dark, prone torso becomes a depiction of a page from a book: a geisha's profile and musical bars and notes. The stag film brings together its own grammar within its own genre and articulates a politics of race that seems different from the original it parodies.

In terms of changes to the narrative, the stag film follows the opera up to the point where Pinkerton leaves Butterfly for the first time. *Menage Moderne du Madame Butterfly* is premised upon his return. Not available in the original text, the sex acts are shown here and explicitly so. Pinkerton actually returns after Butterfly has learned to wait patiently with the help of lesbian love acts with her maid Soosooky. The form of girl-girl sex shows Soosooky servicing Butterfly. Upon Pinkerton's return, the male coolie houseboy also serves him sexually through fellatio and as the recipient in anal sex. The stag film rewrites the opera too when Pinkerton and Butterfly reunite, with Soosooky's physical assistance and the coolie's voyeuristic perversions added to the hard-core version of the scene. The libretto is not simply an object of parody. The stag film makes fun of the opera at the site of the sex act in order to eroticize the taboo of racial otherness and to show the sex acts typically told but not represented. Unlike *Chinese Love Life* and its uses of the features of the face and body, *Menage Moderne* uses the narrating power of Orientalist objects to describe racial difference, not only in the intertitles, but in the visual coverage of the sex acts.

The four major sex acts represented in the film dissect the power dynamics eroticized among the relations between Asians and whites, along with the Orientalist objects framing the action: the cunnilingus between Butterfly and Soosooky; the fellatio and anal sex between Pinkerton and the coolie; the ménage-à-trois between Butterfly, Pinkerton, and Soosooky; and the voyeuristic masturbation sex act by the coolie.[28] In the first sex scene, the reversal works to blur the details of the face and body. The kiss between Soosooky and Butterfly shows them with what looks like white hair and black skin, meeting with white open mouths. The print exists in other formats, and no explanation was available regarding the film reversal version, which intensely highlights the materiality of fabrics in their clothes and the décor in making the women visibly Asian. Their bodies are blocks of color or patterns that help to make the encounter between Oriental women one that is full of pattern and décor. The cultural accoutrements surrounding them, the fans, screen, curtains, and kimonos, are as much a part of the sex scene as the act itself. A number of wide shots capture the fabrics draping the room and the painted screens framing the sex act.

Narrativization also supports the ornamented scene. The close-up of Soosooky performing cunnilingus—of again what looks like black skin and the loud whiteness of the genitalia in this reversal version of the film— is accompanied by an intertitle text that racializes unmistakably: "Proving that the Japanese Peehole isn't cut crossways." The shot is of Soosooky blocking any sight of the genitalia. We cannot see if they are indeed slanted or not. The narrativization introduces this theme of genital difference and helps to make the woman Asian in the first sex scene.

In the second sex scene, the flowing quality of the coolie's gown and the starchy crispness of Pinkerton's military uniform are inserted in the close-ups and emphasized in the wide shots of their sex acts. The coolie, who represents the darker race, wears the white robes while Pinkerton wears the dark military wardrobe. In the wide shots of the sex scene, we see the two men in contrast. Their acts are set against a wall with a wide shoji screen and wallpaper painted with orchid-like flowers. The coolie wears a large peasant cone hat while Pinkerton wears a military hat. Similar to the previous sex scene, we stay wide in order to capture the objects constituting the scene. Wide shots cover the action so as to make use of the accoutrements available to present the sex act as interracial. Rather than the close-up of the genitals, wide shots show the objects of Orientalia that certify the racial difference at play in these scenes.

During the close-ups of the penetration, the ornaments remain in the frame. The fabrics are always included even in the tightest close-up. We must continue to see the objects for us to believe in the difference of the interracial sex act. The pleasure of visualizing interracial sex heavily involves the eroticization of cultural objects. The racial stag film's focus on the meat shot includes genitalia, but it is incomplete if not accompanied by Oriental objects that authenticate the racially illegible bodies. In Tom Waugh's analysis of gender drag in the stag film *Surprise of the Knight,* he describes how "drag eroticism [is] built on role playing, on a sense of play with disguise and gender contradictions. Drag porn presents a basic

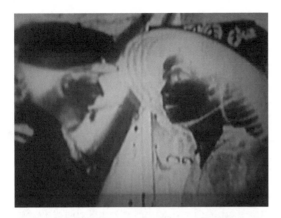

In *Menage Moderne du Madame Butterfly*, the reversal shot emphasizes Pinkerton and the coolie in contrasting colors. The wide shot includes Oriental décor that eventually frames the meat shot.

structural problem: the official uniform of the stag film, nudity, is in contradiction with the play of costume. The gowns get in the way."[29] In the racial drag of yellowface, with all of its layers of fabrics and objects, "the gowns" stay in the way of the meat shot in order to secure racial difference that is otherwise not visible. It is both presentation–based, in terms of the display of genitals and the simultaneous eroticism of objects, as well as narration based, in terms of the necessary framing of race in the intertitles.

The ornate fabrics, objects, and patterns of the mise-en-scène, captured best in the wide shot, are also used to visualize the third sex act; the ménage-à-trois involving Butterfly, Pinkerton, and Soosooky. Their clothes make them visible as racialized sexualities in ways that cannot be claimed as queer projects do, of the documentary quality of stag films for recovering an ancestral past.[30] These versions of Asian women emphasize haphazard Orientalism so that what can be collected is the evidence of hypersexual fantasy surrounding Asian women. What gets promulgated under the sign "Asian woman" has consequences for real Asian women in the sense that these stag films are part of an ancestral past, a collection of fantasies regarding Asian women, whether we claim them or not.

The women are introduced through their clothing and the white flowers in their hair. Butterfly, as the privileged woman, is marked by nudity, unlike Soosooky, who retains all of her clothes. Butterfly's pleasure is ensured. Soosooky does not come; and there is no focus on her face expressing ecstasy. She works throughout this scene. Her visible figure, clothed in the patterned kimono, clearly functions as a sexual servant to the two whose pleasures are prioritized. She moves from caressing Butterfly to servicing Pinkerton's crotch or placing his penis correctly. She eases their burdens of pleasing the other. She moves about the two depending on what service is needed. The shot stays wide in order to capture all the details of the scene. The only close-up that happens is during the final act of cunnilingus by Pinkerton on Butterfly. This shot features Butterfly's ornate shoes and the Oriental carpet below them.

The last sex scene uses the close-up to focus on the coolie's penis as he masturbates. The shot offers detail of the wallpaper behind him so that his penis is directed toward the painted image of a Japanese pagoda. The flowers on the wallpaper continue to be visible. A simple reading of this final act is that the narrative of the masculine, penetrating Western agent and the emasculated, effeminized East ends this stag. Furthermore, Asia is no more than a site of free sex where all Asians are happy to have Pinkerton as a repeat visitor.[31] The film can be read to equate Asians as waiting for the white men to grace them with sexual attention. But even the coolie seems to have more agency—betraying his mistress for favors with the master. The film ends with a scene of pleasure pursued and achieved by the coolie.[32]

For all of the people represented in the film, race is produced through the speaking power of accoutrements such as chopsticks, kimonos, and hairstyle. The décor supports a narrative that produces a particular sexuality for race and gender subjects. They all need to be recognized racially in order for their difference to animate sexuality and visuality for the aim of pleasure. The production design speaks: the shoji screen, an ornate tansu chest, elaborate patterns on costumes, and Oriental-style hair aim to emphasize the visible difference of racial others that is hard to render otherwise. The accoutrements are the smoke and mirrors used to produce a convincing package of the Asian woman. Like the woman in *Chinese Love Life*, they do seem to "look" Asian, but the chopsticks in the bun, the kimono, and the decorations work to authenticate the racialized body.

To indulge in these pleasures within the homosocial and homoracial space of the stag scene is to enjoy them on many different registers. The scene of reception recasts the significance of the racialized meat shot beyond the pleasure of seeing penetration, which is the original goal of the stag film. It also brings up the pleasure of seeing skin not meant to be touched, worlds not meant to be slept in, and people not meant to be sexual partners together so that the space of the stag film interacting with the homoracial and heterosexual spectators becomes an intersubjective interzone, a term Kevin Mumford coins to describe the ways in which disparate groups, differing in race and class, converge for the sake of sexuality.[33] Yet, these liaisons did happen even if they were taboo. Stags contradict the law and generate pleasures from their sight. The illustration of Asian-white sex in this way opens the floodgates to fantasizing the illegalities surrounding sex and race.

CHINA (1930)

Like *Menage Moderne du Madame Butterfly*, the next film, *China*, also uses Orientalist accoutrements to ensure the racialized meaning of the meat shots. Because the genital difference of the Asian woman in the body of the white woman in yellowface is not racially visible, the meat shots themselves require the presence of Oriental objects along with the genitalia in order to establish visible racial difference. This film also uses dance to make visible cultural and racial difference as part of the erotics offered in the sex act. Such grammar takes that racial legibility to say more about Asian-white relations in the world.

China begins within the home of a woman dressed up to appear Asian: she is wearing a bathrobe with Oriental patterns and a large white flower in her geisha-style hair. She opens the door for a white man in a dark Western suit. He auditions her as an "Oriental Interpretive Dancer" and hires her to dance at the Rialto Circus for seventy-five dollars per week. In turn, she rewards him with sex, narrated by the intertitles as "an ancient Chinese way of expressing gratitude."

Through such narrativization and the use of Oriental adornments, *China* incorporates the ways in which previous films racialize the sex act.

The white woman uses costume, hair, makeup, and accessories in order to appear Asian. She also performs actions presented as cultural behavior for Asian women, such as dance and the serving of rice wine. The "Asian" woman lounges in the home while the casting agent searches for talent. She offers him warm and open hospitality by bowing, deferring to his movements, and paying attention to him as the primary actional figure on screen, and then offering him some tea. As he drinks the tea she serves him and shows him her Lao Tze Dance. Close-ups on her gyrating body lead to the hard-core sequence. *China* uses these bodily movements to construct white women as Asian and to sell race as sexual titillation.

Working along with the movements are the accoutrements. The woman is made to be Asian by her heavily embroidered, kimono-style silk pajamas, the big flower (another convention in marking the Asian woman in stag film), her bun-styled hair, and the set design that surrounds her: flowers, paintings, rice wine, and tea cups. As much as possible, a wide shot retains and amplifies the speaking power of these objects in order to remind us of the distinctive racial difference supposedly present. In the pre-sex scene, the Asian woman removes her jacket to reveal a matching dressing gown beneath. The edges of her shirt feature thick embroidery. The garments are themselves used to help establish the seductive aura of the Asian woman by providing recognizable difference in order to fetishize race in porn. Like the coolie and Pinkerton in *Menage Moderne,* the tropes of white male upper classness and Asian female sexual servility are presented through costume. His thin dark suit provides a contrast to her overly embellished figure. The contrast gives the frame visual interest once again in the sense of composition. It is almost like an Eisensteinian shock of patterns and elements in order to create the unexpected poetics of film.

The performances similarly present a marked contrast. While the man is very subdued, she is quite animated. Enthusiastically, she says, "I will show you the Lao Tze Dance." This dance performed by the Asian woman is part of her set of gestures, gyrations, and movements that become classified as Asian. Here I break down the dance in order to ask what is Asian about the following.

1. She rises and releases her overcoat kimono to reveal her matching pajamas.
2. She pushes out her hands, then opens and closes them twice.
3. She places her hands on her hips and shakes side to side six times.

4. The hand on the hip extends to the front then she clap-claps to reach out side to side.
5. She then performs a waterfall gesture in front and center.
6. Her hands sit on the front thighs as she shakes her hips.
7. The swiveling of hips round and round is accompanied by arms up, elbows bending.
8. She shakes her hips more while turning left then right.
9. At the end, she moves up and walks toward him shaking her hips in his face while looking down.

I list the moves she makes in order to show their disorder. There is no such dance—nothing precise about it, which the dancer herself presents as laughable. I am not positing an authentic version of this performance, but I am pointing to the comedic way in which the set of movements is performed. These acts become coded as racial difference based on the cultural objects and racial narrativization framing the sexual acts of the stags. Specifically, Asian women's sexuality becomes framed as both cultural and biological difference; it is a natural attribution of a transcendent culture without a context, which exists to serve the sexual aims of the film.

Exotic dance is actually a form of Orientalism as well. Janet Staiger describes this relationship between dance and exoticizing the other in amusement park peepshows: "In the peephole kinetoscopes that were installed in penny arcades or kinetoscope shops as early as 1894, films were less than one minute long. Showing the gyrations of Dolorita, Carmencita, and Fatima nicely fit the technology's limitations. These dancers were part of the recent fad of reproducing oriental and exotic cultures."[34] The exotic dances caused outrage from the public. Exotic dance is central to the construction of racial difference in the stag film so that the body language of people of color is deemed particularly sexual. Many of the World's Fairs also featured racial Others in dance performance. The dances became a problem because the bodies of people of color overwhelmed the context and negated any educational purpose to the shows. The bodies of women of color are supposedly so essentially and excessively sexual that they cannot be contained by any narrativization.

Several of the Kinsey stags feature the famous "mullata" mentioned by Frank Hoffman.[35] The dance movements performed by this black woman in *Sallie and Her Boyfriend* (1947) and *Dancer's Interlude* (1949) are almost the same as the dances performed by the white woman in yellowface in the film *China*. Is the "Lao Tze Dance" in that film not so authentically Chinese after all? Or is it perhaps more indicative of the dances performed by the exotic dancers featured in stags? So, rather than any authentic representation of cultural difference, the dance indicates its burlesque or stripper origins. The "exotic dance or strip tease" is a staple feature of the stag film, "usually one-reelers featuring a dancer in famous styles" such as those seen in well-known burlesque theaters.[36] The choreography does not seem to mimic whatever "Oriental" dancing may look like since the movements consist mainly of jiggling body parts for the camera in random order.

Janet Staiger, in describing the historical context for such "exotic eroticism," points to the immigration and exclusion laws directed toward the Chinese and Japanese in America. Race suicide fears and the dwindling of Anglo Saxons, who presumably are the rightful Americans, coexisted with the existence of stags featuring interracial sex with racial and cultural Others. The construction serves the white male viewer's fantasy of the Asian woman. These dances, then, do not so much correspond to Asian body language, whatever that is, but rather to its projection and phantasm. In the racialized stag, dance is a form of the sex act for it is a way for the viewer to see and derive pleasure from the bodies of women of color. The racialized body offers visible difference that constitutes sexual pleasure just by autoeroticism. Dance allows the visible difference of the racialized body to show, for it combines the exoticism of the foreign culture with the racially marked body.

The hard-core sex acts work similarly. In *China*'s first sex act, the kissing scene is primarily represented in a wide shot that involves the whole room: the furniture, the fabrics all over the place, and the tea cups on the table in front of them. The woman also takes off her clothes and allows them to frame her body for a while. The ornate Oriental clothes do not leave the frame entirely; they accompany or supplement her. She also peels away the layers of racialized clothing to reveal more clothing in a deliberate showing of herself through the clothes. Finally, when the last of the clothing is dropped, her nudity should really reveal a different kind of skin. It should show her special difference after this huge production, but it does not.

Therefore, the fabric plays an active part even within the sex scenes and the close-up genital shots in the film. These meat shots featuring the Asian women always seem to be accompanied by the kimono, parasol, or fan in order to remind us of the facticity of racial difference that does not

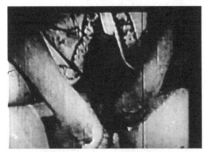
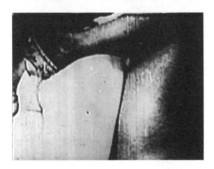

In *China*, the white woman plays
Asian through her costume,
coiffure, and dance. In the genital
shot, the kimono and then the
shoe remind us of her racial
difference before ending with a
pornotopic kiss.

actually exist. In *China,* the clothes, and the ornate embroidery in particular, enter the shot and occupy the frame with prominence, to an unnatural and mannered degree. So the bottom corner of the Asian woman's embroidered kimono-style shirt inserts itself into the extreme close-up of the genital action. The Oriental fabrics frame the genitals during the act of intercourse. To further emphasize the interracial encounter, the intertitle pops up with a name for the sex act that looks no different from any other male penetration of the female: "The Shanghai Gesture." The "Shanghai Gesture," a dance exactly like the last movements of the Lao Tze Dance, needs to be narrated racially as well. Otherwise, the racial difference gets lost. When the bottom of her dressing gown, particularly the part where the two front halves meet, comes together in the meat shot, the patterns form a pattern on the screen as well. The objects remind us of racial difference and also help to aestheticize the interracial sex act.

In *China*'s hard-core sequence, black-and-white contrast delivers visible racial difference for the viewer. The woman in yellowface has a dark, black bottom in close-up against the man's white thighs. She is on top of him on the bed and in the camera frame. This is extremely unusual in terms of the racialized color contrast of genital shots according to gender. Usually the man's penis is darker than the woman's genital area. In *Chinese Love Life,* the man is continually a darker presence. In *China,* the woman's body becomes darker and darker, while the man's penis becomes whiter. Here, she almost has no contrast to the framing of her ass in terms of hue and gradation. There is none at all during certain gyrations—just a black screen with a white shape in and out of that delineated space. The sequence showing how the body on the bottom is lit white and the body on top black makes a point about the deliberateness of the cinematography.

Although there is supposedly no skin color difference, the Asian woman's racialized difference is secured through the coding of black and white in this stag film. She is the darker presence, a reminder of her difference that is similarly secured by the ongoing narrative and the insertion of accoutrements. The visual pleasure of color contrast, the intricate and interesting pattern of objects inserted in art direction, and the humorous narrative emphasize the black and white genitals, which signify miscegenation as a meeting of bodily pleasure. The image is a visual pleasure precisely because of its difference in the social memberships of race, sex, and gender, as well as the formalist aspects of composition that come from the contrast on screen.

The narrative, production design, and cinematography racialize the sex act and also help to create an aesthetic particular to the interracial Asian-white sex act. Narrative and accoutrements team up to assert that what may not be racial difference can be secured as such by external markings. In other typical stag films, such as *Country Stud Horse* (1920), which features primarily white sex, the sight of shoes during sex is a common humorous convention. In *China*, even the shoe is made Oriental through its ornamentation. It functions in a different way; it is supposed to speak racial difference and not just mock the sex act. The shoe is excessively ornate and fulfills its purpose as a racialized sexual object by being effectively inserted into the genital close-ups. The shoe cannot be normal or unmarked; it must emanate excess sexuality, reminding us of the nature of the racialized being performing the act. It is as if the viewers are not allowed to forget that it is a taboo miscegenation that transpires before us.

In another scene, the sex act is humorously attributed to the woman's racial and cultural background, "an ancient Chinese way of expressing gratitude." The narrative supplements the accoutrements in order to remind the viewer of the racial and cultural Otherness of the characters involved. The narrative line marks the sex and seduction as continually racial. However, the need for this line seems to give evidence of the filmmaker's belief that the sex act is not racial in actuality. Nothing of this sort occurs in white stag, where sex is not marked by race. Yet in stag films featuring interracial Asian sex, this theme appears continuously. When the woman and the man strip out of their clothes, the intertitle reads, "When Buddha Smiles." The accoutrements and the narrative both work together to create an intensely racialized sexual scene.

CONCLUSION: STAGS AS RACIAL PORNOTOPIA

The problematization of the racial (in)visibility of sex sees props and narrative eroticizing race as a fetish. Sex itself universalizes all of the differences produced by the end of the films. The films produce visible racial difference in order to erase it through sex. The hard-core sequence in *China* ends in a fully clothed medium-wide two-shot of the couple, loving, post-coital, and domestic. The film ends when the Asian woman and the white man gleefully hug each other and compliment each other specifically in terms of the other's difference. "You have something there," he says as he intimately grabs her bottom. She responds, "And you also."

The racial stag film, like the narrativization of sexual deviance in features at the time, concludes in the coming together of racial and genital difference within harmony. The difference of race and its possible threats to American redefinitions of America's racial and national identity are contained within this particular cultural production. The production of race, indeed, occurs only to be undermined in the film's conclusion.

The visualization of race in the stag film privileges sex and denies racial difference in a problematic positing of a kind of racial pornotopia. That is, racial difference is not fully engaged but is subsumed in a narrative that uses it only for its sexual titillation. It works as a utopic formation without reference to the charged relations it corresponds to in contemporaneous society. So, ultimately, transgressive and transformative meanings of the role of race in sex have no place in the stag film. Instead, the racial difference is but part of a narrative of universal sexual pleasure. Thus, the Asian woman in stag is a contradictory formation, for while she is initially constructed as different, it is her sameness that is finally emphasized. Her sameness seems emphasized in that her race is subsumed within sexual purpose. Yet, her exoticism is an important and celebratory part of the sexual activity—it is present for the sake of the white male viewer's arousal. The stags contain the threat of racial difference and translate it toward different ends. I must point out another stag film from this era wherein the contemporaneous popular culture figure of the diseased Asian body, as described by Nayan Shah in his book *Contagious Divides,* is imagined and eroticized. In *Geisha Girl* (1948–55), a startling white fluid seeps out of the female genitalia in the meat shot. Similarly, *Geisha* (1958) concludes with the white man and yellowface Asian woman kissing with noses and tongues before we see the genital shot of white fluid seeping out of her vagina. The genital shot looks like an aestheticization of the diseased Asian body as part of its erotic grammar.

Janet Staiger argues that representations of non-heteronormative female sexuality in the 1920s and 1930s were tolerated as long as they were condemned within the narrative.[37] In racialized sex, the acts are explored as deviant while their normalcy is simultaneously assured. Does this strong treatment of race in porn as non-difference make the genre utopic? If stags are racial pornotopia, race is then an epiphenomenon to sex within the genre. Precisely because the sex is different vis-à-vis the narrative rather than the image, the act, the costumes, and accoutrements, or the person per se, the role of race in early porn works very specifically as a fetish. Race

In *Geisha*, the couple rubs noses
and tongues before we see a
genital shot with a startling
white fluid.

is there for sexual pleasure and nothing else. I do not mean to say that the
representation of race in visual and sexual pleasure does nothing useful. I
mean to say that the problem of race does not enter the narrative premise
of the film or the visual grammar of its representation. There is a drive to
write it as utopia: that is, "The Sex Life of all races of People are THE same."

If there are no distinctions in the sex acts themselves between white sex
and Asian sex, sexual difference in porn nonetheless uses race purpose-
fully. It mobilizes the economic and historical reasons for the production
of racialized sexuality by making use of fantasy about such illegal entanglements. The fantasy in porn is the assimilation of the racial Other as yet
another sexual companion and the romanticization of sex as a solution to
the problem of race. Representation of race is not a problem but is desirable in the stag film. It is as if race is unproblematic in the world, where
problems of sex are not foregrounded in contrast to other forces where it
is the issue. In the 1920s and 1930s, America entered into modernity fear-
ing sex between Orientals and whites in terms of social hygiene, eugenics,
and race suicide. Stag films contradict such an understanding of race in
contemporaneous society in a way that reflects Linda Williams's observa-

tion that stag films "were cut off from more public discourses of sexuality."[38] I translate this observation to mean that stag films identify acceptable forms of public sexuality, that is, stag films grasp the fears, anxieties, and fantasies about racial others and deliver representations in order to derive pleasure from these public feelings. As Laura Kipnis notes, porn delivers what people want within their historical situations.[39]

All of the objects of discussion in my larger project have a strong connection to history: for instance, the production of *The Thief of Bagdad* and *Shanghai Express* occurred during the height of race panics such as the yellow peril. Stag films, however, offer a strange relationship to history; these narratives function separately from the world. The fears of social hygiene, yellow peril, and real-life miscegenation seem to happen apart from these films. This phenomenon is very different from other engagements such as *Behind the Green Door* (1972), in which audiences at a sex club voyeuristically take pleasure at the sight of an "innocent" white woman engaged in sex with black men. The pornography purports not to talk about the issues while representing the fantasies that spring from the taboo.[40] The taboo sex act directly engages in real world interracial sexual anxieties and issues of the 1970s.

In the stag films, a different racial pornotopia occurs within the specific historical and geographical context of Asian women. In the case of the yellowface Asian-white interracial sex in the stag film, the context is prostitution, race suicide, and social hygiene fears as Asians increased their presence in the United States. These films were made during periods of crisis in American history, specifically in terms of what David Palumbo-Liu calls the management of modernity as the "management of Asian America."[41] Specifically, questions such as "What is America to be?" require reflection about the role of sexual reproduction in the redefinition of American racial identity. Cultural production performed an important role in the "symbolic and ideological maneuvering that sought to tame and accommodate this mutual penetration (of Asians in America and America in Asia)."[42] Itself based on an earlier East-West encounter, *Madame Butterfly* was modernized in stags during a different historical era: the 1920s and 1930s. The original opera coincided with Asian and American/European encounters as indicated in the American exclusion acts that barred and contained Asian immigration to the United States beginning in the 1880s. Similarly, stag films coincided with other acts, such as the 1924 National Origins Act, which barred East Asians from immigrating to the United States, and the 1934 Tydings-McDuffie Act, which classified Filipino Americans as aliens and prohibited them from working in the United States.

Images in *Chinese Love Life* (1921), *Menage Moderne du Madame Butterfly* (1921–30), and *China* (1930) do not capture the ahistorical nature of the stag films. Rather, they capture the defiance of ideology and history by fantasy. Fantasy needs to be unleashed in our understanding of race, sex, and representation so as to inform history. Race provides a specific sexual titillation that seems locatable and identifiable in the body that must be made racially visible. There she is: an Asian woman who must be natural to sex "practiced for centuries." How do certain sexual proprieties come to belong to certain races of women so that their appearances are themselves roles and embodiments they must wear in order to communicate a specific and proper racialized sexuality? In my readings of the Asian woman in stag, accoutrements, narrative, and extreme close-ups of genital shots secure belief that these truly are the sexualities of Asian/American women. Yet such claims are outside history. The genital shots show the racialized sex organ apart from the meat shot and eroticize taboo racial relationships.

A summary of my findings is in order. First, material culture as it functions within the genital shot, particularly the accoutrements of Orientalism, such as wigs, clothes, fans, and other aspects of set design, expose the production of racialized sexuality. For all three films, the racial difference continues as central, even in the most discontinuous and ambiguous hard-core sequences, through the insertion of Orientalist objects and racial narrativization. In racialized stag, the "show" of the genitals features the rarely seen "event" of miscegenation. The sexual difference of racially particular women is secured in both the narrative continuity of the film and the close-ups of the racially particularized genital shots. The narrative is insistent in its interruption of the hard-core shot sequence as if to aggressively announce that she is Asian and he is white—noticing the illegal act of miscegenation. The genitals and the sex act involve partners considered taboo for white men. If the narrative inserts did not exist, would these shots be no different from white sex?

Second, physical actions are made visible as determined by racialization. In the stag show, the genitals do not really belong to racially different women, but instead to white women in yellowface. Whether the women are Asian or white, the "yellowface" masquerade of Asian female genitals in the black and white film shows the need to make racial genital difference visible. The narrative supports this in how it organizes and makes continuous the theme of race in stag. Shots that declare the yellowface woman as the one who proves the existence of slanted genitalia makes fun of Asians through sex and makes fun of sex through Asians. Making fun of Asians indicates the place of Asian women in the stag film. Their bodies are made into cultural objects for the viewers' pleasure and/or ridicule. Their difference provides visual pleasure that comes from seeing objects from afar: exotic items previously unseen for they belong somewhere out there.

Third, narrativization of cultural difference reveals how investments of race and sex charge fantasies of difference and combine ideologies of social hygiene and race panic. These techniques show the beginnings of the tradition of the Asian woman's particular sexuality in pornography. In later pornography, Asian women appear as fantasy images with an ambiguous relationship to history. They are both disconnected and connected; they appear as prostitutes in Southeast Asia during various wars, as madams and prostitutes in plantation porn, as nymphomaniacs in Chinatown during the 1960s, and as drug importers in the 1980s. The threat or problematization of race in the outside world becomes fodder for fantasy and enjoyment within pornography.

So, while porn is a deviant genre, within it there is normalcy as well as perversity. "Multicultural" and other subgenre categories supplement the norm of "vanilla" heterosexual sex. Race signals perversity. If the sex acts are equally the same, as the films ultimately argue, the marketing of racial difference seems to be contradicted. If Asian women do not "do" sex differently, what's the big deal? Race functions as a part of the narrative in the commodification of sex. It is similar to the commodification and valuation of gender morality or virtue in terms of sex in feature films of the time. For example, Janet Staiger discusses the constructions of the vamp, the idolized woman, and the unthinking woman as three popular tropes for women in film.[43] These women are punished by the film's end for being this particular type of woman rather than a wifely, moral, and thinking woman. Racialized commodification and fetishization in feature films of the time work differently. The morality tale is targeted toward white audiences who need to flee from sexually menacing racial others, such as in *The Cheat* (1915), *Birth of a Nation* (1915), and *The Thief of Bagdad* (1924). Race in stag films is narrativized differently. Persons of color or racial Others are not narrativized as immoral. They are not a sexual threat but a sexual treat. They do not correspond to larger ideologies that posit them as the demise of normalcy and of the good social order. The shooting style of the films captures how Asian women are redeployed not as yellow peril but as yellow pleasure.

The racialized stag films function similarly to white stag films for they share the same male gaze.[44] Linda Williams points out the primarily male audience for stags in order to counter gender pornotopia versions of stag history made by Di Lauro's and Rabkin's *Dirty Movies*.[45] In the case of racial representation in the stag film, I argue that racial difference is subsumed in the pleasures of sex in racial pornotopia. Difference is contained in the stag films so that racial fears and anxieties are dampened. This attempt to include racial others as proper sexual objects for the stag's male viewers fetishizes race and eroticizes it as different from the norm. Rather than understanding the stag film simply to reflect anxieties, phobias, desires, and prohibitions about race and sex at the time, the stags offer a pornotopia that says that sex universalizes racial difference.

My search for legacy in this chapter instead finds Asian women's marginality through sexual representation. I have revealed the production of fantasy for the Asian woman as it circulates through its seemingly unquestionable evidence of visible difference. Stag representations of the Asian woman not only show how fantasy is produced from social and economic racial encounters, but they also make use of technologies of the visual to talk about the taboo in different, less anxious ways apart from reproduction and miscegenation. While racial pornotopia assesses the role of race in the imagination, the way race transforms the role of sex in American identity itself and the way racialized sexuality challenges visual technology are not taken up. The donning of race through costume allows for the white performers to play different roles—for the purpose of making sex different. It does not engage the difference of race as articulated by those afraid of it: eugenicists, lawmakers, and the like. The visual play of race is taken up in terms of concrete social relations at the site of the sex act in later productions. Stag films use anxieties about Asian-white sex for their sexual value. Interracial yellowface-white stag films did not simply reflect phobias about the American "Oriental menace" during the 1920s and 1930s, but, rather, they focused on sexuality not only to dampen anxieties but to generate pleasures about race. The important lesson to be garnered in interpreting the production of racialized sexuality in the stag film is the irrational relationship between history, ideology, and fantasy. These films illuminate the production of racialized sexuality and defy the authenticating power of the cinema. And for Asian/American consumers of porn, we are able to see the fantasy performed by white women in yellowface.

5

QUEENS OF ANAL, DOUBLE, TRIPLE, AND THE

GANGBANG ✻ Producing Asian/American Feminism in

Pornography, 1940s–1990s

Asian/American women comprise their own special genre in American pornography. In many video stores, the porn shelves are organized by race under the categories of Asian, black, and multicultural. As such, Asian/American women's sexual subjectivity, practices, and roles in pornography are prominently categorized by race as their foremost signifier. As I show in the previous chapter, pornography is important for understanding racialization as a sexual process. It is a process that continues in later stag films and golden age pornography, wherein we see the visual composition of racial difference. In the recent scene, the Asian/American women porn stars Asia Carrera and Annabel Chong use their sexuality in pornography to comment on the profound complexity of their racialization and use their racialization to comment on the bottomless fluidity of their sexuality. As such, it is not enough to say that we need to study porn to understand Asian/American women's racial formation. The study of porn is also crucial in helping us to recognize the ways in which porn recasts pain, pleasure, power, and the political. It does so through a reminder of the unreliability and unknowability of the experiences of race, sexuality, and representation. To keep open the complexity of images as well as the experience of their production and consumption helps me to formulate a theory of "race-positive sexuality" that takes seriously the challenge of defining sexuality in terms of Asian/American feminist women's practices in pornography. Through the enactment of yellowface, a form of Asian minstrelsy, by "real" Asian women in the 1950s and the performance of polymorphous perversity on the Internet and in video by contemporary pornography's megastars, I show the ways in which pornography helps us to see how race and sex provide the terms for Asian/American women's prioritization of their subjectivities.

RACE AND PORNOGRAPHY

The modern feminist debates on pornography continue from the wars between anti-porn and anti-censorship feminists in the 1980s. Andrea Dworkin and Catherine MacKinnon offered a feminist theory of pornography consisting primarily of a harms-based evaluation wherein pornography enacts violence upon women.[1] Primarily understood as the ultimate objectification of women, pornography is framed as the monster-arm of sexism and patriarchy as exemplified by the popular adage by Robin Morgan that "pornography is the theory and rape the practice."[2] Such rigid analysis that prioritizes victimization in its understanding of the power of both sexuality and representation does not accommodate pleasure, performance, and fantasy beyond accusations of false consciousness. The derivation of anything but pain and oppression from pornography leads to a diagnosis of perversity and pathology inappropriate to the social problems of gender. The derivation of pleasure supposedly results in an agreement to one's own death—as if that experience of having to enjoy one's symbolic death does not in itself indicate women's marginalization as spectators.

In reading pornography differently, sex-positive feminists emphasize a disjuncture between fantasy and reality. Lynne Segal writes, "For pornographic fantasy has no straightforward connection with what may be its 'real-life' enactment, unless it's a stylized 'enactment' (as in consensual s/m) under the fantasizer's own control."[3] Fantasy, as a force, can find politically productive expression, such as in the ways gay men use pornography to seek sexual legacy, redress, and education. Crude definitions of fantasy in anti-pornography feminist platforms do not account for such a productive use.[4] Similarly, feminist film scholars require the watching of pornographic films closely as socially relevant texts and especially as a genre worth studying, rather than a social problem in need of annihilation. For example, through an evaluation of the money shot, or the visible proof of ejaculation that is key to contemporary pornography, Linda Williams identified the problem of visualizing women's sexuality as important to the language and project of pornography.[5] Laura Kipnis encourages the study of porn and its ability to tell us a great deal about power dynamics in society.[6] Furthermore, Susie Bright, Constance Penley, and Naomi Wolf more specifically problematize women's identities and desires in pornography.[7] For example, women desire. Women express different kinds of sexuality. Women participate willingly in perverse practices. Male consumption defies what Wolf describes as Andrea Dworkin's prediction that the proliferation of pornography would lead men to do violence to women. The opposite occurred; pornography instead killed male libido for "real women."[8]

Located between the anti-pornography and sex-positive camps, racialized sexuality in porn remains a problem that needs more serious and more direct address. In the scene of racialized analyses of porn, the simplifications of sexuality, production, consumption, and fantasy and the rhetoric of gender victimization register within the context of the lives of women of color. As Trinh T. Minh-ha argues, women of color live at the intersection of multiple oppressions as they experience racism, gender discrimination, and sexual harassment.[9] For example, the history of racialized sexuality in slavery grounds black feminist responses to pornography.[10] Proponents of sex-positive versions of pornography must not belittle the power of the ongoing legacy of sexual slavery in regard to race. Too easily, racial discourses of pornography are seen as a regressive victimology in an anti-sexuality platform rather as a discourse within history that needs confrontation.[11] This insensitivity to race transpires in rather subtle ways, according to critics such as Susie Bright who comment on how whiteness remains unmarked in discussions of sexuality.[12] Magdalena Barrera proves this when she identifies the exclusion of race in many analyses of sexuality, ranging from popular discourses around Jennifer Lopez's butt to Laura Kipnis's analysis of *Hustler*.[13] Laura Kipnis says porn "does exist, and it's not going to go away. Why it exists, what it has to say and who porn thinks it's talking to, are more interesting than all those doomed dreary attempts to debate it, regulate it and protest it."[14] While Kipnis argues against the likes of Catherine MacKinnon and Andrea Dworkin, we must take care not to conflate anti-racist critique that may look like what she describes as "debate . . . and protest" with anti-sex critique.[15] Sex-positive discourse, proposed by sex workers and cultural critics such as Carol Queen and Annie Sprinkle, is not mutually exclusive from race-positive sexuality as I will discuss later.[16]

Black feminist theories regarding pornography use race and the identification of racism in pornography as the primary lens of analysis. For Tracey A. Gardner, pornography capitalizes on the underlying history of carnal, diabolic, and evil myths constituting the lives of people of color in the United States, such as the myth of the black rapist and the always already consenting black woman. For Gardner, pornography operates a technology of racism, an arm of the monster.[17] Luisah Teish describes pornography as undermining of the black power movement for it aims to pull back advancements gained by the civil rights movement in order to return blacks to non-human ontology.[18] If white women function as objects in pornography, Alice Walker's essay "Coming Apart" identifies a racial grid within pornography that sees black women as animalistic and as less than excrement in the context of white female objectification.[19] She says black women in pornography qualify as less than objects when signifying the scatological. The diagnosis of porn as negative continues in another Walker essay, "Porn," in which the love between a black man and woman becomes undercut by the presence of pornography—so that what empowers black men in the objectification of white women simultaneously disables black female sexual pleasure.[20] Within this work, fantasy proceeds as nothing more than a specter of racism and a distortion of masculinity for taking pleasure and power from female objectification.

Similar to that of black women, Asian/American women's hypersexuality, as "naturally" excessive and extreme against a white female norm, directly attaches to a specific race and gender ontology. At the same time the master narratives that hold for African American women, such as the centrality of slavery, may not necessarily apply to Asian/American women who contend with hypersexual attribution emerging from different colonial histories. While the figure of the black woman in porn as animalistic and intrinsically available lashes out from the historical debasement of black women in slavery, the Asian woman, presented as culturally prone to sexual adventure and exotic difference, emerges from the colonial encounter of war. Like black women, Asian/American women cannot flee from the racial categorization that Alice Walker, Luisah Teish, and Tracey A. Gardner describe in their essays on pornography.

Indeed all women demonstrate sexuality in pornography, but the hypersexuality of women of color knots itself to racial identity and history. Asian/American women's sexuality subsists in history; this history embeds in the sexuality we see on pornographic screens. It is important to recall the historical context of sexuality inscribing the immigration of Asian women into the United States as it significantly informs my exploration of alternative responses to sexuality in the presence of Asian American women in pornography. The historical facts I describe in the introduction warrant repetition in the context of evaluating Asian/American women's formulation of feminist practice vis-à-vis hard-core pornography. Figures of Chinese women prostitutes occupied a prominent place in popular culture to the extent that this imagined threat shaped immigration, resulting in the Page Law of 1870, which curbed their population. At the turn of the century, Chinese women prostitutes were routinely harassed on the streets. Japanese women entered the United States as "picture brides" at the beginning of the twentieth century and as "war brides" after World War II. In Filipino American history, a woman was stoned to death for her adultery, which was considered a gender and racial traitorship.[21] Korean "war brides" arrived in the United States with their American GI husbands after the Korean War. Catalogues introduce mail-order or pen-pal brides from the Philippines today. Specifically because their legal status exists conditionally as part of their marriage to a U.S. citizen or permanent resident, mail-order brides are especially vulnerable regardless of their experiences of domestic violence. And Asian sex workers travel to the United States as transnational sex workers. The process of racialization includes the sexuality of Asian/American women centrally as a subjugating force in ways that can better inform our approaches to race and pornography.

At the same time that we acknowledge the sexuality of women of color in history, and black feminist theory regarding the dangers of pornography, cultural producers who are women of color advocate for "race-positive sexuality," which resonates with the work of women of color in pornography. A formulation that brings together the concerns of black feminist theory regarding pornography and sex-positive discourse, "race-positive sexuality" emerges from the literature of Chrystos, Cherríe Moraga, Audre Lorde, and others who present pleasure, pain, and trauma simultaneously in ways that embrace the liberating possibilities of sexuality while also acknowledging the risks of reifying perversity and pathology traditionally ascribed to women of color in popular culture.[22] The need to talk about pornography from the pain of a particular psychic legacy requires emphasis and the continuity of white indifference to the different racial context for discourses of sexuality needs to be acknowledged.

Race-positive sexuality connects gender and sexuality in pornography to slavery and colonial history while keeping open its anti-racist and sex-positive potentialities. If Lauren Berlant correctly poses the white girl's role in national fantasy as the figure of innocence that must be protected,[23] the Asian girl's extreme perversity occurs in porn as a quality attributed to her ethnic culture and race. Thus, the role of the Asian girl in national fantasy remains that of one who goes without protection. Acknowledging the tradition of cultural producers and critics who are women of color and who present sexuality as constitutive of their racial histories and subjectivities, "race-positive sexuality" argues for the need to acknowledge how sexuality can be pleasurable, powerful, and painful simultaneously. Rather than authorize critics to decide what good and bad sexualities look like for whatever racial agenda, we need to account for the specific ways sexuality works as described by Asian/American women's practices. Rather than advocate for a particular sexuality and representation, I prefer to keep our definitions open so as to make space for those who experience sexual subjugation and are too frequently silenced and those who practice sexual perversity and are too easily dismissed as dangerous bad subjects who damage agendas of racial decency. I propose to listen to the terms posited by Asian/American women working in pornography rather than attend to the fear of ascribing traditional, fixed, and monolithic hypersexuality to racialized images.

In "Race, Gender, and the Law," Kandice Chuh argues that because Asian/American women are produced as always already consenting, they cannot be raped in the eyes of the law. Such a legacy amplifies the stakes for Asian/American women in pornography. If the actual rape of third world women and women of color finds explanation not in terms of white male power but in a natural female propensity for hypersexuality, Asian women's hypersexual ontology becomes described as essential.[24] Thus, to shift the traditional understanding of sexuality and visuality as dangerous and damaging to race and the racialized experience is understandably met with skepticism. What risks emerge in allowing for the possibility that sexuality may be liberating beyond the role of Asian women in national fantasy as aberrant and perverse, which is equated with disempowerment and damage?

Though Earl Jackson warns that pornography "cannot be satisfactorily summarized in any unitary fashion,"[25] race persistently defines the appearance of Asian/American women. Both Asian American and black feminist readings of sexuality must avoid falling into the trap of vilifying race and sexuality, especially in moving images. Chuck Kleinhans says that "fear of images erupts in even the most nominally progressive circles when it comes to sexual representations."[26] Instead, we need to take heed of Laura Kipnis's argument about the value of looking at porn. We must allow the complexities of sex and visuality to surface as part of formulating feminist and anti-racist politics. Asian/American women within pornography experience race as visible and sexual.

Looking at pornography helps us to understand the fantasies and fetishisms regarding Asian/American women's presence in popular culture. Fantasies do not merely unleash domination upon people of color. Fantasies can project desire, open the psyche, and work as technologies of imagination for authors, spectators, and critics of color. As Cynthia Liu and Tasha Oren argue in different contexts, representation should not simply reflect reality but create alternatives as well as compel imaginative interpretation by viewers.[27] Indeed, we should keep open the possibility of redeploying fantasy in the service of making space for those who need to articulate different deviancies and perversities, in the broadest sense of political and social inclusion. Freudian understanding of fantasy emphasizes an alternative different from and at times defiant of reality. Crucial to the formation of subjectivity, fantasy forms the terms with which one relates to the world.[28] If we examine fantasy as part of the racial experience in terms of the perceptions, imaginations, illusions, and consciousness of one's self and others, agency expands as do new levels of analyses regarding racialized sexuality. As Slavoj Žižek evaluates in "The Sexual Act in the Cinema," the articulation of fantasy by the powerful can be seen and evaluated in the sex acts represented.[29] Yet fantasy does not belong to the powerful alone but may be manipulated to express dissatisfaction and other critique. Fantasy, and its expression in pornography, functions importantly in the study of the politics of race, especially as a venue for Asian/American women to redefine the tradition of their hypersexual production in moving images.

In *The Secret Museum* Walter Kendrick asks: What enables pornography in the twentiety century?[30] He describes a shift in sexuality as an analytic subject "in its own right, sorting it out from the moral, legal and religious contexts in which it had hitherto been embedded. Not until very late in the 19th century would the shifting be completed leaving us today with a notion of sex as something like advanced calisthenics."[31] Within this definition, what do we make of "Asian" becoming synonymous with anal sex and other extreme sexual activities, such as the special acrobatics of double and triple penetration and gangbangs in contemporary pornography? While keeping the door open to fantasy and the power of performance in redeploying their meaning, we need to understand the way Asian/ American women are sexualized over time in pornography.

A SOCIAL HISTORY OF ASIAN/AMERICAN
WOMEN'S IMAGES IN PORNOGRAPHY

In the previous chapter, I assess the discourse of Asian women in stag films, which are short, illegally made 8mm and 16mm pornographic films in circulation during the first half of the twentieth century in America and Europe. Here, I study later stag films that require "real" Asian/American women, as opposed to white women in yellowface, to perform the fantasy of Asian women. The Golden Age of porn describes an era wherein high production values reigned, such as the use of film rather than video from the 1960s to the 1980s. In addition, many films of the Golden Age, such as *Deep Throat* (1972), *Behind the Green Door* (1972), and *The Devil in Miss Jones* (1973), made huge profits as couples began to attend screenings in movie theaters together. In this chapter, I link the representation of Asian/American women in the Orientalism of the "genital show," or the showing of genitalia in the stag film, rather than the contemporary money shot, as an adequate goal in early pornography from the beginning of the twentieth century to its continuing use in the production of "yellowface" in the golden age of pornography. In my discussion of later stag films, I describe the enduring role of Orientalism in the production design of the "genital show" as it is shaped by the new historical context of the Second World War. Then I scrutinize what we can claim for Asian/American women in looking at the legacy of these images. In films of the golden age featuring the earliest Asian/American porn stars, I interpret the occurrence of yellowface as a political act. By donning yellowface makeup and costume, applying linguistic approaches such as accents and manner of speech, and enacting peculiar bodily movements, racial difference may seem to establish itself as reliably visible. Within such a problematic formation, however, the juxtaposition of the stereotyped role and the Asian/American woman porn star's body and psyche captures a terrible collision that ruptures the fantasy.

Early pornography problematized racial visibility in its grammar. Since the facticity of racial difference may not register as visibly reliable, pornography finds ways to establish its titillation through production design and narrativization, such as in its intertitle texts or dialogue. These elements work to establish racial difference as the erotic meat of pornography in early stag film. Later, the presence of Asian women defies the fantasy and the stereotype as a prelude to the ways in which Asian women porn stars use pornography to comment on their racialization through sex and their sexualization through race.

As I previously discussed in the genital show of early stag films, Asian women's skin color difference may not appear visibly in black and white depictions of racialized bodies. Thus, accoutrements act as visible evidence of race for the Asian/American woman in stag films, emphasizing her particular difference versus that of other women of color. The sex act in early stag films problematizes the visibility of race as unreliable for Asian/American women. Stag films' use of Oriental objects to establish racial difference helps me to define my concept of the "seeing of race as the seeing of sex." Specifically, these films aim to show us the sexuality of the Asian woman, even though she may be a white woman in yellowface, so as to say something about her race and gender interiority as a being who exists for the white male actor and spectator.

POST-1950S STAG FILMS

The era following World War II witnessed the explosion of pornography out of the stag arena and into mainstream venues. In the 1950s, antimiscegenation laws started crumbling in the United States just as American military men brought home war brides from Asia. The military rest and recreation industry in Southeast Asia began transforming into a commercial industry that saw great global libidinal transactions in its economy. Hollywood produced movies problematizing the interracial love affair. They included popular leading men paired with beautiful Asian women in love stories bound for marriage: *Sayonara* (1957) featuring Marlon Brando, *The World of Suzie Wong* (1960) featuring William Holden, and *Walk Like a Dragon* (1960) featuring Jack Lord.[32] Within this context, the elimination of anti-miscegenation laws and the gradual rejection of the Hollywood Production Code witnessed a new kind of stag pornography from the 1940s to the 1960s. Stag films began to feature "real" Asian women and less white women in yellowface. Two particular trends in the portrayal of Asian women on screen, regardless of their race on scene (such as white women in yellowface), are apparent. First, extraordinary focus on extreme close-ups of her genitalia anticipated the question of the genital "slant" mimicking her eyes, which was presented as the ultimate manifestation of her racial difference. Second, the eroticization of the white male-Asian female marriage became more prevalent in society at the time. The stag film evolved to feature "real" Asian women who must nonetheless traffic in yellowface in order to sell racial visibility that would not otherwise seem apparent. How does yellowface function in these films? When we see Asian/American women putting on the fantasy of Asian women a disjuncture opens. It necessitates a re-evaluation of the reliability of the filmic medium as well as its possibilities for political critique by Asian actresses.

Moreover, we can further see how pornography occurs as a process of racial formation[33] when we examine how Asian/American women present yellowface sexuality in the context of a more dramatic change occurring in stag films from the 1950s. While the technique of illustrating racial difference persists in earlier stag films until the 1950s, the sudden appearance of Asian/American women playing Asian women, especially within the domestic intimacy of the Asian female-white male couple and the absence of Oriental accoutrements on the female body, appears to be significant in the 1960s. In the film *Date Night* (1961),[34] the erotics produce Asian female-white male domesticity. The shift becomes comprehensible if we take account of the historical changes occurring at this time. The white man no longer knocks on the door to encounter the Asian woman because she acts as his wife or girlfriend. Here, the sex scene's lack of Oriental objects in the "genital show" finds revision. While we no longer see Oriental objects decorating the sex scene, the new objects domesticate women who are visibly Asian/American in films with racially unmarked titles such as *Date Night*.

The title of the film confuses at first: *Date Night* hints at a night on the town and the need to prepare oneself by dressing up not down. When the Asian/American woman prepares for a date, she undresses from her day clothes and gets ready to wind down. Unlike earlier stag films where the man, a talent agent, plumber, or external figure, enters from outside the home, the man in *Date Night* enters the home as her husband or boy-friend. We no longer see her opening the door; he simply comes in as if coming home from a long day at work. When he comes in, she does not stand at all, but warmly welcomes him with a smile, without stopping the filing of her nails. The premise of the narrative has completely changed from earlier films where the encounter between the Asian woman and white men transpired within an outsider-insider relation, not only in terms of domesticity but in terms of national belonging as foreigner or citizen.

In earlier narratives of films such as *China* and *Geisha*, the man, usually a stranger from outside the home, encounters an Asian woman, her body racially marked by costume in her racially marked home. She is not American and not normal. In *Date Night*, the woman possesses no racially visible markers on her body or in her home setting. The economy of the couple's physical relationship differs in the intimacy of their greeting—he whispers in her ear and clutches at her robe as she leans in to embrace and kiss him. The genital shot differs the most, however. Instead of Oriental accoutrements, we see a wedding ring, a diamond placed in the depths of the genital show. This very different sort of object present in the sexual relations of the white man and the Asian woman suggests a rewriting of Asian female presence in the later stag film that shows a link to historical events such as the entry of war brides into the United States. As such, history and the unfinished legacies it leaves compel fantasy in pornography.

The sex scene engages the question of racial difference within the couple's interracial domesticity. Significantly different through the increased number of kisses and the genital show, the film establishes a marital sort of relation not present in earlier films while it similarly repeats the display of the Asian woman's genitals again and again as if to anticipate the demand for the visible evidence of her racial difference. The demand, established in earlier stag films through intertitle texts, labels the vagina as slanted and installs anticipation for it herein as part of the erotic language of the shot sequence. The repetition of the genital shot in these later stag films argues that no visible biological difference can be found in the Asian woman's vagina. The racialization that occurs here differs significantly from earlier stags that required the reminder of racial difference. Unlike earlier stag films such as *Menage Moderne du Madame Butterfly* (1921–30), where the intertitles insisted upon a biological difference for

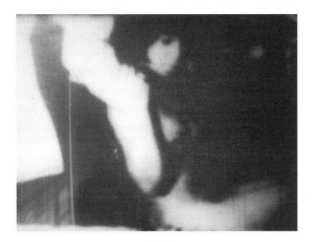

The white man comes home to domestic intimacy,
placing his hands on the Asian woman's shoulders as she
sits at the dresser in *Oriental Girlfriend*.

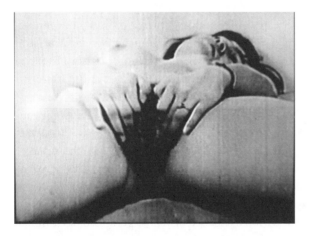

The genital shot in *Date Night* features an Asian woman
with a wedding ring.

Asian women, the stag films of the 1960s worked to establish the lack of it in extreme close-ups, such as the man opening the woman's genitals with his fingers in *Date Night*.

In *Oriental Girlfriend,* the latest among the stag films I study, the white man enters the scene as the woman sits in front of her dresser. His arrival immediately initiates a sex scene peppered with conversation we cannot hear. If we did not account for the historical changes occurring at the time, the reason why this film bears the title *Oriental Girlfriend* would remain a mystery. No racial décor marks the genital show as in earlier stag films, even if Oriental objects adorn the apartment. The sex scenes seem largely reciprocal: they take turns doing the same things to each other in a now rather subdued scene stripped of the garish racial circus of Oriental objects. They register as a couple accustomed to their sexual ritual, and here they keep intent on completing it together. While familiar domesticity frames the couple, fetishization emerges in the interracial sexual coupling itself.

In this section, I have described how the later stag films present sex acts that place Asian/American women within domestic intimacy, in conjunction with the historical development of Asian women marrying American men. That is, in later stag films, a dynamic relationship ties history to the contents of the narrative, or historical phenomena and movements inform and shape pornography featuring racial subjects. The presence of Asian/American women as non-normative wives in contemporaneous history was turned into eroticized relations in pornography. History in the form of Asian and American relations vis-à-vis war, the place of Chinatown in the popular imaginary, and the specialized roles of Asian/American women continue to play in the emergence of Asian women in post-1950s pornography. The depiction of Asian/American women as wives is unlike early stag films' defiance of yellow peril ideology through fantasy or the presentation of racial difference as a sexual treat. In both early and later stag films, however, the Asian/American woman's racial difference makes her more visible and more sexual. Race determines the erotic currency of the films in ways that continue in later pornography. Within this context, racial visibility as crucial to the sexual economy persists in golden age pornography in which Asian women continue a form of "yellowface" initiated by white women in early stag films. The collision of Asian/American women's bodies and the fantasies they embody disrupts the illusion of Asian/American racial visibility in the sex act and the fantasy established in the stag film.

Linda Wong, Mai Lin, and Kristara Barrington appeared in hundreds of pornographic films in the 1970s and early 1980s. Linda Wong worked from 1976 to 1987 in 46 films, Mai Lin worked from 1976 to 1999 in 157 films, and Kristara Barrington worked from 1983 to 1999 in 220 films.[35] Through the production of yellowface in the golden age of pornography, we see the disjuncture between fantasies and the "real" Asian women acting these roles. When pornography attempts to correspond humorously with mainstream films such as *The Deer Hunter* (1978) and *Apocalypse Now* (1979), we can see how both symbolic arenas cohere to establish in the popular imagination perceptions of Asian women as hypersexual. Popular representation, of which pornography is part, helps us to understand racial formation.

The grammar of Orientalism in pornography reinserts itself in the 1970s through the very bodies of Asian/American women who now play these fantasy roles. Relying on Oriental accoutrements, titles, and content, Asian/American women themselves fulfill yellowface scripts. The racialized bodies of Asians are symbolized through Oriental objects such as the jade pussycat and the green lingam. Objects, spaces, and racialized bodies construct the erotics of interracial pornography. Throughout the films, the Asian/American women are referred to by their race. Their sexual acts, practices, and identities are also organized by racial categorization. Race defines Asian/American women in pornography. As such, Asian women porn stars use their racial sexualization in pornography to rewrite their subjectivities. Bound by sex, they use it to open up possibilities for theorizing how they negotiated their roles, stardom, and positions as Asian/American women.

In this section, I survey the various yellowface stagings by each actress. By studying how each fulfilled different yellowface stereotypes, we can see the production of race across time. Along the way, such a collection of scenes demonstrates the Asian/American woman behind the roles in a triangulation: actress, role, and character. As such, porn actresses work to produce characters and fantasies. Such a formulation encourages a theory of representation that should also extend to our spectatorship: we consume roles, characters, and fantasies, not necessarily "real" Asian women. Pornography demands study precisely for the actresses' authorship and performance as exchanges of power and deployments of resistance.

The first Asian American porn star, Linda Wong, starred as a dragon lady in films such as *Oriental Babysitter* (1976), *The Jade Pussycat* (1977), *China Lust* (1976), *China De Sade* (1980), and *The Erotic World of Linda Wong* (1985). These films mimic and parody Hollywood movies such as the James Bond series as well as *The World of Suzie Wong*. Within these films, Linda Wong's race becomes classified as Oriental not only in her personal description as a star but in the language of the film and its erotics. Race determines her sexuality and her role within the films, in which she established a reputation for welcoming all sorts of sex acts. This brand of sexuality makes up the erotic thrust of her sexual relations compared to other women in that race defines the roles she plays: the innocent "Oriental" babysitter, the Chinatown sex expert, the dominatrix, the spoil of war, the dragon lady, and the spy. In each, she represents the ultimate deviant. Racialized not only within her roles but by the narrative, props, costume, makeup, and the racial intensification of the genital show and the money shot, she also occupies the role of an exceptional Asian who meets white normative standards of beauty.

In one of her most popular films, *Oriental Babysitter,* Linda Wong plays a teenager whose babysitting jobs lead to sex with her white male and female employers. The film opens with an introduction by Wong, who looks directly at the camera and narrates her escapades from the position of a sexually insatiable, but otherwise innocent young woman. "When I was younger, [I had] many fantasies . . ." she says as we see her caught in the middle of a fight between a white husband and wife. The man "looks towards me at any chance." He comes home early to find Wong sleeping on the sofa and gently seduces her into sex by telling her to be "quiet . . . [I won't] hurt you, [I want to] hold your body . . . for an Oriental girl [you've got] large breasts." She retroactively narrates the scene with pleasure. While her face expresses surprise and a little fear, her voice emphasizes the willingness and desire awakened in her. "The gentleman of the house . . . fondling my breasts," she describes it, while his hand covers her mouth. She feels sorry for him for being drunk, "poor man." Constructed as a scene of coercion, she responds to him with a kind of recalcitrant passion, gyrating and welcoming him while saying, "Don't please . . . stop, please." The sex scene supposedly turns consensual during cunnilingus, while at the same time the shot emphasizes her youth: her smiling face in pleasure as ribbons in her hair unravel. He comes on her belly. She then describes how the man apologizes for taking advantage of her—which she

Linda
Wong smiles
as ribbons
unravel from
her hair during
cunnilingus
in *Oriental
Babysitter.*

counters in the voiceover as actually the fulfillment of her desires. She "really lived out one of [her] fantasies."

Linda Wong delivers her narration in a soft-spoken, sexually inflected tone without an Oriental accent. She delivers the following line adorned with jewelry and big coiffure rather than racialized adornments: "After a few more babysitting jobs, I thought I learned a lot. I would suck a man's penis with dignity and total love." The title *Oriental Babysitter* racially classifies her so that nymphomania, a common ascription in pornography, links to her racialization throughout the film. The racialization continues from the title to her lovers' responses to the emphasis on her Asian face as the punctuation to every sex scene in an intensification of the money shot. In the 1970s, the face becomes necessary to the porn convention of the money shot, or the proof of the man's ejaculation on the woman's face as it expresses her pleasure. When accompanied by the discourse of the Asian face as the "zone" of contact by David Palumbo-Liu,[36] the money shot has racial implications. The proof of the man's pleasure on the woman's face, as the vehicle of her sexual expression, serves as evidence of both the man's and woman's collective pleasure. For the ejaculate occurring on the Asian face, as the terrain where racial interiority manifests externally, mobilizes the language of racial difference to infuse the proof of pleasure with racial eroticism.

In *The Jade Pussycat*, Linda Wong plays a traitor to her white male lover who secures a long-lost cultural treasure, the aptly named Oriental object, the "jade pussycat." We first see Linda Wong doing fellatio for an extraordinarily long amount of time, with special emphasis on her face throughout the sex scene. Her face expresses ecstasy with her eyes closed and mouth open during intercourse. Her face is framed by her thick, long black mane and her fingers with long nails press against the man's arms. She supposedly achieves pleasure before her lover ejaculates all over her belly. As they linger together in bed, Linda's comrades, a pair of Chinese men, arrive on the scene, revealing her traitorship. Like in the James Bond films, where the sexual encounter leads to a betrayal, so does the sexual encounter between Linda Wong's femme fatale character Jasmine and her lover in this Johnny Wadd, private detective series. Her lover finds out about her traitorship too late and she remains suspect throughout the story in terms of her allegiances. So the first Asian American porn mega-star plays a dragon lady in the sense of being untrustworthy and villainous in a continuation of Anna May Wong's roles from earlier in the century.

In a later scene, a German dominatrix played by the porn star Georgina Spelvin "requires" Linda Wong's presence. The diminutive Spelvin commands the larger-bodied Wong: "Little Chinese girl with the name of a flower, undress and show me your body." Wong's Jasmine willingly and enthusiastically complies in a conflation of Asian women's essential servitude and dragon lady treachery. Cunnilingus ensues. Spreading apart Linda's legs, Spelvin asks a question perennially rehearsed in porn, "Is it true what they say about Chinese girls?" "Take a look," responds Jasmine as we see a close-up of her genitals. The racialization of acts and genitalia extends to identities. Within the film, Johnny Wadd refers to Jasmine as the "Oriental chick." The Asian characters ultimately remain supplementary to the film's conclusion of white sex remaining the norm as Asians are discarded. Similar to their plight in Hollywood movies, the "sneaky little Chinaman" plays a rapist and the dragon lady fails in her goal to undermine the white hero. White order restores a narrative of racial adventure in pornography. Racial identification overdetermines Wong's sexuality in conjunction with other problematic themes, such as the production of her otherness as perversity: dragon lady, lotus blossom, or racial traitor.

The Asian/American woman represents the ultimate perversity for other deviant sexualities. In *China Lust*, another Oriental object, a "green lingam" actually symbolizes the sexual nature of the Orient and its "ancient sexual rites." Set in San Francisco's Chinatown, *China Lust* features a gang of hustlers seeking the lingam for its powerful magic. It brings the "good-hearted joy" and makes "the bad-hearted miserable." Within the

Linda Wong's face
in ecstasy before she
betrays her lover in
The Jade Pussycat.

The Asian woman
and the green lingam
are surrounded by
Oriental décor in
China Lust.

film, hustlers, lesbians, and a plethora of diverse characters use it in order
to access the sexual power of the female Asian, who comes to represent a
transcendent hypersexuality desirable to others. The sexually fueled search
for the green lingam in the narrative concludes with a sex scene between a
black man and an Asian woman, their racial visibilities fueling the eroticism of their climactic encounter. The closing scene locates Linda Wong's
character within an enclosed space filled with Oriental objects such as
plants with long, thin, cascading leaves, long scrolls with calligraphy hanging on the bamboo walls, large wooden cherry framed photographs of
jade elephants, and a bed covered in silk sheets. Within this space, she
wears a short, tight cheong-sam. The black man enters this room and finds
her as a kind of prize. In a film that features a racial and sexual mix
of characters, the two extremely perverse hypersexual beings fulfill each

other. The pairing of two taboo subjects who are also racialized sex objects conveys racial fetishism. The racialized nature of the taboo coming together to join forces arranges the erotic power of the film's culmination.

The eroticization of racialized and cultural historical events such as the Vietnam War and the poverty of the third world provide erotic fodder for Linda Wong's other films, such as *China De Sade.* Set "somewhere in Southeast Asia" during the Vietnam War, the scenery of riverboats, thatched roof huts on stilts, and coconut and palm trees organizes a tropical setting for erotic interracial relations. The music is similarly primitive, drums evoking the grand scenes of *Apocalypse Now* and the crew's journey on the river. The sex scene set in an unspecific Southeast Asia features a blonde white woman threatening a white man with a gun; she forces him down as Linda Wong performs fellatio on him. A knife is pulled out and the white man is bleeding everywhere—blood drips all over the white man and the Asian woman's hands. The Asian woman massages the blood all over her body as she stretches her neck back. The white woman joins in the sex and we see a knife cutting a slit across the man's arms. This sex scene enables me to show how the Golden Age of pornography is a moment in the making of porn where acting, directing, design, and filmic craft took priority in the making of sexually explicit material. The high production qualities come together to establish the Asian women's perversity through her racial difference.

Colonial history informs the sexualization of race and the racialization of sex for erotic aims. Within *China De Sade,* the poetic use of blood explains the history of colonialism and war framing interracial Asian-white relations. *China De Sade* is about a veteran lieutenant seeking his long-lost Asian female lover, Ming Lee. It seems to be inspired by war films such as *The Deer Hunter* and more closely *Apocalypse Now. China De Sade's* villain, Captain Krieg, evokes Marlon Brando's general in *Apocalypse Now* in the performance of a sadist who surrounds himself with multiracial others. Here, they become sex slaves and masters. A black male guard with a gun rapes the captain's daughter in a scene later revealed as sex play between lovers. Ming Lee works as the captain's dominatrix, commanding others to have sex while serving him sexually as well. The lieutenant reunites with Ming Lee and they have sex in a cage while he is bound. The captain captures Ming Lee and the lieutenant and forces them to have sex while the daughter whips both of them. In these scenes, the lieutenant asks "Why do I love seeing her [Ming Lee] in pain?" as he

The Asian woman massages blood all over her breasts in the opening scene of *China De Sade*.

extracts sexual enjoyment from her physical suffering during sex. The pain on her face, as legacy of colonial war history enacted on her body, seems to be part of Ming Lee's attractiveness to the white male lead. The sex performed is directly tied to colonial relations where the Asian woman is both dominant and dominated.

The Erotic World of Linda Wong, completed before her death reputedly from a drug overdose, features her long awaited comeback as the first full-fledged Asian American porn star. Older, she continued to act while speaking without an Oriental accent, wearing her black hair extremely long and holding on to her extraordinary beauty. Gorgeous, tall, and long, she was an unusually good-looking woman not only in comparison to Asian women but to other women with whom she engaged in sex. Wong's beauty, however, while clearly of an Asian woman, was not typical of an Asian woman or any other woman. Instead, she was an exceptional figure whose stardom capitalized on her visible Asian-ness, noting that her extreme beauty turns her simultaneously hypervisible and invisible in terms of her race. In comparison to other Asian women such as Mai Lin and Kristara Barrington, both Linda Wong and Asia Carrera are the bigger stars. Wong and Carrera are also closest to meeting the white ideal of beauty. More clearly, they look whiter, whether in stature or in features, and thus their stardom speaks of the marginalization of Asian women in porn who must meet impossible standards of beauty.

Porn stars like Mai Lin did not fulfill more typical standards of white beauty. In her use of Oriental accoutrements, Mai Lin asserted a different form of racialized beauty and sexuality. In the late 1970s and early 1980s, a set of films starring Mai Lin continued themes from the Vietnam War and other scenes of inequality wherein race comprises part of the sexual enjoyment. Mai Lin, also known as Maile and Miki Moto, started her career in the mid-1970s and frequently featured extra long dagger-like nails in the style of Anna May Wong, who was said to bear the "longest nails in Hollywood." Having starred in over one hundred movies, Mai Lin deployed Oriental self-decoration in a form of racialized sexuality. Her roles as the maid, the prostitute with a heart of gold, the sex expert, the mysterious, forever foreign Chinatown girl, the masseuse, and the dragon lady in a Bond girl type of situation are all racialized as different from white sexuality.

Excalibur Films describes Mai Lin as insatiable, frequently having sex even when the cameras are off. "She's a woman who revels in raunchy, raw sex and she'll happily participate in group scenes, back porch, kinky sex, double penetrations—you name it, and Mai Lin's done it many times."[37] Well known for experimenting with the widest range of acts with great enthusiasm, Mai Lin plays a maid seduced by her master in *Sexcapades* (1983). While pornography regularly rehearses the maid and master trope, race shapes the power dynamics represented. As the maid, Mai Lin's racial difference plays a role in her sexual response and her desirability. Dressed in a black cheong-sam underneath a white apron and shifting her long hair, Mai Lin responds to his question about "his cock": "Yes, it is very big . . . I am scared." She bows with servility and inquires if there is anything she can do for him. While she looks at him directly, her face is full of deference, waiting for his command. She emphasizes her smallness in contrast to his much bigger size. Her response also gauges the dynamics of power fueling the sexual encounter. Her innocent pleas "not to get in trouble" with the mistress for messing around with the master thrill him. He fetishizes not only her employment status but also her racialized body parts, wondering how she cleans with her long, long nails and stiletto heels. She resists his overtures by deferring his proposal.

He directs her to carry out various acts. "Touch yourself," he commands. She responds with a mix of resistance and compliance. She says, "I don't want to make any trouble . . ." and then asks for clarification regarding his directions, as she touches herself. "Here?" she asks coyly, skillfully negotiating her clitoris. In these scenes, race and class difference are thrilling factors in the sexual act for they inform her inflections of servility, as evident in her lines, pose, and expressions, all of which seem to anticipate

Mai Lin wears a maid's apron over her cheong-sam dress in *Sexcapades*.

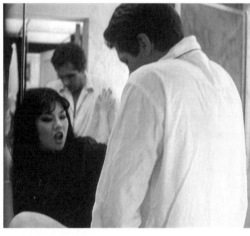

The apron comes off and hair comes down during sex with the master, who says, "Come, Mai Ting," in *Sexcapades*.

her intent to fulfill whatever his commands may be. The master eroticizes her exotic name when he asks where he should fuck her and all the while narrates his actions by uttering her name, "I am fucking you, Mai Ting . . . Come, Mai Ting." In these scenes, her visual presence, decorated with the Oriental symbols of long black hair and long nails are designed to signify erotic meaning. They racialize her sexuality. Racial difference counts significantly in the sexual eroticism presented in the film.

Mai Lin seduces a tourist with the lures of Chinatown and the attribution of sexuality particular to Chinese culture in *Rated Sex* (1986).[38] She delivers lines like "What do you expect—this is Chinatown!" Her racial identity provides erotic power to the sex scene through its difference from typical white sex. The tourist says, "I've never had an Oriental girl before ... never seen one ... just in the movies ... Suzie Wong" as Mai Lin glides her long nails along his body. She gives him "a nice Chinese massage" and then reverts to the dragon lady persona when she leaves him all tied up. In these porn titles, different fantasy scenarios are enacted and Asian women are merely part of the various special options available. Racial difference relegates Asian female presence in the Golden Age of pornography to the realm of "special" desires, practices, and identities. Unlike the norm in porn where white women don various costumes, Asian women must always wear their race in terms of sexuality.

In the early 1980s, the mixed race Asian American porn star Kristara Barrington, also known as China Lee, played roles both marked and unmarked by race in over 150 films.[39] Born in 1965, she supposedly retired in 1987 but continued to make films somehow until 1999.[40] In films such as *Oriental Jade* (1987), *China and Silk* (1984), *Samurai Dick* (1984), and *One Night in Bangkok* (1985), she stages the Asian prostitute, or spoil of war, entangled with Americans during wartime relations in ways wherein her costumes and the settings contributed to the erotic grammar of the scenes. *Oriental Jade* opens like *China Lust,* on a boat along a river of Southeast Asia. We see a white man and an Asian woman having sex in the open air as the boat glides along the river in a direct reference to *Apocalypse Now,* even in the style of the voiceover. The narration we hear contextualizes the scene as a memory and describes the hypersexual ontology of the Asian woman.

> I met her in the last months of the war years ago. Sex was the only commodity cheaper than human life ... for a few ... you can fuck anything you want ... she was something different. Jade was a whore all right, what else was there to be, but she had this real special quality with me like she was really getting off and somehow it wasn't an act. At least that's what she made you believe. I think back on how much I hated that hell and then I remember her. Shit, maybe I wasn't in love but I was sure as shit hella in lust.

The narration emphasizes her enjoyment of sex as natural. The boat stops as they have sex and we hear sounds of monkeys, roosters, and other animals. The setting and the sound design contribute to narrating a particular sexuality for the Asian woman assigned as natural to her biology and her geography. Like Linda Wong, Kristara Barrington's roles as a spoil of war argues for Asian women as the ultimate female deviant whose sexuality connects to the black man, who is also marked as racially Other through sex.

Barrington also acts as a madame of a San Francisco bordello. The history of Asian prostitution in San Francisco during the late nineteenth century plays into the scenario of *Yankee Seduction* (1985), a film set in the South after the Civil War in which a Chinese prostitute takes over a brothel in a racially harmonious conclusion to a film set in an intensely tense racial scene. Barrington orders a black man to strip so that she may fellate him. He speaks to her with deference. He asks: "May I fuck you Miss Lee?" Race once again operates as a sexual treat for spectators who consume two hypersexual beings. She also fights with a white woman who calls her a "San Francisco reject, traitor, criminal" and a (former) bordello whore before they engage in lesbian sex themselves. In the context of the Vietnam War and the history of Asian female prostitution, the sexuality of race limits Asian/American women in porn. Race operates as a titillating force in the cross-racial sexual encounter.

Race supersedes any other identification even for biracial Asian/American women in pornography. Kristara Barrington's films included her racialization as Asian as part of their erotic offerings. While race may seem indeterminate for her as a biracial woman, race inevitably determines Asian/American women in porn. Barrington played roles marked as Asian biologically as well as historically. While Asian women grew visible in pornography, they did so as Asian/American women. Distinct because of race, Asian women are forever foreign against American men, black or white. They play roles that seem like one-dimensional fantasies such as dragon ladies and spoils of war. They possess cultural traits in their sexual skills. Decorated with Oriental accoutrements, they are fetishized for their visibility as Asian women who are exceptional to their race. Myths of servility imbricate their sexuality in ways the women contradict or fulfill but must nonetheless engage.

Race binds Asian/American female sexuality in pornography. Asian/American women cannot flee its hailing. By studying Asian/American women in pornography, we reveal the connections between history and fantasy. Within history and fantasy, Asian women must answer the call to race, as imagined within their racial identity as a special category. Within these roles, they must carve unique presences. They cannot but work against or within the parameters of the maid, the innocent lotus blossom, the servile wife/maid (the latest incarnation of these two roles), and the dragon lady that describe their legibility. What political lessons can we draw from this bind?

Josephine Lee argues in the context of enacting stereotypes that the

Asian American actresses' bodies exceed the stereotype and reveal its construction.[41] The achievement of stereotypic yellowface sexuality in pornography reveals the fantasy of Asian women as different from Asian/American women. While we see each actress donning the stereotype of the Asian woman in different films, her Asian/American body shows the construction of fantasy. This production of sexuality by porn stars developed in the contemporary scene wherein porn stars enjoy celebrity status in multimedia form. In contemporary pornography, two megastars show different ways of working within such racial legacy, using a multiplicity of media, toward political ends.

CONTEMPORARY ASIAN/AMERICAN WOMEN IN PORNOGRAPHY

Within contemporary pornography, race continues to organize Asian female sexual acts, practices, and identities. Two Asian female porn megastars from the 1990s defy this cacophony of racial fantasy and fetishism in rewriting themselves through the Internet and in rewriting sexuality through self-authored pornography. Through their self-authorships, I argue for reclaiming racialized sexuality in ways that prioritize Asian American feminist expression in pornography. Asia Carrera, who also worked under the names Jessica Bennett and Asia, acted in 369 films from 1993 to 2005 while Annabel Chong acted in 51 films from 1994 to 2003. While acting in significantly less films, Annabel Chong established a notorious career that shot her into prominence not only in popular culture beyond pornography but also in academic circles. Unlike previous Asian American porn stars, both women are also listed in the Internet Adult Film Database as directors: Asia Carrera directed two films in 1997 and Annabel Chong directed two films in 1998 and 2000.

The Internet becomes a new technology in these women's authorships. Whether as writing, directing, or creating new genres, Asia Carrera uses the Internet to create a unique brand of racialized sexuality. By redefining sexual normativity through a program of embracing polymorphous perversity, she fulfills Katrien Jacobs's argument that politics finds expression in porn if female porn stars create new public spaces for sexual expression and for redefining sexuality.[42] In the 1990s, Annabel Chong initiated the program of the gangbang, taking the hypersexuality of Asian women to the extreme by embracing whoredom as a feminist practice rooted in her particular racial and cultural situation. She relinquished control of her commodification in favor of forwarding what I call a theory of unknowable subjectivity and unreliable representation. Using a term deployed by Katrien Jacobs in her analysis of lesbian sadomasochism, I show Annabel Chong's self-presentation as a "monstrous revolt" that diagnoses the results of the hypersexual tradition of Asian/American women in moving image representation and offers a new theory of sex that can better accommodate the politically productive perversity of her role as a feminist porn star and an avatar online. Unlike white feminist pornographers such as Nina Hartley and Candida Royalle, who make works that aim to create a different and new sexual economy for women's pleasure, Carrera and Chong do not shy away from images that seem to reinscribe the tradition of hypersexuality as essential to race. Rather than creating images that are simply opposite to traditional representations, Carrera and Chong present existing fantasies of Asian women as crucial to their self-perception and social legibility. Precisely because they teeter on the edge of the acceptable, in varying degrees, they offer truly new forms of sexuality as Asian American feminists working in pornography.

The term "Asian" holds particular significance as part of a racially based organization of sexuality in contemporary pornography. Based on a study of *Adult Video News* reviews and Internet pornography database searches of "Asian," the most common current themes of Asian and Asian American women emerge and reflect a relationship to contemporaneous history and globalization: girls from the Orient, young girls (uniformed school girls or poor enslaved girls forced to sell their bodies), the fetishized racial difference in interracial sex, spoils of war, prostitutes, anal sex, and the discourse of stereotypes such as the model minority, the good student, and the small servile body as a pre-feminist haven.[43] While these images are occupied with different kinds of presence, one generalization emerges: race takes precedence over any category of identification organizing the appearances of Asian women in pornography.

Within this limited gamut that includes the work of popular porn stars such as Mimi Miyagi and Kobe Tai, the porn star Asia Carrera appeared in hundreds of films.[44] She has also written and directed at least two films, *Apassionata* and *Last Little Whorehouse*.[45] Biracial like Kristara Barrington, Asia Carrera's appearance resonates with Linda Wong's, for they possess extraordinary forms of Asian beauty and exceptionally beautiful bodies that adhere to white idealized standards compared to their white and nonwhite female counterparts. Like Linda Wong, Asia Carrera presents a racially different body that nonetheless fulfills normative standards of beauty. She chronicles the production of beauty through plastic surgery on her website, presenting the aesthetically pleasing body as part of her profession.

Like Linda Wong, Carrera's face plays an important role in the money shot in terms of emphasizing the racial difference at the moment of providing proof of pleasure. While the money shot typical in feature pornography indeed relies on the woman's face, Asia Carrera functions doubly in order to provide evidence of racial difference and her particularity as an Asian sexual presence. The camera returns to find in it a particularly coy and innocent expression: eyes wide open and framed by false eyelashes as semen ejaculates all over her face. Close-ups on her whole face show her tonguing the semen as a form of beauty shot. Her face occupies the central object of vision. Linda Williams argues that the money shot offers a solution to the problem of visualizing female pleasure. That is, pornography problematizes the difficulty of representing proof of women's pleasure, as exemplified in the search for clitoral visibility in films such as *Deep Throat* (1972).[46] The proof of ejaculation occurs on the woman's face as she expresses pleasure. Asia Carrera's visible expression of pleasure while maintaining perfect makeup extends this shot to the realm of glamour and beauty extraordinary to pornography. Her beautiful stardom also capitalizes on her reputed brilliance, "her good head."[47] Hers is an identifiable face loaded with meaning: model minority, exceptional beauty, dirty pictures. Together, these three characteristics help to constitute the erotic power of her stardom.

In *Phantasm* (1995), Asia Carrera co-stars with one of the most popular (white) porn stars ever, Jenna Jameson, also a "Vivid" girl. Vivid girls represent the famed high-end production company, and the women present a new breed of porn star: they do not look like typical down-on-their-luck porn stars but rather Hollywood movie stars in full glamour. This difference is brazenly advertised in billboards all over Los Angeles; this was especially the case around the mid-1990s. When porn came to be very widely acknowledged as entering mainstream acceptance, Vivid girls came to exemplify this crossover. In the video directed by Bud Lee, Asia appears in money shots that simultaneously foreground her beautiful face in a merging of the conventions of romantic comedy and pornography in terms of porn featuring particular stars with their trademark looks. In a racially unmarked role, the narrative line focuses on her production as a sex machine. She comes to possess intrinsic qualities for achieving and generating great sexual pleasure.

In the film, couples enter a sex club and join a contest for individually demonstrating the best sexual abilities in a variety of scenarios. Asia is presented as an unwitting character who is not as excited to join the sex club as her eager boyfriend. Soon enough, she awakens to the passions of multiple sexual encounters. Possessing innate abilities for achieving pleasure, Asia Carrera's character wins. Throughout the film, her vanilla quality, or her seeming innocence within the culture of her sexual adventure, is highlighted. Her fabulous face, glamorously made up, expresses joy in the sexual scene as if her own sexuality surprises her. Her big hair with bangs, her wide-eyed look, and her enormous smile provide a contrast to her leather bondage gear and generate great appeal. In one shot, she turns toward the camera, and so her clear-eyed and smooth-complexioned look of innocence and wonder is particularly amplified. Her boyfriend does not do so well until the end, when they both combine forces to give pleasure to the madame-dominatrix played by Jenna Jameson. Both Jenna Jameson and Asia Carrera are presented as the exceptional beauties of the film. The other characters do not meet the traditional standards of beauty in mainstream popular culture and are presented as secondary characters. Carrera and Jameson, in contrast, exceed the normal expectations for beauty and are shot accordingly. Asia Carrera, beautiful like Jenna Jameson, displays particular talents for moving her body well into the shots. They both traffic in the currency of porn in terms of possessing beauty both typical and excessive of their racial group, such as their black or blonde long hair and their exceptionally tall and seemingly surgically altered bodies. In another shot, Asia is surrounded by attractive women who worship her from below so that she towers over them and seems superior in beauty and power.

Thematizing gender and sexuality, Asia Carrera also directs and writes her own films with her now ex-husband Bud Lee, credited at times as Bud Carrera. The wife-and-husband team of Asia and Bud Carrera directed *A Is for Asia* (1996) and *Apassionata* (1998). Both films purport to present autobiographical themes. For example, *Apassionata* showcases her talents as a pianist while telling the story of a runaway that is very similar to that published on her website. *A Is for Asia* presents a narrative about "Asia's First Anal" while presenting the very act itself, several times. In the opening shot, we follow a woman's legs outfitted in white stilettos as they walk

Asia Carrera's wholesome face contrasts with the leather bondage wear to comprise her appeal in *Phantasm*.

Three attractive women surround Asia Carrera's naked figure in a tribute to her exceptional beauty and sexual prowess in *Phantasm*.

along a dingy alleyway. Revealed as Asia Carrera, the woman approaches two men, presumably drug addicts, as one lays on the ground while the other rummages through a dumpster. We hear "Cut!" and Bud Lee enters the scene to give Asia further direction. The title sequence then shows the behind-the-scenes processes and equipment required in making the film. We see a white male crewmember's hands in very dirty gloves collecting cable, setting up c-stands and lights, and handling a Makita drill. The credits show us that the film is written, directed, and produced by Asia and Bud as he enters her dressing room to give specific prompts about her craft as an actress. He says, "Your man tells you 'You're not cool enough to be with his friends and family.'" So dressed in white stilettos, fishnets, and a dress, she flees her fiancé to have sex "with guys like these . . . [with whom I] know what I'm getting." The scene continues with the same opening shot of stilettos until she has sex with both of the men from various angles and positions. The clever behind-the-scenes approach allows for the crew's inclusion in the shooting of the sex scene. We see camera operators maneuvering intricately and acrobatically in order to illuminate the particular angles we subsequently see.

Throughout this scene, as she supposedly plays herself, Asia Carrera acts with a kind of bright, cheerful wholesomeness constituted by her enthusiasm, energy, and great flexibility. In every moment, she actively engages her partners and directs the action. She summons one to carry out an act while she positions herself to involve the other. She actively initiates and composes actions in the sex scene. In this scene, Asia's work shows how women as stars have a role in the authorship of their pornography. The choreography of sex needs full coverage in terms of shooting from a variety of camera angles. The film highlights quite centrally the sexual partnership between actors working together to do what feels right while selling the work of sex. Orgasm also requires her craft. The sex scene ends with Asia Carrera's flawlessly and heavily made-up face as she licks semen while looking very happy, open, and flirtatious. The bright lighting emphasizes her wholesomeness, and her freshness seems to authenticate her enjoyment not only of sex but of porn stardom.

Afterward, she and Bud discuss what happened. She explains her creative choice in acting and the direction she pursues as an actress: "I thought you wanted a nasty finish. You didn't like it?" He concurs, "You're right." She responds, "You're not pissed at me . . . [I followed] the heat of the moment . . . fans will love it!" In this discussion, Asia and Bud establish the collaborative and creative process in the production of pornography. Asia Carrera authors sex scenes herself in an explicit demonstration of agency and authorship of her sexuality as well as an engagement of the question regarding the primacy of the actress or the framing of the director and writer. As such, writing and directing a film about the making of the film demonstrates a conscious acknowledgment and engagement of the power dynamics in pornography. Bud Lee suggests the idea of "being in this business two years now . . . doing something outside yourself . . . [a real] attention getter." Asia responds "no" immediately, indicating the difficulty in deciding how far one goes with one's stardom. The film subsequently follows the process of her first anal scenes accompanied by a shooting style that "exposes" the processes of porn stardom.

The money
shot featuring
Asia Carrera's
cheerful and
smiling face in
A Is for Asia.

In the next scene, Asia defends her choice of shooting her first facial cum shot as "know[ing] what sells!" in order to present her self-
authorship within pornography. A discussion about the anal sex scene
shows her fictional husband's inappropriate possessiveness. Demonstrating savvy business practice regarding self-reinvention, she says, "I want to
give my name some lift as an adult film star." Jonathan Morgan, who plays
her husband, belittles her by saying, "Knowing Bud [the actual director/
husband who plays the fictional director/non-husband], it'll probably be
a DP [double penetration]." Asia asserts her power to shape her own career
by responding to his sexism and using it as an opportunity to forward a
non-moralistic and feminist definition of sexuality: "If I want to do an
anal scene, [for] a broader fan base [I will]." Her fictional husband describes the anal act as "the only thing I have with you." Her response
vacates her sexualized area of any such investment. Asia asserts, "Let's not
equate my love for you with my asshole. It's more than any sex act. I love
you with all my heart and not my ass, okay? You've got the best parts of
Asia Carrera." She convinces him to agree. The film presents the anal sex
scene as a revelation of a private Asia executing a brand new, never-before-
seen or done sex act in her home space. This enables the shooting of two
anal scenes as Asia's first time. Moreover, her wholesome persona seemingly so antithetical to porn fuels the erotic nature of the scene. The porn
star is a wife and a woman who thinks through her career in strategic and
careful ways. Her expression is serious, strong, and vulnerable when she
engages her husband in the movie.

The movie ends with Asia's anal with the porn star Tom Byron and double penetration with two dildos as her fictional husband watches. Framed within her autobiography, the reconciliation scene demonstrates what her actual husband and co-director Bud (Lee) Carrera declares on camera as the end credits scroll: "Another happy ending to another movie in Carrera-ville!" Through this scene, we learn about Asia's engagement of gender in pornotopia. In the postmodern presentation of film within a film, the play between Asia Carrera's porn life and true life provides erotic fodder. Bud's taking on of Asia's name also signifies an acknowledgment of her star power and the gender power dynamics raised in their working relationship as husband and wife.

The commodification of her autobiography also informs the next film she wrote and directed. Co-directed, written, produced, and composed by Asia Carrera, *Apassionata* follows the life of a runaway homeless girl and her fantasy life as a racially unmarked princess in the time of Mozart. Produced with high production values, the period piece begins with Asia dressed in a white wig and ball gown in a scene that establishes her as royal princess under the tutelage of Mozart, with whom she has a torrid affair. In this role, Asia Carrera shows off her abilities as a pianist. We realize these period scenes are fantasies for they are intercut with the stories of a runaway, living in a van or a campground while hitching rides on the highway with a face brazenly full of hope. Shamelessly imagining a future away from home, she trades her musical talent for food. Dressed in combat boots and overalls, rather than Oriental accoutrements, Carrera stands out as racially distinct among the cast. She also stands out on the roadside as a frontier she intends to conquer. Moreover, this shot illustrates her personal narrative of being a teen runaway, an experience described in her website bio.[48]

Asia Carrera's star persona as a model minority—she is a member of Mensa (the high IQ club recently acknowledged her membership) and a piano prodigy—inserts itself into the language of porn. Indeed, part of her popularity comes from her racialized history: she played piano at Carnegie Hall in her early teens and taught English as a teenager in Japan—all details inserted into her porn-star biography. Through these details, she continues to appear in the exceptional vein, whether as an extraordinary beauty strikingly non-typical as Asian or as someone typically Asian in her background. These biographical details highlight her exceptionality: What is such a good Asian girl doing in porn? Her racialization occurs

Asia discusses her first anal scene with Jonathan Morgan, who plays her husband in *A Is for Asia*.

Dressed in a wig and a Victorian gown, Asia Carrera plays the piano in *Apassionata*.

Asia Carrera hitchhikes with a hopeful face in *Apassionata*.

differently. It plays into the marketing of her stardom in pornography in a commingling of the intimate and the Other. The image of the girl-next-door combines with the image of the model minority in ways that further indicate her success as a celebrity.

Asia Carrera chose to retire from porn stardom in 2005. She runs an extremely popular website and blog where she sells videos and other products as well as propagates a sexual polymorphous perversity critical of heteronormativity. She aims to control her own commodification by presenting testaments regarding her sexuality and lays bare anxieties about her career decisions: Should she return to porn?, for example. Her blog includes seemingly frank sexual self-presentations. For example, she describes her "luck" in being vaginally orgasmic. Her published wedding vows, humorous and irreverent as well as serious, reflect sexuality far from puritanical norms. Unapologetic about her profession, she rejects moralism blatantly in an embrace of seemingly contradictory identities that I describe as polymorphous. She embraces and finds no contradiction in her positions as mother, wife, porn star, exhibitionist, and Internet entrepreneur.

Between 1996 and late 2006, Asia Carrera's website received 23 million hits. Characterizing herself as a self-taught nerd, she proudly designs her own website, which she markets as the primary mechanism for getting to know her outside her films. It features her wedding vows with her new husband, Don Lemmon, a description of her creative process as a co-director with Bud Lee (she handles the "creative" work and "motivating crew" while he handles the technical aspects of the work), recent pictures in Hawaii after she gained twenty pounds in her post-retirement transition, a humorously written blog that chronicles her weight gain during her pregnancy, a chat room (without private chats available), frequently asked questions, and a biography that lists her membership in Mensa. The site details her National Merit finalist award and full scholarship to Rutgers University, a confession of her plastic surgery exploits, and a testimony on "Why I Do Porn Even Though I'm Very Bright and Could Have Done Whatever I Wanted."[49] There are numerous photographs available for free or for pay. We see her working on her computer and posing in the nude. She sometimes brings the two images together: porn star geek. In all, she presents a critique against moralistic approaches to sexuality and commodification of her racialized identity.

In my analysis, I acknowledge how web-based self-representations work like self-publishing. They tend to present more idealized and edited versions of the self. Asia Carrera's website testimony focuses on a racialized childhood that leads to sexual freedom. She describes a struggle similar to Evelyn Lau, the award-winning writer of *Runaway: Diary of a Streetkid*. Both Asia and Evelyn describe strict Asian American/Canadian households. Due to the demands of her parents, Asia ran away from her strict upbringing as a "model minority" Asian American child. Asia shows her response to such conditions to be an American one and in the process she positions herself as part of and surviving an Asian American interpellation:

> I was grounded for every "B" I got, and beaten for getting anything lower than that. I was not allowed to socialize at all, or go to parties, because they said there'd be time for that after I got into a good college. Well, I did what any red-blooded American kid would do, I'd sneak out. And get caught. And get beaten. And get grounded again. Without launching into too much detail, let's just say I was unhappy. (I tried to kill myself a lot) (Asian kids everywhere have e-mailed me to verify that this is standard practice in Asian households —what a relief to find out I'm normal, huh!) . . . Sometimes I fucked people I didn't want to, so I could have a place to sleep, or a good meal. I gritted my teeth a lot, and did what I had to, rather than crawl back home and grovel for my folks' forgiveness.[50]

In the passage above, she identifies with other Asian Americans, especially youth, almost like a role model. The experiences she details are not only racial and cultural but also gendered. Both rebelling against her parents' policing of space and coping with her dire situation as a runaway through sex describe a gendered experience. She battles moralistic judgment of her choices and her situation by highlighting her financial autonomy, her eye for the future, and her "love for life."[51]

Such testimony in Asia Carrera's very personal website attests to the particular stardom she occupies, one not present for other Asian women in pornography. While Asian/American women constitute a huge special genre in pornography, racial fetishism confines their appearance unless they are exceptional like Asia Carrera, who asserts her personal history in her authorship, directing, and acting. Asia Carrera celebrates race-positive living, an intelligent analysis of racial subjection, and a critique of moralism regarding the experiences of sexuality and race. On her website, we also see a successful entrepreneur negotiating her commodification in a form of feminist power.

Through her initiating the massive gangbang in the porn industry, the Asian/American porn star Annabel Chong shot to the attention of popular culture critics and scholars. She appeared on *The Jerry Springer Show* and occupied the focus of a documentary premiering at Sundance. Today, hundreds of essays on her work are available on line from academic journals to film reviews to newspapers to blogs. Chong achieved fame particularly for her affinity for doing perverse acts while proclaiming herself a feminist. Like Asia Carrera, she receives regard as a "thinking" porn star in a kind of eroticization of the model minority stereotype—especially since she worked in porn while an undergraduate at the University of Southern California. Unlike Carrera, who enjoys recognition as having a "good head on her shoulders," Chong encounters a more questionable reception, for both anti-pornography and sex-positive feminists may claim her. In her most famous film, *The World's Biggest Gang Bang* (1999), the expressive contortions of her face and body demonstrate the unreliability of representation in terms of making distinct the appearance of pain or pleasure. In various publications, she resists commodification by forwarding a deeply contradictory identity that negotiates not only the binds of pain and pleasure but good and bad. She also does so in nicely spoken ways that seem to counter well her affinity for nasty sexual practices. As such, she receives more of a contested response for pushing the buttons of acceptable sexuality even within pornography.

In "The Child Defiled: The Annabel Chong Story," an article by Gary Morris in the *Bright Lights Film Journal*, the tag line to the article reads, "Liberated Porn Queen or Psychological Wreck?"[52] Annabel Chong's record of putting on extreme acts can be assessed in her well-known films such as *I Can't Believe I Did the Whole Team!* (1994). Having acted in over fifty porn films, Chong established her fame in *The World's Biggest Gangbang,* in which she set the first world record for the most sexual partners for a single woman in one sitting (251 men). When the "intense, disturbing"[53] documentary about her experiences entitled *Sex: The Annabel Chong Story,*[54] premiered at Sundance, it sealed her stardom outside of pornography. The caliber of Annabel Chong's stardom, parallel to that of Linda Wong and Asia Carrera, secured itself on different grounds. Unlike Wong and Carrera, who fulfill white standards of beauty in porn, the smaller, shorter, and darker (more visibly Asian and less racially ambiguous)

In *The World's Biggest Gangbang*, Annabel Chong's face contorts in pleasure or pain during sex.

Chong fulfills the extremely perverse expectations for racialized sexuality in order to offer a radical critique of commodification and stardom.

The World's Biggest Gangbang touts itself as an unique project and no less than a historic event establishing a world record number of sex partners (soon broken by others if not immediately). It begins as the director and crew prepare for the shoot scheduled for the next day. The director explains that the gangbang is Annabel Chong's idea. Chong explains the project's aim quite succinctly: to prove women can work as "studs" not "sluts." Accordingly, the set celebrates the extreme athleticism in her claim to power and evokes Greece and the Olympics with its white pillars and statues. We meet Annabel Chong, who seems an alert, aware, and self-possessed young woman as she surveys the scene of her dressing room and her set. Dressed in a suit and speaking loudly in a British accent of sorts, she walks confidently through the sound stage. Later we see her emerge into the gangbang lifting her arms up, smiling in her luminous gold lamé dress, and we hear her speak of her goals for the project and her life as a student. Her navigation of contradictory words and worlds—wholesome, intelligent student speaking in a certain educated manner coexisting with porn stardom and the specificity of her fame as based on extreme perversity—combine to contribute to her recognizability.

"The industry's attraction to Grace Quek (Annabel Chong's real name) is clear—she's very pretty, naïve-looking, agreeable, a kind of Asian child bride—and the lure of defiling this image is clearly the driving force."[55] Chong's voice and appearance stand out not only in person but also

Annabel Chong enters the arena of *The World's Biggest Gangbang.*

within the industry. The writer Kimberly Chun explains: "Whatever her motivation, an ad for nude models in the *L.A. Weekly* led to meetings with directors such as Ed Powers, director of *Dirty Debutantes* and John Bowen, the director of *World's Biggest,* who talks about taking 'this girl with an Asian look and an English accent' and making her into the nastiest porn star ever, who stages particularly extreme acts."[56] Her director, in the passage above, measures the performance of perversity by Chong within fetishistic and patriarchal logic. That is, he finds worth in her ability to complete men's sexual aims based on her looks and abilities for particular acts. An Internet porn star biographer lists Annabel Chong as "the one porno starlet who it can be said specializes in gang bangs, having appeared in lots of kinky group gropes for Bone [director John Bowen]. . . . She is a kinky, crazy sexual dynamo who is one of the most popular Asian porno stars ever."[57] This perception both confirms and differs from her platform as a feminist who works in pornography, according to her interviews, so as to say something about moralism, sex, power, and gender. In one of many interviews, she offers the following critique: "I really believe that when you talk about banning porn because it's exploitative of women or because it's obscene, then it's terribly fascist."[58] While delivering such critique, she also delivers what may seem a contradictory statement. A CNN.com article states, "Quek . . . says she likes being treated 'like a piece of meat.'"[59]

Chong aims to confront the myth of the "passive female"[60] in a critique of gendered and racialized expectations for women's sexuality. In doing so, she also offers a more egalitarian, "multicultural equal opportunity" approach to the porn process. In *The World's Biggest Gangbang,* she proves the sexual abilities of women like herself with a multitude of partners. Claiming to have mastered "triple penetration," an act involving vaginal, anal, and oral sex, Chong occupies a new face of feminism, worlds apart from the anti-pornography feminists Dworkin and MacKinnon and the black feminists Walker, Garner, and Teish.

A wide range of interpretations from enslavement to empowerment surround the presence of feminism in the commodification of Annabel Chong. In *The World's Biggest Gangbang,* the director lauds her entry: the beautiful Annabel Chong! In other scenes, she seems ridiculed by other individuals.

> Scenes [of] her sidling up to [porn star Ron] Jeremy [emcee of the gangbang] and others in the porn industry as if they cared about her are undercut by interviews [in *Sex: The Annabel Chong Story*] in which it's clear that she's been totally commodified in their minds—Bowen doesn't even pay her for the gangbang video that he himself calls the best-selling video in porn history. Once her record of 251 guys is eclipsed, she's dismissed as "all washed up," and ends up gaggling with second-rate pornmeisters over a few hundred bucks.[61]

The World's Biggest Gangbang's most noticeable and enduring image must indeed be her contorted face, expressing what most certainly looks like pain, with enough ambiguity, however, so that it may also turn out to be pleasure. Her facial expression of pain cannot serve as factual evidence of her oppression when the facial expression of pleasure looks similar. The picture of her face presents much more complexity. She demands for the men to fuck her or summons them to her. Her commanding power in inciting the men to give it to her competes against the extreme close-up shots of her face in pain (or pleasure). Since we cannot read pleasure or pain, we must keep in mind the possibilities her critique offers, no matter how contradictory. Rather than follow the pornographers who dismiss her feminism in service of her commodification, I acknowledge the powerful way Chong brings to light the hypersexuality of Asian women within her career experience. In this film, Chong seems to successfully appropriate technologies of the camera and the contest for perversity in porn in order to diagnose conventional understanding of female sexuality as bound and limited. She presents herself as an unreliable subject. So if anti-pornography feminists claim her as a victim, she counters their appropriation by offering a more contradictory subjectivity: a porn star who enjoys seeing herself sexually represented as a feminist claim to power.

Critics call the documentary about Grace Quek, aka Annabel Chong, entitled *Sex: The Annabel Chong Story* "difficult to watch and utterly compelling" within the same breath that questions the subject's reliability: "feminism's heroine or patriarchy's victim?"[62] The film documents her experience of filming the gangbang and follows her for the next two years. Directed by her then-boyfriend, the documentary shows Annabel Chong being jeered by the audiences of *The Jerry Springer Show*. When she is asked why she has sex with so many men, she answers "why not" matter-of-factly. The film recollects the shooting of *The World's Biggest Gangbang* and her declarations of reclaiming promiscuity for women and relinquishing the classification of "slut" in order to claim "stud."[63] A set of interviews on campus and in her home, a motel room apartment of sorts, allows us to hear Chong speak further on her feminist platform. We also hear from her classmates and a professor. In contrast, we see porn producers with incredible valley views from their homes as they comment on Chong. The disenfranchisement between actress and producer becomes particularly revealing when we discover that she never received payment for her work in the gangbang. We then follow Chong as she returns to England, where she was raised and also, significantly, gang raped, and then to Singapore to "come out" to her parents as a porn star. Chong herself understands the film as a somewhat "fair" but skewed image. Indeed, the discourses around the film center on her victimization and feminism.

Critics note that Annabel Chong's contradictory "double life" as a porn star and an academic needs to be appreciated in the study of the film. In her *Asian Week* article, Kimberly Chun asks: "How does this woman reconcile her third-wave feminist studies with the objectification of porn; her Christian upbringing as a Chinese girl in Singapore with her toils as sex worker in the raw, Gen-X gonzo porn genre; and her speeches about sexual freedom as female empowerment by the adult industry's overwhelmingly male producers and directors?"[64] She reconciles those contradictions with what Chun describes as hints of substance abuse. Critics admire the quality of her openly sexual personality as well as her assertion of female "love for sex and control of her life" as a critique of "puritanical" ideas about sexuality.[65] Regarded as suspect, others describe her affect as "both unsure of herself and in total control at the same time."[66] Critics ask if the producers of *The World's Biggest Gangbang* duped and used her: two years after the gangbang, she still had not received payment for her work. Chun illustrates Chong as far away from her spunky self at the end of the film: she seems "ready to be directed" rather than commandeer her life.[67] Moreover, the film culminates in a dramatic revisiting of the site of the gang rape. By concluding the film with Chong's return to her past, the filmmaker connects the gang rape with the gangbang and constructs the gangbang as Chong's reenactment of a character-defining act of serial violence. Perhaps this construction of Chong's character in the film produces a victimized subject that denies her power.

In Annabel Chong's work, an important critique of pornography and documentary presenting the regime of truth of Asian/American women as a "special genre" emerges. Chong offers a feminist platform that prioritizes sexuality as a critical analysis against the victimizing discourses that tend to dismiss her critique. The prioritization of sexuality and her voice within the film both argue for a new subject of feminism: the Asian female sexual pervert. Her figure presents perversity as a feminist position. She "defies the lure"—to borrow Morris's description, of Asian/American women as passive victims by becoming the active participant in sex.[68] In this, the difficulty in assessing the pleasure or pain of her expression becomes politically productive practice in terms of our interpretation. Precisely because of the difficulty in assessing her facial expression, we should not forget that the encounter between others across difference cannot be assumed. Especially as Chong's iconicity remains rife in debate as monstrous or feminist, we must keep her meanings loaded with possibility.

Where this engagement leads needs further examination. In *Sex,* Chong confirms that she felt presented in a limited way. Later, we find out from other sources such as Morris and Chun that Chong was sleeping with the film director Gough Lewis during some of the making of the film. Chong says this film should more appropriately use the title *Sex: The Gough Lewis Story* as told through her body and life.[69] If a racialized porn star can remain spoken over in documentary, what happens in porn that she neither directs nor owns? Annabel Chong understands the importance of performance. She presents Grace Quek, documentary subject, and Annabel Chong, porn star. This occupation of an unstable subjectivity that shuttles from one position to another needs serious study for its political possibility. Rather than remaining stalled within the shocking nature of the sex acts, we can see the dynamic process of producing and creating them. Her voice remains strangely perplexing, however. As an unreliable subject, seemingly affected by drugs and alcohol, she makes the question of her agency difficult to answer. Why do we need to find her agency, or political possibility, as a sex worker or a porn star?

Through the force of unreliability, Chong rewrites racialized sexuality beyond victimization in favor of achieving an elusive and out-of-grasp subjectivity. It turns out to be too tempting to relegate Annabel Chong to victimhood: to frame her gangbang with the gang rape highlighted in *Sex: The Annabel Chong Story* and to say she did not succeed in turning the slut into a stud, especially since she did not get paid, and the violence continues to overdetermine her identity. In her own words, she dispels the appropriation of her position as raped and victimized in *The World's Biggest Gangbang*. Because she is someone in front of the porn and documentary cameras, her economic exploitation silences her powerful intellectual and anti-commercial critique. Like the actresses on Broadway, the Hollywood Asian American femme fatales, and the porn stars preceding her, Annabel Chong is bound by the processes of race, sex, and representation as well as money. From this position, she directly provides an intellectual, social, and philosophical critique of these technologies and categorizations. Hypersexuality accompanies her powerful critique, developing it as an unstable and contradictory position that attests to the complexity and ambiguity of sex, race, and representation.

Chong's interviews offer a nuanced critique of the filmmaker of *Sex: The Annabel Chong Story* as well as the porn industry and restrictive Asian cultural values. Not only does she want to critique gender limits for her own sexuality and for sexual roles for women, she presents a major race-sex-and-gender critique: " 'Don't you think,' she says, 'that by putting women on this terrible pedestal, where they're all pure and perfect, is kind of terribly constraining on women? It really puts this terrible limit on what they can do in life. It's just another way of controlling—limiting the avenues of exploration that women are allowed to do.' "[70] In this statement, Annabel Chong, porn star and social critic, provides an explanation for why she tests the bounds of hypersexuality. In claiming hypersexuality as political and personal critique, she is rendered unacceptable. It makes sense that since then Annabel Chong no longer makes herself available and instead presents another persona entirely. The writing on her website offers an even more effective refusal of the question of her resistance.

Annabel Chong's own words and own voice reject further inquiry regarding her character Annabel Chong. Like that of Asia Carrera, Annabel Chong's website has represented her voice in cyberspace since her retirement in 2003. I quote most of the very brief site here in order to give an indication of Annabel Chong's complex understanding of her self-formation, especially as an avatar, announcing "game over" to those pursuing her further. She chooses a new anonymity in cyberspace.

Whatever happened to Annabel Chong?
Annabel is dead, and is now replaced full time by her Evil Doppelganger, who is incredibly bored with the entire concept of Annabel, and would prefer to do something different for a change. From her shallow grave, Annabel would like to thank her fans for all their love and support all these years, and to let them know that she will never forget them.

In that case, what is this Evil Doppelganger up to nowadays?
The ED is a diabolical yuppie who is working as a web developer and consultant. She specializes in ASP and .NET with C#, Database Development and also does web design. While the divine Ms Chong was busy doing her Annabel thang, the ED was surreptitiously going to computer boot camp to pick up some skills, so that she can permanently kill off Annabel Chong and begin her new life of peace and relative obscurity. Now she is making a pretty decent living being a horrible geek and all that, proving that there *are* second chapters in American life, to hell with F Scott Fitzgerald.[71]

In the above short passages, Annabel presents multiple subjectivities within the same racialized and sexualized Asian/American female body. She seems to confirm her unreliability as well as the political power of her position as a bound subject. In direct contrast to Asia Carrera, Annabel Chong's refusal to traffic further in self-commodification speaks to her particular significance in pornography.

Katrien Jacobs uses the term "monstrous revolt" to describe the work of the sadomasochistic lesbian performance artist Maria Beatty.[72] The monstrous "assume[s] that women are urged through false consciousness to act out and improve their fantasies in relation to the 'original' heterosexual act." Instead Jacobs "show[s] how Maria Beatty commands complex processes of desire, bodily exchange, how she fictionalizes and aestheticizes her sex life in order to reinvent definitions of female sexuality which can be stimulating and negotiable for women." Monstrous revolt may not be appropriate to use for the life and work of Annabel Chong. Chong does, however, more than any other figure I study, teeter on the edge of the real and the imagined. As unreliable, she rewrites sexuality outside of race as simply victimizing. As monstrous and outside legibility, however, her meaning registers as primarily bad, undesirable, and powerless.

Where deviancy and hypersexuality stand as the norm in porn, race provides the difference. Through their racialization, we see that Asian American female porn stars craft their own personas, direct their own videos, and insert Asian American female priorities in pornography and their websites as feminist and anti-racist critique. Through mainstream pornography, we can ultimately see that the vocabulary of pleasure does not exceed politics. Asia Carrera and Annabel Chong show us how the embrace of bad womanhood does not occur uniformly in its political critique. By studying their work, however, the dynamics of fantasy, fetishism, money, power, and history in pornography can point to how we may expand Asian women's roles in the national imaginaries to include their work of redefining race and sex in pornography. As feminist practices, they expand our understanding of how sexuality helps to define race and how pornography opens up space for the study of Asian/American women's power.

To reiterate the terms I prioritize in my study, what if we study Asian/American women's representations by centering sexuality as their own, even if that sexuality looks different from what typically constitutes the normal and the acceptable? Within racialized communities, acknowledging perverse pleasures and enjoyment in sex as well as in viewing, performing, and criticizing offers a more viable politics of recognition. At the same time, the experience of pain and the fear of reinscribing images through the power of cinema must remain part of our analyses. When we see the production of fantasy for Asian women in early stag films, the production of yellowface in Golden Age pornography, and the performance of perversity by Asian/American porn megastars, we recognize an intensely racialized formation of sexuality in representation. Asia Carrera and Annabel Chong emerge from this hypersexual legacy in order to provide two different political engagements with pornography. Annabel Chong especially challenges acceptable forms of politics and power: she insists on the unreliability of representation and the unknowability of the race, class, gender, and sexual experience. She shows this complexity by exposing her vulnerability as difficult to pin down. Then, she runs away. I surmise that her flight is an attempt to flee the oppressive power of classification and to keep the debates about her power or powerlessness open. Along the way, she opens space for the formulation of race-positive sexuality that attests to the need for us to maintain the complexity of representation.

To center the sexuality of Asian/American women in pornography as a feminist critique of racial and sexual representation rightly and more accurately complicates the process of viewing as simply an act of violence upon the viewer. We can acknowledge images of Asian women as perversely and pathologically sexual in the Western cinema industry and from there argue that the condemnation of non-normative sexuality and the simplification of the process of viewing a film do not sufficiently illustrate the political possibilities raised in watching race and sex on screen. The space between bondage and freedom in defining racialized sexuality proves vast, ambiguous, and complex, in ways we need to sustain as ever mysterious and surprising in terms of its political possibilities.

6 ✤

"LITTLE BROWN FUCKING MACHINES POWERED BY RICE" OR SEX TOURISTS WITH MOVIE CAMERAS AND PROSTITUTES WITHOUT MOVIE CAMERAS ✤ Politicizing the Bottom in Southeast Asian Sex Tourist Movies

Watch what happens when she gets a complete load of my cock . . . as big as her arm.—*101 Asian Debutantes: Volume 1* (1995)

You can't beat the attitude of these girls. There's no girl in the world that will give you a shower, give you a blowjob, fuck your brains out, and fold your clothes with a smile on her face. Dammit, nowhere!—An American john in *The Good Woman of Bangkok* (1991)

Describing popular perceptions of Southeast Asian women as small, sexual, and servile, the quotes opening this chapter resonate with the U.S. military adage that Asian women are "little brown fucking machines powered by rice," a saying popularized as various Southeast Asian countries came to be sites for international sex tourism.[1] In rest and recreation spots such as Angeles, Olongapo, and other U.S. military bases scattered all over Southeast Asia, street vendors display hats and t-shirts emblazoned with the long phrase or simply the abbreviation LBFM as souvenirs of wild times, wild women, and wild places.[2] Each attribute in the phrase "little brown fucking machines . . ." describes an important criterion comprising the Southeast Asian female prostitute's commodification.[3] Her smallness emphasizes the Western john's largeness. Supposedly, the brown color of her skin somatically signals a perverse sexual economy, an epidermal schema magnifying a presumed love for sex directly attributable to ethnic culture and racial constitution. Her insatiability, an objectified assignation linked to her colonial subjection, constructs her as non-discerning sexual performer. In the deployment of this description, the women love fucking so much they exhibit an energetic and excessive sexual drive that is machine-like, for the Asian woman's sexual being is for the man. According to such logic, the Asian woman is a slave or a bottom. She delivers a sexual being in service of masters or tops. Furthermore, this sexuality is "powered by rice," in an eroticization of the women's situation in the underdevelopment of nations such as the Philippines, Thailand, and Korea. Her third world status not only positions her in a way that eroticizes her poverty within national underdevelopment but also naturalizes for her a torrid tropical constitution. The appellation LBFM mobilizes attributes that help define the kind of Asian womanhood desirable to the West, which is persistently and repeatedly available as a tradition in Western moving image production.

In the famous "documentary fiction" *The Good Woman of Bangkok* (1991), Dennis O'Rourke uses prize money from the Australian Film Commission in order to "meet a [Thai] prostitute and make a film about that." More than ten years after the release of *The Good Woman of Bangkok,* I take it up in conjunction with a different work of cinematic sex tourism— the video series *101 Asian Debutantes* (1995–98). Self-advertised as the "#1 selling Asian series" of gonzo, or popular cinéma vérité, pornography, *101 Asian Debutantes* presents an ethnically ambiguous white American or European male named Jean Marc Roc filming his sexual liaisons with prostitutes in Korea, the Philippines, and Thailand.[4] He primarily works as both the john and the camera operator for the video series. On his website, Roc promotes the series as featuring "sex in Asia" with "real girls that we aspire to, dream of, love and hope to love. Presented to be admired, desired and longed for in ways that the gold-chained, loveless, filth craving ASSHOLES of the coast [Los Angeles porn industry] could never imagine ever existed."[5] Although their names are near homonyms, the white male filmmakers Jean Marc Roc and Dennis O'Rourke author different kinds of works on the Southeast Asian sex tourist industry; however, both the gonzo pornography and documentary fiction genres assert sexual relations as sites for speaking about Southeast Asian prostitutes.

The Southeast Asian women speak from a position of hypersexuality in both of these "reality-based" sex tourist movies being that the site where they live and work is the Southeast Asian sex tourist industry—a place mythologized for the hedonism available to Western men in novels such as *Fox Girl* (2002) and documentaries including *Sin City Diary* (1992), *Camp Arirang* (1996), and *The Women Outside* (1996). In the case of *The Good Woman of Bangkok,* we see the women dancing on bars, caressing customers and flirting, performing genital shows, and expressing drunken laughter. Young girls gyrate against much older men, cringe at their kisses, and sit on their laps as part of their work in the bars. In *101 Asian Debutantes,* we see them fucking with enthusiasm, achieving orgasm, expressing physical enjoyment through grunts of pleasure, masturbating, engaging in intimate pillow talk, bickering, experimenting with various positions, and actually articulating likes and dislikes for particular sexual play as well as preparing themselves for sex or sexual performance by the application of lotion and other rituals. Rather than simply diagnose these scenes as authentic evidence of particular proclivities for sex—or the victimization of these women by representation, among other forces, under colonialism, militarism, and patriarchy—I examine the politics of white male filmmakers' claims of granting access to and making visibly legible Southeast Asian prostitutes' subjectivity as well as Asian women's engagement of the moving image apparatus. The white male filmmakers make these claims by capturing their liaisons with the gaze of their cameras, which are authorized by what the filmmakers proclaim as speaking from the intimacies of sexual and emotional relations. The Asian women engage the camera differently in ways that contradict and corroborate the filmmakers' agendas. Rather than speak for these women, I highlight their unknowability as subjects and the unreliability of representation as a process. I aim to accomplish a form of "speaking nearby" rather than "speaking for" these subjects.[6]

In this chapter, I critique the ways Dennis O'Rourke's practices are ultimately premised on a hermeneutic project, that is, the knowability of the Asian woman prostitute through a particular method he configures in order to assess the power relations between the filmmaker and the prostitute vis-à-vis the power of the camera. I evaluate close readings of the movie's reviews and interviews with O'Rourke himself in terms of advancing a discourse of transcendental love that ultimately recenters the filmmaker and relegates the women as supplementary to men. Why is this missed in existing analyses? In addition, I evaluate the filmmaking practices of Jean Marc Roc's *101 Asian Debutantes* as a work that does not hide its hermeneutic agenda of constructing Asian women as "little brown fucking machines" and, as such, actually fulfills O'Rourke's promise of self-indictment through sex and film. Through close readings of his films and his statements online, I show how Roc speaks for Asian women in terms of their sexual desirability to white men. In pornography representing sex acts between the filmmaker and the prostitute, what we can more clearly assess is the shared attempt by O'Rourke and Roc to produce the Asian woman's hypersexuality in order to establish a particular white masculine heroism that further marginalizes Asian women. Finally, I privilege dissecting the films' grammar, specifically of bodily movements, design, and cinematography (composition, movement, and lighting), in order to provide interpretive readings of the different prostitutes' gazes and bodily voices in order to explore how Asian women perform against and/or corroborate the transcendental claims made by the filmmakers. In so doing, I explore how the expression of the Southeast Asian prostitute's desire indicates a semiotic excess, or an abundance of material describing the situation of power and intersubjective unknowability, or the inability for both the filmmaker and the prostitute to know the other in the politics of representing Southeast Asian sex tourism—so that any claim of authentic racial-sexual representation, *including my own,* must fall short. As a contribution to recent transnational feminist debates concerning whether or not prostitutes of color can resist as subjects within globalization,[7] my approach centers on an evaluation of the prostitute's gaze and bodily voice as important engagements with white male sexual and scopic regimes.

As part of larger debates about the role of the third world woman intellectual raised by Gayatri Spivak's classic essay "Can the Subaltern Speak?" I examine what it means for a woman of color in the United States to see resistance to commodification and subjection precisely through the material that targets Western male pleasures at squalor, poverty, and otherness. This also enables me to reflect more fully on my interdisciplinary methods of close intertextual reading and auto-ethnography in terms of the role of the critic, especially as an Asian American feminist viewer of global and historical racial sexualization, in offering a theory of use to any reader regarding the bondage of hypersexuality for Asian/American women. While hypersexuality haunts Asian American women's sexualities in order to produce different responses that range from Margaret Cho's and Evelyn Lau's to Nancy Kwan's and that of the viewer I fought with after watching *Miss Saigon*, how does this hypersexual demand function in globalization and in formulating transnational feminism today? How can an Asian/American feminist viewing practice of Asian women in pornography step back from accepted definitions of racialized sex as harmful and the viewing experience as an infliction of violence in order to better understand different contexts of sexuality? What can we learn from the representation of subaltern Asian women that helps us make sense of hypersexuality in transnational representations?

SEX TOURIST WITH A MOVIE CAMERA 1: THE GOOD WOMAN OF BANGKOK

In *The Good Woman of Bangkok* (1991), the acclaimed filmmaker Dennis O'Rourke, a middle-aged white man, travels to Bangkok, hires a prostitute, and makes a film about their relationship, which he describes in interviews as "love." With guaranteed prize money from the Australian Film Commission, given to established, high-achieving filmmakers, he intended to make a film that would otherwise never be approved for funding. He describes his "documentary fiction" as a critique of nonfiction film practices that celebrate the filmmaker as a "teller of truth." Supposedly, instead of occupying the position of hero, he wanted to indict the filmmaker as unavoidably complicit with the social problems that documentary practices aim to expose "objectively." That is, rather than shoot the film condemning these practices, only to participate in them off-camera, O'Rourke became a john on camera in order to speak as a filmmaker.

The main issue that arises in discussions of the film is why he had to fuck her in order to make a film responsive to the situation of inequality. If we were to make a film about firefighters, would we fight fire ourselves? Or about boxing, would we become boxers and hit our subjects? Others, such as the writer Jessica Berens, who speaks as the painter Sebastian Horsely in "Nine Inch Nails" regarding his crucifixion in the Philippines: "How can you paint the crucifixion without being crucified? To me it makes perfect sense to get close to it."[8] In speaking from the site of sex tourism, these two approaches dramatize the ethical conundrums created by the films, demanding that we ask: What is an ethical practice regarding the representation and study of othered subjects, especially at the site of sex for sale? Do we need to implicate ourselves, whether as porn connoisseurs or johns, in order to say something valid about issues and problems within sex work? And how does this differ by race and gender?

Does the intense moralism that pressures sex industries and organizes Asian women prostitutes' place in society prevent them from relating to others unless those interviewers and/or filmmakers are also deemed immoral participants in the sex industry? In this line of questioning, O'Rourke's sexual engagement is justified by an anti-moralist platform to understanding sexuality. However, I suspect such a practice if it leads to a celebration of white men who use Asian women as grounds for their own self-discovery and self-aggrandizement. Even in Berens's voice, the Philippines and Filipinos are the stage and props for white male self-discovery, experience, and expression. Even the local food is rendered distastefully so that Filipinos remain the terrain for centering white male subjectivity. In my analysis, I am interested both in recognizing how Asian women use the technologies of their subjugation by white men to question that subordination by representation and in centering the subjectivity of racial subjects who are caught in the bondage of hypersexuality and the bind of representation.

In the tradition of progressive filmmaking practices for which he is known, in highly regarded works such as *Cannibal Tours* (1988), O'Rourke in *The Good Woman of Bangkok* aims to capture the freedom of Western men in their encounters with constrained Southeast Asian women at the particular and personal site of commodified sexuality. Repeatedly, he insists on his different agenda apart from other filmmakers and other sex tourists: "A lot of the clients of these women, and this is alluded to in the film, actually make videos of their fucking the girls which they can take home for their own delectation. That was not my interest. I just wanted to have some kind of visual record of being in this process with hundreds of other men. I am ostensibly no different to them. The only difference is that I had another agenda, which was to make some kind of work out of the experience."[9] Furthermore, "Foreigners are making pornography all the time. There was a group of men in the Rose Hotel where I was staying who were busted while I was there for doing porno movies in their rooms.

They do it all the time. Just get the girls out of the bars and shoot video or magazine stuff. The police are usually paid enormous bribes not to interfere."[10] But O'Rourke claims to have a different agenda: "I decided my film would be different. I wouldn't be there saying how terrible it all is and then behind the scenes go and fuck the woman. I'd start by fucking her and then I'd try to rescue myself."[11] In these statements, O'Rourke emphasizes his focus on understanding the john's viewpoint, rather than representing the prostitute in the sex industry.

The relationship between the filmmaker Gough Lewis and the sex worker Annabel Chong described in the previous chapter resonates here. As O'Rourke describes above, the sex practices of documentary filmmakers are usually placed in the background of nonfiction films. That is, they shoot the scene as a problem before turning off the cameras and fucking the women. O'Rourke proclaims that he did not hide his power; he supposedly prioritizes the telling of the prostitute's life *after getting sex out of the way*. In effect, he is already a bad subject who enables the audience to enter a life he knows and of which he is a part. Being part of the industry as a filmmaker enables him to communicate lives therein. What needs to be debated, according to O'Rourke's method, is not the sex for sale but the problems and conditions these women face in their work and the role of the white male sex tourist and filmmaker in that world.

Before being redeemed by feminist and postcolonial film scholars, Dennis O'Rourke's controversial film at first generated outrage, signaling a fall from the grace of progressive circles. For example, in *The Filmmaker and the Prostitute*, Laleen Jayamanne describes how the horrified response to the film "fails to read its structure, how it works and condemns it on the basis of a priori beliefs."[12] Clearly, she identifies the outraged response to the film as a kind of race panic about sex, especially in its forsaking of good analytic viewing practices. Reading the film as visible evidence of (North) Western masculine power and (South) Eastern female subalternity becomes a premature and unproductive diagnosis that too easily befalls sexual representations within postcolonial and racial scenes of inequality. Similar to the premise of *The Hypersexuality of Race*, regarding moral panic precluding the work of critical reading, what was originally diagnosed as a film exploiting the social and historical fact of sex tourism is later read more productively and politically.

However, how does the Asian female subject fare in such accolades for the filmmaker? In becoming a valuable self-conscious meditation and mediation by the filmmaker, about himself, through the available-for-purchase fantasy and fact of the Asian woman as the "little brown fucking machine powered by rice," the film raises the challenge of how to privilege cinematic and performance literacy in ways that center the Asian woman's subjectivity. The prostitute Aoi's authorship needs to be clarified. In *The Good Woman of Bangkok,* the first time we see Aoi she is on the bus on her way back to Bangkok, where she puts on makeup, then takes off her glasses to dust off the excess powder with her palms and fingers. Without her glasses, her face is more visible and we notice that only one eye works; the other is lazy. Immediately, through Dennis O'Rourke's construction of the introductory sequence, she truly registers in this shot as a person with a situated specificity, a hometown, a family, and a history—with the help of interview and footage. Moreover, the emphasis on her unseeing eye is particularly telling on O'Rourke's part. If the goal of the film is to capture the prostitute's speaking or looking back at the john with the camera, this particular prostitute can only half do so, as one eye cannot look back. Another interpretation is that one of her eyes always looks askance at O'Rourke, his project, their relationship, and the filmmaker/spectator.[13]

The only shot of O'Rourke in the entire film is of himself shooting from inside the cab as it winds through the city—we see his reflection in the small mirror—with his eye behind the camera shooting the scene of Thailand as an arriving tourist would. While we see only one eye, his eye behind the camera organizes our perceptions. Overall, O'Rourke seems to lay bare his power versus her lack of it—responsibly, artfully, and visually—in the intertitles as well as the sequence of shots. So it is the filmmaker's eye introducing him in the film; while her unseeing eye introduces her immediately after as an effective commentary on whose gaze is more privileged. To make this more explicit, his one-eyed mirror shot mimics Aoi's one eye. The filmmaker and the prostitute each screen each other's motives within their relationship in the film.

If we stick to reading the film as a solitary text, indeed what O'Rourke sets out to do is more complicated than other documentaries on sex tourism. Through various devices, Dennis O'Rourke successfully situates us in a physical, intimate space within sex tourism that implicates his access and privilege. It is precisely this seemingly great achievement of self-reflexivity that the film uses to celebrate itself as a special revelation of Aoi's authenticity to the audience. As her lover, O'Rourke's subjectivity is privileged by bringing us closer to Aoi's subjectivity. Thus, a seemingly

Aoi makes up her face in *The Good Woman of Bangkok*.

self-deprecating move by the filmmaker who says he is not a hero actually elevates the filmmaker, especially in light of what he will ultimately say in the film's conclusion about the prostitute who refuses his gifts in order to return to her work. An intertextual analysis introduces new questions.

What is the role of sex acts and practices in such an approach? O'Rourke shoots their relationship in a film that will not feature any sex acts between them. In doing so, what we learn about the unequal power relation is the ubiquity of power in that relation. If his sleeping with her is such an important premise for his project, why not show it? Perhaps we would then see that he is not outside power, or we would feel differently about the heroism attached to the white male filmmaker upon such a sight. If he has to fuck her to tell the truth about his "guilty" versus innocent position, why won't he show himself doing it? In the visual record, he remains the clean, heroic filmmaker.

I insist on this crude visualization as compelled by an intertextual reading of the film through close readings of interviews with Dennis O'Rourke in *The Filmmaker and the Prostitute*. Therein, he speaks of Aoi in terms of mutuality, consent, and collaboration so that we begin to see that a discourse of transcendent love haunts O'Rourke's description of their particular relationship. It brings to light his decision to emphasize the need to fuck her versus the possibilities and perils of their collaboration. specifically what I see in her authorship through usurping the camera from his stated agenda:

> My film won't be one of those futile television documentaries that talks to prostitutes and to lying government ministers and then after giving the audience a voyeuristic thrill, concludes that prostitution is bad. I hate and despise that kind of cinema—films that give people their truths as fantasies.

What interests me are the possibilities of love. The emotional possibilities of a love that must cross the barriers of race and sex and class and language. *I honestly believe such a love is possible. I'm in love with Aoi, and she knows that—though I've told her from the beginning I cannot stay with her once the film is completed* [my emphasis]. My film is about the kind of love that can be created between prostitute and consumer, a love that starts from a position of fake sexual intimacy.[14]

It is through his assertion of "emotional love" and a peculiar sexual intimacy emergent from paid sex that he claims to give us her "truth." But what kind of love is this? While it seems based on their structural locations, how does it ultimately disregard their social positions in this scene? O'Rourke moves us into the dangerous territory of transcendental love and an illusory kind of intersubjectivity in his description of the film and their relationship rather than the deconstruction of power highlighted by critics. Because he moves us into a place of abstraction, we must return to the concrete place that authorizes his speech.

While the film certainly presents moments where Aoi asserts herself and seemingly defies him, we can never know entirely what this relationship is about, as the film critic John Powers writes after visiting the couple. Upon close reading of his own interpretations and responses to the film, however, I believe Dennis O'Rourke relies on Aoi's removal from relations of power in order to center his own subjectivity.[15] They are just two people in love: "Our love affair and our sexual life was the same as any other. It was just [as] transcendental as any love affair I've had."[16] Here O'Rourke understands love to be "transcendental," as he tries to verify that once Aoi and he are in love, they are removed from the world. Alona Wartofsky notes how O'Rourke uses this framework in order to classify himself as a fellow sufferer, depicting his love for Aoi as a sacrifice and thus further articulating his victimization, much like René Gallimard's love in David Henry Hwang's play *M. Butterfly*.[17]

Like *Madame Butterfly, Toll of the Sea,* and *Miss Saigon,* wherein the Asian woman's love is understood as unworthy, Dennis O'Rourke characterizes his love in the opening titles as exceptional, in the form of "love without pain." For example, he further claims that he willed himself into falling in love with Aoi so that he could become a "victim" to her moods. In a statement that could be true, he claims, "I loved her more than she loved me, I imagine."[18] Finally, he defends himself against accusations of manipulation in order to retreat to "love," quite a fraught concept within a history of representation featuring Asian women's unrequited love, which usually ends in suicide.[19]

For O'Rourke, love and emotion is the ultimate agenda in combining the concrete subject positions of the filmmaker and his subject. There is a suspension of power required for his equation to work: "To say I manipulated her is to ignore the 9-month relationship" and the emotions that existed between them.[20] In the end, his justification is that "things happen in the chaos of life!"[21] Chaos, whether in meaning or in life, does not negate how Aoi is still a prostitute and O'Rourke is still a john. While I believe that he destabilizes his identity in order to connect with her, I believe he ultimately chooses to protect himself from her by rendering himself familiar as opposed to her racial and sexual otherness. He remains clean and reliable while she is presented as the dirty prostitute who refuses his offers to save her so as to return to prostitution.

Why not expose the process of operating from the same plane, as he claims? He says, "I had to deliberately collapse that fake moral distance and critical distance between me and my subject. I had to align myself as much as possible on the same plane."[22] What does this look like? He becomes part of her world as a john and as a filmmaker concerned with power and art. Sadomasochistic scenes may be played here, but he does not characterize his representation as such. He shies away from the complexity of their relationship to render a more traditional binary encounter between filmmaker and prostitute rather than filmmaker/john with filmmaker/prostitute providing a complex intersubjectivity that would better problematize the process, poetics, and politics of representation for raced and gendered subjects.

In actuality, O'Rourke describes a long rehearsed version of white male-Asian female love that has a concrete limit. Like Pinkerton in *Madame Butterfly* and Chris in *Miss Saigon,* he will not stay. Enabled by such male characters, he acknowledges this legacy as a postcolonial position. Both characters practice a form of love for the Asian woman that O'Rourke easily disengages in his work and life. Similar to what exists between Cio-Cio San and Pinkerton in *Madame Butterfly,* and Chris and Kim in *Miss Saigon,* it is a love reserved for the "fantasy" of the Asian woman, "different" from what can be felt for the white woman in that it is founded in disposability and abandonment. And as he says above, O'Rourke pronounces this limited love—especially in terms of work—at the beginning of his relationship with Aoi. Yet, the frame of a more innocent kind of love persists in his claims regarding Aoi's resistance and refusal. To him, their relationship is a testimony of their love simply as a man and a woman.

O'Rourke very clearly defines a particular kind of love between Aoi and himself as an incomprehensible love. For O'Rourke romanticizes his first meeting with Aoi: "She had all the external qualities of victimhood, but her strength was obvious from the first night. It was 3 a.m. when the pimp introduced her to me. He said I could take her for 500 baht ($20) and keep her until the afternoon. I gazed at her for a long time. The pimp's words meant nothing. I was in the process of meeting a woman." The above statement is the edited version of what shows up in the intertitles of the film that I analyzed earlier. In the film, he announces that their meeting is situated within sex tourism. Yet, in interviews about the film, he discusses this moment of personal experience as transcendental, a statement that can be understood in light of performances taking place within the inter-actions between prostitute and john. O'Rourke describes meeting Aoi in a romantic way, where the pimp's words "meant nothing" at the moment of meeting her "as a woman."[23] O'Rourke at this point captures the individual relations occurring in prostitution that are frequently not described in primarily economic analyses. Indeed, these categorizations are very much part of the eroticism between them as a man and a woman in this highly charged scene. For example, in his relations with other prostitutes, he realizes that Aoi performs a script designed to extract more money from him. He tells the story of another prostitute, Tam, who almost became the subject of his film. Although he has a memorable night with her, six months later she does not remember him. When she again performs this same tear-jerking drama on their second encounter, his connection to her, and his recollection of their first all-night emotional bonding, shatters. The accompanying tears and the sob story are clichés articulated to the individual as an entity: the Western john who must be milked for money. He says: "The whole process was something new for me and I was com-pletely delirious. I didn't realize that she was working on me the same way that these women work on all their customers."[24]

Similarly, she is also treated as an entity: the prostitute who provides services for the john who pays. In such an unequal situation, both the prostitute and the john are agents in unequal ways. The prostitute is a worker in the situation of sex tourism but what is her part of the bargain within the film? While she may write her own benefits into the bargain (she gets two rice farms, not one!), the claim of transcendent love needs to be problematized in such a relation. Awareness of this hermeneutic agenda moves us beyond Linda Williams's useful assertion that since he is a white male filmmaker, he can only tell the film if he articulates and demonstrates his privileged position. That is, since we do not have anything else to provide a solution to the messy morass of sex, video, and inequality, this film should be touted for this methodological achievement.[25] Such a reading privileges the subjectivity and voice of the white male filmmaker and relegates the Southeast Asian prostitute to a secondary status, marginalizing her yet again in the guise of new knowledge.

In *The Good Woman of Bangkok,* despite the claims of destabilizing subject positions, Dennis O'Rourke returns to the stable position of offering us unmediated access to Aoi's life. We are supposed to have gotten the inner life of a prostitute of the lowest strata and recognize her as an incredible person, through him.[26] As such, his is a statement of love for a "native of another culture [he] was trying to comprehend."[27] But he seems to acknowledge fault in this when he then offers an abstraction, thus making a mystery about their relationship, which is inaccessible, unexplainable, and distinct from their socially situated locations. While O'Rourke deserves credit for making the discussion of Aoi possible, his insistence on a form of transcendental love and reinstalling white male heroism (despite his failure to save her) introduces new limits to what we may know about the Asian woman in her sexual representation.

This frame of mutuality—mutual recognition and victimization—is a prevalent diagnosis of relations in the Southeast Asian sex industry. For example, Jeremy Seabrook interviews johns and prostitutes in Southeast Asian sex tourism scenes who decry each other and render themselves as the other's victim.[28] *The Good Woman of Bangkok* reveals a parallel structure, as O'Rourke's rowdy interviews with crowds of johns in the bars contrast with Aoi's soliloquy of quiet suffering in the hotel room. One can also see that the discourse of love undergirding the film all the way to its end reveals a similar binary via the creation of a utopian space untouched by power. Yet even if O'Rourke claims that he and Aoi are emotional equals, we are still left with the question of what the role of emotions are in terms of power. In any case, this easy equalizing is also apparent in his declaration that "everyone's a victim in prostitution."[29] And in discussing his decision to come to Bangkok, we note this type of move as well: "Did I have a free choice in what I did?"[30] Thus, are johns and prostitutes—and by extension, filmmakers and subjects—all equally victimized? In confronting this impasse, we might be able to move beyond this paradigm of mutual victimization if we were allowed to evaluate the complexities of their relationship through a bolder, more explicitly sexual filmmaking practice. Does moral panic similarly govern O'Rourke in his choice of methods? Is he prevented by fear that explicit sexual representation has no place in philosophical or social inquiry?

To share the intricacies of the intimacies of O'Rourke's entanglements would provide a new assessment of the role of moving images in seeing sex and race power dynamics. Two scenes come to mind. John Powers and Alona Wartofsky in *The Filmmaker and the Prostitute* recall the scene of Dennis O'Rourke's "ashen-faced and furious" outburst at Aoi, in which he yells at her for not laundering and ironing his clothes—"duties" that are part of their contract. John Powers rationalizes the outburst as an emotional bonding in front of him that the two needed to enact.[31] Alona Wartofsky, in contrast, won't let the moment pass.[32] After she asks O'Rourke about the moment, he once again becomes "ashen-faced and furious," bursting out at her, "Do you ever iron anyone's trousers? Do you ever do anything for anybody else?" He then proceeds to describe this moment as something that the West—represented by viewers and critics outside the film production—would not understand. When he says, "She just knows how it is with men. That's what she knows and that's what's in the film," we can see how such a scene, if represented, would more fully represent the dynamics of their relationship. Such a critique recalls Tracy Quan's accusations of Western self-importance in understanding other sexual cultures.[33]

In O'Rourke's written description of the process of looking for his film subject, he "tests" a number of prostitutes by sleeping with them. In his recollection of Tam, the woman I described earlier, who almost became the subject of his film, he expresses a struggle with his various positions as a john, a filmmaker, and a (white) man: "There was the act of prostitution —fucking I mean—and there was talking about who I was and why. Most of it was my just playing the role of the filmmaker in an attempt to conflate the ego of the man behind the camera and the man who lusted after the prostitute. This is not to say that the two were immutably separable and always will be."[34] If O'Rourke had showed this process of interrogating the dynamics of the self as a subject-in-struggle, a complex triangulation, within the cinema, he would have avoided what *The Good Woman of Bangkok* currently accomplishes: recentralizing the white male subject position as the Good Man of Bangkok and further marginalizing the Asian woman. Why deprive us of wrestling with these complexities?

Through a close reading of his interviews, I gather that O'Rourke misses the potentiality to articulate the limits of intersubjective relations and representation by backing away from the image he describes to John Powers: that he will film himself rolling a condom on his penis in order to establish his participation in an industry frequently condemned by filmmakers before partaking in the enjoyment themselves.[35] In choosing not to show the process behind his selection of Aoi (which entailed fucking a number of prostitutes) or to show even the sex acts between them that centrally come to provide the basis for his truth claims on her behalf, he stabilizes white male subjectivity, which frequently remains innocent in the transaction of prostitution as a john. If we were to see the sex act auditions with other prostitutes, such as Tam, his position as the filmmaker and the man who brings Aoi to us would be much more open to the critique he aims to accomplish: the failure of the white man to save even himself.

An ethical filmmaking, in terms of imagining other realities and interrogating power, would directly problematize through representation, in ways that the issue deserves, the fact that he does fuck her, for that relationship to be established in all of its brazen display of the dynamics of power in the contemporary transnational age. How much can we learn from seeing such a scene of racialized sexuality? Or how else can we know that he is not simply fucking her within the limited intersubjectivity of their relation as prostitute and john? What do a first world man and a third world woman look like together—how would their conjoined representation capture the dynamics of power circulating between them? What surprises me about O'Rourke's insistence that his position is admirable because he fucked her is that he does not show us the dynamics of their "love," the shifting power dynamics that allow him to claim victimization as well, as part of his project for her as a prostitute to be heard talking, with her clothes on, and looking at the mirror mediating our gaze. We also do not see, as I point out with the prostitutes in Roc's films, the sometimes effortful and even tedious process of getting the john off, the body belying whatever pronouncements anyone might wish to make about "love" or sexual proficiency. In closing my analysis of O'Rourke's film and his commentary on it, I propose that we continue to question the permissible and accepted ways of representation, not only in terms of what can be spoken about others, but also in terms of how sexual representation and, specifically, the throes of their everyday relations even in sex enrich our understanding of the relations between Western men and Southeast Asian women at the site of sex tourism. O'Rourke's sensational deployment of sex would also be exposed for its delimiting of Aoi's subjectivity solely as a prostitute. O'Rourke's selective refusal to show sex acts really limits agency within the film and reserves it for the filmmaker alone. He omits the sex scenes in order to cover up his own subjectivity as a john. The john remains clean in the extra-diegetical operation of the film itself. "Love" is the fig leaf that rationalizes the invisibility of O'Rourke's naked sex act. His claims of exposing his guilt and breaking down the filmmaker as hero are really reinscriptions of the white male author of Southeast Asian women.

Differently from his interviews, O'Rourke fetishizes Aoi when he purports to represent her solely as a film object and not as co-author within the film. If she helps to construct the film's scenes, as he claims, why not show them in the process of deciding how to play the scenes? How did they come to agree on the shot? If he were to show how the authorship happens, the construction of making the fiction is exposed rather than just announcing it in the credits. "Documentary fiction" seems to me to be a gratuitous declaration at the closing credits when he does not show the process of deconstruction. Overall, the question about what is fact and what is fiction remains ambiguous in his discussion. Instead, what he actually does is offer Aoi in all her purported authenticity, through her very own speech acts in the mirror, all enabled by a problematic love that attributes to the camera a positivist value that captures—no matter how shaped by the filmmaker—her presence.

To take to heart the assumption that we do not look at sex through a moralistic lens, the site of sexual interaction should be but another site of encounter to help us see and better understand dynamics of power. To show sex between the filmmaker and the prostitute is to come clean regarding the limits of what we can know about each other and what we can see even in the most intimate of acts and encounters. I would buy his indictment of himself as a filmmaker–as–unreliable subject and as a white man evaluating himself if he broke open the taboo of representing the sex act that he chooses to participate in for the making of his film. If it is her job to have sex with him, as it is his to shoot the scene, sex would be a valid site for our evaluation of white male and Asian female power relations. I now move from a film with barely any sex acts to a video with mostly sex acts in order to explore the argument about how seeing sex is to see power, bursting in complexity.

Gonzo pornography may be best described as cinéma vérité or "reality"-based professional-amateur pornography, wherein the filmmaker also acts as the john in representations of the sex acts. Situated in the Southeast Asian sex tourism scene, gonzo pornography sells the "truth" of Asian women to consume in the privacy of one's own home. That is, these "realistic" tapes purport to provide the visual as powerful uncontestable evidence of Asian women's "naturalized" biologic drive for deviant sex as well as her cultural propensity for hypersexuality. Southeast Asia as a site of erotic fulfillment finds particularly telling expression in the gonzo. Requiring few resources to make immense profit, the genre threatens to eclipse traditional pornography in financial terms, as evidenced by the rise of two of the major pioneers, Ed Powers and John "Buttman" Stagliano, to prominence and power in the industry.

Set on location in Thailand, Korea, and the Philippines, the series *101 Asian Debutantes* features Jean Marc Roc—an ethnically ambiguous Western man, director, actor, and performer—as he secures Asian female prostitutes for sex on tape. He is ambiguous precisely because of his seemingly French name, which is contradicted by his American accent. What is more certain is that the women are caught up in the global industry of sex tourist work fetishized by Jean Marc Roc in his series of four tapes featuring approximately six sex scenes with four to ten women per tape. The women are from clubs in the streets of Patpong and other multinational brothel towns. In these videos, Jean Marc Roc is a Western man with money who films pornography with women in the sex industry.

In these tapes, Jean Marc Roc pursues personal enjoyment and profit as a filmmaker and man who travels to Southeast Asia in search of sex—without actual acknowledgment of his power. This is in contrast to the ways in which O'Rourke aims to premise his film as the breakdown of the heroic status of the filmmaker as a reliable narrator. Roc persists in speaking for the women outside of the structures of inequality and ascribes to them "love of a nice guy and good hot sex." For the sake of comparison, I cite and perform close readings of Roc's first four tapes in the series *101 Asian Debutantes*. While the first tape brings together women from Thailand, Korea, and the Philippines, the others in the series focus on a particular group of women in a particular country. Thus, the second tape features

Thai women, the third tape focuses on Filipinas, and the fourth shows Korean women. In Roc's website as well as on the cover packaging of his materials, he purports to counter the "sleaze" of contemporary pornography practiced in the United States. He writes, "The L.A. industry is boring and out of touch. Full of tired, denigratory [sic], and hardened attitudes towards the sexes that all those who make the trek to ASIAEROTICA seeks to escape. Could somebody please tell me what the hell is sexually stimulating about watching 300 jerks in a room line up to fuck Jasmine St. Clair [the porn star who dethroned Annabel Chong] like so many men waiting to releave [sic] themeselves in a public toilet? . . . I despise this crap. I despise the industry that profits from bringing all of us down to the lowest levels of humanity."[36] In his work, Roc purports to present images that celebrate Asian female sexuality and womanhood as an alternative.

Each tape features trailers for the next tape. Using humor characteristic of pornography in titles such as "come-ing" this fall, the videos also poke fun at third world political conditions, such as civil war. The first shots of the trailer in the second tape, for example, feature military vehicles spilling over with men with guns. The voice-over says, "One man caught between the thighs of women he loves . . . he is the thriller in Manila," while the intertitle reads, "Sex and Revolution on Videotape." The video image shows two small women servicing a tall, big, white man. The camera is placed so that we see the naked bodies and faces of the women all over the man, whose head and face we cannot see. The voice-over continues as representations of the exteriors of brothels are shown: "Come walk the streets of Manila with Jean Marc Roc . . . When Jean Marc Roc walks the streets, you always know what he's going to find." We then see close-up shots of two Filipina women with white semen all over their faces as they stare at the camera. Ultimately, we can regard the trailer as a microcosm of the video with the squalor and political strife of the third world countries framing the sex scenes and eroticizing the situation of the Asian women. Unlike O'Rourke, who seeks a single subject for his film, Jean Marc Roc displays these women for their varied sexual styles and how they may fulfill his sexual interests. Unlike O'Rourke, who declares that he does not hide his agenda, Roc truly does not hide himself as a sex tourist who aims to speak for Asian women. Targeting an audience, he constructs them as idealized objects and comes to prove them to be what has been described as "little brown fucking machines powered by rice."

In the beginning of the second tape, a title establishes the setting as

Bangkok, Thailand. A series of shots offers up visions of the exotic and faraway. We see old women in loose colorful clothing as they peddle vegetables from their boats. In the middle of their work, they look at the camera without saying anything while their faces register emotions closer to exasperation rather than pleasure at being taped. A mountain of melons sits on a boat with a man and a child, and the river is full of traffic. Another shot is composed entirely of peasant hats. As a contrast to these pastoral scenes, Roc offers up the Bangkok cityscape, complete with shots of street traffic, congestion, and smog. The next set of images establishes old Eastern architecture intercut with shots of peddlers on the streets selling kites, birds, and other goods. These daylight shots frame the night-life scenes.

Disco balls rotate and various lights flash over the women dancing to the pop song "One Night in Bangkok." Roc speaks from the position of a tour guide who leads us around sex tourism scenes: "Here we go again, fellas, in Bangkok, Thailand. Glad you could make it. Pull up your chair and join me while I take you around." The song itself is part of a culture industry that references sex tourism in Asia. At this point, the following lyrics are made prominent: "One night in Bangkok, makes a hard man stumble, not much between despair and ecstasy. . . ." Under this song are images of Thai men dancing on the streets, loitering, and hanging around the vendors. One of them looks at Roc's camera, makes a gesture with his middle finger, and then grabs his crotch while laughing wildly. As we see more women walking the streets and men from all over the world roaming around and riding in jeeps looking at the women, Roc continues his voice-over with characteristic incoherence about Thailand's character as a culture and a country.

Unlike O'Rourke, Roc does not interview people in the scene. The visible images are collected to authenticate the location where the sex acts transpire through a very prominent voice-over. He states: "Seems like they always play this song . . . Thailand [is] more a state of mind . . . Enjoy . . . I want to take you to a bar. A very interesting tale took place there." Like O'Rourke's film, Jean Marc Roc's narration makes him the materiality of the film itself. That is, while we do not see him in these scenes, he organizes our perceptions as the director, star, narrator, and cameraperson. He tells us a story that takes place in the bar, framing the encounters within a particular narrative line that makes prominent his mediation.

Inside the Blue Hawaii Bar, a very thin, dark girl with blonde streaks in her long black hair dances very slowly around a pole on the bar. Similar to O'Rourke's film, we do not see Roc's body on screen. Roc shoots openly, while O'Rourke sometimes seems to shoot with a stealth camera, perhaps at his waist. However, we do still see from their point of view as cameramen in both situations. In any case, the girl in question dances for Roc's gaze by looking boldly, directly, and unflinchingly at the camera. It is an intense physical experience to watch her gaze. For me, her gaze rejects his commodification, as if she wants not only to witness but reject his eclipse of her person. Or she may be drugged out, unavailable, or unaware of the significance of the camera beyond the john. However, other viewers may simply see this look as part of her seduction not only of Roc but of the viewer. It is precisely this human exchange in the look, interpreted differently by various viewers, that fuels the power of this image.

The camera continues to present a mediated look upon the prostitute. Roc focuses on her as she performs leg splits, raising her legs high around the pole. She wears a g-string, a skimpy loose pink top, and black leather high-heeled booties. He takes turns focusing and lingering on each of the clothing items and body parts. A button pinned on the center of her chest indicates that she is number 71. She opens her shirt for him and sits with the pole between her thighs. She pulls up her g-string, turning to capture his attention before coming down from the bar. She bends over so that we see her buttocks before she faces him. He does not say a word throughout the first part of their meeting. At this point, we can again make comparisons between the two filmmakers.

Unlike O'Rourke, Roc shows the situation of their meeting rather than presenting it via intertitles. Like O'Rourke, he must undergo some sort of transaction for paying her bar fine to the pimp. After the bar scene, we then see her suddenly fully clothed and standing outside the bar next to fruit at an outdoor store. Dressed in jeans and a loose long shirt, she looks at the camera (him) curiously, but without disdain. Through the logic of the edited shot sequence, he shows that you can purchase this woman, take her out of the bar, and have sex with her in your hotel. The next scene shows the young woman stripped down to her dancing clothes, performing a slower, private dance on the bed inside a hotel room. In a sense, the events do unfold like an instructional manual for finding sex as a tourist in Southeast Asia.

Moreover, Roc eroticizes the women's poverty and fetishizes their squalor as evidenced in recording their outfits. He spends a great deal of time focusing on the Asian women's tattered and old clothes and shoes as a kind of foreplay (for the viewer) to establish more information about the women before the sex acts. For example, he focuses on Number 71's pink shirt with white diamond-shaped patterns scattered all over it. He shows us that she has cut two larger diamond-shaped holes just above her nipples as an inventive way of making the frilly top more functional for arousing customers. In the bedroom of the hotel, we see details of her clothing more closely. He focuses on her red sequined underwear with the pink heart sewn over the crotch. The close-up also reveals her extraordinarily bony thighs. I use the description "bony" deliberately—for the video seems to establish this as significant in its lighting and composition. Throughout the tapes, deciding whom he chooses to shoot and what body parts authors his desires for a particular Asian woman. Similarly, in *The Good Woman of Bangkok* Dennis O'Rourke shoots in the bathroom of a bar where women are fighting about their clothes; one prostitute complains about the fleas in her jacket, stolen from someone else because she's "so poor." He films them from the perspective of one standing among them. Soon he reveals his presence, when one woman notices, "That foreigner is filming us." O'Rourke also seems to fetishize the women's poverty so that a voyeuristic gaze operates in the "behind-the-scenes" of the bar. It is yet another mirror scene and he mediates the scene before us, his filmmaking surely enabled by his status as a Western white male john.

While all of the women in both works are poor, the two filmmakers are not equally rich. O'Rourke shoots in Thailand for almost a year, both on film and video, with a much higher budget. Roc seems to shoot his video sex tours in various countries occurring over a period of years. Indeed, Roc's is a less sustained project that allows him to tape some women regularly or annually, rather than over a prolonged period of time that would require ghastly production expense. O'Rourke shoots Aoi, her hometown, her communities, and her relatives. While O'Rourke and Roc differ in terms of budget and perhaps their differing class positions as well as the status of respectability afforded their respective genres, the way poverty functions is similar but not the same in their works. Roc makes erotic—at the moment of the sex act—the women's squalor. And O'Rourke's focus on poverty itself is fetishized so that an aesthetics of squalor informs the filmmaking in locations indicative of the women's poverty. For O'Rourke, Aoi's poverty is authenticating of her status as a subaltern subject, and for Roc, the poverty is part of the sexual titillation.

I'm so poor
I wear this lousy jacket.

The bargirls complain about their clothes in a behind-the-scenes shot of Bangkok nightlife in *The Good Woman of Bangkok*.

That foreigner's filming us.

The bargirl identifies O'Rourke and his camera behind the scenes in *The Good Woman of Bangkok*.

Money indeed informs the primary relationships represented in both works. *The Good Woman of Bangkok* involves the payment of two rice farms for the single subject of the film. *101 Asian Debutantes* features various women who cost, for example, ten dollars for two at a time. The financial arrangement is indicated at the beginning of the first tape in the series *101 Asian Debutantes* and also in the website when Roc describes paying nothing at all because he supposedly seduces and because they simply "love good hot sex." In the bar sequences of *101 Asian Debutantes*, however, the women are visibly for sale; that is, Roc situates the relations in the bars and identifies the women by numbers indicated with buttons pinned to their bathing suits. Money enables O'Rourke to shoot endless footage in his portrait of Aoi, talking with her for hours in order to reach dramatic heights in her performance. In spending less time with the women, the quality of Roc's portraits is more limited but nonetheless quite telling of a number of the women's performances.

While poverty is told through Aoi's narration, poverty suffices in the visual narration of the various women in *101 Asian Debutantes*. Some embody Roc's preference for smallness and youth, a particular type of Asian woman among a population more heterogeneous in size, look, age, and attitude. While Roc's sampling of women is quite limited toward showing the appellation LBFM as manifested in their very bodies, some of the women are older and do not meet stereotypical standards. For these more anonymous prostitutes, their representation requires sexual labor without the humiliation of having to reveal their "inner" or "truthful" kernels of the self. It seems to me that a more demanding, difficult, and self-exposing labor is required of Aoi, who must expend emotional work for the camera. For example, in the sex scene with Number 71, Roc and the young woman maintain their silence. Any instructions for her happen off camera. Neither speaks across the ambience of the hotel room, so that the sound of her bracelets is amplified.

Number 71 ultimately negotiates some kind of voice in her performance primarily through her establishment of a relationship with the camera. She ignores the filmmaker and works with the camera to compose her body within the frame and to perform acts for it, all the while staring at the lens in ways that pierce the viewer with a powerful gaze. In one shot, she looks at the camera unflinchingly as he penetrates her from behind. His voice-over attempts to narrate her story, which her stare seems to contradict. Then she begins to look at the camera as a mirror, playing with her hair and looking at her reflection. At one point, she sticks out her tongue to the camera in a taunting manner, or perhaps in relishing a sexual moment. These images show the woman within the sex acts occurring within the sex tourism industry. She engages the camera directly by staring at it unflinchingly in ways that speak to me powerfully. The second image shows her authorship in adjusting her visual self-presentation. She demonstrates awareness of the camera and her ability to shape her presence even in a minute manner of fixing her hair and checking her appearance.

At this juncture, I must again remind the reader that this gaze functions differently for the more typical viewer that it does for me as an Asian American feminist viewer. My reading of her gaze may emphasize my own desires for a particular response in the voices of these women, while for

The prostitute stares at the camera as she is penetrated from behind by Jean Marc Roc in *101 Asian Debutantes*.

The prostitute in *101 Asian Debutantes* plays with her hair and looks at the camera, us, or herself while Jean Marc Roc penetrates her.

The prostitute sticks out her tongue at the camera as Jean Marc Roc adjusts her legs in *101 Asian Debutantes*.

others her gaze may simply cause ejaculation. In terms of performances by the other prostitutes in *101 Asian Debutantes,* some do initiate touching and other sexual action while others anticipate his needs and follow his instructions. While one laughs with him and seemingly achieves orgasm multiple times, another is ignored and chastised when she requires a condom. Exhibiting docility, another looks at him, in the fourth tape, with hesitation and waits for his direction. Another instructs him to tape her a certain way, contradicting a more servile demeanor. While the prostitutes provide varied performances, Jean Marc Roc attempts to discipline this diversity and new possibilities of subjectivity by privileging his own representation.

Jean Marc Roc attempts to direct and delimit how we see these differently responsive women, perhaps in order to organize his male viewers' reception. While Jean Marc Roc shows himself through voice-over and point of view rather than direct representation, he works hard to hide himself, particularly his face, during many of the sex acts within the film. Through this absence, he uses the women's presences to represent a particular masculine version of himself. Rather than his face, he prefers to present himself as the phallus; that is, he shows his body to be extensions of the penis in the sense of phallic power. Showing the erect penis bolsters masculinity and patriarchy in pornography. Carole Vance discusses why seeing the flaccid penis undermines the phallus in pornography.

> Against feminist anti-pornography discourses of the power and danger of male sexual domination, it is crucial to emphasize how the phallus as a symbol functions primarily to hide as well as to create and sustain, the severe anxieties and fears attesting to the penis. The question is whether the public display of the fragility of the penis (as an appendage only precariously available for men to use in heterosexual engagement) can work to undermine the notions of the phallus (as ubiquitous concept connecting masculinity to power).[37]

If the center of action is Roc's erect penis, it represents the phallus as idealized masculine power where all body parts emanate. While we see the women in their entirety, the filmmaker remains hidden. I believe this is a deliberate construction that requires conscious set-up and a great deal of work to accomplish. When he does catch his face on screen, he spends time in post-production to eliminate its trace. In this video, Roc shows his penis, leg, arm, thigh, and other body parts against parts of her body. By choosing not to show his face within the sex acts, he shows himself only as the hard, erect penis. He hides his face, distorts his voice-overs, and makes his body function as an extension of the penis. During the sex acts, Roc places his penis against parts of the prostitute's body, such as her arm, thigh, or face rather than the wider stomach, back, or shoulders so as to emphasize the difference in their particular shapes and sizes. As part of the eroticism, he looks bigger against her smallness. He works to create a visual language that provides this visible evidence. The composition and the visual racialized difference are important to the erotic grammar of the relationship and the visual representation. Access to his face or emotionality cannot be included—and this is perhaps true of the eroticism as well.

Unlike the gonzo films situated in the United States—such as Ed Powers's *More Dirty Debutantes*—the man in *101 Asian Debutantes* is unidentifiable on the cover and in the footage. In the scene of U.S. gonzo, the men are stars themselves who anoint new women into the profession, sometimes even stardom. In the sex tourism gonzo scene, no such stardom is available. Applied in post-production, a wipe-effect covers Roc's face, which is blurred like a criminal in hiding. These are conspicuously placed whenever his face threatens any form of appearance. For example, when he is having sex with a woman, he sometimes leans down as he gasps with pleasure or as he reaches down into a new and more pleasurable position. At the moment when his face enters the frame, a black strip covers it up. In most cases, we are disallowed the sight of his face.

As stated earlier, we never directly see Dennis O'Rourke's face in *The Good Woman of Bangkok* either, even if we do get sense of him through Aoi's responses to the man behind the camera. The only times Roc enters the scene are as a penis or a fragmented body of the director. He comes in to fix a woman's pillow so that we see her face as well as her genitalia when she masturbates. When they are engaged in intercourse, he enters the scene as a penis. This is the part of his body that is prioritized so that it functions as a metonym of his body. Apart from the power of anonymity he achieves, he covers up his face for it is in direct competition with his penis. The penis, then, is the organ that expresses the filmmaker. We do not see his face in the entire series, for it would return his identity to the ground, short of the phallus.

What we see in representations of explicit sex that O'Rourke shies away from are the women's performances and how they contradict the Western filmmaker Roc's attempts to discipline their presence. In this context, if we assume that sex is neither immoral nor a violence thrust upon women in its visual representation, the wide-ranging diversity of Southeast Asian women's performances shows them utilizing sex and technology in order to establish a new presence and performative power on screen. If what we learn is the performance of white masculinity and the performative power of Southeast Asian women's representation, the use of technologies of sex and cinema helps to establish new morphologies of racial representation that I will discuss more closely in a comparison of the Southeast Asian women's bodily voices in both works.

THE BODILY GAZE OF PROSTITUTES WITHOUT MOVIE CAMERAS

Rather than accessing any truths of Asian women prostitutes vis-à-vis Roc and O'Rourke, most likely we are getting performances of race, class, gender, and sexuality in *101 Asian Debutantes* and *The Good Woman of Bangkok*. Within these performances, the Southeast Asian sex worker enacts a very potent political performativity as one who does not bear the camera, saying something through its technology, and as one overdetermined as a little brown fucking machine, making an intervention within the terms of her hypersexuality, or her sexual acts. Developed significantly by Judith Butler is the notion of performance and performativity regarding the social production of gender norms—particularly women's access to power. Performance refers to enacting gestures, acts, and bodily movements that comprise our understanding and expectations of particular identities, such as demureness in women or boldness in men. The theory of performance as theorized by Butler identifies how repetition of these acts over time naturalizes identity categories such as gender.[38] The performative, as a theory of subjectivity, aims to capture the feasibility of refiguring the limited bounds of race, sexuality, and gender scripts. Within the performances by prostitutes that display awareness of the camera, a break in the scripts of expected roles for third world women may occur and thus result unexpectedly in the emergence of new subjectivities that may challenge our preconceived ideas and understanding of third world prostitutes. In my formation of agency through speaking in racialized sexual representation, I am informed by Saba Mahmood, who posits "agency not as a synonym for resistance to relations of domination, but as a capacity for action that historically specific relations of subordination enable and create."[39] The performative, and the regulation of identity acts, is essential to this project of locating third world women's agency in bodily voices articulated within the moment of the cinematic sex act in gonzo pornography.

In the representations of prostitutes establishing a particular Western masculinity, the presence of female desire challenges our understanding of the power dynamics at work in race, sex, and cinema. In the sex scene with Number 71 in *101 Asian Debutantes*, Jean Marc Roc's hand enters the frame to fondle her nipples. He places a pillow behind her head so that she can see herself in the video monitor. She rubs herself and says "come on," motioning for him to come toward her from behind the camera. She looks at herself in the monitor, evoking similarities to the scene involving the mirror O'Rourke uses so that Aoi can watch herself "confess." Again, Number 71 asks Roc to come over. He flips her over so that we see their intercourse from above. When he lifts her up, her face expresses what looks like pain. She opens her mouth, squinting her eyes as if he is ripping her apart. The expression is accompanied by sounds of pain and by the motion of her hands pushing, as if instinctually, to counter his weight. The black wipe-effect covers his face as her face expresses pain. While we cannot truly discern if the expression is of pain or pleasure, the question of suffering is raised in this moment. Does she suffer in the sex act as part of the erotic power sold by the film?

Elaine Scarry writes of pain's resistance to expression whether in descriptive language or others' cognition.[40] A phenomenological approach to *101 Asian Debutantes'* representation of the prostitute's expression is to focus on what may be transpiring before the viewer, and to note that something certainly is happening that destabilizes viewing as well as the dynamics within the scene being watched, whether it be pain or pleasure. The certainty of intercourse and physical contortions of pain as well as the undeniable sounds of intense pleasure destabilize the established experience of viewing with the instability of meaning. Something significant is transpiring and begging to be read. My appropriation of the phenomenological method and my application of it to viewing resists the transcendental impulse in O'Rourke's understanding of love, especially when I situate viewing practices within power relations.

In the scenes where sexual pleasure is declared by the prostitute, the question of suffering or enjoyment is answered by the possibilities of pain present at the moment of her bodily expressions. She watches him and fondles her breasts as if to ease his force. With her other hand, she supports his weight as he plunges into her. Soon she smiles and says, "Oh yeah" as she stares and stares at the camera with deep intakes of breath as he continues to penetrate her. He makes sure to lift her head, so that her hair falls away and frames her face. Her expression of what may be pain and pleasure is powerful in grounding the viewer in the certainty of his or her body—whether in horror or satisfaction. In *Watching Rape,* Sarah Projansky identifies representations of rape as sites for political critique.[41] Watching the detailed transcription of power relations at the site of sex tourism enables better understanding of the vast sea of experience within frameworks of bondage and freedom framing such sexual relations.

We see that Roc and the prostitute converse during the sex acts: he asks if she likes it, to which she responds, "Yes, I like it." Or he uses words that indicate a director-actor relationship, in the sense of instructing her and making sure she knows the reason: "Put your face over here so I can see it." She follows his instructions as if invested in finding the best way to show off her ecstatic face or simply to follow well his commands as part of earning her pay. The ambiguity of pleasure and suffering establishes the Asian woman's subject position within visuality. While it may be hard to read her experience, we can see that pain and pleasure are undoubtedly important within the establishment of her presence on screen.

The scenes with Number 71 include a considerable amount of time in which she masturbates and plays to the camera with various positions and angles to show off her actions, her face, and her body at the moments of ecstasy. The visibility of women's orgasm is problematized in pornography in ways that are aggravated in the site of Southeast Asian sex tourism. Shot in real time, as is the convention in gonzo pornography, forty minutes of fondling the woman's nipples, cunnilingus, full body caressing, clitoral stimulation, and intercourse produce results that capture physical, psychic, and emotional responses, whether pleasure or pain in the expression of the face and the bodily contortions and convulsions. While the human body produces recalcitrant responses to stimulation, we cannot forget the context of the sexual encounter represented in porn, where sex workers understand that there is an expectation of the performance of pleasure and where we cannot be certain of what else transpired before or after the shoot. In one scene in *101 Asian Debutantes,* a prostitute turns her face away from the camera as she supposedly orgasms. Her expression is hard to assess in performances of sexuality, especially by professional sex workers whose jobs are not only sexual service but selling sexual fantasy.

What is seriously at issue in the vision of the prostitute's body in ecstasy within the scene of sex tourism, however, is the threat of providing evidence for establishing the essentialism of the "little brown fucking machine powered by rice." Again, what we may be able to deduce from watching these scenes is the impossibility of telling pleasure from pain and vice versa as an especially important theme that arises in representations of Asian women in porn discussed in the previous chapter, wherein pain is so closely—yet somewhat unclearly or ambiguously—linked to pleasure. Indeed, pain is inextricably linked to the pleasure associated with the mystery of Asian women as they are sold and described in gonzo pornography. As an Asian American female spectator of the contradictory spectacle of professional performance and innocence and pleasure and pain, I interpret the women's agency and assertions of subjectivity as emergent. I believe that conventional viewers of this genre read these moments less in terms of identification and more in terms of their sadistic viewing pleasure or interpretations of women's masochism. The phenomena of the prostitute's subjectivity are essential to gonzo pornography, which eroticizes the women's status, their poverty, and their desperation. This is in contrast to the different genre of American porn such as the glossy Vivid films wherein such semiotic excess would not be apparent or even part of its appeal. Indeed, gonzo pornography in the sex tourism scene depends upon, if not relishes, the access to the women's third world dependency through their sexual labor.

Within the scenes of sex tourist pornography, the crux of what we learn is the ultimate unknowability of relations across difference and through moving image representation. That is, in concrete analysis of the relations in sex tourism, an element of the unknowable in our analysis would prevent speaking for these women. Within this site, where there is no clear-cut binary between pleasure and pain, desperation and enjoyment, and power and subordination, the women's voices are not containable. A semiotic excess and ambiguity operates so that the women's subjectivities are not quite accessible. The cinematic inaccessibility to knowing the other rejects interpretations based on a binary frame of power and powerlessness or pain and pleasure. In the study of moving image representation of race and sexuality, the factors of unreliability include the difficulty in gauging performance aspects of race, gender, class, and sexuality as well as the limits of the medium in adequately representing the situation's complex inequality. Transcendental love, however, differs significantly from the reminder to accept the limits of what we can know.

As such, through the bondage of hypersexuality and the bind of representation, the women in the documentary fiction and gonzo pornography can be read as complex entities: simultaneously actors as well as subjects and objects of desire. I find further evidence in *The Good Woman of Bangkok,* wherein I isolate the women's performances on screen during group interviews. The shameful looks practiced by Aoi's friends when conversing with her (and him) about their sexual experiences, show the contesting on-camera subjectivities, evident in their different bodily relations to the camera. Mainly, the other women look down and avert their eyes and heads away from the camera, barely able to speak or take up space in the frame. The male interviewees look ahead and push toward the camera. With faces dominating the small frame, they yell out with saliva striking the lens. Critics of *The Good Woman of Bangkok* have recounted the men's speech frequently: brazen, proud, guilty, and fun filled. They range from justifying the use of the women, to complaining about Western women, to celebrating Asian women as servile. And the women's speech seems to reveal the shame and the humiliation of their forced consent to paid sex, as well as resentment, anger, regret, resignation and feisty, everyday banal interactions with each other. In one discussion with Aoi's friend, we hear Dennis O'Rourke ask about her popularity in the bars. Aoi coaches her to respond with "sometimes good and sometimes bad." The scene is very quiet and calm in comparison to the club scenes. The women speak to each other directly and intimately.

At an outdoor restaurant, Aoi recounts to the camera her experiences with various foreign men. Her friend Nee, a thin, brown, quiet woman with disheveled hair and no makeup who is dressed in a red sleeveless shirt, loose white shorts, and big glasses, enters the frame. Her mannerisms indicate a cautious awareness of the camera and the man behind it. She catches quick looks at the lens but never sustains a stare. In plain view, right before sitting next to Aoi, she fixes her hair before she sits at the edge of the frame and never looks up. She looks down, in direct contrast to Aoi, who speaks loudly and directly to the camera in a carefree, matter-of-fact way. Face forward, she places her hand under her chin and inclines her head as she smiles and smirks. She actually laughs at the end of one story about having to pry five dollars from a man after she has provided her services. In contrast, her friend sits rigidly at the edge of the frame while trying to light a cigarette and not occupy too much space in the frame. Aoi soon asks for her help in recounting another tale: "What's the name of that

Aoi directs her friend
to answer Dennis
O'Rourke's question in
*The Good Woman of
Bangkok*.

Aoi discusses sex work
with her friend in
*The Good Woman of
Bangkok*.

hotel not far from here?" The woman looks afraid and puzzled before she responds softly, "Bangkok Center." She looks at Aoi the whole while, waiting attentively to be cued or addressed. Aoi continues, "Yeah, Bangkok Center is no tip. Chinese man is no tip. I stay all night." In her confession, Aoi then includes her friend, who now smokes a cigarette while averting her gaze. When addressed, she faces Aoi with full attention. In between her responses to Aoi's questions, she closes her eyes and looks down a lot, especially when discussing a particular scene in which, after a ménage-à-trois, they did not get a tip. Aoi brazenly declares "He fucked me twice and you once" before her friend bows her head.

The conversation is rich with the description of negotiating power in the sex tourism scene. Indeed, our access to it is precisely through O'Rourke and his relationship with Aoi. Throughout this conversation, Dennis O'Rourke reminds us of his presence as a mediator not through voice-over, such as provided by Roc, but through the placement of the camera and the occasional, actually rare, insertion of his interview question. We see the two women from the point of view of the filmmaker, who sits across from them on the other side of the table. The camera must be right at his chest for the women keep looking at him, right next to the lens. He is right there, the choreography announces, among these prostitutes in Thailand. He brings us to the table as these women talk "candidly." The conversation is somber; however much of this is due to the friend's palpable discomfort and slow hesitant speech. When she speaks, she looks intently at Aoi and smiles awkwardly, as if unaccustomed to speaking about their work so publicly, especially in front of a camera held by a Western man. When not speaking, she appears distressed as she sucks on her cigarette. The women both look down at the end of their conversation. And then Aoi looks up at the filmmaker, waiting for his cue as if to ask: have you gotten what you wanted? In these scenes of public intimacy, we may assess the limits of their collaboration, his mediation, and her representation. But because sex and "love" with the prostitute authorize our entry into this public discussion of sex, the sight of that foundational relation would enable us to see the dramatic relation of power.

Within the scenarios represented in *101 Asian Debutantes,* the visible physical expressions of Asian women's bodily and psychic torments as well as pleasures provide contradictory assessments. Roc's explicit speech is required to tame the perceptual truths of sex tourism displayed in the images. Words narrating the women's smallness, brown-ness, and shape create a tension against the visual representation that overflows with the political economic situation of sex tourist exploitation. In conversation with Roc's narration, the visual powerfully presents the unequal conditions that force these women into sexual labor while also presenting the women in the throes of pleasure. While the ability to say no as a prostitute within the sex tourism scene is quite limited, the recalcitrant body speaks powerfully to remind us of the laboring dimensions and physical demands of human relations within prostitution and sex tourism. The work presents structures of inequality in place, while displacing the seeming solidity of linguistic and bodily speech and conveying personhoods and relationships transpiring in the scene of sex tourism.

Like Dennis O'Rourke, Jean Marc Roc in *101 Asian Debutantes* presents the Asian women as his "collaborators," for he supposedly records them in an unbiased way through the "gonzo" form. I isolate the bodily presence of the prostitute through which Roc focuses entirely on narrating and showing her body in its sexual being. Supposedly, Roc simply delivers who these prostitutes already really are. This same purposeful construct describes female labor in international tourism, whose conglomerates benefit from the availability of sexual services as a major source of revenue. But as we see from Aoi's speech, women's movements into the sex industry are motivated, as always, by the need to support families and the need for survival through work. This runs contrary to Roc's claim that they desire to serve white men and perform "exotic" sex.

The sex and gender order in the neocolonial political economy shows up in sex tourist hard-core gonzo through the performance of sex acts as labor, the dire settings where actions occur, and the representation of poverty such as in the paucity of the women's accoutrements against the wealth required for the shoot. At the same time that the john commodifies the Asian woman's size, body, hair, and skin in the interests of constituting a Western male masculinity (as powerful and big), the very same problematic representation speaks also to the particular subjectivity of the Asian woman. The Asian woman demonstrates that she has some access to the power of representation through her visual presence in terms of location, her clothing and cosmetics, and her relationship with the director and the camera as indicated in her performance.

In terms of location, the prostitute is a being of the particular space, meaning that she could not be the subject required if it were not for the accoutrements, objects, and space surrounding her. Her status and identity are secured by the horrible cheap motel room, the thin yellow sheets, noise from the cars, and the street too close by, as well as the bar. One speaks through her dress and her use of underwear so big that she can fold it easily into an inventive thong. Some of the other women wear very feminine, up-to-date, or fashionable lingerie. Their nails are long and manicured. Their bodies are well-groomed, featuring shaved pubic hair, stylish haircuts, and skillfully applied makeup in a specific fashion of bright red lips or other, more natural, but nonetheless made-up looks. Frequently the means of production are apparent in the sex scenes as the women lie on wires and microphones and negotiate tripods placed close to the bed.

What I will call "prostitute portraiture," reminiscent of colonial photographs such as in the work of Malek Alloula, intersperses the tapes by Jean Marc Roc.[42] The scenes are a way for the women to be introduced as a kind of advertising for the upcoming sex scene or for the next tape wherein the particular woman is featured. For example, in the fourth tape, individual women are featured lounging in soft lighting, as if for a formal portrait. The first woman is dressed in white lace lingerie with a garter belt, panties, and a flimsy bra. In a characteristic shot by Roc, the camera pans across her entire body as she poses on her side. Her face, made up in brown eye shadow, arched eyebrows, blushing cheeks, and red vibrant lips, is framed by silky lavender sheets. Her red manicured nails graze her face as she begins to caress herself all over her body and masturbate. Eventually, Jean Marc Roc joins her, asking her to try out his penis. Later on, she changes to a black, short corset-style bra and a matching thong as she masturbates again. These beauty shots act as sexual portraits of the women, who seem to enjoy their own sexual stimulation within a setting lit and set up for the individual, before engaging in intercourse with Roc. At the end of the fourth tape, Jean Marc introduces "a sneak peak at Jeana, she's hot!" Located in a comfortable room that contains a futon, Jeana casually lounges to show off her body, which is dressed seductively. Her hair is tousled and her face completely made up. She looks at the camera with sexual confidence, boldness, and self-assurance. The glamour shots of her face looking at the camera intently are interspersed with shots of her face with semen all over it. While the women work with the camera in a particular self-presentation that Roc appropriates as non-victimized (in other words, he presents them as simply willing and sexual beings) in his video catalogue, he sells their primary purpose: to be universally and perpetually available sexually.

Roc gives the women the opportunity to speak directly to the camera. One describes herself as if meeting a pen pal or a potential husband. (On his website, Roc mentions the willingness of some women to "hook up" with Asiaerotic.com members, those who share Roc's fetish for Asian women.) One Filipina-looking woman says she would like to meet someone. Soon after, Roc has sex with her. Whether this is the third take or the only take, the construction of the woman as desperate is underlined. The shoot captures humiliation to extract eroticism. The prostitute speaks nonetheless and articulates a subject position that expresses desire to meet someone from the West and perhaps stop this kind of work. It lends a kind of authenticity to the tape in the sense that the consumer can actually get this very same woman for himself. While the prostitute understands that she reaches out to the camera and the consumers out there, beyond the room, she engages the camera within the sex scenes as well.

The women's bodily engagements with the camera are extraordinarily diverse so that questions about their experiences cannot be generalized into one experience. One woman masturbates while finding the best way to show off her vagina and fingers in relation to the camera position. Jean Marc Roc often shoots the same women, from tape to tape, months and years apart. In the fourth tape, he tapes a couple of Korean women in 1988 and again ten years later. Their camaraderie appears in their conversations, in which there is plenty of joking around. However, he still directs, commands, and instructs them. The women display a familiarity with his parameters. While he directs a camerawoman to get a close-up, one of the women interrupts and says, "No, I will show you. I will show you. I will show you, the close-up" as she manipulates the movements of his body and hers. It is uncertain if the camerawoman is a westerner or another prostitute in occasional scenes in which Roc performs both roles as john and camera operator. At this juncture, this lack of clarity says a great deal about the speaking that is possible for the prostitute. While Roc does not purport to craft art or make political work, the gonzo porn as largely shot in real time may allow for more room for the women to represent themselves.

To continue the scene, Roc then attempts to kiss the prostitute, and she says, "No, this is better" and motions toward their genitalia in intercourse. In one part, he tells the larger of the two women that she has a "good pussy" and that he "likes it." She responds positively and they have sex, wherein she gyrates and works to please him as they embrace and kiss each other. The thinner woman is entirely professional in demeanor while this occurs and "helps" by pumping his penis with her hand and caressing his testicles. The bigger woman shields her face in myriad ways throughout the scene. She turns away from the camera and hides behind the thin woman and her own disheveled hair. She even retreats from the scene entirely. The thinner woman's performance as an eager participant is emphasized by the distance of the larger woman. While the conversations are friendly, the work relationship is never forsaken. When the larger woman retreats from the camera, Roc commands her to come here, "Now!" The sex scene ends with a "thank you" from one of the women as they laugh, lounge, and look in the mirrors to evaluate their post-coital appearances as Roc lingers on.

In earlier tapes where Roc brings in women he's previously engaged, he describes their previous sexual relationships and which particular activities they enjoy while performing them. For example, he describes Number 26 as having facial expressions that express enjoyment. The scenes begin with women grooming themselves, putting on makeup, adjusting their outfits, and fixing their hair. There are scenes where he simply masturbates them to the point of orgasm, which is signaled by audible results and physical convulsions that seem out of control. He uses a diversity of dildos that the women supposedly love and at times steal. And he does not come himself. Another woman in the fourth tape grabs his head to pull him down closer as he performs cunnilingus.

In the second act of the second tape of *101 Asian Debutantes*, the prostitute Number 26 demonstrates awareness of aesthetics for the purpose of arousal. Huge granny underwear transforms into an interesting contraption of rolled fabric acting like a g-string. She is thin, as thin as he is thick. She moves with caution as he moves without, brashly throwing sheets about as she sits or stands quietly with full attention toward him. The visual registry of plain sheets, the extreme smallness of the room, and its sparseness signal loud and clear the cheap, red-light district quality of a room for sex. The proximity of the outside is constant and close. Cars seem to be right outside the window, with cops whistling and the sounds of general bustling. If one were to draw the curtain, the street might fall into the room. In spite of his narration of her love for sex over the need for money, these scenes cannot be understood outside her role as a worker. As articulated by Sturdevant and Stolzfus, the women of the third world are there to serve men who are at play—despite Roc's words to the contrary.[43]

At the end of the first tape, a Filipina woman reclines comfortably with Roc, her face cradled in the nook of his shoulder as she looks at herself in the camera monitor, adjusting her facial position to be more flattering as they lounge. They have a long conversation about whether he should use a condom. She attempts to cajole him into using one. The sex they eventually have does not include one. In these scenes, while a certain familiar relationship is obvious between the john and the prostitute, the power dynamics still bring into question the politics of collaboration. The visual unreliability of the women's orgasm also puts in doubt their pleasure. But to deny the prostitutes' abilities to converse with Jean Marc Roc or other customers, to laugh as they do, to experience sexual pleasure, and to have a relationship is to ignore the complexity of their subject positions or to totalize them into a victim identity without the contradictions of projecting fantasy on the johns as the johns project fantasy upon them.[44]

I now return to the Asian woman numbered 71 whose gaze warrants attention as represented in the first sex scene of *101 Asian Debutantes*:

Babes in Thailand, the second video in the series. Roc tapes her as she masturbates for him and the camera. Throughout this long scene, she looks at herself in the monitor and adjusts herself within the frame. She keeps looking at herself, arranging her hair in various ways as she composes the frame that we see. She changes her position and then looks at the camera to check what it looks like. She smiles at one particular arrangement of herself. Prompting him to come into the scene, she continues to stare and stare at the monitor. Then she begins to the stare at the camera herself, while he penetrates her from behind. She no longer stares at the monitor that mirrors her, but at the camera that acts as a stand-in for the viewer. Her face is the central site of emotional expression. And her look, unyielding and focused, is powerful. While it secures the bodily pain and pleasure she feels in the moments of sex, I wonder if her stare makes uncomfortable the arousal extracted from a sexual transaction between the powerful and the less powerful, or if it creates a discomfort for the viewer as it ruptures the narration of the "little brown fucking machine," or if her look at the camera heightens the eroticism for male viewers interested in consuming her specific status. For me, her humanity emerges in contrast to Roc's fetishization of her exterior. The extent of the prostitute's speech in the scene above is "Me horny" and "I like it" and "Do you like it?" "I like you." "Thanks." "You're welcome." In *The Good Woman of Bangkok,* the speech performed by both men and women discount each other in their oppositionality. In this scene, her limited words contradict a more complex experience in the sex act. The contradiction attests to her situation as bound by sex work, caught in sexual servitude that also produces physical pleasures and the possibility of desire for her client.

CONCLUSION

In both *The Good Woman of Bangkok* and *101 Asian Debutantes,* the films' overwhelming visual representation of inequality is accompanied by pleasure and enjoyment as well as pain. The first film offers the intimacy of representing the sexual subject fully clothed and not engaged in sex; the second series offers sex itself—fucking, kissing, physically connecting—captured by a combination of vérité and traditional porn and documentary practice. The work presents the structures of inequality in place, while displacing the seeming solidity of linguistic and bodily speech and conveying complex personhoods and relationships transpiring in the scene of sex tourism. What is captured is a world of desperation coexisting with enjoyment.

These films show the difficulty of assessing race, sex, and representation. What we learn is that each act and each representation is a site of power relations. For each subject, the quality of unknowability and unreliability have different implications. Furthermore, the filmmakers' speech cannot capture the excessive facticity of the visual world. By shooting in the gonzo style within the scene of sex tourism in Southeast Asia, both filmmakers expose the gross inequality between Western men and the objects of their desire. Within these films, the place and the people speak with their looks, their very presence, and their world, in ways that contradict the film-maker. In a sense, the filmmaker and his terms can be superfluous against the world of Asian women speaking as both seeing subjects and viewed objects, especially to particular viewers. However, the viewer too cannot simply claim multiplicity in viewing position, for the terms of representation are limited by the inequalities organizing these stories.

From an intimate authenticating position, O'Rourke claims to capture the veracity of the situation, while Roc works hard to discipline the location and the women so that they succumb to his terms. Both film production and viewing are intersubjective experiences within and between each other. Film itself is a subject that acts in every situation of its viewing. And like the native before the viewer, it also sees back and creates a powerful response.

The intersubjectivity possible in these films is the unknowability of relations across difference rather than their directability and containment. In *The Good Woman of Bangkok*, Aoi has a presence that can be felt in concrete terms not contained by the director. She has an ambiguity that we sense is not captured by O'Rourke's words. While we cannot know the Other, there are ways in which the Other speaks within and against the constraints of the film. Film creates corporeal presences before the eye and in the space of the camera that speak volumes about the personhoods before us. Unlike O'Rourke, who presents her as somewhat knowable, we must remember the limits of representation. In *101 Asian Debutantes*, the prostitutes refuse the filmmaker's narration through the disturbing power of their own returned gaze and the enactment of pain or enjoyment articulated through sexual performance. Furthermore, the gaze and the body speak of certain beings historically situated through their clothes, choreography, gazes, and the ways in which they mobilize their surroundings. The power of the prostitute's visual situation within her world implicates the filmmaker in ways that he cannot easily control.

Although complex and fascinating, the possibilities of resistance in these films are quite limited, telling us something different about agency itself as fleeting and difficult to assess. The white male filmmakers attempt to direct their representation of women in ways that render themselves heroic. My concerns are for the possibility of the women's agency to remain more open—not quite tangible yet nonetheless possible. The central issue is to accept the limits of representation, especially when emphasizing the power of interpretation from our specific viewing position and when filmmakers claim the special position of presenting these women in representation. In *The Good Woman of Bangkok,* defiance of the conventions should also demonstrate a critical awareness of the filmmakers' limits as well as the limits of representation so as to avoid ultimately relying on the presentation of authentic, collaborating subjects. I make this demand in order to hold out for an ethical filmmaking not premised on the secondary status of Asian women. My readings of the various technical aspects of the cinema—performance, directing, camera work, and design—offer multiple presentations of the Southeast Asian prostitute that make any authenticity hard to claim. In presenting themselves as enjoying sex with johns, or eroticizing their pain and poverty, or participating in "collaboration," the prostitutes in these films present a multiplicity of Asian women whose truths are actually more inaccessible than is acknowledged by the Western male authors who claim to present their authenticity. Different voices emerge for me as an Asian American feminist viewer.

The problem is not so much a matter of whether Western men can say anything at all about sex tourism, as Linda Williams frames.[45] The question is, when Western men present these images as collaborations, how much awareness, not only of the power dynamics but of the limits of representation itself to communicate ethical conundra, is accounted for? While both Dennis O'Rourke and Jean Marc Roc claim to love their subjects, both also describe their work as collaborations with prostitutes. And for both, the disjuncture between the object and the intertextual opportunities to open up discussion of the representational process is not adequately taken up. That is, while both of these Western male filmmakers purport to discuss the uniqueness of their position, they nevertheless present essentially sexual identities for Asian women, thus ensuring their further marginalization.[46] Considering the popularity of these works in speaking for these women, the contentious meanings of the physical and emotional expression of the prostitutes must be part of cultural discourse.

I conclude this meditation by emphasizing the importance of interpretation. Sex is the primary site of contestation over the making and unmaking of Asian female legibility in popular culture. Focusing on the prostitute's gaze, speaking back in defiance of representation, allows us to recognize the possible subversion of pornography and documentary conventions from unintended spectators, such as me, who attempt to center the lives and representations of third world women, and to open up to their powerful presence in representation. While the prostitutes' "speech" in Roc's work may not be intentionally or ultimately political or subversive, I assert the importance of an Asian Americanist feminist reading to recast the meaning of their voices beyond the transcendental through the insistence on situating the physical and psychic responses of the viewer and of the subjects viewed. Like other feminist theorists who assess the possibilities of resistance by the marginalized, I insist that Southeast Asian prostitutes are not beings simply overdetermined by race and economics, but subjects who engage technologies of the visual and the sexual in order to write themselves into the historical record. They do so as bound subjects, caught in the business of sex while also demonstrating contradictory acts, including desire and enjoyment simultaneously expressed within a dynamic of labor/leisure and pain/pleasure.

7 ❋

THE POLITICAL POWER OF
HYPERSEXUALITY IN ASIAN AMERICAN
FEMINIST FILMS

The film *La Señorita Lee* (1995) begins with Jeannie, a short-haired Korean American woman in Daisy-Duke shorts and combat boots who works in a grocery store, strutting across the rough, dirty, and brown streets of Los Angeles. Though pregnant by her Mexican lover, who must leave the country, Jeannie faces pressure to marry a "dull doctor" approved by her family to cover up what they deem improper whorish behavior. Playing the lead role, the Asian American feminist filmmaker Hyun Mi Oh films herself naked in the mirror as the character contemplates her newly pregnant body, the fleshy evidence of her carnal desires and the subject of condemnation by her community. She's staring herself down in the mirror. At stake in the collision between her needs and her family's reputation is her self-definition. Within the nature and function of sex in Asian/American women's lives and the representation and aesthetic of sex in cinema and performance, how do discourses of panic and fear regarding Asian female hypersexuality marginalize women who wrestle with the contradictions, traumas, and joys of the racial experience of which sexuality is intrinsically a part? A deeper, more contradictory, and complex definition of sexuality and representation needs to inform discourses of race so that fantasy exceeds a determining relationship to reality when we approach sexual representations. As Lynn Segal argues, "There is no straightforward connection between dynamics of desire as fantasy and the satisfactions sought in material reality. Rather, fantasy is its own object in the sense that it allows for multiple identifications across differing people [and] positions."[1] Fantasies are individual and group idealizations and projections of desire. Frequently, the terms of one's fantasies are grounded in but also exceed one's circumstances. If we understand hypersexual representations by Asian American women as articulations of fantasies, they present enabling new freedoms and new subjectivities, especially in redefining the tradition of hypersexuality for Asian/American women.

Fantasy, representation, race, and sexuality need to be understood as complex formations, especially in terms of understanding Asian American feminist filmmakers who produce "bad objects," or representations of "improper" sexual acts and "inappropriate" identities, as social critiques of gender, race, bourgeois, and sexual heteronormativity. Through bad object production, Asian women feminist filmmakers assert struggles for recognition that build from the work of Asian queer filmmakers who "center the margins" by privileging non-normative experience, such as Richard Fung, Midi Onodera, Mari Keiko Gonzales, Shu Lea Cheang, and Pratibha Parmar—most of whom, notably, are film practitioners based outside the United States.[2]

In *The Love Thang Trilogy* (1994), Mari Keiko Gonzales successfully narrates the complexity of desire in Asian American lesbians' lives. Speaking from the specificity of very particular stories, her experimental narratives achieve a complex layering of race, gender, class, and sexuality. In the first vignette, desire for another Asian lesbian behind the frozen yogurt counter is expressed within a self-conscious assessment of the power of looking at an Asian woman within the context of violence against Asian women. The next piece, *Skydyking,* celebrates the outburst of sexual expression for another, a desire that must be silenced within the woman's family. The final vignette, *Eating Mango,* problematizes desire across racial and cultural difference. In these stories, the subjectivity and desires of the Asian lesbian protagonist are unapologetically presented as worthwhile and fun stories to tell.

Similarly, but not in the context of Asian American lesbianism per se, the filmmakers I discuss in this chapter—Helen Lee, Grace Lee, and Machiko Saito—prioritize their characters' own individual sexualized needs and redefine the terms of their legibility in a world where Asian women are too frequently rendered as secondary subjects within ethnic, feminist, and film studies. Moreover, the women in their films claim a diversity of sexualities in order to reject normative definitions of proper womanhood and proper racial being. Most importantly, these filmmakers insist on representing sex as central, perhaps even a dominant undergirding thematic in the narratives of their films. Sex is the site where racial subjectivities form and reform, class collides, and gender unravels as the self forms and transforms. These filmmakers offer a redefinition and expansion of sexuality as an aesthetic and as an organizer of race, class, and gender experiences.

The films by Lee, Lee, and Saito certainly depend on and are enabled by works that emerge from women of color film authorships by Hyun Mi Oh, Dawn Suggs, Cheryl Dunye, Julie Dash, Frances Negron, Shu Lea Cheang (and her queer women of color filmmakers' group, ET Baby Maniac), Midi Onodera, Mari Keiko Gonzales, and Pratibha Parmar. In these other women's works, sexuality is explicit, intrinsically part of one's subjectivity and a key site for pleasures and politics. Sexual desires, identities, acts, and communities are represented in films that assert that the racial experience of Asian women and women of color is imbricated and bonded with gender and sex. So rendering of the bondage of sexuality and the bind of representation as both traumatic and pleasurable is not solely found in the work of Asian American feminist filmmakers but is also found within a transnational comparative cultural context, especially alongside films by Clint Black, Nguyen Tan Hoang, Isaac Julien, Marlon Riggs, and other makers of color, primarily queer, working boldly in the explicit visualization of racialized sex acts as events that bind and liberate bodies, tongues, and consciousness.[3]

Close readings of the racialized sexuality in the films of Helen Lee, Grace Lee, and Machiko Saito show how they rewrite norms for properly racial, gendered, and sexual women by disconnecting their racialized sexuality from their ontology. That is, the attribution of hypersexuality as "natural" to their race and gender does not capture the process of subjection they must undergo. So while the Asian female characters in their films may be sexually available and sexy, their subjectivities are forged within and beyond their racial-sexual bonds. In their films, as well as within my interviews with Lee, Lee, and Saito, I then focus on the ways in which they assert a new epistemology, or ways of knowing Asian women, in terms of moving image and living image representational practices and methods.

Finally, I show how Asian American feminist filmmakers who represent sexually explicit moving images create new morphologies or new forms and structures of legibility for Asian women in representation. Their reclamations of hypersexuality describe struggles for recognition that require corporeal understandings of race, sexuality, gender, and representation. The definition of aberrant and perverse sexuality offered by these independent filmmakers returns us to everyday, ordinary sexuality that plays an integral part in Asian/American women's lives.

In the last six chapters, hypersexuality is defined primarily through Hollywood and other institutions as well as white male fantasies of Asian women in pornography. In this chapter, my study of the zipless fuck, the one-night stand, the easy Asian girl, and the incest survivor shows how Asian American feminist filmmakers define and characterize Asian American women's sexual representations through identities critical of bourgeois heteronormative tradition but which, in their presentation of practices, are not overdetermined by their sexual choices. Beyond aspiring to the normal, or returning to Renee Tajima's demand for more ordinary representations of Asian women in film, I long for redefining ordinary not to mean fearful asexual politics.[4] Rather, a redefinition of sexuality must transpire to include what has been typically classified as perverse, whether queer sex acts, lesbianism, sadomasochism, prostitution, asexuality, masturbation, or other non-normative identities, acts, and practices that do not demand morality, chastity, and demureness that discipline women.

SEX AND FUCKING IN ASIAN AMERICAN FEMINIST FILMS

The works of the three filmmakers concluding my study exemplify independent Asian American feminist films concerned with the production of sexuality for Asian/American women in cinema and performance. The first set of works is by the important filmmaker Helen Lee, whose body of work spans a significant fifteen years, an amazing feat for any independent filmmaker. Grace Lee, one of the most prominent emergent independent filmmakers working today, as cited by *Filmmaker Magazine,* initiated her career by making the documentary *Camp Arirang* (1996), a film about "base women" or prostitutes working near U.S. military bases in Korea. She received a Student Academy Award for her narrative film *Barrier Device* (2001), and she continues to make films about Asian American female subjectivity, as evidenced by her recent documentary, *The Grace Lee Project*

(2005), a film about people named Grace Lee—whom she describes as the "quintessential Asian American woman."[5] Machiko Saito considers film just another avenue for expressing and exploring life. In award-winning, internationally screened experimental films and a visually powerful everyday persona, Saito's works emerge from the San Francisco queer, film, and youth communities in order to create spectatorial and authorial discomforts that lead to broader and more inclusive definitions of sexual and other diversity.

For the filmmakers Helen Lee, Grace Lee, and Machiko Saito, the public tradition of racialized sexuality in Western representation shapes the subjectivities of Asian/American women in their work. What ties these Asian female filmmakers together are the ways in which they explore the meaning of sexuality and race as deeply mired in each other. They present Asian female characters as sexual beings in the sense of desiring bodily pleasure within the context of pain—expressing and building upon the bind of representation that emerges from a moving image history of Asian American female hypersexuality. Informed by the cinematic legacy of Asian female-white male liaisons of hypersexuality, these Asian American filmmakers craft different relational formations. For example, the filmmaker Helen Lee starts at the point of masturbation, critiques white male objects, prefers black male objects, and presents hypersexuality as a mole to scrape away. Such struggles for recognition are also present through reimaginings of hypersexuality in the Asian female fetish via domestic and transnational interracial sex with various nonwhite men in Helen Lee's *Sally's Beauty Spot* (1990), *Prey* (1995), and *Subrosa* (2000) and with an Asian man in *My Niagara* (1994).

In the other films, how do filmmakers construct racialized sexual difference—between two Asian women characters in Grace Lee's award-winning film *Barrier Device* as well as her new work, *The Grace Lee Project*, and in Machiko Saito's powerful auto-ethnographic performances? My discussions of their works are also supported by interviews conducted with Helen Lee in Toronto, Seoul, and Santa Barbara in 2001–2004, Grace Lee in Santa Barbara in April 2004, and Machiko Saito in San Francisco in June 2004 and Santa Barbara in 2005.

REWRITING ASIAN/AMERICAN WOMEN IN THE SEX ACT:
THE FILMS OF HELEN LEE

Helen Lee's first film announces the arrival of a body of work that renders a different Asian female than the hypersexual one established in popular culture. In *Sally's Beauty Spot,* an Asian woman obsesses about *The World of Suzie Wong* (1960). This popular Hollywood hit established in contemporary terms, as well as in expressive colloquialisms, the fantasy of the sexy self-sacrificing Asian woman. Peter Feng describes it as the film Asian Americans "love to hate." In his essay, "Recuperating Suzie Wong: A Fan's Nancy Kwan-Dary," Feng capturing the "quandary" faced by spectators who find themselves enjoying this film. Defying criticisms that remain in the realm of whether the film is racist or not, or even analyses that deny pleasure at Suzie's sassy subversions and compliance, Feng identifies the complexity of engaging in visual culture as spectators. He describes the process of reconciling his political criticism of racist films with his fan status: "To be a fan of Nancy Kwan, the spectator of color has to forget more than she or he remembers, and to flatter oneself as a resistant spectator is to be forever aware of the narrative context from which one has mentally excerpted images of defiance."[6] Feng captures the conundrum of taking what is useful and leaving what is painful, presenting it as a difficult and perverse spectatorial process employed by spectators of color. Following Jessica Hagedorn's appreciation of Suzie Wong's sassiness, sauciness, and stylishness,[7] Feng opens the discussion of the rich relationship between spectator and actor, moving beyond discussions of the relationship between spectator and film. Helen Lee furthers this discussion by speaking as a filmmaker directly to the powerful image of Suzie Wong within her own images.

Within the film *Sally's Beauty Spot,* a voice asks the protagonist why she loves the movie *The World of Suzie Wong* so much. Sally responds, "It has always been there ever since I was a little girl." So the film acknowledges how representation provides a historical context for her subjects as well as for her authorship in confronting the powerful legacy of Suzie Wong. Lee develops a multilayered cinematic language to express how film shapes the Asian woman's self-recognition in the mirror as well as her interracial heterosexual relationships. *The World of Suzie Wong,* as a wide-reaching cultural exemplar, is presented as shaping what people know about Asian/American women and how such knowledge extends to the level of intimate relations. Lee does not, however, render a direct link between representation and the real in a film that is situated within a story of one woman scrubbing her mole (a symbol of Asian female fetishism) and her self-perceptions via the movies and a number of interracial relationships.

Made in the early 1990s, *Sally's Beauty Spot* fits squarely within the outburst of experimental film work by women of color.[8] Experimental in a form aimed to capture how cinematic representation shapes the roles, traumas, and pleasures of hypersexual representation for Asian/American women, the three visual and aural thematic threads constituting *Sally's Beauty Spot* are shots of Sally by herself or in relation to a black or a white man, shots of women with moles on their faces, and distorted excerpts from *The World of Suzie Wong*. The audio involves various voice-overs of conversations between Sally and others, readings of text from the postcolonial theorist Homi Bhabha, the feminist film critic Tania Modleski, the philosopher Emmanuel Levinas, and conversations from *The World of Suzie Wong*. Lee stitches together these scenes and conversations in order to represent the Asian woman through the black mole on her body as a fetishized vision of Asian/American women.

Helen Lee uses the mole to represent the Asian woman as a fetish, a mole staining skin and psyche abrasively. It is especially apparent as the body encounters others who interpellate Asian female racial visibility as signifying a particularly hypersexual ontology. The mole is a fetish or an unsuitable sexual substitute for the desired Asian woman herself. I define fetishism according to Freud, who describes the process of replacing the normal sexual object "with another, which bears some relation to it, but is entirely unsuited to serve the normal sexual aim."[9] The Asian woman, not ideal to white reproduction, fulfills the non-normal, especially compared to the white woman. In *Sally's Beauty Spot,* the mole functions as the projection of the Asian woman's desirability by others, such as the fascination with her fragmented body parts. As a fetish, her subjection is an objectification, a sexual aberration that causes distress in a discourse apparently internalized. In the film, others see her as a sexual object with the help of emblems from popular culture such as Suzie Wong, a ghostly figure who interrupts the scene of life through her presence as fantasy. Suzie Wong is a fetish within the narrative of *The World of Suzie Wong* and the film as well—as the character is fetishized upon in *Sally's Beauty Spot*. In this sense, the Asian woman is a fetish herself: an unsuitable sexual substitute for the Asian/American woman who lives under the sign of Suzie Wong but who does not fulfill her sexual objectification properly.

Helen Lee establishes a world where popular images about the Asian woman inform relations with others as well as one's own body. The image of Suzie Wong plays continuously as the Asian woman in *Sally's Beauty Spot* stares at herself in the mirror and voice-overs link her to Wong dancing at the bar and flipping her hair as she moves in a sexual manner.

The black silky hair becomes a marker of the Asian woman's sexuality. In the shot, Suzie exudes a powerful sexuality and desirability by wagging her hips side to side and swaying her hair as she turns. The scene is choreographed so that the sexy Asian woman is in the center of the room and the focal point of the shot with the light organized around her as the key figure. The academic text, in voice-over, pushes this point further by saying that signifiers such as "silky and black hair" unify the Asian woman on screen and the Asian woman watching the film. The set of looking relations, to use Jane Gaines's term, between Suzie, Sally, and the mirror, shows the Asian woman on screen as a production of sexuality that the living Sally, the Asian American female subject, cannot embody.[10]

In *Sally's Beauty Spot*, Asian women cannot live up to the production of sexy womanhood. The footage of Sally combing her hair becomes a sequence of close-ups of other Asian/American women with moles on their faces. The freeze-framed, still shots show the women looking directly into the camera with serious expressions on their faces. The voice-over going along with this series of shots is an interview with Sally regarding her mole, with eerie and suspenseful music:

> INTERVIEWER: Tell me, Sally, when did you start becoming aware of it?
> SALLY: When my breasts started to grow.
> INTERVIEWER: And how did you feel about that?
> SALLY: The growing?
> INTERVIEWER: No, the blemish.

The eyes of the Asian women with various moles look directly at the camera as the voice-over continues. A fetish for the Asian woman herself, the mole is, to use Lee's word, a "blemish" they live with, in a clear and persistently present way, as is argued by the film. An exhilarating illustration of the specter of hypersexuality Asian women live under, the collection of faces represents a dazzling diversity of women who share similar markings that occupy their faces differently. The voice-over directly posits the incongruence between the lives of Asian/American women and the sexual fantasy about Asian women. The film then focuses on how the mole traumatizes Sally, showing her in a close-up in which she is naked from the mole up, washing it scrupulously. She says, "It's the first thing I see when I look in the mirror" as she rubs it vigorously, as if trying to erase it and scour it away as it threatens to engulf her own coming of age. She covers it with liquid makeup, but the black won't fade.

Sally attempts to cover her mole
in *Sally's Beauty Spot.*

Through sex and the role of her mole within the sex act, Sally recognizes
her own status as a fetish. Sally kisses an unnamed white man. In the
frame, they enter from opposite sides in a medium close-up. These shots
are intercut with the violent confrontation between Suzie Wong and Robert Lomax about her European dress. He chastises her, "You look like a
cheap European streetwalker!" She yells back, "You shut up!" We cut to
Sally and her white man trying to meet lips. We return to Suzie on the
receiving end of Lomax's strangely violent rage. In disgust at her Western
clothes, Lomax yells, "Why not put a ring in your nose too!" At this
juncture, the academic voice-over punctures the scene by describing the
desirable and lovable quality of the horrific. Slavoj Žižek describes any
intimate relation of touch and sexual intimacy as a shocking scene we
must cope with through fantasies about ourselves and the Other in the
sexual act.[11] The coexistence of these seemingly contradictory characteristics makes further sense when we recall the volatility of the subjects' inner
lives before the sex act even transpires. Recall the triangulation of Suzie
Wong as character, actress, and person. So while Suzie may be a prostitute,
she is also the "good woman," different from the Western woman, and
different from the prostitute herself. The scenes of her sexual encounters
with white men is loaded with the exchange of power. Helen Lee's film
extends this dynamic to Sally and the unnamed white man as they return
to the frame while almost kissing with open mouths. The sex scene is
isolated in order to capture its location as a meeting point for different
subjectivities. Moreover, to intercut the kissing scene with the Hollywood
film shows how the popular enters the intimate. And the production of sex
for the Asian woman by the white man enters the authorship of an Asian
Canadian filmmaker concerned with Asian women. The kissing scene

between the white man and the Asian woman is undercut, however, as if to say *Sally's Beauty Spot* should not have to bear the burden of this traditional representation.

In the kissing scene, the accompanying voice-over provides a link between the self/other meeting in the Suzie Wong film and in Sally's own sexual interaction with a white man.

> MAN: Were you born with it? Can I see how it feels?
> SALLY: Don't touch it please.
> WOMAN (suddenly): Have you considered surgical methods of removal?

Inside the moment of the kiss, representing the intimacy of her relation, the white man's voice remains at the level of the fetishistic. The mole fascinates the white man within the sex act, a comment regarding the way fetishism works. He is not focused on her subjectivity but on her objectification as part of his sexual aims. Again, Suzie Wong herself is a fetishized object. In the *Suzie Wong* scene intercut into *Sally's Beauty Spot,* we see that the white man rejects Suzie's Western costume. Lomax is linked to the unnamed white man in *Sally's Beauty Spot* for they both prefer an essential Asian woman to fulfill their desires. They both reject the women standing before them, preferring the fantasy. Lomax, in *Suzie Wong,* falls for her truly, vanquishing all resistance, only when she becomes the woman he wants, traditionally outfitted in the gown of a Chinese empress.

Sally's Beauty Spot closes with an exploration of interracial kissing between the white man and the Asian woman in the *World of Suzie Wong.* We intercut to Suzie and Lomax as she now wears a traditional Chinese outfit. Suzie then kneels on top of the stairs and Lomax stands before her in awe. She instructs him on how to kiss her properly despite her large headdress. "You tilt your head," she says. He responds, "Clever, these Chinese." Lomax then sweeps Suzie off her feet and kisses her deeply as she lies in his arms. She is the disciplined Asian woman now, existing for him as entirely good, entirely ancient. She returns to the premodern construct, erases her status as prostitute, and becomes eligible to be his wife. As such, the scene deals with perceptions of the fetish and the exotic among two individuals. Helen Lee critiques this scenario by refusing the white man's kiss within her own film and instead accepting the black man's—and in doing so, she rewrites the established "white knight" scenario well argued by Gina Marchetti.[12]

Rather than pairing Asian female sexuality with a white man's, her sexuality is partnered with a black man's in *Sally's Beauty Spot*. The kiss and the embrace, for the black man in *Sally's Beauty Spot*, reverses the violence done unto the Asian woman by the misrecognition and self-erasure symbolized by *The World of Suzie Wong*. Sally smiles, her lipstick matte thick. Helen Lee edits together love for the black man versus the violence of self-hating comments about the body. In the film, the Asian woman prefers the realm of shared Otherness, or mutual recognition, rather than objectification by the white man. The film, however, does not simply counter white-Asian pairings. It also establishes a critical spectatorial relationship to *The World of Suzie Wong* as a misrecognition of Asian female sexuality through Sally's reflective response.

Helen Lee describes the role of sex in the film as follows: "In *Sally's Beauty Spot*, the sexual thematics of the piece are treated lightly, allusively and symbolically, with various almost-kisses that lead up to the final one with the black lover that finally breaks her illusions."[13] The sex act in this sequence, the kiss between the black man and the Asian woman, comments on the way fetishization of the Asian woman finds hypersexual commonality in that of the black man. She recognizes herself in his Otherness and, presumably, he recognizes himself in hers—both rendered in hypersexuality. In a sense, the Asian woman's sexuality is constructed like that of the black man and here linked in mutual desire.

The academic voice-over comments, "Good object—which object?" as the black man and Asian woman kiss on screen. In the final shot of the sequence, the black man's lips occupy the whole screen. Sally's lips, outlined severely with matte color, dissolve onto his. She smiles. The black man's lips and the Asian woman's matte lips meet in the film as a recognition that the fetishization of their body parts, as substitutes for the whole Other, works similarly for the racialized sexuality of the black man. They are both bad object choices, as lovers, and in their choosing each other as a better match than the white male-Asian female formation, they question the very forces of their objectifications.

In order to recognize herself, Sally meets with others who are similarly fetishized. Helen Lee describes the sex act in *Sally's Beauty Spot* as the moment where Sally comes "to realize the process of her objectification." She continues: "The sexual dimension has an inexorable quality—of being propelled by social circumstance or driven by personal pursuits. Sexual identity [is] inextricably tied to racial, social dimensions of the self. As a

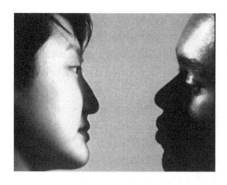

The Asian woman chooses the black man in *Sally's Beauty Spot*.

filmmaker, I try to bring a more subversive or playful quality to these scenes without them being overtly either, to keep things ambiguous and alive."[14] In the film, Sally's response to it is not rage but ambivalence. She herself finds Suzie fascinating and uses the footage from the film to fuel her sexual life. In this short film, Lee signals the importance of sexual racialization as experienced by the Asian woman vis-à-vis popular film. This awareness is exemplified in the character's fascination and love for the movie *The World of Suzie Wong*, which is playing in reverse or distorted form and thus speaking to its haunting power. Sally looks on with fascination as Suzie serves the artist Lomax some food and ultimately refuses the character's brand of sexuality and womanhood. Committed to formulating a visual language based on the Asian woman's subjectivity, the film thematizes self-introspection and relations with other racialized sexualities—white men, black men—and relates them to the sexual visibility of her difference as an Asian woman. In Lee's films, the obsession with the subjectivity of the Asian female hinges on the axes of race, sex, gender, and visuality. This theme continues in her next films, which centrally feature sex with nonwhite men and Asian women in domestic and transnational scenes.

In *Prey* (1995), the mutual objectification between lovers of color leads to mutual recognition when a Korean Canadian female grocer (property owner), played by Sandra Oh, confronts a Native Canadian male drifter (shoplifter), played by Adam Beach, both of whom are successful actors of color. Their encounter turns into a different kind of relationality when they engage in sex soon after their meeting. As a matter of fact, their relationship transforms in the most radical sense, especially regarding property and ownership. The characters are reconstructed through sex and, in effect, step deeper into their assigned social and racial roles at the moment of the sex act—in order to rewrite them. The store owner's daughter Il Bae and the drifter Noel meet in the store and initiate an intimate relationship that ends in a confrontation between the new couple and Il Bae's father.

Each character is constructed as different from the other, in ways apparent in the camera movement and choreography, primarily in terms of their relationship to property. Lee introduces the characters in her film as they are situated within their space: the woman is bound to the store. The film begins with the jarring sound of an alarm bell and then a phone. Grunting and groaning from sleep, a lamp is turned on to reveal Sandra Oh's grumpy morning face. Calmly rising from sleep in a Greyhound bus, a drifter wakes up gently to no fanfare. He quietly and casually looks around and makes sense of where he wakes. He's a drifter on a bus. As characters on the opposite poles of propertied and non-propertied, their polarity organizes their coming together in sex and the recognition that crosses distances at the moment of the sex act. While they are opposites of each other, they also share displacements and marginalization. She is ambivalent about her property and he is wary of stealing: he says that he would not steal if he did not truly need it. Sex is the site where class and culture collide but most significantly transform.

Soon after the first meeting at the store, the encounter between Il Bae and Noel leads to a sex act. The construction of such an easily accessible sexual availability in the protagonist rejects the dismissal of such characters. That is, in her easiness or sexual availability, a life nonetheless emerges beyond her sexual enthusiasm, and it is worthy of telling. Hypersexuality, when taken on as behavioral choice, should not be discounted for it is a site of subjectivity where we can learn about race. The dialogue situates their sexual meeting as the coming together of two who chip away at their respective Otherness. The representation of their relation moves beyond Otherness as erotic fodder toward substantiating their knowledge and their recognition of each other's differences. For example, the scene preceding their sex scene is of Il Bae's discovery of Noel's displacement and lack of power when they must leave his sister's Native doll in the pawnshop for lack of money. She takes him home, where they preside over the making of tea. Rather than an exotic ritual in which an Asian woman serves a man such as in the stag films, the drinking of tea in a regular cup represents a social meeting in a cultural context that needs no exotic

Oriental accoutrements. Tea is a matter of everyday sustenance that needs no qualification. It is also used to block, or choreograph, the actors in relation to the camera prior to their sexual meeting.

All transpiring within one shot, the characters are established in the process of recognizing each other in various displacements as they make and drink tea in the two-shot. Il Bae begins on the left of the screen when they intertwine, and she ends the long shot on the right of the screen. While not explicit, the scene prepares us for the sex act by showing the intimate space between the two as they come to be tied together. This is established primarily in their movements, as if a rope binds them tightly and winds them together. In the delivery of dialogue, they pay attention to each other's sentences, as if to keep the sexual current moving between them through the linking of words. The tea is made, then consumed as they become more close.

NOEL: Nice place.

IL BAE: Nice shirt.

NOEL: Why'd you change your name anyway?

IL BAE: It's the name I was born with.

NOEL: Does it mean anything?

IL BAE: It's a boy's name. My father thought I was going to be a boy.

NOEL: Why did you change it . . . Il Bae.

IL BAE: Yeah, why, you can't even pronounce it.

(Beat. They stare at each other with desire.)

IL BAE (confidently): That's okay. I'll teach you.

The sex act occurs in the context of cultural shame—the narrative indicates that Il Bae changed her name to a normalized English name and abandoned her heritage as a Korean in the West. They continue to look at each other in a sexually charged pause before the sex act, which is set up as a significant site for their mutual recognition.

During sex, he tries to pronounce her newly reinstated Korean name, his linguistic attempts punctuating the acts of penetration. Similar to the last shot featuring their flirtation, their fucking transpires in one single shot. The camera moves alongside and up their contrasted bodies: his golden brown skin on top of her lighter skin. Beneath him, her hand lingers on his bottom and moves up his back, motivating the camera to follow the movement. They begin to kiss deeply as she rolls on top of him with her hair falling all over his face. He tries to say her name, Il Bae, at the

Il Bae drinks tea with Noel in a two-shot before they begin to intertwine in *Prey*.

Il Bae and Noel switch positions in the two-shot as they meet eye-to-eye before the sex scene in *Prey*.

Noel attempts to say Il Bae's name during sex in *Prey*.

In *Prey*, Il Bae teaches Noel how to say her name by way of their mouths and tongues meeting.

same time that he attempts to catch his breath. Within this face-to-face close-up, she says her name in the correct way. They kiss and kiss, so that he finally learns to say her name. Lee describes how "the scene in bed with Il Bae and Noel acts as a kind of bridge or segue for the characters to enable them to get to another stage with each other, via the tongue (creating intimacy through kissing and language)."[15] Within this single shot, Lee establishes how the sex act is the site where Noel learns how to say Il Bae's name as an important cultural meeting beyond, yet precisely because of, the sex act.

The sex act enables a kind of coming together of two individuals who represent very different sectors of social life. Lee describes how the "sexual statement or a sexual act often acts as a pivot—in story or character or thematic terms. It's an assertion of the body, the racialized and genderized [sic] figure who may be socially subjugated in my films, but there the private, sacral moments between lovers . . . can't be 'judged.' "[16] How do we understand the moment of intimacy in the sex act as a moment not to be "judged?" Do lovers relate to each other in sex in ways apart from their specific identities, or do they step deeper into the roles and scripts of race? In Lee's films, sex is a place to study relationality between subjects who are also individuals engaged in a specific, contingent moment. The relations therein may not be predictable, so that judgment must be suspended in order to identify the individual relationality at work between the Native male and the Asian female. Within the sex act, they do not leave their specific identities but forge new relations through this particular engagement —as grounded in their corporealities, which also fuel their desire. This desire based on difference differs from Dennis O'Rourke and Aoi, whom we never see in sex, but whose intimacy requires transcendence of their locations.

The moment of the sex act between Il Bae and Noel, as a site of social transformation and self-fashioning, disrupts the binary, not only between public and private, but also between fantasy and social reality. The bodily pleasures consumed and performed by Noel and Il Bae occur within a specific social order where Others do not mix. These Others are constructed within specific backgrounds and embodied by actors whose bodies demarcate poor and rich, Native and immigrant, man and woman, and propertied and poor. As such, the film confronts the general tendency to fear and flee from complications netted by sexuality in racial discourses of representation that continue to this day. We see the sex act as a site of political, narrative, and aesthetic strategy that moves the characters to further connection and alliance.

Rather than flee from sex or ignore race, the racialized sex act is treated as a scene where racial identities fracture and transform in the realms of the intimate as well as in the larger world. Racial subjects do not remain coherent but shift and change at the moment of encounter with others. In this relation, they are no longer Other to each other but are aligned through intimacy into a different form of knowing. To study sex acts actually recasts the meaning of sex in racial self-formation as consti-tutive—in both repressive and formative ways. The sex act offers recogni-tion of the Other in a way that matters to the external world. After Il Bae and Noel have sex, they unify behind a gun, pretending to shoot it at the mirror. In effect, they are shooting at themselves. From here, the film moves on to three-shots as they begin to encounter, as a couple, other individuals, such as her grandmother and then her father, neither of whom understand the kind of cultural meeting and recognition now pres-ent between the two. The mirror shot, featuring intertwined bodies and smiling faces as they play with the gun, anticipates the kind of misrecogni-tion they encounter in the larger public realm.

The sex act, having significance outside itself in terms of her family and larger relations in the world, reconstructs the two main characters within their given social roles while maintaining their racial and ethnic differ-ences. The two meet in a scene of mutual displacement that makes mutual recognition possible. Their sexual relations transpire within one-shot sce-narios wherein they negotiate the space inside the frame and focus on each other. The sex act is not romantically egalitarian—they do not share the frame but remain situated within their own specificity. Within their en-counter, identities form across shifting power relations and mutual trans-formations in a very different form of love for the Asian woman than the white-Asian love in *Miss Saigon, The Good Woman of Bangkok,* and *Ma-dame Butterfly.* In this sex scene, Helen Lee rewrites the terms of throwaway love, premised on abandonment and disposability, and usually reserved for Asian women in popular culture, in favor of a politics of recognition in the sex act.

In the film's conclusion, a misidentification between the father and the lover ensues. Noel mutters Il Bae's name with the correct pronunciation and her father repeats Noel's pronunciation in shock. He recognizes the intimacy indicated by that familiarity. In this final confrontation, the sex

The two hold a gun together in a
two-shot after sex in *Prey*.

act between the two lovers, as a site of recognition, introduces itself to the
external world. Sex is the site where meetings can be possible and where
they do not exist separately from other relations. Not only are they a
matter-of-fact part of life in Helen Lee's world, but they are essential to it
in a world full of misrecognition across race, class, gender, and sexuality.
Situated within the specific lives of racialized, classed, and gendered subjects, Lee's characters show the possibilities of recognizing difference,
meeting across unequal power relations, and creating new alliances.

The question of what is a viable politics of visibility for Asian Americans
can be answered by the need to attend to form and how it could be of
service in dramatizing racial, sexual, and other subjections. Specifically,
Lee uses sexuality as a way to frame intergenerational and interracial relations, defining sex as a powerful force that shapes the self and the relations
presented within the film. Unlike the previous chapter, in which O'Rourke
and Roc tell the story of the filmmaker and the prostitute in terms of
mutual victimization, Lee narrates a meeting between an Asian woman
and a Native man as a relationship in which power shifts between the
lovers. Unlike O'Rourke and Aoi, and Roc and the prostitute, where one is
vulture and the other prey, both characters in Lee's film are simultaneously
vultures and prey to each other. In *Prey*, interracial Native-Asian sexual
encounters offer the possibility of mutual recognition only after the lovers
encounter each other and pay attention to their power and difference.

In Helen Lee's latest short film *Subrosa* (2000), a Korean American
adoptee returns to Korea in search of her mother in a narrative that
genders and sexualizes the contemporary documentary topic of Korean
adoptees' homecoming.[17] The female adoptee ends up in the red-light
district, which is frequently represented in documentaries about Asian sex

tourism by Asian American feminist filmmakers; *Sin City Diary* (1992), *Camp Arirang* (1996), and *The Women Outside* (1996) are three such documentaries. In *Subrosa*, the Asian American woman becomes the sex tourist when she sleeps with a sexy Korean bar owner who barely speaks English. Her sexual liaison clarifies her confusion, displacement, and sense of loss and also reveals to the viewer the central character's unheroic complexity.

Although the unnamed character is not racially mixed, the adoption agency leads her to the sex district where American GIs hire Korean women for "rest and recreation." The choice of writing and casting a character that is not of mixed-race Asian descent indicates a more complex picture of sex tourism as that which also occurs among Asian men and Asian women. The scene of sex tourism as a site for figuring Asian American female subjectivity is uncanny. The sight of a Korean American woman looking for her history in this site of Asian American transnational politics is an incredible juxtaposition because the site of Asian sex tourism already occupies an important part of Asian American feminist platforms as Asian American women contend with their power differentials against Asian women in Asia. The best example is Rachel Rivera's *Sin City Diary*. In the middle of a documentary primarily made up of interviews with prostitutes, Rivera inserts her own homecoming as a Filipina American. Zooming into her passport photo, she problematizes the power differentials between her as a filmmaker and her interviewees. She indicts herself for being no more than a tourist who leaves the subjects anyway. Similarly, *Subrosa*'s mise-en-scène unleashes not only the presence of the sex industry within the narrative of the Korean adoptee, but also the haunting of sex industry cultures in Asian American feminisms. The unnamed character in the film, who is underdressed and not made up, interviews a prostitute, who is overly made up. The figures constituting the identity position of the Asian American woman and the Asian woman find themselves sharing a frame in this film. The women look in the mirror and see in their reflection hauntings by their others in the Asian sex tourism scene.

Unable to secure any information from the prostitute, the unnamed woman wanders into a bar as a customer. In front of bar exteriors similar to those shot by Dennis O'Rourke and Jean Marc Roc, the Asian American woman enters only after being prodded by a Korean man to come inside. Inside the bar, the Asian American woman encounters men and women who stare at her, unsure of her visibly different but racially similar presence. The bartender, actually the owner, is a very tall and muscular Korean man dressed in tight black clothes who comes over and buys her a drink. She drinks tentatively and looks him up and down. Like Il Bae in *Prey*, the unnamed character ends up having sex with him soon after their meeting. "Other" to each other in terms of language, he does not speak English and she does not speak Korean. Unlike the previous sex scene in *Prey*, the Asian woman does not connect with the man through speech but through fucking itself. Counteracting the idea that sex is liberatory at all occurrences, sex in *Subrosa* is an act of confusion. The Asian American woman looks for resolution to her search for personal belonging and ancestry through casual sex.

Emphasized as a much smaller figure, the unnamed Asian American character bounces vigorously on top of the broad shouldered and muscular Korean bartender during intercourse. She demonstrates an intense and powerful physicality as her facial expression indicates concentration on the mechanics of the sexual act. The unnamed character is a picture of an Asian/American woman as a desiring and very actional sexual subject. She closes her eyes and rides the man, who is mainly represented as a chiseled and desirable male body below her, whose contorted face and body we see from above his head. The sex scene is shot from one angle, at the head of the yoh or futon-like mattress, and focuses entirely on her extraction of pleasure from the man with whom she cannot speak. At the end of their sex scene, he gets ready to leave her sparse and lonely room while she sleeps. She watches him as he quietly walks away, then laughs out loud at herself. With exasperation and a bit of amusement as well, she says, "All this way for a fuck. Pretty amazing!" He concurs it was amazing before bolting out the door. Throughout the film, her expression is somber and overwhelmed. Now, she laughs at her failed attempt at emotional and psychic connection.

In the next scene, the unnamed woman jumps into the Han River, misleading us to a suicide ending. But in *Subrosa*, the sex scene is both a central and a peripheral act of subject formation: her jump is an attempt to reconnect with the womb of her mother and her country. As her body falls deeper into the Han River, she hears her biological mother's voice welcoming her into the world (again) in a form of rebirth or self-birth. The shot of drowning repeats the beautiful birthing opening to the film; her mother's words soothe her as she is born again, violently rising out of the river. In *Subrosa*, the unnamed woman in search of her past fully realizes her alienation through sex. Sex is where the character decides to do something about her situation, as wrongheaded as jumping in the lake may be. It is how she returns to her mother and makes sense of her homeland by immersing in it fully—she looks around, with eyes wide open, in its waters.

In *Sally's Beauty Spot,* a sexually charged relationship transpires between a single Asian American woman and various men. With the white man, her kisses are tentative, and with the black man, a different form of meeting occurs in their kiss. A Native Canadian male drifter and a Korean Canadian female storekeeper resolve their displacements through sex in *Prey.* And in *Subrosa,* a transnational adoptee's search for belonging in Korea culminates in sex occurring in the red-light district. Informed by stereotype discourse, sites of exile, conditions of displacement, work, and family, Helen Lee's films speak from a particular historical place of Asian American and Canadian female self-formation in the late twentieth century. Within these historical situations, sex acts are represented as a source of both pleasure and pain in the context of much larger lives.

Sex is a central wound in Helen Lee's films. She authors a particular kind of wound as a gathering site or a constellation of narratives that make up the Asian woman's life. *Subrosa, Prey,* and *Sally's Beauty Spot* all use sex as one of many social forces that constitute Asian women, including race, class, and transnational and cross-racial desire. While sex significantly constitutes Asian female subjectivity, it cannot completely determine her. Sex makes sense in the context of other categories of experience such as race, gender, and class. Indeed, the Asian women made by Lee combat such a production of sexuality. Sex makes them up just as other forces do. As such, sex cannot and must not be ignored in the exploration of Asian female subjectivity in film. While sex may be fascinating and overwhelming, the total life of the Asian/American woman exceeds sexuality at the same time. *Subrosa,* compared to Lee's previous works, emphasizes the equation between sex, race, and gender in more dynamic terms. Lee refuses to prioritize one social categorization over the other. Instead, she shows characters engaging with and confronting the complexity of their lives through sex in *Sally's Beauty Spot, Subrosa,* and *Prey.*

Within her films, Helen Lee presents sex acts as sites for self-fashioning for raced and gendered subjects. She inserts a gender and sex narrative into racial situations where both men and women transform at the site of the sex act. Her films show intercourse and other intimate acts in an artful way that registers beyond a moralistic realm and makes robust the debates about race, sex, and visuality by featuring Asian female characters seeking sexual pleasure and at times failing. Lee employs a particular understanding of sexuality that is dialectic in how it makes and unmakes people. She describes her construction of sex for the Asian woman: "Generally, I try to avoid the sexual victimization of the lead character, even when the sex doesn't have a good end [*My Niagara, Subrosa*], because I feel that that is too easy. Sex surely can complicate matters but also clarify. It's after sex that Julie Kumagai [in *My Niagara*] realizes the limits of her commonality with Tetsuro; that the nameless main character in *Subrosa* realizes that her longing and need for connection cannot be satisfied through a casual sexual liaison with the Korean bar owner."[18] In a way that counters race and sex panics regarding visuality, Lee presents sex as an important everyday part of life for the Asian woman in her films. In her films, including *My Niagara*, Helen Lee strips her Asian female characters out of their clothes and engages them in sex acts, alone or with various men, in order to articulate the lives of Asian women beyond the binary of servile submission and femme fatale-ism.[19] She visualizes Asian female subjectivity grappling with the self as an object of fetishism, fantasy, and otherness in scenes in which the Asian woman's inner life is emphasized. By appropriating the position of objectification by others, she remakes herself primarily through sexual relations with others and the mutual recognitions, objectifications, and subjections found in the encounter. Sex is a site where relations with others are captured and negotiated, particularly in how the Asian female—as a specific character bound within the film—encounters other racialized sexualities, specifically those of nonwhite men.

Sex, instead of destroying them, gives them reprieve. The act itself is a space and time where the self can experience and analyze the social. Helen Lee presents sex as a place where some of the other social categories shift and change. It is a place where one can learn at least some parts of the self. Instead of romanticizing it, she recasts it as useful and integral within racial scenes. While representing explicit sex acts and body parts, she does not forego how fantasies about sexy Asian women inform intimate self-images. She asserts the importance of desire as a way to explore Asian female subjectivities. By figuring Asian women as desiring subjects, constituted at least in part by sex, among other things, Lee fulfills demands articulated by Asian American feminist scholars on representation while also employing the analytics of visuality articulated in feminist film theory.

Helen Lee's work identifies sex as that which binds Asian women but also sets them free within the realm of experience and representation. The historical context that interpellates Asian women as excessively sexual should not foreclose other avenues of exploring her subjectivity, such as in cinematic language. In Lee's films, sexual acts function as the pivotal points of the narrative, where Asian female characters transform and recognize themselves and others so that representation itself is a technology used to articulate other uses and possibilities for sexual subjectivity. While sex is very important in Helen Lee's work, what is hypersexual about it? Asian female engagements with what are "normal" sex acts for white women become perverse in the racialized gendered context. They become perverse in the sense that "normal" sexuality has not been available to Asian women in cinema. As such, I refine my deployment of perversity as a political critique of the hypersexual tradition of Asian/American women in popular representation. Helen Lee perverts the established representation and demands access to more realistic, contemporary sexual identities that make sense on screen, responding to fantasies of Asian women as well as scenes of Asian/American women's everyday lives, in which sex functions practically, pleasurably, and painfully.

BREAKING THE DRAGON LADY/LOTUS BLOSSOM DICHOTOMY:
GRACE LEE'S ASIAN/AMERICAN WOMEN

Helen Lee and Grace Lee both practice a bringing onto the screen of more ordinary yet immensely complex Asian/American women, in comparison to such femme fatales as Anna May Wong, Nancy Kwan, and Lucy Liu. That is, their characters would not be shocking to see on the street as would be the characters of Hollywood femme fatales if they stepped off screen. In my film *The Fact of Asian Women,* for example, I direct actresses, in full costume, to walk the streets of contemporary San Francisco evoking Anna May Wong in *The Thief of Bagdad* and *Shanghai Express,* Nancy Kwan in *The World of Suzie Wong,* and Lucy Liu in *Charlie's Angels.* The disjuncture between the performance, the fantasy, the role, and the women to which they correspond in the streets is so immense. The image on screen comes to life in order to reveal itself as a fantasy.

Loni Ding focuses on the subject of casting in ways relevant to Helen Lee's own choices within the context of sexy Asian women preceding hers on screen: "I think selecting your on-camera personality is akin to asking the question, whose face is mine, whose face could be mine? . . . The very ordinariness of our camera subjects is their humanity, which affirms and extends ours. . . . Whether a film is fiction or documentary, I see it as storytelling. On-camera persons—actors or interviewees—are chosen for their ability to be convincingly themselves."[20] The women in Helen Lee's and Grace Lee's films look like regular women in the sense of their costume and makeup. Although the films are heavily stylized, Helen Lee's costume design works under a different economy than that of Hollywood films. In *Subrosa*, the Asian woman wears a baggy down jacket, jeans, and a backpack perpetually hanging over her shoulder. In *Prey*, Il Bae looks like she never got up from bed or the grunge era. Unlike Anna May Wong with her elaborate costume designs, or Nancy Kwan with her matching bags, shoes, and dresses, or white women in yellow face, or the prostitutes with their numbers and inventive clothes, or Lucy Liu with her leather outfits, these women register as everyday women, as called for by Renee Tajima in her classic essay "Lotus Blossoms Don't Bleed." Unlike Tajima's prioritization of the ordinary as normal, which does not quite counter well the problem of hypersexuality, Helen Lee's ordinary Asian women engage in sex and risk verifying hypersexuality in order to find more viable subjectivities otherwise unavailable to them. To be clear, the works of Asian American feminist filmmakers such as Helen Lee correct the possibility of veering to the puritanical side by claiming their right to the sexual life of "normal" American women—at least that of women we see in the popular cultural imagination. Another example is the Asian Canadian filmmaker Mina Shum's *Double Happiness* (1994). In her award-winning role as Jade Li, Sandra Oh risks hypersexuality by aggressively enjoying her zipless fuck with the white male lead.

While multidimensional in their complexity, Grace Lee also works with "regular" Asian women in casting her films. Moreover, I believe her characters are premised on rejecting the categorization of Asian women—ordinary, hypersexual, or extraordinary—in a larger vision of the inadequacy of gender, race, and sexual types. What are Asian American filmmakers asserting beyond these categories? I believe it is the inadequacy of any racial categorizations of the complexity of sex.

Prior to and in her becoming a filmmaker, Grace Lee has frequently identified the force of categorization in framing Asian/American women on screen. This categorization comes to be a challenge that Grace Lee engages and confronts in films that resonate with large, generalized audiences. With the success of her narrative *Barrier Device* (2001), she encountered many managers and agents who said, "I don't know what to do with you." They compartmentalized her as interested in making films "only" about women or "only" about Asian Americans—as if these groups and topics are limited and uninteresting to others. Within industry pitches, ideas she considered incredibly funny, such as "a Korean family in the Midwest," with its premise of rich cross-cultural encounters, were not considerable within a framework of "only Asians" or "only women." The lives of these compartmentalized groups are not perceived as complex. Stereotyped and simplified, they do not register as dramatic or comedic. They are overdetermined by categories.

Likewise, Grace Lee encounters the force of categorization shaping the options of Asian American actresses when she watches a sitcom featuring such an actress, otherwise outgoing and bold "in real life," from whose mouth bursts forth a torrent of words with a strange Asian accent. Grace Lee cringes in her seat, sweating with the realization of the suffocating box Asian women must fit into, realizing that "it would be too weird for . . . [the general American audience] to see [an Asian American] without an accent." In this moment, Grace Lee's statement registers a particular understanding of the stereotype that goes far beyond the identification of negative and positive images. Stereotypes are the ground for articulating Asian Americans in the popular imagination. Considering the history of stereotypes delimiting audience expectation, there is a particular logic to shaping characters who are recognizable in order to have the opportunity to say something with and about them. That is, a giant leap is required in framing Asian Americans beyond the stereotype. In reconfiguring the limits of roles available, we must use that knowledge in order to construct characters that undo those very limits.

So if Asian/American women are bound by hypersexuality in their roles, filmmakers cannot but traffic and must traffic in hypersexuality, for it is the basis of their recognizability and the ground for undoing such established tropes. In doing so, the work of the filmmaker is clear. However, she must, like Grace Lee, assess the force of categorization as a "positive challenge, not an obstacle." What Grace Lee's realization clarifies is that we must confront categorization continuously in order to operate in the world and proceed knowing there is drama, conflict, tension, and comedy in lives dismissed as simple and known, and in the very work that must be done to prove that claim. However, in making my claim about the bind of hypersexuality, I want to be very clear that the acknowledgment of the stereotype must be made alongside a commitment to dismantle it and to point to its inadequacy in defining the complexity of any identity or subjectivity, group or otherwise, in representation.

Since stereotypes are the ground of representation for filmmakers of color, and sexuality the terms of legibility for Asian women subjects, the force of categorization leads to conceiving *Barrier Device,* a film about a tightly wound Asian woman sex researcher who unravels when she realizes that her research subject, a carefree and sexy Asian American woman, is getting married to her ex-fiancé. Lee describes the context of hypersexuality framing her formulation of the characters as well as the perceptions of Asian women she experiences firsthand as a research assistant herself. She conceives the film's setting while working as an interviewer, having been hired by a researcher because people supposedly feel comfortable talking with Asian women. What makes people comfortable talking with Asian women about their intimate stories? And furthermore, how can this attribution exist alongside Asian/American women's hypersexuality?

Barrier Device sets up an encounter between two Asian American women in order to confront that convergence. Grace Lee describes how the film allows her to comment on what binds Asian women:

> We all know that Asian women are always these hypersexualized beings, especially on screen. I like that there were two regular people [in *Barrier Device*]: a researcher and a girl. And they could talk intimately and clinically about sexuality. Rather than [the conversation] becoming so sexualized, they could just relate. . . . This was important. I like that there was a guy [between them] who was not there, and I wanted to see two women dealing with each other, because you don't see that often on screen either.[21]

Within the context of hypersexuality, Grace Lee formulates characters who are "regular" people, grounded in jobs, families, and homes—their lives are fully detailed and carefully contextualized. Establishing the characters carefully allows for the exploration of the relationship between Asian women across sexuality, race, and gender in a film focused on homosociality between women, which occurs over a shared sexual object in a way that mimics male homosociality that is grounded in shared sex objects.

Within this social relation, Grace Lee's *Barrier Device* breaks the binary understanding of Asian women in film as dragon lady/lotus blossom. Audrey, played by Sandra Oh, is a model minority Asian female character who is professionally admired for her sophisticated and rigorous research methods. In the beginning of the film, her personal life comes undone when her fiancé leaves her for being "too cold," for working long hours, and for being too focused on her work. As she interviews research subjects, Audrey meets Serena, played by Suzy Nakamura, an actress and a waitress at a hip Asian hotspot and a confident hypersexual figure who has several lovers and a carefree attitude toward her sexual and emotional love life. Audrey and Serena represent different poles in the sexual range of experience within the historical repertoire of available sexual subjectivities for Asian women in the U.S. film industry. They share a man, Audrey's ex-fiancé, who is now one of Serena's lovers. And through their conversations, we recognize the way in which each woman responds to her interpellation as lotus blossom or dragon lady.

Grace Lee presents a relationship between two Asian American women who evoke these polar sexual personas in order for them to cohere and ally and for that dichotomous formation of the dragon lady/lotus blossom to be broken forever in hopes of new alternatives. The scene introducing the two characters transpires during an interview about sex practices; the women are facing each other across an office desk. Explicit sexuality is immediately present in the film in its very introduction and construction of characters. They are deeply connected to each other, sharing a lover they seem to know about at the moment of his disclosure during the interview. The upright and uptight Audrey interviews Serena, a casual, relaxed, and disheveled person. Audrey asks Serena matter-of-factly about her sexual practices. Serena is unashamed to admit multiple partners and her enjoyment of sex, spilling over with details regarding her sex life. Unfazed by Serena's responses, Audrey suddenly recognizes her necklace on Serena's neck and is visibly shaken. Given to her by her grandmother, Audrey left it at her ex-fiancé's house. No longer able to conduct herself ethically as a researcher, she cannot but exploit her position to find out about Serena's sex life with her ex-fiancé, for whom Audrey still pines. Serena divulges all of her sexual and emotional life to Audrey and soon they become intimate friends. The more she knows Serena, the more Audrey struggles to disclose her relationship to the man they refer to as "J." A caller I.D. mishap reveals Audrey's identity to Serena and a passionate confrontation ensues in the research office in the presence of another research subject. The encounter threatens the unraveling of each character—Audrey's professional integrity and Serena's carefree and trusting personhood.

Sex acts in *Barrier Device* evidence the limits of lotus blossom/dragon lady characterizations within each character. The main sex scene, understood against Serena's prowess in the film, features Audrey and her white male colleague Dwight. Upset by Serena's "sex journal," which chronicles the escalating and explicitly hot romance with Audrey's ex-fiancé. "J.," Audrey invites her Dwight out and they subsequently end up in bed—very fast to bed like Il Bae in *Prey* and the unnamed character in *Subrosa*. Asian American women are easy in these films. While Audrey researches and encourages the use of the female condom and for it to be introduced with care, her actual practice in using it fails. Unprepared for a safe sexual encounter, she grabs the female condom with exasperation. She moves away from Dwight brusquely, her face contorting to express frustration as she turns off the light. Returning to the space between them in bed, she alienates him with her abrasiveness. The sex scene unravels quickly and the intimacy between them dissipates. Unable to maintain her partner's sexual attention, she loses sexual social decorum by yelling at him for not being able to complete the sex act. He moves away. She's frustrated.

While Audrey fails, quite uncomfortably and traumatically, at sex with her colleague, Serena describes successful sex not only with Audrey's ex-fiancé but also with another lover. Serena's vibrant drawings in a research diary provided by Audrey describe sexual prowess and adventure in ways that culminate in a deeper relationship with Audrey's ex-fiancé. The two women are sexually imbricated to each other; sex binds them to each other as friends and as Asian women so that by the end of the film they acknowledge to each other that bondage.

The incredibly emotional confrontation in which the characters recognize themselves within each other provides a new Asian female relational formation on screen. The two individual Asian women are mutually constituted by the other so that they may better understand themselves. In the confrontation, the women unleash anger and frustration with each other. That is, while Serena yells at Audrey for betraying her trust, she must acknowledge that she was aware of the pain she caused Audrey by wearing Audrey's grandmother's necklace. Serena expresses her rage, being no longer carefree; and Audrey loses control by breaking down in her professional setting. Serena and Audrey achieve better understandings of themselves and each other in the redefinition of the binary of the lotus blossom and the dragon lady. In the process, they recognize an alliance or friendship through their sexualities. Not only are they part of each other, but they are to one another the self-sacrificing lotus blossom and the cruel

In *Barrier Device*, Audrey loses her composure in the sex act as Dwight loses interest in her. Serena and Audrey confront each other.

dragon lady—contradictory and complex in their sexualities. Such is the way the stereotype works, binding the dragon lady and the lotus blossom to each other, as the model minority and the coolie are bound to each other in Robert Lee's *Orientals*.[22]

Like Helen Lee, Grace Lee continues to work on the subject of Asian women as a deep and incredibly rich subject of inquiry. In *The Grace Lee Project*, Grace Lee problematizes Asian/American women's categorization in a truly compelling way that innovates film form intertextually. The documentary moves from her upbringing as racially unique in her mostly racially homogenous hometown of St. Louis, Missouri. In leaving home, she discovers the incredibly ridiculous commonness of her name. A pattern emerges in others' descriptions of her namesakes: shy, quiet, overachieving, and ultimately unknowable despite what is known about her. Frequently, Grace Lee is hated by others. Upon further research, not scientific by any means, she draws a cartoon character of Grace Lee—5'3", college educated, and so forth. By reaching out to other Grace Lees through the website gracelee.net, thousands of other Grace Lees reach her. The documentary captures this dynamic transnational encounter while offering specific portraits of an entire group of Asian American women and particular versions of Grace Lee that take dents at the stock version of Grace Lee. We meet a long time civil rights activist who works in the black community, a dynamic news reporter, a vivacious pastor's wife, a teen artist obsessed with "dark images," and a Christian youth organization leader with clear-cut plans for her life. Through the lives of these women and interviews with a variety of people, the filmmaker Grace Lee identifies the shared fantasies and projections of identity for Asian women. Even the nice, smart, quiet, wholesome image that seems most complimentary exceeds and plays against the norm in a pathological formation. As such, it captures how particular Asian/American women deal with those tiresome expectations. In the homogeneity of Asian/American women named Grace Lee lies a deep heterogeneity.[23]

Based on interviews, descriptions gathered of the standard Grace Lee include a good girl, quiet, attractive, submissive, overachieving, and a typical model minority. The fantasies of Grace Lee collide with the lived realities of Grace Lees. The filmmaker Grace Lee, in the face of typical good girl Grace Lees, needed to find more inspiring figures. The most striking figures who defy the assumptions about Grace Lee are the lesbian Korean American activist who relocates to Korea and starts a prominent lesbian organization and lesbian bar, and the Korean American adoptee Grace Lee, now a deaf, middle-aged single mother who endured physical abuse as a child, fled a great deal of domestic abuse, and now lives in a new family formation with another woman. Interviewed in the early years of her project, the Korean American lesbian now refuses to be part of *The Grace Lee Project* for she is no longer a lesbian and refuses to bring shame to her family. In my interview with her, the filmmaker Grace Lee tells me that she forgets that the deaf single mother, who speaks with so much integrity, resilience, and strength, is also named Grace Lee. That is, the filmmaker is so overwhelmed by the power of her story that she forgets how she came to be in her presence to tell her story. In *The Grace Lee Project*, the good girl Asian image is challenged and destroyed by the lived realities of these particular Asian/American women who must survive and exist as subjects of perverse sexuality, race, and gender. I point to these two final women in order to show how sexuality continues to hold its power for Asian/American women in the form of heterosexism and domestic abuse, the latter which silences Asian women and curtails their possibilities.

Against the assumption that Asian women are not the regular vehicles of the narrative within their perpetually supportive roles, Grace Lee speaks from specificity as well as generality. That is, she makes films she wants to see featuring "regular" Asian women but with a large audience in mind. She recognizes that Asian women are part of a general audience. She notes how we, broadly, across all kinds of differences, laugh as audiences together, as well as differently. Her interests lie in getting different kinds of people to respond to her work. Specifically, Lee wants to reach the largest audiences possible while maintaining a voice committed to Asian American women. The subject is overflowing and well energized by a tradition of hypersexuality that represents Asian American women and by established theories that frame the political power of hypersexual representation inadequately, especially as authored by Asian/American women.

Hypersexuality binds the women together so that the ordinary women in Helen Lee's and Grace Lee's films live complex lives that involve, among other things, sex—in small or large ways. It does not consume or subsume them entirely but its presence certainly organizes their worlds. Through the Asian/American actresses who stand for them, Helen Lee and Grace Lee show sex as a way to discuss the complexity of everyday lives caught in conundrums of race, sexuality, postcoloniality, class, and other social forces. Their narratives are situated within Asian American feminist quandaries regarding visual objectification, loss and melancholia, intergenerational conflict, and friendship between women. In their films, sex itself opens up to various wide-ranging and relevant politics. Sex opens the floodgates to richly nuanced lives deserving of equally compelling forms. To represent sex, sexualities, and sex acts in order to locate subject position and formation is to show the full range of complexity in Asian/American women's lives. The filmmakers show how sex is imbricated in Asian women's histories of transience, immigration, or cross-cultural meeting in both an aesthetic and political project. Moreover, Helen Lee and Grace Lee reveal how, as Helen Lee describes, "sex is never the culmination or endpoint." Rather, it is the pivot where social forces are made unstoppable, relentless in their possibilities for making women recognizably Asian to themselves and to others in multiple ways beyond servility, submission, and hypersexuality.

Wearing blue lipstick, fake eyelashes, silver eyeshadow, bound into a neon blue corseted leotard with silver straps, and, of course, wearing her trademark big long black hair, Machiko Saito is negotiating a camera and framing the scene for us. In another shot, she sports long nails and rehearses a different expression on her face. The movie documents Machiko Saito's process of filmmaking. Next she's making love with a gorgeous man in Berlin. The scene is shot in what looks like a squat or tenement. Perennially focused on lives in the margins, *Hart Schell und Schon* (2003) celebrates a nomadic, urban, and cosmopolitan racial and sexual being. In *Pink Eye* (2000) Saito appears in a pink wig and fetish gear, breaking a camera and peering through a fish eye lens with her face to the floor. By shooting herself in the process of making film and negotiating her ability to use technology, Saito attempts to illustrate and articulate other facets of her life, including the celebration of sexuality and the problematization of technology in visualizing race and desire. In *Premenstrual Spotting* (1997), she is naked, drunken, singing from the musical *Chicago*, masturbating, and bleeding on the bathroom floor. In *Femme TV*, she's at the Folsom Street Fair where assless chaps and duct tape suffice on all different types of bodies before she takes us to a scene of sex where women strap on dildos and punish each other—with love. She expands our bounds of the normal and the acceptable in her celebration of different acts and identities.

The award-winning experimental filmmaker Machiko Saito screens her films and wins prizes in prominent experimental film festivals all over the world while working as a filmmaker who defies the very classification of "independence" by barely distributing her own work and resisting the commercial aspects of marketing herself. Saito's experimental film *Premenstrual Spotting* features a racialized sexual subject whose history of family sexual trauma registers visibly in a playful, powerful, disturbing, and defiant presence on screen. Working with a definition of sexuality that insists on the simultaneity of pleasure and trauma, the drunken Asian/American woman in Saito's film renders the damaging power of sexual abuse and the pain one must endure from it—before any kind of transformation or consciousness can be realized. I conclude this chapter with a discussion of Machiko Saito's *Premenstrual Spotting*, for it challenges approaches to racialized sexuality in Asian American, film, and feminist

Machiko Saito frames herself in *Hart Schell und Schon*.

Machiko Saito shows off her long nails and tries a different facial expression in *Hart Schell und Schon*.

studies that render sexual representations of the racial experience as damaging rather than as productive political practice. Her emphasis on the pain of sexual experiences also amends sex-positive frameworks that do not account for the different experience and history of racial subjugation via sexuality.

The opening of *Premenstrual Spotting* suggests a traditional Asian American autobiographical nonfiction film. The camera zooms into the still image of family life; soon, this traditional revelation of the documentary subject is interrupted by a tall, angular female figure in leather fetishwear whipping her own long body taut. She is ambiguous—is this a drag queen or a woman playing at a man in female drag? The editing is cut fast, as if to the beat of a strobe light, and set to jarring music that announces that this is not a typical confessional nonfiction piece. It provides a counterpoint to what Lisa Lowe calls the generational framework of history telling in Asian American narratives.[24] Familiar images of family in home movie footage are intercut as the strikingly tall, amazingly long-haired thin figure poses in the shocking white light: images of the father smoking at the dinner table and the mother wearing a haircut from the 1960s are juxtaposed with images of the daughter (the figure in drag) ultimately in fetish gear or naked. The contradiction between the images productively poses the disjunctures between the spaces she occupies now and her family memory and history. The present images collapse time and space: we do not know where this strobe-lit scene takes place. The place where she takes off her black clothes so that her breasts spill out looks green and otherworldly. Another shot looks orange and her body bent over naked looks like an iris. Another image is superexposed. The colors are bleeding. It features her naked, covering her face with her arms, but her breasts are showing completely. She is unavailable but also brutally self-exposed. Saito is thoughtful about what she shows. The world of the present, from which she speaks or looks to the past, looks artful and crafted. Cinematically beautiful, it is not so much placeless, but it is certainly a world possessing a different mood and a different way of life.

We now enter the world where the character lives in the present. She is wildly made up and flaunts a confrontational attitude with the camera by enacting show tunes in full performance mode of arms flinging and long, long hair teased and displayed. In voice-over, the narrator describes getting drunk every night as an adult and the elaborate performance of fetish wear as rehearsing "child's play" through a "superhero" sexual persona.

In fetish gear, Machiko Saito drinks while performing show tunes in *Premenstrual Spotting*.

Machiko Saito sings show tunes in *Premenstrual Spotting*.

She plays with gender instability and ambiguity so that we never quite pin her down. What we see is the collision of her two worlds. It can be described in terms of an old sexual terror that will not go away, haunting her current world as it explodes with expressions of pleasure in her body's movements and favorite show songs.

The movie is difficult to watch for there is a specter of violence through-out the film in terms of her physical performance—drunken, she falls all over the place, simulating masturbation and describing graphic sex acts in the sexual abuse by her father. Premenstrual spotting actually refers to what her mother renames the daughter's vaginal and anal bleeding when she is just six years old. She describes the comfort she feels in bathrooms as spaces that "lock—[so she can] breathe again." Show tunes from the musi-cal *Chicago* featuring the refrain "I'm Here!" register the coming together of terror and subjugation with self-acceptance emerging from those very conditions. The ending of the film features, for example, the reinterpretation of fellatio and sodomy with her father, performed as a six-year-old girl, so that the final shots we see are the money shot in porn but with blood all over her face as she lays spread-eagled in the very bathroom where she plays and performs earlier within the tape. She re-enacts the violence and renders the proof of male pleasure a violence on to her: the male ejaculation in the money shot on the woman's face becomes her own blood. It is in the final moments of the tape that we understand the title as the misnaming of evidence in order to hide the crime. I use this word deliberately in order to isolate the politics of perversity that is advocated in Machiko Saito's films. It is not limitless. The issues of consent remain important as well as the need to evaluate how perversity can be productive depending on the ethical issues and power dynamics involved in each situation.

In the case of *Premenstrual Spotting,* the mother deliberately classifies the blood in her daughter's genitals, evidence of sexual abuse committed by her father, as nothing but "premenstrual spotting." In this classification designed to protect the integrity of the family and disregard the daughter's pain and experience, we see that the daughter is unimportant and negated. The film's language of sexual play and visual pleasure emerges from the violence upon the daughter. The film evaluates the intense trauma regarding surviving sexual violence at home from the hands of a loved one; the formulation of her artful life is one that emerges from surviving pain. The coexistence of expressing the pain of trauma and belting out the joy (of survival) is similar to the trajectory of this book itself—reminding us of the pleasure in sexuality as well as the pain and suffering found therein. The representation of surviving and acknowledging rape becomes a call for recognition of one's subjection and one's crafting of creative work that recasts that experience.

Machiko Saito's *Premenstrual Spotting,* shot almost entirely by herself, is the first of four films. She describes her process of filmmaking: "I shoot, direct, edit and create, write, perform, and act—whatever I feel like—I don't think I have a specific agenda with my four pieces. *Premenstrual Spotting* was a big experiment, a learning of technology, learning how to shoot and edit, play with myself on camera . . . with no intent for anything other than what happens in the moment, to put on an outfit, to put on a [light] gel."[25] For Machiko Saito, making the film is about engaging herself

Spread-eagled on the
bathroom floor, Machiko
Saito performs a scene in
Premenstrual Spotting.

Machiko Saito performs a
bloody form of the money
shot in *Premenstrual
Spotting*.

as a visual artist or finding another venue as an expressive person. She aims to capture what she sees, which the camera does not always get. Based on the fact that lives like hers are not represented well, she enacts film experiments. *Premenstrual Spotting* did not start out as a film about abuse, but abuse reared its head in the final moments of the film, when she records her voice-over to make sense of the images she captured.

In terms of distribution, after making the film alone "99 percent of the time," in what Saito calls an "isolating experience," a curator discovered her work when passing by her editing booth at Artists' Television Access. He saw a shot as she opened and closed the door of her editing room. It was a moment in which he saw one frame and immediately asked to program her film. The incident was purely accidental, for she guarded the film fiercely: "I did not think about entering in film festivals."[26] In its premiere at the giant and highly regarded queer of color festival MIX NYC, she "felt vulnerable" as the image of herself "star[ed] back at me in the front row—it actually was surprisingly *quite* painful."[27] She describes a highly bodily response to the corporeality of the film itself. Her viewing in New York is informed by the context of the film's production in San Francisco. Machiko Saito explains that the sexuality of the film is "not intentional . . . naked does not equal sexy. There's a line in *Premenstrual Spotting*, 'learning to enjoy sex.' " In the celebration of sex in popular culture today, Saito says, "I feel I was doing it in a way but [also] not. This town [San Francisco] is so sex positive, sex parties . . . Can we do other things than fuck each other on stage?"[28] Her film makes a critique where pleasure is emphasized, at times, at the expense of pain and sexual trauma. In describing the film as a process of discovery, rather than a piece intended to discuss sexual violence, Saito describes sexual trauma functioning like the return of the repressed. Her first film, again, addresses sexual violence as something that rears its head in the final postproduction process.

As a filmmaker, Saito says that there is "not a lot of stability" in terms of negotiating industry and independent work: "I live a simple life I make complicated."[29] From this position and as one who defies race, class, gender, and sex norms—dressed flamboyantly in a tiara, cowboy hat, and black western-style leather gear—Machiko Saito continues to establish her critical presence as a filmmaker. She makes her own clothes out of plastic bags and establishes a powerful presence on the street and on stage. In her work, Saito offers a definition of hypersexuality that emanates powerfully from all of her films. For her, sexuality is "an innate quality that should be protected, appreciated, enjoyed and not exploited. . . . It's really unfortunate . . . happens to all women, we feel we have to mask our sexuality to protect ourselves. . . . Sex should be fun, intense, dramatic. . . ." Saito's engagements with race, sexuality, and visuality as forces central to life as we currently know it offer new forms of power and pleasure in wrestling with the Asian woman's sexuality on screen, making and unmaking her in ways that testify to her resilience in the face of her assignation as a marginal subject of race, sex, and gender.

POSING GOOD QUESTIONS IN THE MAKING OF BAD OBJECTS

The work of Asian American women filmmakers who express experiences of sexuality and sexual desire, acts, and identities in representation requires more specific formulation regarding how we understand representations of racialized sexuality today. These women's works defy the logic of race panics regarding sex and visuality by insisting on the use of explicit sex as the grounds for articulating and redefining their identities through the political power of representation. If Asian women are overdetermined by hypersexuality, these filmmakers take on that premise and show how that sexuality needs to be considered in order to express and understand Asian women today. They use sexuality and representation to point to the inadequacies of frameworks that reject the importance of their experiences and expressions.

By studying these women's works, I formulate that sexual and scopic pleasures are essential to defining and understanding the sexual experiences of Asian women and the problem of their representation. As such, we must reject any accusations of race traitorship, false consciousness, and complicity that can arise when looking at the works of feminist filmmakers who embrace sexual perversity. Asian American feminist filmmakers imagine different futures beyond violence against women and the tendency to frame women as derivative to men in perception and analyses. By embracing pleasure as political and sexuality as crucial to race and identity, I use these works to include the role of sexuality and visuality in expanding the definitions of Asian American experience.

Moreover, the Asian American feminist filmmakers I study are not only committed to representing explicit sex acts as sites for the recognition of oneself and ones' relations within and beyond hypersexuality but also to innovating their form to best express their passions for Asian/American women. Helen Lee's short films *Sally's Beauty Spot, Prey,* and *Subrosa* pivot on sex acts, intercourse itself as well as kissing and touching, as acts of identity transformation. They are scenes of connection and affirmation as well as loss, confusion, and dissatisfaction. The primary relationship in Grace Lee's film *Barrier Device* transpires between two Asian women whose personal transformations dispel the dichotomous framing of Asian women as dragon lady/lotus blossom. *The Grace Lee Project* studies the categorization of Asian American women as limited and emphasizes sexuality as key in marginalizing them. Machiko Saito's experimental films articulate a racialized sexuality that is simultaneously terrorist and terrific. Her redefinition of sexuality challenges the parameters of Asian American studies' conceptions of gender and sexuality in an important way. It artfully provides the evidence we need to make sure the sexual experiences of women, no matter how uncomfortable and difficult, are accounted for in our definitions of racial agendas and communities. The discomfort Saito aims for is the ultimate goal for a filmmaker: to create space for subjectivities previously marked as worthless and undervalued for they do not meet standards of normalcy for good (Asian) women.

By surveying the ontology of Asian women in the films of Lee, Lee, and Saito, I show how the filmmakers do not so much seek to get out of the bind of racial hypersexuality and representation itself as to assert the importance of engaging explicit sex in racial representation as crucial to understanding Asian women in fantasy and public culture. The filmmakers Helen Lee, Grace Lee, and Machiko Saito engage hypersexuality as a site of trauma as well as pleasure and all engage film as an expression of ways of looking, seeing, and making their presence known as racialized and sexualized women. In their works, sexual acts and identities are where vulnerability and strength are negotiated as racialized and gendered subjects— within a frequently irreverent Asian American feminist film practice and a challenging hypersexual aesthetic, both of which provide important innovations to contemporary American cinema by asserting a new morphology, that is, new forms and structures of legibility—for Asian/American women in film, public culture, and national fantasy.

In representing sexual subjectivities and desires, Lee, Lee, and Saito evaluate them as collisions, encounters, and sites of subject formation that capture the unknowability, difficulty, pleasurability, and emotionality of racialized sexuality in representation. In creating new relations of race, sex, and cinema, they avoid the pitfalls of anti-sex, anti-feminist, and race-evading platforms circulating today. Scopic and sexual pleasure must be part of political critiques of race and representation. In these films, the relationship between sexuality and race is not premised on repugnance, victimization, or damage. Rather, Asian American feminist filmmakers demand that we, in the broadest sense of any audience, acknowledge as central different sexual practices in the experiences of gendered and racial subjects. This position strongly counters the hypersexuality we Asian women inherit in popular screens and stages. It reclaims sexuality as enabling and essential to any imaginings and articulations of the self. As such, it challenges us to rise toward creative spectatorships and authorships regarding Asian female subjection. That is, we need to imagine sexuality as not antithetical to the politics of race but essential to its envisioning.

8 ❖

NEW HORIZONS

IN RACE-POSITIVE

SEXUALITY

Sexual images of Asian women are extremely powerful in representation. As spectators, actresses, and producers, we can wrestle and remake established images in order to alter them or make them serve our variant needs. The sites of cultural production—from Broadway actresses to Hollywood femme fatales, from "yellowface" performers in stag films to porn megastars, from documentary fiction to gonzo porn, from popular films to independent films—whether marginal or mainstream, need to be studied and engaged. Within these works, Asian women filmmakers show how they are spoken for through sex and thus speak in sex in order to provide an untangling from as well as an embrace of the binds of hypersexuality and representation. Speaking in one's own terms as made by one's context of hypersexuality can better explain and celebrate Asian American women who embrace perversity as productive. In their works, a passionate engagement of perverse sexuality ultimately embraces self-acceptance.

In the works I analyze throughout this book, sexuality is redefined to be both tensely knowable and unknowable, full of pleasure and unpleasure, emotional and cold—as such, limited as well as powerful. The actresses, spectators, and filmmakers who engage in struggles for representation demonstrate powerful investment in representation itself, especially within the formulation and innovation of film languages, while remaining aware of representation's contradictions and limits in binding and categorizing Asian/American women. To dismiss explicit representations of racialized sexuality stifles the articulations of improper desires and unwieldy sexual subjectivities made by women who engage and experiment with sexuality and race, whether in industry, independent and experimental films, or performances, in order to seek better representations and realities. Asian/American women's performances and filmmaking are political practices that question the role of Asian/American women in public culture and fantasy. Sexuality is centralized not only as sexual identities but as practices of play and pleasure as well as subjugation and oppression, especially as they present challenging new subjects of sex, race, and cinema.

More recently, the work of the actress Sandra Oh in theater and increasingly prominent venues such as award-winning hit movies and popular television shows continues to challenge us as viewers. In the face of Asian women characters who choose to kill themselves when forsaken by white men in *Madame Butterfly* and *Miss Saigon,* Sandra Oh's most notable scene in the hit movie *Sideways* (2004) reverses the legacy. She will not die for the white man who relegates her love as worthless. Instead, she will beat him up till he bleeds. She establishes a viable subjectivity that brings together the gaps between fantasies of Asian women and the lived realities of Asian American women.

While Sandra Oh's roles in acclaimed shows such as the HBO series *Arli$$* and the hit television series *Grey's Anatomy* (2005–) and successful movies such as *Under the Tuscan Sun* (2003) are all not racially marked, they are also not disregarding of race. She is not playing an Asian woman with a strange accent or contorting her body in ways that are essentialized to a racial or gendered ontology. Oh performs roles wherein she is a specific socially situated subject that includes but is not entirely determined by her racial and sexual identity. While she is not the main character in these films or television series, she establishes a powerful presence as a racialized and sexualized woman not overdetermined by either category. In 2006, she won several acting awards that signal her emergence. Upon receiving the Screen Actors Guild Award in January, for her role in *Grey's Anatomy,* she expressed gratitude that the cast reflects the diversity of the United States while delivering one of the most comic and feisty speeches.

Along with the primary ensemble of the show *Grey's Anatomy,* Sandra Oh graced the cover of *Los Angeles Magazine* in 2005. She is particularly prominent in both the cover and the article given her recent nomination for an Emmy. In the interview, she states, "I'm happy to be working on a show where if you're not white, you don't have to explain your existence . . . I'm really tired of that." The same magazine interview opens with a focus on Sandra Oh's mastery of her craft. She demonstrates various ways of delivering one line so that the meaning of the scene changes in each performance. And the success of the scene, in terms of presenting identifiable characters, definitely depends on her ability to offer different interpretations and creative choices. At the end of the shoot, the writer and executive producer James Parriott is very impressed with the wide range of emotions she deploys as Dr. Christina Yang, exclaiming, "Wow, she's a Ferrari." The scene is opposite the actor Isaiah Washington, an African American man who plays Oh's boss and lover. Washington's character is as socially unskilled as Oh's is socially dominant. While the most recent reports indicate that Asian Americans are presented in television as socially incompetent uber-professionals, Oh's character displays complexity as a doctor whose bedside manner has much to be desired. Yet she also leads her cohort of medical residents with an appealing and sassy frankness. In her sexual relationship, she is blunt and clear-headed about her desires and expectations while Washington's character is confused and more tentative.

Within Sandra Oh's acclaimed films, her roles are not merely a springboard for others' development or simply a caricature; rather, they are characters begging further discussion. In *Sideways,* for example, four characters in their thirties and early forties reach crucial junctures that will decide how they will lead the rest of their lives. Miles, the best-man-to-be, takes Jack, his soon-to-be-married friend, to the Central Coast wine country of California to celebrate with wine and golf the groom's last week of bachelorhood. A former television star, the groom Jack seeks sex with any (and many) willing women. A divorced wine expert and school-teacher, Miles continues to pine for his ex-wife while lying about publishing his recently completed novel. They meet two women: the waitress-cum-graduate student Maya, a divorced white woman who cultivates her new love for wine, which is emblematic of her new independent life; and Stephanie, an Asian American single mother working as a pourer in a winery while raising a biracial daughter. When we meet Stephanie's white mother, we realize that as part of a complicated and unexplained back story, Stephanie must be an adoptee.

Quite easily, Sandra Oh's character may mistakenly be dismissed as another hypersexual Asian woman. The requisite characteristics are present: perverse sexuality, disposable love interest, and marginal subjectivity as adoptee and single mother of a biracial child. It is easy to dismiss the work if we approach the scene of Stephanie getting fucked in a contorted position at the motel, Jack's line about fucking her like an animal, and her sexual accessibility to him in isolation. For example, while Jack professes his love for Stephanie, he also characterizes her as quintessentially hypersexual: "She tastes different . . . she fucks like an animal." Meanwhile, she regards him differently, spending family time with him, her daughter, and her white mother. And he installs himself in her life, putting her daughter to sleep and charming the grandmother. Within the context of the narrative, and upon closer reading of the film, the character history, and the performance, a very full life emerges from Sandra Oh's character. While we do see the bachelor Jack regarding her as nothing more than hypersexual, we see the painful experience of such a classification for her. Even more powerfully, she rejects the classification and explodes with rage at the conclusion of the film. She becomes not only the measure of a particularly undervalued life in society; she is also the litmus test for Jack's depravity. As the poor single mother, she has less appeal for him if he must become responsible to her and her daughter. He would have to be a parent rather than remain the coddled fiancé of a privileged daughter. Stephanie's situation allows for us to measure his unethical behavior. That is, Jack becomes more truly unappealing by behaving irresponsibly and selfishly. Stephanie ultimately is a character who must cope with perceptions that mistake her for a hypersexual woman, a figure who holds no value for men like Jack.

While reviews of the film primarily focus on the other characters within the Screen Actors Guild award-winning ensemble of *Sideways*, Cynthia Fuchs in popmatters.com (2005) and Peter Travers in *Rolling Stone* (2004) describe Sandra Oh as "dazzling," "feisty," "sexy" and "sassy."[1] Oh surely establishes her presence. Travers characterizes Stephanie as "Jack's equal in carnal come-ons." Although they are sexually compatible, she is quite disadvantaged by Jack's intentions for nothing but a last-minute fling. It is rewarding to see Oh's character Stephanie exacting revenge in one of the film's most powerful scenes. When Stephanie discovers that he is about to get married, she charges at him with great rage. Looking dangerous and strong straddling her motorcycle, she drives into Jack's motel parking lot and beats him ruthlessly on the head with her helmet. She breaks his nose and he is bleeding everywhere. She unleashes the dragon lady, for reasons that make dramatic sense.

A different embrace of perversity occurs for Asian/American women in the recent film *Saving Face* (2005) by Alice Wu. It centers on two sexual deviances for its two Chinese American female leads: for the older woman, single motherhood and having a much younger lover; and for her daughter, closeted lesbian sexuality. The film offers new visions and subjectivities that redefine good and bad womanhood for Asian/American women. Wilhelmina Pang is a young surgeon who attends the elaborate weekly family ritual gathering where mothers gossip, generations mingle, and the various young people are paired up on the dance floor under watchful eyes. Closeted as a lesbian, Wil draws amusement from her mother's match-making shenanigans until she meets Vivian, another Chinese American woman, with whom she falls in love. She hides their relationship. The various older men consider Wil's widowed mother, identified only as "Ma" and played by the actress Joan Chen, to be very attractive. A scandal breaks when Ma is discovered to be pregnant out of wedlock, causing shame to her own father, the leader of the community. He promptly kicks her out of the house and into Wil's apartment. Finding it increasingly difficult to hide her sexual identity, Wil fixes her mother up with a husband in order to alleviate shame in the family and to get her out of the apartment. Wil reverses positions with her match-making mother. Ultimately unable to compromise their desires, both women choose to reclaim shame and silence by coming out to the community. At her arranged wedding, Ma reveals her relationship with a young lover; Wil kisses Vivian at the weekly family gathering. The two couples incorporate what was previously shameful in order to redefine their new family formations with these defiant acts. They are also accepted into the community fold.

Issues of sexuality in Alice Wu's debut film complicate the American narrative of immigration. Most significantly, the perverse is subsumed into the normal, in an era of intense conservatism. As exemplified in the film, today's civil rights struggles entail fighting for the right to be normal, as with the battle to legitimate gay marriage. The critique present within alternative lifestyles is subsumed into the need for recognizing such formations as acceptable relations. While the critique of heteronormativity and normalcy remains in lesbian and other unconventional partnerships, minority subjects are focusing their struggles within their rights to claims of normalcy. Marginalized subjects such as lesbian women and marginalized formations such as unconventional partnerships between older women and younger men still face shame and ill repute today. When we prioritize the needs, experiences, and desires of such marginalized subjectivities, we expand our ideas of acceptable identities, relations, and desires. In May 2006, the porn star and adult video director Mimi Miyagi filed her candidacy as a Republican candidate for governor of Nevada. Dressed in a pillbox hat and hot pink suit, she led an entourage of campaign hotties. Prominently outlining her political views from homeland security to a variety of other topics, she made claims for the browning and sexing of America through the sex-positive leadership of an immigrant porn star.

Through the sexualities of Asian/American women on scene and screen, I engage the lives of marginalized subjects in all their complexity. My work aims to open the door for the future study of Asian/American women who confront sex, not so much with fear, but with the bold spirit of recognizing its meaningful place in everyday life as a wound, a scar, a mark, a stain, and a source of joy. Ultimately, I hope that the engagement with sex in representation and the real also comes to inform and foster more imaginative relations. If sex is embraced in the visual cultural production of racialized subjects, may it also mean inclusion of those who are further marginalized by sexual subjugation in their racial experiences at the center of our politics and everyday life.

The screens and stages I discuss help to shape the everyday. They are sites for imagining alternative realities. They host sets of relationships of interdependency and contestation between subjects who author, consume, and criticize the productions. The important arena that needs to be studied is the way in which processes of authorship, spectatorship, and criticism are about the forging of relations between subjects and objects as necessarily intersubjective. We are not dominated by representation but are compelled by it to respond, to think, to shape our lives in protest or agreement, and to act in a wide range of available options. The questions of relating across others and recognizing oneself and others within the world are old questions that the sites of contemporary racialized sexuality in representation extend and excite in meaningful ways. The relationship created by racialized sexuality in the cinema and performance is best described as bondage between pain and pleasure, interdependent and mutual—a formulation that I find perfectly enabling and clarifying for the problem of Asian/American women's hypersexuality in representation and in intimate, private, and public relations. Its power is not absolute but rather holds the possibility of refashioning the self with the very reins of one's bondage.

Asian American women feminist cultural producers rewrite social expectations for Asian women that are "demanded" by hypersexual images. When a different and even pleasurable form of recognition occurs for them through sex or sexual interpellation, a new vista opens. Sexual or scopic pleasure cannot be denied at the same time that the pain and subjugating power of sexuality and moving and living image representation need to be acknowledged. The conscious engagement of both pleasure and trauma in sexual experience and its representation reflects a forwarding of consciousness from within bondage. In performing, authoring, viewing, and criticizing the sex act, it is constructed as a crucial site for constituting the self for Asian/American women. Within this site of sexuality, Asian women recast wholly different dynamics of sexuality that are also about self-fashioning, laughter, recognition, and redemption.

We lose a great deal when we avert our attention from what Asian American women have to say about sexuality and race, especially when they defy or even yearn for the norm. They constitute what Eve Oishi calls "bad Asians," or what Viet Nguyen calls "bad subjects," for they bring forward a racialized sexual aesthetic that describes the power of representation to inform one's most intimate ideas about oneself, in a discourse that should be opened up and populated with the play and pleasure—as well as the pain and trauma—that is both sexuality and moving image representation.[2] To look at the representations by Asian/American women who specifically engage hypersexuality is to see testimony of the power of representation in articulating one's subjectivity and the power of sexuality itself as the articulation of hope as it arises out of pain and the desire for pleasure and play. In claiming perverse subject positions, they offer critiques of the silence and normativity that typically stifle Asian/American women.

Engaging in the objectification of Asian women as hypersexual figures could potentially bring an autonomous sense of self by using the very terms of one's subjection. Seeing films as vehicles of consciousness allows for feelings and emotions to emerge from within certain sites of sexual subjection that exceed the project of domination or submission. In the master-slave dialectic, the primary mechanism available to the slave for transformation out of the terror of slavery is work. In the case of engaging figures of mastery on screen, independent interpretation becomes a form of work that introduces the possibility of transformation. The potential process in which actresses, spectators, and critics can embark on a transformation out of racial, sexual, and representational bondage is the claiming of the critical and creative work of interpretation located within the practices of authorship, spectatorship, and criticism.

Drawing pleasure from seeing Sandra Oh's performances, and the lives of the mother and daughter in Wu's film, and the bold declaration for inclusion indicated by Mimi Miyagi's candidacy for governor, we can see how the reclamation of sexuality in the scene of racial representation aims to capture how desire makes consciousness embodied. It makes the self flesh in the presence of the other and through the other, in concrete relations of sexuality. Touching, kissing, and expressing sexual identity and desire is not just physical, but is a meeting and colliding of consciousness and a possible site of transforming our realities. The sex act, whether unfulfilled in *Sideways* or satisfyingly life-altering in *Saving Face,* shapes consciousness as racialized and sexualized bodies are engulfed in situations of power, speaking of worlds organized by desire and the desire for recognition. As Frantz Fanon states, "As soon as I desire, I am asking to be considered."[3] The political power of Asian American feminists' engagement of sex as viewers, makers, and performers is the articulation of a desire to address social inequalities undergirding their hypersexuality and the recognition of the need to get out of their secondary status. Asian American feminist filmmakers and other engagers of popular culture present their understanding of racialized sexuality and representation itself through assertions of their needs and redefinitions. Race-positive sexuality —the representations of Asian women fucking, touching, kissing, and engaging in other bodily acts by themselves or with others—can be deployed toward new freedoms, forms, and structures of recognition and legibility in culture, fantasy, and imagination.

1 ❖ the hypersexuality of asian/american women

1 *The World of Suzie Wong* (1960) and *Flower Drum Song* (1961).

2 See Gonzalves, "Unashamed to Be So Beautiful." See also Parreñas Shimizu and Lee, "Sex Acts"; and Parreñas Shimizu, "Theory in/of Practice."

3 See Oishi, "Bad Asians."

4 For a trajectory of the "Butterfly" construct for Asian/American women, see de Lauretis, "The Stubborn Drive," 851–77; Yamamoto, "In/Visible Difference," 43; and Heung, "The Family Romance of Orientalism," 158–83. *Madame Chrysanthemum* (1887) was published by Pierre Loti in France and is widely seen as inspiring *Madame Butterfly* (Giacomo Puccini, 1904). See Lucy Liu's star-making turns as a fire-spewing lawyer in the hit television show *Ally McBeal* and as a dominatrix in various forms in such feature films as *Payback* (1999), *Charlie's Angels* (2000), *Kill Bill: Vol. 1* (2003), and *Kill Bill: Vol. 2* (2004).

5 For a wonderful analysis of Margaret Cho's performance of the racial, gendered, and politically sexual body, see Rachel Lee, "Where's My Parade?"

6 Cabreros-Sud, "Kicking Ass," 44–45.

7 Quan, *Diary of a Manhattan Call Girl*, 274. In a recently published article on the new link between sex work and popular culture, Quan clearly states that she would "never recommend prostitution as a career to anyone, even the most enthusiastic would-be call girls," in order to remind us of the power dynamics at stake not only in sex work but also when women author hypersexuality in popular media. Quan, "Raunch and Its Discontents," http://fifthestate.co.uk/2007/02/raunch-and-its-discontents (accessed February 28, 2007).

8 Quan, *Orientalia*, and *Diary of a Manhattan Call Girl*.

9 See Kempadoo and Doezema, *Global Sex Workers*; and Kempadoo, Sanghera, and Pattanaik, *Trafficking and Prostitution Reconsidered*.

10 Foucault, *The History of Sexuality*.

11 This dialogue in the film is taken verbatim from Lau's book *Runaway*,
158–60.

12 Hall, "New Ethnicities"; Wallace, *Invisibility Blues*; Julien and Mercer, "The
Last Special Issue on Race."

13 While these Asian women share a complex understanding of hyper (het-
ero) sexuality, their differences in ethnicity and class must be acknowledged
as well as the question of agency—which is never uniform nor universal but
creative and local. A prostitute runaway teenager writer writes from a
marginal class position that shapes control of her sexuality in ways radically
different from those in different class, age, gender, and race positions. The
radical sex feminists Gayle Rubin and Jill Nagle warn of the dangers of
conflating differences regarding sexual choices and conditions. See Rubin,
"Thinking Sex"; Rubin, "The Traffic in Women"; and Nagle, *Whores and
Other Feminists*.

14 See Kang, *Compositional Subjects*; Lynn Lu, "Critical Visions"; Hagedorn,
"Asian Women in Film"; and Tajima, "Lotus Blossoms Don't Bleed"; as well
as the film *Slaying the Dragon*, directed by Deborah Gee and Asian Women
United.

15 See, for example, Hershatter, *Dangerous Pleasures*, a history of prostitution
in China; Carby's work on blues women in *Cultures in Babylon*; and Zelizer,
The Purchase of Intimacy. I am indebted to Estelle Freedman and her course
on the history of sexuality in the United States for helping me to chart these
debates.

16 Marriott, *On Black Men*, xiv.

17 See films such as James Foley's *The Corruptor* (1999), which featured numerous dead Asian women, and recent movies such as Paul Haggis's *Crash*
(2005), where Asian women appear in boat or truckloads as illegal immigrants whose sexual slavery looms as possible.

18 In Asian American feminist discourse, the relationship to representation is
typically rendered as such. See interviewees in Deborah Gee and Asian
Women United's *Slaying the Dragon* (1989).

19 I make a distinction between the issues at work within a heterosexual site of
study, with its emphasis on chastity and modesty placed upon women
today, and an at times undiscerning celebration of queer sex that does not
address gender asymmetry within the queer experience of sex. While queer
critique celebrates sex, we must recall Nayan Shah's thoughtful reminder
on the "hard and wonderful" work of making sure sexism and gender
privilege are not forgotten in queer critique. We must pay attention to the
different ways sex operates in differently gendered contexts. Women continue to live under the demands of moralism on their sexual identities and

practices that any queer valorization of sex must not overlook. See Shah, "Sexuality, Identity and the Uses of History." Queer of color critique is especially nuanced in approaching the limits as well as the liberating power of sexuality. Sexuality continues to be severely delimited in our society today—while queer and porn culture may be valorized in superficial or ultimately heteronormative ways publicly, policy regarding sexuality continues to be governed by moral panics. Moralism continues to fuel debates in feminist studies—specifically sex traffic discourses, attitudes about sexuality in school, debates about prostitution, compulsory heterosexuality, or representing homosexual style as supplementary to heterosexual aims. The recent International Association for the Study of Sexuality and Culture (IASSC), meeting in the United States for the first time, focused the entire conference on moral panics and sexual rights (San Francisco State University, June 21, 2005). Queer scholars of color such as Gayatri Gopinath, Martin Manalansan, Jose Esteban Muñoz, and Nayan Shah continue to remind us of the dangers of marginalizing race, ethnicity, women, and gender issues in queer studies and of the need to account for homophobia and heterosexism in feminist and race studies.

20 The work of Kobena Mercer in *Welcome to the Jungle* and Suzanna D. Walters in *All the Rage* problematizes the notion of visibility in gay and lesbian contexts.

21 See Siobhan Somerville's study of the intertwined emergence of race and sexuality as crises, categories, and scholarly fields in the late nineteenth century and the early twentieth. She identifies the challenge in studying race and sexuality to be the avoidance of edifying one category to privilege the other (Somerville, *Queering the Color Line*, 5). The fear of sex and representation has a history in the study of racialized and colonial subjects according to Stoler, *Race and the Education of Desire*, and in ways taken up by Kamala Kempadoo and others.

22 In the last few years, defense of marriage amendments are being proposed and fought over in the United States. See, for example, George Bush's Healthy Families Initiative. Stacey, "Scents, Scholars and Stigma."

23 The literature is rich across the disciplines ranging from the work of Robert Lee, *Orientals*; Palumbo-Liu, *Asian/American*; and D'Emilio and Freedman, *Intimate Matters*.

24 For example, spectatorial pleasure is not simply locatable in a false consciousness acceptance of the fantasy figure of Suzie Wong or in the oppositional strategy of finding possibilities of resistance in Nancy Kwan's performance, as Jessica Hagedorn and Peter Feng argue. Hagedorn, "Asian Women in Film"; Feng, "Recuperating Suzie Wong."

25 For a rich and nuanced critique of the construction of Asian women's images, see the chapter entitled "Cinematic Projections" in Kang, *Compositional Subjects*. Kang argues that we must recognize the production of race

and sexuality in these images rather than understand them as corresponding directly to "real" Asian American women.

26 Palumbo-Liu, *Asian/American*, 1.

27 Kang, *Compositional Subjects*, 3.

28 Kim, "Dangerous Affinities"; Cheung, "The Woman Warrior versus the Chinaman Pacific." Leslie Bow further explicates this debate in *Betrayal and Other Acts of Subversion*.

29 Hirata, "Free, Indentured, Enslaved"; Peffer, *If They Don't Bring Their Women Here*; Rosen, *The Lost Sisterhood*, chapters 5–7 and the epilogue; D'Emilio and Freedman, *Intimate Matters*, chapter 5; and Yung, *Unbound Voices*.

30 See Kayo Hatta's film *Picture Bride*; and Glenn, *Issei, Nisei, War Bride*.

31 See the Bancroft Library and Paul Cressy boxes cited in Parreñas, "White Trash and the Little Brown Monkeys."

32 See Constable, *Romance on the Global Stage*; Valerie Soe, who uses text from mail-order bride catalogues in her film *Picturing Oriental Girls* (1992); and Tolentino, "Bodies, Letters and Catalogs."

33 See Abraham, *Speaking the Unspeakable*.

34 See Keller, *Fox Girl*; and the film *The Women Outside* by Takagi and Park.

35 See Rubin, "The Traffic in Women"; Rubin, "Thinking Sex"; and the Fifth Annual Conference by IASSC on Sexual Rights and Moral Panics, San Francisco State University, June 21, 2005.

36 See Ting, "The Power of Sexuality."

37 In terms of such sex acts and identities, Richard Fung's pioneering essay on pornography defines for gay Asian men the position of bottom as a passive one. See Fung, "Looking for My Penis." By equating the bottom to the undermined, the discourse follows patriarchal logic regarding sex practices. Thus, limited definitions of masculinity and power surface in his otherwise important critique. If the receiving position is always passive and disempowering, then women who receive, as well as men who receive, are always powerless. However, both Nguyen Tan Hoang's video *Forever Bottom!* (1999) and essay on the porn star Brandon Lee, "The Resurrection of Brandon Lee," describe a more complex and critical "bottomhood" for Asian men both in pornography and everyday practices. Redefining the position of the bottom as not entirely powerless helps reframe women of color's complex occupation of their racialized sexuality outside phallocentrism.

38 See Chuh, "Rape and Asian American Women."

39 According to Michel Foucault, "Sexuality is part of our behavior. It's a part of our world freedom. Sexuality is something that we ourselves create—it's our own creation, and much more than the discovery of a secret side of our desire. We have to understand that with our desires, through our desires, go new forms of relationships, new forms of love, new forms of creation. Sex is not a fatality: it's a possibility for creative life." Foucault, *Ethics*, 163.

40 It is easy not to think about power differentials when it comes to the intersections of race, class, sex, and gender analyses. For example, Nayan Shah, in his book *Contagious Divides*, also cautions us against the valorization of sex, especially in queer critique, if it ignores the sexual and gendered marginalization of women. Martin Manalansan's work on public cultures of homosexuality such as *Will and Grace* and *Queer Eye for the Straight Guy* also offers a similar cautionary critique. He asks us to interrogate what kind of sexuality is celebrated. How are queers and especially queers of color marginalized when celebrating homosexuality as handmaidens to normative heterosexuality? See Manalansan, "Race, Violence and Neoliberal Spatial Politics in the Global City."

41 Marks, *The Skin of the Film*, 29.

42 Russell, *Experimental Ethnography*, 25; Jay, *Downcast Eyes*, 3; Ono, "Re/membering Spectators," 131.

43 Fung, "Center the Margins."

44 So that white sexuality may be defined as normal, the racialized sexuality of women of color and of Asian women in particular must be constructed as pathological: excessive, aberrant, and deviant. Sander Gilman argues that the link between blackness and sexual "concupiscence" traces back to the Middle Ages so that a "pathology" of racialized sexuality (Abdul JanMohamad's term) or sexual racism (as used by Kevin Mumford) links biological difference to cultural difference in order to shore up the contemporaneous racial regime. JanMohamad, "Sexuality on/of the Racial Border," 94; Mumford, *Interzones*, xvii. For example, black women are blamed for an intrinsic lasciviousness that corrupts white men in order to place blame for prostitution on women of color and to sanction legalized rape of women of color. Gilman, *Making the Body Beautiful*, 228.

45 JanMohamad, "Sexuality on/of the Racial Border."

46 A particular conflation of Asian and Asian American women occurs in Hollywood and its images wherein Asian American ethnicities stand in for one another. Asian American actresses have commented on this phenomenon in various interviews. In her *Bitch* interview in April–May 2005, for example, Sandra Oh contextualizes her taking on Asian American roles responsibly, carefully describing the nature of her craft in representing any character. Moreover, while radically different, Asian American and Asian women have shared interpellations as sexualized beings. Accordingly, Asian American feminists Elaine H. Kim ("Sex Tourism in Asia"), Miriam Ching Lowe, Chandra Talpade Mohanty, and Pamela Tomas describe Asian American feminism as engaging transnational appreciation and problematization of its connections to Asian women. Neferti X. Tadiar carefully proposes vigilance in maintaining distinctions and privileges across Asian and Asian American feminisms in "Filipinas 'Living in a Time of War,'" her recent essay on Filpina/American feminisms. Laura Hyun Yi Kang intro-

duces the formulation of Asian/American women to account for the distinctions and linkages between Asian and Asian American women in her book *Compositional Subjects* (2002).

47 See Kondo, *About Face*; Josephine Lee, *Performing Asian America*; and Shimakawa, *National Abjection*.

48 For further discussion on trauma as historic, personal, and intertwined, see Caruth, *Trauma*; Caruth, *Unclaimed Experience*; and La Capra, *Writing History, Writing Trauma*.

49 See Warner, *The Trouble with Normal*.

50 In today's era of battling for gay marriage and other queer civil rights, fighting for the normal occupies a prominent place in queer platforms for social justice. While fighting for such rights in an era in which the pathology of queer people is still asserted, holding on to the vision of social and political critique that queer life proposes needs to be maintained.

51 As an expansion of Linda Williams's idea of "onscenity," or the public saturation of sexuality, rather than the private notion of obscenity in visual culture, I am interested in the scene of spectatorship whereupon these stage figures further live. See Williams, "Pornographies on/Scene, or 'Diff'rent Strokes for Diff'rent Folks,'" 233–64.

52 See the films *Sally's Beauty Spot* (H. Lee, 1990) and *Pink Eye* (Saito, 2000).

53 Robert Lee, *Orientals*, 88.

54 Eng, *Racial Castration*.

55 See Warner, *The Trouble with Normal*.

2 ❖ the bind of representation

1 See the important psychological and philosophical discussions of the concepts of normalcy and pathology in Canguilhem, "Do Sciences of the Normal and the Pathological Exist?"

2 I argue for the notion of hypersexuality as a bond of mutual recognition in the article "Master-Slave Sex Acts."

3 My usage of the term "Asian women" refers to the trajectory of fantastic figures found within representational images rather than "real" women. My study aims to provide evidence for rethinking particular models in their interpretation. Through the specific notion of Asian women as a discourse of fantasy, I use race, sex, and gender to show how the production of meaning in the process of representation is complicated. For a genealogy of the suicidal Asian woman in the theater from *Madame Chrysanthemum* (1887) to the *Mikado* (1885) to *Madame Butterfly* (1904), see de Lauretis, "The Stubborn Drive," 873; and Heung, "The Family Romance of Orientalism," 160.

4 I believe that the Asian woman's innocence, versus the white woman's innocence, is made perverse when she is also a prostitute.

5   Berlant, *The Queen of America Goes to Washington City*, 58–60.

6   At the end of the musical, the curtains close as Ellen, the American wife, reaches out to Tam, Chris and Kim's biracial son.

7   Yoshikawa, "The Heat Is on Miss Saigon Coalition," 277.

8   See Kondo, *About Face*; Schlossman, *Actors and Activists*; and Shimakawa, *National Abjection* for excellent studies of the *Miss Saigon* controversy and activism.

9   See Rubin, "Thinking Sex," 297. Using Jeffrey Weeks's term "moral panic," Rubin describes how fervent social fears translate to scapegoating sexual minorities. In this ground-breaking essay, Rubin identifies the limits of feminism and the need to study sexuality as a system of oppression distinct from a gender system that prioritizes the victim status of women in its study of sexuality.

10 J. Lee, *Performing Asian America*, 56.

11 Kondo, *About Face*, 228–35.

12 Pao, "The Eyes of the Storm."

13 Schlossman, *Actors and Activists* is an excellent historical address of activism accompanied by careful analysis of content in *Miss Saigon*.

14 Ibid.

15 Ibid.

16 See Angela Pao and Behr and Steyn as cited in Shimakawa, *National Abjection*, 46.

17 Schlossman, *Actors and Activists*, 149.

18 Quan, foreword to *Orientalia*, 8–13.

19 Ibid. Tracy Quan accuses white feminists of xenophobia for attempting to contain the sexual adventures of Western men. She also critiques the victimized representation of prostitutes, both Asian and Asian American.

20 Shimakawa, *National Abjection*, 188. Shimakawa builds off of the French feminist theorist Julia Kristeva, who defines abjection as "both a state and process—the condition/position of that which is deemed loathsome and the process by which that appraisal is made or the means by which the subject/the I is produced; by establishing perceptual and conceptual borders around the self and jettisoning that which is deemed objectionable, the subject comes into and maintains self-consciousness" (188). In my work, I assert that sexuality abjects Asian women as racialized and gendered subjects and that this hypersexuality leads to a race panic when it comes to discourses of representation.

21 Following Jose Esteban Muñoz, who describes the agency of queer spectators and producers of color, my experience may indeed be called a kind of "disidentification" practice. Muñoz, introduction to *Disidentifications*, 4. I use identification in the psychoanalytic sense of seeing oneself in another in a kind of recognition or in identifying oneself with another on stage as a substitution of the self. Freud defines identification as a position that is

directly tied to the original object, which then undergoes a process of substitution, until finally, the meaning of the object becomes tied sexually to a person. See Freud, *Group Psychology and the Analysis of the Ego*, 50.

22 Schlossman, *Actors and Activists*, 151.

23 I am interested in the politics of pleasure in the experience of enjoyment as a rich and contradictory site that diagnoses politics, power, and resistance. I am especially compelled by Slavoj Žižek's discussion of pleasure at the site of subjugation. See Žižek, *For They Know Not What They Do*, 159–60.

24 For a theory about the multiplicity of viewing positions, see Josephine Lee, *Performing Asian America*.

25 Wolf, *Problem Like Maria*.

26 As I am talking about the fantasy of the Asian woman, rather than measuring what "real" Asian women feel, the case of Filipina American performers and spectators on Broadway provides a specificity of the raced actress who performs against a white male script.

27 While the contemporary cast is composed of a varied number of other ethnic Asian women, I note the hugely significant presence of Filipinas. My status as a Filipina American scholar surely enabled my intimate conversation with the actresses I interviewed. The historical and social context of constructing Filipinos as "the entertainers of Asia" is yet to be developed more significantly.

28 Tajima, "Lotus Blossoms Don't Bleed" identifies the minor roles of Asian women as a mainstay of the Asian female stereotype: faceless hordes that signify essential qualities to whole groups of Asian American women.

29 Stanislavsky, *Building a Character*, 5.

30 Chekhov, *On the Technique of Acting*, 156.

31 Stanislavsky, *Creating a Role*, 93–94.

32 Stanislavsky, *Building a Character*, 269.

33 Strasberg, *At the Actors Studio*, 327–28.

34 Again, my focus on Filipina actresses is primarily for empirical purposes, since the interviews and anecdotal accounts emerge owing to the predominance of actors and actresses of this ethnic background in *Miss Saigon* and the particular access provided by my own ethnicity. In November 1999, I met Edmund Nalzaro in New York City's Broadway Theater. I interviewed him in New York City on October 2000, along with the actresses Luzviminda Lor and J. Elaine Marcos.

35 Marcos, personal interview, October 2000.

36 Wang, "Oh My!" 15.

37 Lor, personal interview, October 2000.

38 See Mani, *Contentious Traditions*; and Sunder Rajan, *Real and Imagined Women*.

39 Schlossman points to how Edward Behr reports that "Boublil, Schönberg and Hytner were determined to have as many real-life Asians in the cast as possible; Madame Butterfly-type make-up, though suitable enough for

opera, would, they knew, be inadequate, *especially for female members of the cast.*" See Schlossman, *Actors and Activists*, 141, emphasis added. And in the same work, Angela Pao describes how Asian women are "exotic songbirds played authentically and Asian men are ciphers for whites to play" (152).

40 Lor, personal interview.
41 Marcos, personal interview.
42 Ibid.
43 Ibid.
44 Ibid.
45 Lor, personal interview.
46 Ibid.
47 Ibid.
48 Lor, personal interview.
49 Marcos, personal interview.
50 Lor, personal interview.
51 Ibid.
52 Wolf, *Problem Like Maria*, 141.
53 Lacan, "The Mirror Stage," 2.
54 See Mercer, *Welcome to the Jungle*, and Hall, *Representations*.
55 I am referring to racial discourses of representation criticized by Michele Wallace, who points to the limits of negative/positive image demands by communities of color. My theory of misidentification builds upon her critique and offers concrete solutions that account for the complexity of images that she prioritizes in her work. See Wallace, *Invisibility Blues*, 1–4.

3 ❈ the sexual bonds of racial stardom

The quotation from Anna May Wong that opens this chapter is from See, "Anna May Speaks," 195–96. The Nancy Kwan quotation is from JoAnn Lee, *Asian American Actors*, 207. The Lucy Liu quotation is from Chambers, "Lucy Liu."

1 For a discussion of theater and film representations of the butterfly trope, see Heung, "The Family Romance of Orientalism," 158–83.
2 The definition of sexuality I subscribe to includes a Foucauldian understanding of the pervasiveness of sex and a Freudian psychoanalytic understanding of the centrality of sex to explain the frenzy and rupture of identity as it applies to a racial and gendered scene. See de Lauretis, "The Stubborn Drive," 873; Foucault, *History of Sexuality*; Freud, "Fetishism"; and Lane, *The Psychoanalysis of Race*.
3 See Nancy Kwan's interviews in Deborah Gee and Asian Women United, *Slaying the Dragon*; and JoAnn Lee, *Asian American Actors*.
4 Ogunnaike, "The Perks and Pitfalls Of a Ruthless-Killer Role."
5 Leong, *The China Mystique*, 62. Graham Russell Gao Hodges's biography

Anna May Wong: From Laundryman's Daughter to Hollywood Legend provides the historical context of the intense racism that shaped her life as well
as her reception within the Chinese American community. Caught between
a Hollywood system that " 'bound' her talent with restrictive, demean-
ing roles that accentuated a western, often sadistic eroticizing of Chinese
women" (232) and racial and national politics that magnified the impact of
her roles and drew resentment from Chinese American and Chinese communities, Anna May Wong nonetheless demonstrated critical agency in
commenting on racism and writing "articles in fan magazines and newspapers on significant topics including interracial love, Hollywood careers,
and Japanese aggression" (xxi). Karen Leong's *The China Mystique* studies
the gendering of American Orientalism in Anna May Wong's negotiation
of transnational forces in formulating her own subjectivity. Leong astutely
evaluates Wong's choices to pursue acting and to lead an unconventional
racial and gendered life against the conventions faced by other Chinese
American women (to marry early and work within the family laundry,
typically). Leong characterizes her scene-stealing performances in *Shanghai Express:* "Wong portrayed the stereotypical role of the stoic Chinese
prostitute with passion; expressing inner strength and depth beneath the
seemingly placid visage, she stole scenes from Dietrich" (65). Moreover,
Wong's life involved a political process of becoming Chinese American (77)
and a critical commentary on the limits and perils of participating in
popular representation. Anthony Chan's *Perpetually Cool* traces the career
trajectory of Anna May Wong as she negotiated community and industry
in establishing her visible presence in Hollywood and the world.

6 Negra, *Off-White Hollywood*, 8.

7 Homi Bhabha focuses on the ambivalence of the stereotype. The stereotype
must repeat itself "in changing historical and discursive conjunctures; informs its strategies of individuation and marginalization; produces that
effect of probabilistic truth and predictability which, for the stereotype,
must always be in excess of what can be empirically proved or logically
constructed." See Bhabha, *Nation and Narration*, 66.

8 Mercer, *Welcome to the Jungle*; Hall, *Representations*; and Wallace, *Invisibility Blues*.

9 Homi Bhabha defines the stereotype as an "arrested" representation in
Nation and Narration, 77.

10 For example, images of Japanese and Chinese Americans were influenced
by U.S. foreign policy, particularly when it needed to decry an enemy so as
to justify national relations. See Eugene Wong, *Visual Media Racism*.

11 Denise Uyehara is a Los Angeles-based performance artist who focuses on
Asian American bisexual female identity issues. Her performances include
Hello Sex Kitty (1999), which traveled widely to universities and other
exhibition spaces.

12 See Ma, *The Deathly Embrace.*

13 See Read, *The Fact of Blackness.*

14 For a phenomenological approach to film, see Russell, *Experimental Ethnography*; Marks, *The Skin of the Film*; Sobchack, *The Address of the Eye*; and Williams, *Viewing Positions*, for an intersubjective approach to cinema. In addition, Williams, *Viewing Positions*, includes essays that critique dominant paradigms of viewing such as the male gaze, and various works by the Frankfurt school that refuse to grant agency to spectators and ignore the intersubjectivity of the reception experience.

15 I must note that I formulate this particular racial sexuality within a feminist discourse that excludes the Asian woman and within a racial discourse that ignores her sexuality. This is a problem in terms of theorizing the Asian femme fatale's seemingly eternal presence as wild and corrupting sex.

16 See the works of Kim, *Asian American Literature*; Hagedorn, *Dogeaters*; Hahn, *Earshot*; Parmar, "That Moment of Emergence"; Trinh T. Minh-ha, *Woman, Native, Other*; Zarco, "My Worst Fear" and "Once Upon a Seesaw with Charlie Chan"; Chrystos, *Not Vanishing*; Davis, *Women, Culture, Politics*; Hammonds, "Black (W)holes and Geometry of Black Female Sexuality" and "Race, Sex, AIDS: Construction of 'Other' "; Hine, *Dangerous Women*; Jordan, *Living Room*; Lorde, *Black Unicorn* and *Uses of Erotic: The Erotic as Power*; Moraga, *Loving in the War Years*; Sapphire, *Push*; and Ntozake Shange, *For Colored Girls Who Have Considered Suicide When the Rainbow Is Enuf.*

17 This reclamation of Anna May Wong as a "bad woman" and a feminist icon of sorts is a historically bound project within our "post-feminist" world. That is, in proposing alternative ways of defining Wong's performance, her role within feminist and racial politics of representation changes. I am working in a vein similar to that of Patricia Hill Collins, who traces the black body in popular imagination from the Venus Hottentot to Josephine Baker to Beyoncé Knowles and Jennifer Lopez. She describes the conundrum regarding problematic definitions of black sexuality and the agency and resistance of these women in engaging this definition. See Collins, *Black Sexual Politics.*

18 Racial others such as black men play roles that significantly require their racial visibility. An extraordinarily large black man is the main guard of the palace and is framed in contrast to the smaller "Mongols" or "Eastern" men.

19 See *Slaying the Dragon* wherein clips and stills of Anna May Wong are used as examples of "bad" stereotypical representation without contextualized analysis.

20 In the previous chapter, I identify the viewing position of misidentification as the rejection of the ideologies presented in the cultural text in favor of the viewer's own identifications, desires, and needs.

21 Karen Leong describes how Anna May Wong's racial heritage influenced,

and at times, overdetermined her comportment and movements in her film roles. See Leong, *The China Mystique*, 72.

22   See Negra, *Off-White Hollywood*; and Leong, *The China Mystique*, 64.

23   As the thief progresses toward upright stature as a reformed prince, he becomes more clothed.

24   *Toll of the Sea* (1922), *Thief of Bagdad* (1924), and *Shanghai Express* (1932) are Anna May Wong's most significant film roles that led to supporting roles in major films as well as lead roles in B movies.

25   In a queer reading of scenes such as the one in which Shanghai Lily grabs the knife from Hui Fei, my student Mary Trieu suggests that Hui Fei saves Shanghai Lily because they are lovers. Unpublished, untitled paper.

26   Feng, "Recuperating Suzie Wong," 42.

27   Cheng, "Beauty and Ideal Citizenship," 56–57.

28   Ford and Chanda, "Portrayals of Gender and Generation, East and West: Suzie Wong in the Noble House," 119.

29   Law Kar, "Suzie Wong and Her World," 68.

30   Ibid., 69.

31   Marchetti, *Romance and the "Yellow Peril,"* 116.

32   Ibid., 120.

33   See Koshy, *Sexual Naturalization*.

34   Anne Anlin Cheng theorizes the triangular formation of various racial womanhoods in the musical. See Cheng, *The Melancholy of Race*. My student Mary Trieu is developing an astounding, illuminating reading of the film of *Flower Drum Song*, arguing that Helen is a bisexual/lesbian character caught in queer relationships with both Mei Li and Linda Low.

35   Linda Low is reimagined by David Henry Hwang in his remake of the musical on Broadway in 2001. Linda Low no longer represents a corruptive, man-hungry figure but is a more complex and largely ambiguous female figure seeking artistic expression outside the community of Chinatown.

36   Similar to Anna May Wong's career, Nancy Kwan's decelerated after these first successful forays into leading roles.

37   Another movie trailer, for *Very Bad Things* (1998), also features an unknown Asian woman who falls to the floor with a great thud in a close-up that is supposed to be a funny shot. Others have speculated the actress to be the porn star Kobe Tai. In my viewing in several theaters, people laughed a lot at such a racially loaded scene. The character in the film is a prostitute who is killed by too vigorous intercourse with several white men, who end up killing her black bodyguard as well.

38   Fuchs, "This Epic Battle."

39   In my interviews with moviegoers who had seen *Charlie's Angels*, I attempted to collect responses to this scene of Lucy Liu performing a massage. While many viewers express resentment at this stereotypical role, they

also appreciate Liu's performance as "ironic" or "sarcastic." Other viewers also point to how Lucy Liu was the only one among the Angels capable of playing the role, because her racial background was necessary for making it "believable." The responses index varied appropriations of meaning for this scene. See my film *The Fact of Asian Women*, whose world premiere was at the Silver Lake International Film Festival, Los Angeles, 2002.

40   For a visual representation of the argument in this chapter, see my video *The Fact of Asian Women*.

41   I use the term based on the U.S. military description circulating in Southeast Asian sex tourism scenes: "little brown fucking machines powered by rice." L. M. H. Hing discusses the "sex machine" in terms of the development of global hypermasculinity as one of the most powerful manifestations of imperialism within globalization today. See Ling, "Sex Machine."

42   The critic Cynthia Liu and the novelist Lisa See studied the late actress's papers in archives at the University of Southern California, Paramount, and the Library of Congress, including interviews in the fan magazine *Photoplay*, in order to fuse the powerful images of sexuality with the much less sexual voice of the actress herself. Based on research on Anna May Wong's many interviews, and quoting directly from those interviews and Wong's other public statements, Lisa See honors Wong's belligerent voice and direct criticism of Hollywood. Cynthia Liu studies closely Anna May Wong's interviews and captures a sassy, irreverent presence that is political and powerful. See C. Liu, "When Dragon Ladies Die, Do They Become Butterflies?," 23–39; and See, "Anna May Speaks," 195–96.

43   See, "Anna May Speaks," 195.

44   C. Liu, "When Dragon Ladies Die, Do They Become Butterflies?," 23–39.

45   See, "Anna May Speaks," 195–96.

46   Lisa See describes the historical context of anti-miscegenation laws, the significance of Wong's stardom in Europe, the Chinese and Chinese American responses to her stardom as "negative images," and her search for home as a woman both integrated into and excluded from American culture.

47   *Peter Pan* (1924), *The Crimson City* (1928), *Across to Singapore* (1928), *Tiger Bay* (1934), *Java Head* (1934), *Daughter of Shanghai* (1937), *Vitaphone Novelty: Thrills from the Past* (1961), *The Savage Innocents* (1959), *Portrait in Black* (1960), and *Silents Please: Old San Francisco* (1961).

48   Asian and Asian American women were referred to as Oriental women during the time when Anna May Wong was working in film.

49   Leong, *The China Mystique*, 61.

50   Ibid., 82.

51   JoAnn Lee, *Asian American Actors*, 207.

52   Dadyburjor, "A Thing for Ling."

53   Dyer, *Stars*, 182.

54 Rob Medich, "Just Who Is Lucy Liu?"

55 As cited in Chihara, "There's Something about Lucy."

56 "Q the Interview: Lucy Liu," *Independent Sunday* (London), features section, June 29, 2003.

57 Feng, "Recuperating Suzie Wong,".

58 Foucault, *The History of Sexuality*, vol. 1, 95.

59 JoAnn Lee, *Asian American Actors*, 210–11.

60 I do this in my digital film *The Fact of Asian Women*.

61 Anna May Wong occupies the position of icon in many articles and cultural productions, such as *China Doll*, the play by Elizabeth Wong.

62 Butler, *The Psychic Life of Power*, 7–10.

63 Ibid., 7.

64 According to Butler, "The subject is the linguistic occasion or the individual to achieve and reproduce intelligibility—the linguistic condition of its existence and agency." See Butler, *The Psychic Life of Power*, 10–11.

65 Ibid., 243.

66 Gordon, *Ghostly Matters*, 179.

67 Sobchack, *The Address of the Eye*, 129.

4 ❖ racial threat or racial treat?

1 Queer white male discussions of stag representations emphasize both the unwieldy nature of meaning in hard-core pornography as well as the possibility of authenticating self-identity in sexual representation. In gay discourses of pornographic representation, Earl Jackson argues, the "visibility of gay men is predicated on acts"—in terms of becoming an "identifiable gay male subject. . . . The figures on screen owe their visibility to their voluntary submission to the gaze of the other and the desire of the other." See Jackson, "Graphic Specularity," 139. Jackson describes the dynamic engagement between viewers and the performers on screen as entangled subjects: "it is precisely as a representation that the screen image offers the viewer a range of psychical realities as phantasmatic possibilities for articulating subject positions within the spectatorial situation, especially because the viewers' drives themselves are, fundamentally, representations" (149). Tom Waugh's study of gay male eroticism also shows the racial difference in relating to sexual representation. Waugh discusses the potential for "political pride of a stigmatized minority rediscovering a cultural heritage, as magnificent as it is lurid." See Waugh, *Hard to Imagine*, 285.

2 See Harris, *The Stag Film Report*; Williams, *Hard Core*; and Hoffman, "Prolegomena to a Study of Traditional Elements in the Erotic Film."

3 See essays by Penley and Williams in Williams, *Porn Studies*.

4 See the websites of various porn stars such as Mimi Miyagi, who complains

about being the lowest paid performer on shoots. In the case of black women in porn, see Miller-Young's "A Taste for Brown Sugar."

5 See Magdalena Barrera's critique of Laura Kipnis in "Hottentot 2000"; and MacKinnon and Dworkin, ed., *In Harm's Way*.

6 Kipnis, *Bound and Gagged*, xii. The possibilities can be opened up to dissect the production of hypersexuality creatively—as indicated in the mock pornography tapes by Greg Pak. In *All Amateur Ecstasy* (2001) and *Asian Pride Porn* (2001), sexuality is both politically conscious and humorous about race. In the first tape, a number of Asian and other women appear to be having orgasms. Only at the end of the short film do we realize that their head bobbing shots culminate in sneezes. In *Asian Pride Porn*, the series of trailers advertise porn tapes based on typical Asian roles on popular television such as the Chinese delivery boy sex scene in order to install racial pride in yellow porn.

7 de Lauretis, "The Stubborn Drive."

8 Walter Kendrick historicizes the debates about pornography from Plato's and Aristotle's competing understandings of the power of culture to the present. "Plato makes art out to be something like poison, slowly accumulating in the system and strangling it. In the Aristotelian view, art is homeopathic medicine, to be taken as needed and put back on the shelf" (*The Secret Museum,* 40). He states that knowledge is at stake in the critic's stand on pornography "also by implication, to any representation of whatever kind, in whatever medium" (40). Claims about the power of representation and sexuality that Earl Jackson makes reflect this equation. In gay studies of representation, for example, the power of affirmation and the identification of heritage for a sexually oppressed and categorized group through representation must be available. See Jackson, "Graphic Specularity." Tom Waugh argues, for example, that within stag films, gay spectators have the opportunity for visual pleasure, self-identity, and self-legitimation" in terms of acknowledging a kind of treasure trove of treats for a minority without visible history of its love, passions, and actions. See Waugh, *Hard to Imagine*, 319.

9 See Rubin, "Thinking Sex."

10 Linda Williams describes "the quintessential stag film shot: a close-up of penetration that shows that hard core activity is taking place." Its aim was the "genital show" of sexual penetration, and not so much proof of pleasure such as the money shot or proof of ejaculate that one can see in contemporary feature pornography. See Williams, *Hard Core*, 72.

11 A number of stag films at the Kinsey Institute feature interracial sex between whites and blacks, including *Darkie Rhythm* (1928–30) and *Two Nights and a Day* (1953), but the established discourses about stag do not attend to racial difference in their studies.

12 Only in the years after World War II, coinciding with the large migration of Asian women coming to the United States as war brides, do Asian women come to play themselves in *China Babe* (1950), *Oriental Girlfriend* (1965), and *Date Night* (1961). In all of the stag films featuring Asian-white interracial sex, skin color difference does not play out either.

13 For an extensive study of social hygiene, race suicide, and eugenics as it mattered to Asian immigration and American modernity, see Robert G. Lee, *Orientals*; Palumbo-Liu, *Asian/American*; Shah, *Contagious Divides*; and Yu, *Thinking Orientals*.

14 Hoffman, "Prolegomena to a Study of Traditional Elements in the Erotic Film," 144.

15 Kendrick, *The Secret Museum*, 27.

16 The couple is indeed Filipino in *Philippino Couple* and Korean in *Korean Couple*, as opposed to interracial pairings in the representation.

17 Waugh, *Hard to Imagine*, 297.

18 Ibid., 298.

19 Ibid., 298.

20 Ibid., 298.

21 Structuring recuperation of Asian stag films for Asian male or female viewers is not possible in the same way that critics have approached gay spectatorship and subject formation. I have not found data available for Asian American male or female spectatorships of these stag films, as they were viewed in the predominantly racially segregated spaces of the American Legion and frat houses.

22 Hoffman, "Prolegomena to a Study of Traditional Elements in the Erotic Film," 145.

23 Martha Harsanyi worked as the Kinsey film curator from 1970 to 1975. I interviewed her on June 2000 in Bloomington, Indiana.

24 Palumbo-Liu, *Asian/American*, 93–94.

25 Fanon, *Black Skin, White Masks*; and Bhabha, *Nation and Narration*.

26 See Heung, "The Family Romance of Orientalism."

27 Waugh, *Hard to Imagine*, 315.

28 These are the major sex scenes in the film. They do not include the title cards or the brief monster shots after the first title cards. I am referring to the still shots of a penis and then a vagina at the start of the film.

29 Waugh, *Hard to Imagine*, 314.

30 Ibid., 315.

31 Such a trope is referenced in Hwang, *M. Butterfly*.

32 See Fung, "Looking for My Penis." What would Fung's essay—on passivity as no way for pleasure—say of this particular concluding sex act? See Nguyen Tan Hoang's film *Forever Bottom!* and its reclamation of the passive sexual position as politically strategic.

33 Mumford, *Interzones*.

34 Staiger, *Bad Women*, 56.

35 Hoffman, "Prolegomena to a Study of Traditional Elements in the Erotic Film."

36 Olsen, "How Those Stag Movies Are Made." For additional information on exotic dance, see Shocket, "Birth of the Blues."

37 Staiger, *Bad Women*.

38 Williams, *Hard Core*, 84.

39 Kipnis, *Bound and Gagged*, x–xi.

40 Such stag film pornography is race positive in the sense that its entanglement with race is superficial. In *Hard Core*, Linda Williams defines three different forms of utopia written in pornography: integrated, dissolved, and separated. In the dissolved and separated forms of utopia, the point is that sex occurs "behind the green door." See Williams, *Hard Core*, specifically the chapter entitled "Utopia" (166–82).

41 Palumbo-Liu, *Asian/American*, 17.

42 Ibid.

43 Staiger, *Bad Women*.

44 Williams, *Hard Core*, 59.

45 Ibid., 58.

5 ✳ Queens of anal, double, triple, and the gangbang

1 MacKinnon, *Only Words*; and Dworkin and MacKinnon, *In Harm's Way*.

2 Morgan, "Theory and Practice," 139.

3 Segal, "Sweet Sorrows, Painful Pleasures," 70.

4 Waugh, *Hard to Imagine*.

5 Williams, *Hard Core*.

6 Kipnis, *Bound and Gagged*.

7 Bright, "White Sex"; Williams, "Porn Studies: Proliferating Pornographies On/Scene"; Wolf, "The Porn Myth"; Penley, "Crackers and Whackers."

8 Wolf, "The Porn Myth."

9 Trinh T. Minh-ha, *Woman, Native, Other*.

10 See generally Hine, *The African American Odyssey*; Higginbotham, *History and Theory*; and E. Brown, *Black Women in America*.

11 This is a particularly intense experience at some conferences wherein white feminists respond to my prioritization of race as sex negative and feminists of color fear what the priority of sexuality threatens in terms of reifying the traditional pathology ascribed to women of color.

12 Bright, "White Sex." See also Williams, "Porn Studies: Proliferating Pornographies On/Scene."

13 Barrera, "Hottentot 2000," 407. The Kipnis analysis of *Hustler* may be found in Kipnis, "(Male) Desire and (Female) Disgust."

14 Kipnis, *Bound and Gagged*, xii.

15 Ibid., x.

16 Queen, *Real Live Nude Girl*; Sprinkle, *Annie Sprinkle: Post-Porn Modernist*. See also Rubin, "The Traffic in Women" and "Thinking Sex."

17 Gardner, "Racism in Pornography," 105–6.

18 Teish, "A Quiet Subversion."

19 A. Walker, "Coming Apart," 41.

20 A. Walker, "Porn."

21 Rhacel Parreñas, " 'White Trash' Meets the 'Little Brown Monkeys,' " 115, 132 n. 7.

22 Chrystos, *Not Vanishing*; Cherríe Moraga, *Loving in the War Years*; Lorde, *Sister Outsider*. The work of these authors demonstrates the context in which women of color write about their sexuality. They assert the need to redefine sexuality in their own terms.

23 Berlant, introduction to *The Queen of America Goes to Washington City*.

24 See Chuh, "Rape and Asian American Women."

25 Jackson, "Graphic Specularity," 129.

26 Kleinhans, "Teaching Sexual Images," 119.

27 C. Liu, "When Dragon Ladies Die, Do They Become Butterflies?"; and Oren, "Secret Asian Man."

28 LaPlanche and Pontalis, *The Language of Psychoanalysis*, entry on phantasy, using Freud, "Formulations on the Two Principles of Mental Functioning." More generally, see Freud, *The Interpretation of Dreams*.

29 Žižek, "From the Sublime to the Ridiculous," 171. Žižek discussed the process of composing the sex act in cinema by actors and producers in order to assess its unrepresentability (176). For example, pornography is "codified" rather than "spontaneous" (177). In his discussion of the sex act between Willem Dafoe and Laura Dern in *Wild at Heart* (1990), Žižek discussed how he may see power dynamics in the sex act (185). Dafoe's character demands that Dern's character state her consent to his sexual demands, and then rejects her. Through the focus on her hand, we see her resistance unravel toward willingness, what Žižek calls the "sign of her acquiescence, the proof that he has stirred up her fantasy." His surprising rejection, according to Žižek, further humiliates her—in a demonstration of the power dynamics in the moment of the sex act.

30 Kendrick, *The Secret Museum*, 33–66.

31 Ibid., 65.

32 See Deborah Gee's film *Slaying the Dragon*; and Marchetti, *Romance and the Yellow Peril*.

33 Omi and Winant, *Racial Formation in the United States*.

34 *Date Night* is also known as *Chinese Babe* and *Oriental Girlfriend*.

35 From the Internet Adult Film Database at http://www.iafd.com (accessed September 28, 2006).

36 Palumbo-Liu, *Asian American*, 81–115.

37 See http://excaliburfilms.com/pornlist/starpgs/Mai_Lin.htm (accessed May 23, 2006).

38 See information on Mai Lynn on film and Mai Lin in the video's cover.

39 Kristara Barrington played roles that included a Chinatown girl and a spoil of war. Asian women's racial difference, established both in the costume and in the narrative, persists in the grammar of seduction in other films such as *Samurai Dick* (1984). In that film, Ron Jeremy offers an "American hotdog" to her "sashimi." The Asian women in the film act as "little girls" dressed in kimonos having sex to Oriental muzak. In *One Night in Bangkok* (1985), Kristara Barrington has an Oriental accent of broken English within a narrative where soldiers compare the whorishness of Asian women to the innocence of the white women they left behind at home.

40 See http://adult-pornstar-mall.com/starpgs/Kristara_Barrington.htm (accessed May 23, 2006).

41 Josephine Lee, *Performing Asian America*.

42 Jacobs, "The Lady of Little Death," 13.

43 *Adult Video News*, http://www.adultvideonews.com (accessed May 23, 2006); Google search results, http://www.google.com/search?hl=en&lr=&q=pornography+asian&btnG=Search (accessed May 23, 2006).

44 Less recognizable in the mainstream but popular Asian/American porn stars like Mimi Miyagi, Kobe Tai, Mika Tan and others must perform roles that fall clearly within limited parameters. In screening compilation films like *All Star Asians*, the selection of films is unified by the overdetermination of race in presenting Asian female sexuality in pornography. Like the fetishization of their body parts such as in the smallness in stature of Kobe Tai in *Haunted* where the male performer does not demonstrate connection to her as a subjectivity but as merely a body to use. In *Ancient Sex Secrets* directed by Ralph Parfait, Kia and John Dough perform sex within the context of yoga and breathing exercises. The dialogue employs the "ancient forces," "yin and yang," "jade stalk" and "jade gate" and the action involves Oriental massage. In *John Friendly Big and Small*, directed by John Friendly, the Asian women act as extremely enthusiastic energetic servile sex partners coded as third world subjects. While Asian women constitute a huge specialized genre in pornography, their appearances limit towards racial fetishism unless they are exceptional stars like Asia Carrera who asserts both a personal history and subjectivity other than race, such as gender dynamics in a marriage for example.

45 For a comparison, Nina Hartley has directed approximately fifteen titles.

46 Williams, *Hard Core,* 130.

47 *Asia Carrera* xxx Buttkicking Homepage, http://www.asiacarrera.com (accessed September 30, 2006).

48 http://www.asiacarrera.com/bio2.html (accessed September 30, 2006).

49 http://www.asiacarrera.com/bio.html (accessed September 30, 2006).

50 Nakamura, "Big Money Shot."

51 http://www.asiacarrera.com/bio2.html (accessed September 30, 2006).

52 Morris, "The Child Defiled," 29.

53 Ibid., 1.

54 Annabel Chong also directed two films I have not seen, *Office Cruelty* (Impressive 2000) and *Pornomancer* (New Machines Studio 1998).

55 Morris, "The Child Defiled," 2.

56 Chun, "Sex," 2.

57 See http://www.worldsexhosting.com/pstars/annabel.html (accessed May 23, 2006) and http://www.megawallpapers.org/gallery/242/annabel-cong?show=full (accessed September 28, 2006).

58 Askew, "Life Thru a Lens."

59 Clinton, "Sex Sobers in Controversial Sundance Documentary."

60 http://www.ruthlessreviews.com/movies/s/sex.html (accessed May 23, 2006).

61 Morris, "The Child Defiled," 2.

62 Williams, "Review of *Sex: The Annabel Chong Story,*" 53.

63 Chun, "*Sex: The Annabel Chong Story,*" 3.

64 Ibid.

65 Penny, "One on One with Annabel Chong."

66 Clinton, "Sex Sobers in Controversial Sundance Documentary."

67 Chun, Kimberly. "*Sex: The Annabel Chong Story.*"

68 Morris, "The Child Defiled."

69 Penny, "One on One with Annabel Chong."

70 Chun, "*Sex: The Annabel Chong Story.*"

71 http://www.annabelchong.com (accessed May 23, 2006).

72 Jacobs, "Katrien Jacobs Fleshes Out Maria Beatty."

6 ❖ "Little brown fucking machines powered by rice"

1 See Enloe, *Bananas, Beaches and Bases.*

2 Similarly, t-shirts emblazoned with "Sex Tourist" are also available for sale. See Louie, *Orientalia.*

3 For a discussion of the economic reasons and motivations for women in Asian sex tourism, see Truong, *Sex, Money and Morality*. It is primarily through an economic lens that she investigates the problem. I am interested

in the fantasies circulating in and the desires manufactured for it in visual culture.

4 Gonzo, the popular contemporary genre of professional-amateur cinéma vérité or "reality-based" pornography, features hard-core sex between white male sex tourists and Southeast Asian female prostitutes.

5 Roc, http://www.asiaerotica.com/editorial.html (accessed September 26, 2006).

6 See Trinh T. Minh-ha's discussion in Chen, "Speaking Nearby."

7 See Brennan, "Selling Sex for Visas"; and Bales, "Because She Looks Like a Child."

8 Berens, "Nine Inch Nails," 270.

9 Berry, Hamilton, and Jayamanne, *The Filmmaker and the Prostitute*, 149.

10 Urban, "Dennis O'Rourke and *The Good Woman Of Bangkok*," 158.

11 Souter, "The Bad Man of Bangkok?" 121.

12 Jayamanne, "Reception, Genre and the Knowing Critic," 27.

13 Thanks go to Cynthia Liu for suggesting this interpretation of looking askance.

14 Powers, "An Unreliable Memoir," 108.

15 See Hamilton, "Mistaken Identities"; and Cohen, "Brecht in Bangkok."

16 Wartofsky, "The Trial of Dennis O'Rourke at Patpong," 161.

17 Wartofsky, "The Trial of Dennis O'Rourke at Patpong."

18 Urban, "Dennis O'Rourke and *The Good Woman of Bangkok*," 161.

19 Heung, "The Family Romance of Orientalism."

20 Urban, "Dennis O'Rourke and *The Good Woman of Bangkok*," 156.

21 Ibid., 152.

22 Wartofsky, "The Trial of Dennis O'Rourke at Patpong," 161."

23 Urban, "Dennis O'Rourke and *The Good Woman of Bangkok*," 150.

24 Urban, "Dennis O'Rourke and *The Good Woman of Bangkok*," 149.

25 Williams, "The Ethics of Documentary Intervention," 81–83.

26 Urban, "Dennis O'Rourke and *The Good Woman of Bangkok*," 157.

27 Ibid., 164.

28 Seabrook, *Travels in the Skin Trade*.

29 Williams, "The Ethics of Documentary Intervention," 81–83.

30 Urban, "Dennis O'Rourke and *The Good Woman of Bangkok*," 156.

31 Powers, "An Unreliable Memoir," 111.

32 Wartofsky, "The Trial of Dennis O'Rourke at Patpong," 161.

33 Quan, foreword to *Orientalia*, 9.

34 Urban, "Dennis O'Rourke and *The Good Woman of Bangkok*," 149.

35 Powers, "An Unreliable Memoir," 106.

36 http://www.asiaerotica.com/editorial.html (accessed September 29, 2006).

37 Vance, "Negotiating Sex and Gender in the Attorney General's Commission on Pornography," 83.

38 Butler, *Gender Trouble*; and Butler, *Bodies That Matter*.

39 Mahmood, "Feminist Theory, Embodiment, and the Docile Agent."

40 Scarry, *The Body in Pain*.

41 Projansky, *Watching Rape*.

42 Alloula, *The Colonial Harem*.

43 Sturdevant and Stolzfus, *When the Good Times Roll*.

44 See Kelsky, *Women on the Verge*.

45 Williams, "The Ethics of Documentary Intervention," 81–82.

46 An example of an ethical work that captures the dynamics of power and history as well as the dialectics of cultural translation and relations in the encounter between third world prostitutes and white men is Tracey Moffatt's film *Nice Colored Girls*.

7 ✻ the political power of hypersexuality

1 Segal, "Sweet Sorrows, Painful Pleasures," 70.

2 For foundational essays on queer of color filmmaking perspectives, see Fung, "Center the Margins," and Parmar, "That Moment of Emergence."

3 My next book project, *Race and the Moving Image Sex Act*, continues the phenomenological approach I take up in this first book. It compares the production of race and sexuality across African American, Asian American, Chicano, and Native American cinemas in the United States and beyond through a study of touching and its power as a racial threat and treat in the cinema. In this comparative race and sexuality film project, I specifically group together popular psychosexual feature film dramas, the new adult film, and blaxploitation from the 1960s and 1970s (including Richard Quine's *The World of Suzie Wong* [1960], John Huston's *Reflections in a Golden Eye* [1967], Just Jaeckin's *Emmanuelle* [1974], Richard Fleischer's *Mandingo* [1975], and Steve Carver's *Drum* [1976]) along with the contemporaneous and contemporary emergence of the independent work of filmmakers of color in the United States, which features strong sexual themes in their representations of the U.S. racial experience. Specifically, these films expand sexual fantasy about people of color in the development of a racial politics that requires a corporeal understanding of the racial experience in all of its carnality.

4 Tajima-Peña, "No Mo Pomo and Other Tales of the Road," 55.

5 Grace Lee, personal interview, Santa Barbara, Calif., April 21–22, 2004.

6 Feng, "Recuperating Suzie Wong," 50.

7 Hagedorn, "Asian Women in Film."

8 I refer to classics of the 1980s, including *Nice Colored Girls* (1987) by the Australian aboriginal filmmaker Tracey Moffatt, *Illusions* (1985) by the African American filmmaker Julie Dash, and *Sari Red* (1988), by the South

Asian British filmmaker Pratibha Parmar. With the help of media organizations in the post–civil rights era, such as Los Angeles's Visual Communications, San Francisco's NAATA, New York's Asian Cinevision and Women Make Movies, and London's Sankofa and Black Audio Film Collective, these women of color in the United States, Canada, the United Kingdom, and Australia produced political personal works. In their body of work, they also developed an exciting visual language important to the history of the film craft that engaged the complexities of race and gender subjectivity, colonial experience, and immigrant life. The works screened in film festivals such as Women in the Director's Chair in Chicago; the Asian American festivals in New York, Los Angeles, San Francisco, and Chicago; queer festivals such as MIX in New York and Los Angeles; and the long-running Women of Color Film Festival at the University of California at Santa Cruz.

The 1980s and 1990s heralded the community of women of color filmmakers that inform such important media organizations as Third World Majority and Women of Color Film Collectives working today. A tradition of Asian American filmmaking innovation also enables the rise of others. For example, Helen Lee came into filmmaking inspired by the work of Pam Tom, a pioneer Asian American filmmaker trained at the UCLA Film School. Lee's work was also facilitated by her training at NYU's Tisch School of the Arts (Cinema Studies) and involvement with Women Make Movies, an independent media organization based in New York City that continues to distribute her short films. In my interviews with her, Lee described her work as situated in the independent media scene. She is also committed to narrating the lives of Asian women in complex visual ways: "When discovering Women Make Movies, shortly before I worked there, watching Pam Tom's *Two Lies* left me pretty thunderstruck, that someone could deal with issues personal to me—she was speaking to me—in cinematically interesting terms. Her craft as a filmmaker, I respected enormously. The mood and atmosphere and texture of life she is able to create in half an hour stunned me, inspired me." Additionally, her kinship with other Asian American women filmmakers in New York City and Los Angeles helped to form her as a filmmaker: "Striking up friendships with Shu Lea Cheang, Rea Tajiri and Christine Chang in New York City in the early '90s, they were formative years for me, and feeling a bond between their work and mine. We should have started an Asian women's filmmaking collective back then! I also met Hyun Mi Oh, who also inspired me with her writing. She had just graduated from UCLA, shortly after Pam Tom, at the time. Her writing was incredibly strong, forceful, pungent, very Korean!"

While I do not wish to locate the solution to the problems of race and representation entirely in the hands of independent filmmakers, I conclude with the works and words of Helen Lee and others for they exemplify a commitment to politics as well as craft.

9 Freud, "Three Essays on the Theory of Sexuality," 100. Freud defines the fetish as a sexual substitution associated with the sexuality of the object. According to Lynn Segal in "Sweet Sorrows, Painful Pleasures," "What is substituted for the sexual object is some part of the body (such as the foot or hair) which is in general very inappropriate for sexual purposes, or some inanimate object which bears an assignable relation to the person whom it replaces and preferably to that person's sexuality (e.g., a piece of clothing or underlinen). Such substitutes are with some justice likened to the fetishes in which savages believe that their gods are embodied" (70).

10 Gaines, "White Privilege and Looking Relations."

11 Žižek, "From the Sublime to the Ridiculous," 183–84.

12 Marchetti, *Romance and the "Yellow Peril."*

13 Helen Lee, personal interview.

14 Ibid.

15 Ibid.

16 Ibid.

17 In her take on a topic explored in successful documentaries such as the PBS film *Passing Through* (1999) by Nathan Adolfson, Lee chooses to tell the narrative in ways that prioritize not only gender and sex but also narrative drama.

18 Helen Lee, personal interview.

19 In *My Niagara*, a Japanese American woman resolves her melancholia through her sexual relationship with a Korean-Japanese man.

20 Ding, "Strategies of an Asian American Filmmaker," 48.

21 Grace Lee, personal interview, April 2004.

22 While intertwined in their sex lives, the characters are also situated within a consciously racial understanding of the social world. That is, both Audrey's and Serena's backgrounds are contemporary and situated specifically in the academy and in the flight of Koreans after the race riots in Los Angeles in 1992, respectively. In a scene where Serena picks at Audrey's white hair while nestling her head on her lap, Audrey cannot get enough of finding out more about Serena, whose parents left the United States after the L.A. riots, returning to Korea so that Serena must care for her younger brother. While both female characters exemplify different poles of sexuality, their specificity and background provide more whole and complex characterizations. The crucial representation in the film is the way in which the characters recognize their polarities and their perfection in each other's eyes.

23 Grace Lee describes how she is persistently mistaken for other Asian women. "On a really basic level, no, we don't look alike and we are not all the same. That's just such a basic thing that happened to me personally, especially

where I grew up and being mistaken, even in film school, when I was called [other film students' names] . . . I'm like, 'C'mon, I'm totally different.' It's one of those nagging realities that happen a lot, and in taking that, it's so simple to me. Yes, let's set up the argument and then disprove it. Who is Grace Lee? Who is Asian American women? Maybe at the end of it, you just sort of think, 'No we really can't define them as one thing.' Then I think I'm successful." Grace Lee, personal interview.

24 Lowe, *Immigrant Acts*.
25 Machiko Saito, personal interview, May 2004.
26 Ibid.
27 Ibid.
28 Ibid.
29 Ibid.

8 ❖ new horizons in race-positive sexuality

1 See Fuchs, "A Picture about Lying," and Travers, "Review of *Sideways*."
2 Oishi, "Bad Asians"; and Nguyen, *Race and Resistance*, 143.
3 Fanon, *Black Skin, White Masks*, 218.

BIBLIOGRAPHY

personal interviews

Harsanyi, Martha. June 2000.
Lee, Grace. April 2004.
Lee, Helen. May 7, 2001–July 23, 2004.
Lor, Luzviminda. October 2000.
Marcos, J. Elaine. October 2000.
Nalzaro, Edmund. October 2000.
Saito, Machiko. May 2004 and 2005.

film, video, and performance

Across to Singapore. Directed by William Nigh. MGM, 1928.
The Adventures of Buttman. Directed by John Stagliano. Evil Angel, 1989.
A Is for Asia. Directed by Asia Carrera and Bud Carrera. 4-Play, 1996.
All Amateur Ecstasy. Directed by Greg Pak. Atom Films, 2001.
Apassionata. Directed by Asia Carrera. Adam and Eve, 1998.
Apocalypse Now. Directed by Francis Ford Coppola. Paramount Pictures, 1979.
Arli$$. HBO, 1996–2002.
Asian Pride Porn. Directed by Greg Pak. Atom Films, 2001.
Baise Moi. Directed by Coralie Thi Thanh. Pan European Productions, 2000.
Barrier Device. Directed by Grace Lee. Hypnotic/*www.gracelee.net*, 2001.
Behind the Green Door. Directed by Artie Mitchell. Mitchell Brothers Film Group, 1972.
The Birth of a Nation. Directed by D. W. Griffith. Hollywood Classics, 1915.

Camp Arirang. Directed by Diana S. Lee and Grace Yoon Kyung Lee. Third World Newsreel, 1996.

Cannibal Tours. Directed by Dennis O'Rourke. Direct Cinema Limited, 1988.

Casting Couch. Kinsey Institute Film Archive, 1924.

Charlie's Angels. Directed by Joseph McGinty Nichol. Flower Films, 2000.

Charlie's Angels: Full Throttle. Directed by Joseph McGinty Nichol. Flower Films, 2003.

The Cheat. Directed by Alfred Rolfe. Australian Photo Play, 1915.

Chicago. Directed by Maurine Watkins. Music Box Theatre, 1926.

China. Kinsey Institute Film Archive, 1934.

China and Silk. Directed by Steve Scott. Image Entertainment Inc., 1984.

China Babe. Kinsey Institute Film Archive, 1950.

China De Sade. Directed by Charles De Santos. VCX, 1980.

China Lust. Directed by Summer Brown. VCX, 1976.

Chinese Love Life. Kinsey Institute Film Archive, 1921.

College Coed 1. Kinsey Institute Film Archive, 1952–54.

College Coed 2. Kinsey Institute Film Archive, 1952–54.

The Corrupter. Directed by James Foley. New Line Home Video, 1999.

Country Stud Horse. Kinsey Institute Film Archive, 1920.

Crash. Directed by Paul Haggis. Lions Gate Films, 2004.

The Crimson City. Directed by Archie Mayo. Warner Brothers, 1928.

Cuban Dream. Kinsey Institute Film Archive, 1950–55.

Dancer's Interlude. Kinsey Institute Film Archive, 1949.

Darkie Rhythm. Kinsey Institute Film Archive, 1928–30.

Date Night. Kinsey Institute Film Archive, 1961.

Daughter of Shanghai. Directed by Robert Florey. Paramount, 1937.

Deep Throat. Directed by Gerard Damiano. Arrow Productions, 1972.

The Deer Hunter. Directed by Michael Cimino. MCA Home Video, 1978.

The Devil in Miss Jones. Directed by Gerard Damiano. VCX, 1973.

The Diary of Evelyn Lau. Directed by Sturla Gunnarson. Canadian Broadcasting Corporation, 1994. Broadcast premiere March 13, 1993.

Displaced View. Directed by Midi Onodera. MCANO Film Artists, 1998.

Dirty Laundry. Directed by Richard Fung. Video Data Bank, 1996.

Double Happiness. Directed by Mina Shum. Fine Line Features, 1994.

Drum. Directed by Steve Carver. Dino de Laurentiis Corporation, 1976.

Emmanuelle. Directed by Just Jaeckin. Distributed by Vestron Video, Canal Plus, and Image International, 1974.

The Erotic World of Linda Wong. Directed by Charles De Santos. Stardust Industries, 1985.

The Fact of Asian Women. Directed by Celine Shimizu. Self-distributed, 2002 (re-edited version released 2004).

Fire. Directed by Deepa Mehta. Zeitgeist Films, 1996.

Flower Drum Song. Directed by Henry Koster. Universal International Pictures, 1961.

Forever Bottom! Directed by Nguyen Tan Hoang. Frameline Distribution, 1999.

Geisha. Kinsey Institute Film Archive, 1958.

Geisha Girl. Kinsey Institute Film Archive, 1948–55.

The Good Woman of Bangkok. Directed by Dennis O'Rourke. Direct Cinema Limited, 1991.

The Grace Lee Project. Directed by Grace Lee. Women Make Movies, 2005.

A Grass Sandwich (A Free Ride). Kinsey Institute Film Archive, 1915, 1917–19.

Grey's Anatomy. ABC, 2005–.

Hart, Schnell und Schon. Directed by Machiko Saito. Pro Dom Productions, 2003.

Hello Sex Kitty. Performance piece. Directed by Denise Uyehara. Los Angeles, 1999.

Her Uprooting Plants Her. Directed by Celine Parreñas. Third World Newsreel, 1995.

I Can't Believe I Did the Whole Team! Directed by John T. Bone. Fantastic Pictures, 1994.

Illusions. Directed by Julie Dash. Women Make Movies, 1985.

I'm the One That I Want. Written by Margaret Cho. Directed by Lionel Coleman. Cho Taussig Productions, Inc., 2000.

Indian Giver. Kinsey Institute Film Archive, 1958–62.

Indochine. Directed by Regis Wargnier. Sony Pictures Classics, 1992.

The Jade Pussycat. Directed by John Chinn. Caballero Control Company, 1977.

Japanese Rape. Kinsey Institute Film Archive, 1970–71.

Java Head. Directed by J. Walter Ruben. First Division, 1934.

Kill Bill: Vol. 1. Directed by Quentin Tarantino. Miramax Films, 2003.

Kill Bill: Vol. 2. Directed by Quentin Tarantino. Miramax Films, 2004.

Korean Couple. Kinsey Institute Film Archive, 1967.

Last Little Whorehouse. Directed by Asia Carrera. New Sensations, 1997.

The Love Thang Trilogy. Directed by Mari Keiko Gonzales. Frameline Distribution, 1994.

Madame Butterfly. Written by Giacomo Puccini. 1904.

Madame Chrysanthemum. Written by Loti Pierre. 1887. Opera by David Belasco in 1904.

Mahal Means Love and Expensive. Directed by Celine Parreñas. Self-distributed, 1993.

The Making of Miss Saigon. Directed by Richard Wright. HBO Studios, 1991.

Mandingo. Directed by Richard Fleischer. Dino de Laurentiis Corporation and Paramount Pictures, 1975.

Masters of the Pillow. Directed by James Hou. Avenue Films, 2004.

M. Butterfly. Directed by David Cronenberg. Warner Brothers, 1993.

Menage Moderne du Madame Butterfly. Directed by Bernard Naton. Kinsey Institute Film Archive, 1921–30.

Mexican Honeymoon. Kinsey Institute Film Archive, 1937.

The Mikado. Libretto by W. S. Gilbert. Music by Arthur Sullivan. Gilbert and Sullivan Archive. First produced at the Savoy Theatre on March 14, 1885.

Miss Saigon. Written by Alain Boublil and Claude-Michel Schonberg. Produced by Cameron Mackintosh. Directed by Nicholas Hytner. First produced at Theatre Royal, Drury Lane, London, September 20, 1989.

More Dirty Debutantes. Directed by Ed Powers. The Nasty Brothers, 1989–.

"My Dreams Were Limited." In the one-woman show *Notorious C.H.O.* Written by Margaret Cho. Cho Taussig Productions, Inc., 2002.

My Niagara. Directed by Helen Lee. Women Make Movies, 1994.

Negroes at Play. Kinsey Institute Film Archive, 1948.

Nice Colored Girls. Directed by Tracey Moffatt. Women Make Movies, 1987.

Night in a Turkish Harem. Kinsey Institute Film Archive, 1931.

Office Cruelty. Directed by Annabel Chong. Impresive, 2000.

101 Asian Debutantes: Volume 1. Sex in Asia. Directed by Jean Marc Roc. Asia-Erotica.com, 1995.

101 Asian Debutantes: Volume 2. Babes in Thailand. Directed by Jean Marc Roc. AsiaErotica.com, 1995.

101 Asian Debutantes: Volume 3. Manila Nights. Directed by Jean Marc Roc. AsiaErotica.com, 1995.

101 Asian Debutantes: Volume 4. The Koreans. Directed by Jean Marc Roc. Asia-Erotica.com, 1998.

101 Dirty Debutantes. Directed by Ed Powers. The Nasty Brothers, 1989–.

"One Night in Bangkok." In *Erazor*. Directed by Murray Head. Zyx/Shift Music, 1984.

One Night in Bangkok. Directed by Paul Vatelli. Caballero Control Company, 1985.

Oriental Babysitter. Directed by Leonard Burke. Essex Productions, 1976.

Oriental Girlfriend. Kinsey Institute Film Archive, 1961.

Oriental Jade. Directed by G. W. Hunter. VCA Pictures, 1985.

Passing Through. Directed by Nathan Adolfson. Center for Asian American Media, 1999.

Payback. Directed by Brian Helgeland. Paramount Pictures, 1999.

Peter Pan. Directed by Herbert Brenon. Kino Video, 1924.

Phantasm. Directed by Bud Lee. Wicked, 1995.

Philippino [sic] *Couple*. Kinsey Institute Film Archive, 1970–71.

Piccadilly. Directed by Ewald André Dupont. Milestone Films, 1929.

Picture Bride. Directed by Kayo Hatta. Miramax, 1994.

Picturing Oriental Girls. Directed by Valerie Soe. NAATA, 1992.

Pink Eye. Directed by Machiko Saito. Pro Dom Productions, 2000.

A Place of Rage. Directed by Pratibha Parmar. Women Make Movies, 1991.

Play It to the Bone. Directed by Ron Shelton. Walt Disney Video, 2000.

Pornomancer. Directed by Annabel Chong. New Machines Studio, 1998.

Portrait in Black. Directed by Michael Gordon. Universal, 1960.

Premenstrual Spotting. Directed by Machiko Saito. Pro Dom Productions, 1997.

Prey. Directed by Helen Lee. Women Make Movies, 1995.

Rated Sex. Directed by Robert McCallum. Essex Home Video, 1986.

Reflections in a Golden Eye. Directed by John Huston. Warner Brothers/Seven Arts, 1967.

Revolution. Written by Margaret Cho. Directed bv Lorene Machado. Wellspring, 2004.

Sallie and Her Boyfriend. Kinsey Institute Film Archive, 1947.

Sally's Beauty Spot. Directed by Helen Lee. Women Make Movies, 1990.

Salt of the Earth. Kinsey Institute Film Archive, 1950s.

Samurai Dick. Directed by Kaye Vie. VCA, 1984.

Sari Red. Directed by Pratibha Parmar. Women Make Movies, 1988.

The Savage Innocents. Directed by Nicholas Ray. J. Arthur Rank Film Distributors, 1960.

Saving Face. Directed by Alice Wu. Sony Pictures Classics, 2005.

Sayonara. Directed by Joshua Logan. MGM, 1957.

Scherezade [sic] *and the Sultan*. Kinsey Institute Film Archive, 1936.

La Señora y la Criada. Kinsey Institute Film Archive, 1938.

La Señorita Lee. Directed by Hyun Mi Oh. Cinema Guild, 1995.

Sex Bowl. Directed by Shulea Chang, Ela Troyano, and Jane Castle (as Et Baby Mamal). Video Data Bank, 1994.

Sexcapades. Directed by Henri Pachard Bero. VCA, 1983.

Sex Fish. Directed by Shulea Chang, Ela Troyano, and Jane Castle (as Et Baby Mamal). Video Data Bank, 1993.

Shanghai Express. Directed by Josef Von Sternberg. Paramount Pictures/ Universal Studios, 1932.

Sideways. Directed by Alexander Payne. Fox Searchlight Pictures, 2004.

Silents Please: Old San Francisco. Produced by Paul Killiam. Gregstan Enterprises / ABC, 1960–61.

Sin City Diary. Directed by Rachel Rivera. Women Make Movies, 1992.

Slaying the Dragon. Directed by Deborah Gee and Asian Women United. Center for Asian American Media, 1989.

Some Questions for 28 Kisses. Directed by Kip Fulbeck. Video Data Bank, 1994.

Squanto. Directed by Xavier Koller. Buena Vista Pictures, 1994.

Stretchmark. Directed by Veena Cabreros-Sud. Third World Newsreel, 1996.

Subrosa. Directed by Helen Lee. Women Make Movies, 2000.

Super Flip. Directed by Celine Parreñas. Progressive Films, 1997.

Ten Cents a Dance. Directed by Midi Onodena. Women Make Movies, 1986.

The Thief of Bagdad. Directed by Raoul Walsh. Douglas Fairbanks Pictures, 1924.

Those Fluttering Objects of Desire. Directed by Shulea Cheang. Video Data Bank, 1992.

Tiger Bay. Directed by J. Elder Wills. Associated British Film Distributors, 1934.

Toll of the Sea. Directed by Chester M. Franklin. Grapevine, 1922.

Tongues Untied. Directed by Marlon Riggs. Frameline, 1989.

Two Lies. Directed by Pam Tom. Chinema Productions, 1990.

Two Nights and a Day. Kinsey Institute Film Archive, 1953.

Under the Tuscan Sun. Directed by Audrey Wells. Walt Disney Video, 2003.

Very Bad Things. Directed by Peter Berg. Polygram USA Video, 1998.

Vitaphone Novelty: Thrills from the Past. Directed by Robert Youngson. Warner Brothers Pictures, 1954.

Walk Like a Dragon. Directed by James Clavell. Paramount Pictures, 1960.

West Side Story. Directed by Jerome Robbins and Robert Wise. MGM, 1961.

What About Sex? Asian Heterosexuality. Directed by Lok C. Siu, Anna Coe, Sari Yoshioka, and Jason Chung. Undistributed, 1992.

Who Killed Vincent Chin? Directed by Christine Choy and Renee Tajima. Filmmakers Library, 1988.

Wild at Heart. Directed by David Lynch. MGM Home Entertainment, 1990.

The Women Outside. Directed by J. T. Takagi and Hye Jung Park. Third World Newsreel, 1995.

The World's Biggest Gangbang. Directed by Greg Alves. AMZ, 1999.

The World of Suzie Wong. Directed by Richard Quine. Paramount Pictures, 1960.

Yankee Seduction. Directed by Jerome Tanner. Western, 1985.

Year of the Dragon. Directed by Michael Cimino. MGM / UA Entertainment Company, 1985.

print

Abraham, Margaret. *Speaking the Unspeakable: Marital Violence among South Asian Immigrants in the United States*. New Brunswick, N.J.: Rutgers University Press, 2000.

Aguilar-San Juan, Karin. *The State of Asian America: Activism and Resistance in the 1990s*. New York: South End Press, 1993.

Alloula, Malek. *The Colonial Harem*. Minneapolis: University of Minnesota Press, 1986.

Althusser, Louis. "Ideology and Ideological State Apparatuses." In *Lenin and Philosophy and Other Essays*, 85–126. Translated by Ben Brewster. Introduction by Fredric Jameson. New York: Monthly Review Press, 2001.

Ansara, Martha. "A Man's World." In *The Filmmaker and the Prostitute*. Edited by Chris Berry, Annette Hamilton, and Laleen Jayamanne, 21–24. Sydney: Power Publications, 1997.

Askew, Robin. "Life Thru a Lens: Robin Askew Meets the Star of *Sex: The Annabel Chong Story.*" *Spike Magazine,* http://www.spikemagazine.com/1000annabelchong.php (accessed May 23, 2006).

Bales, Kevin. "Because She Looks Like a Child." In *Global Woman.* Edited by Barbara Ehrenreich and Arlie Russell Hochschild, 207–29. New York: Metropolitan Books, 2002.

Barrera, Magdalena. "Hottentot 2000: Jennifer Lopez and Her Butt." In *Sexualities in History.* Edited by Kim M. Phillips and Barry Reay, 407–17. New York: Routledge, 2002.

Benjamin, Jessica. *The Bonds of Love: Psychoanalysis, Feminism, and the Problem of Domination.* New York: Pantheon Books, 1988.

Berens, Jessica. "Nine Inch Nails." In *Inappropriate Behaviour.* Edited by Jessica Berens and Kerri Sharp, 263–71. London: Serpent's Tail, 2002.

Berlant, Lauren. *The Queen of America Goes to Washington City.* Durham, N.C.: Duke University Press, 1997.

Bernstein, Elisabeth. "The Meaning of the Purchase: Desire, Demand and the Commerce of Sex." *Ethnography* 2 (September 2001): 389–420.

Berry, Chris, Annette Hamilton, and Laleen Jayamanne, eds. *The Filmmaker and the Prostitute: Dennis O'Rourke's* The Good Woman of Bangkok. Sydney: Power Publications, 1997.

Bhabha, Homi. *Nation and Narration.* London: Routledge, 1994.

Bishop, Ryan, and Lillian S. Robinson. *Nightmarket.* New York: Routledge, 1998.

Bogle, Donald. *Toms, Coons, Mulattoes, Mammies and Bucks: An Interpretive History of Blacks in American Films.* 4th ed. New York: Continuum, 2001.

Bow, Leslie. *Betrayal and Other Acts of Subversion: Feminism, Sexual Politics, Asian American Womens' Literature.* Princeton, N.J.: Princeton University Press, 2001.

Brennan, Denise. "Selling Sex for Visas: Sex Tourism as a Stepping-stone to International Migration." In *Global Woman.* Edited by Barbara Ehrenreich and Arlie Russell Hochschild, 154–68. New York: Metropolitan Books, 2002.

Bright, Susie. "White Sex: Pornography and the Politics of Fantasy in America." *Village Voice,* May 18, 1993, 34.

Brown, Laura. "Not Outside the Range: One Feminist Perspective on Psychic Trauma." In *Trauma: Explorations in Memory.* Edited by Cathy Caruth, 100–112. Baltimore: Johns Hopkins University Press, 1995.

Butler, Judith. *Bodies That Matter: On the Discursive Limits of "Sex."* London: Routledge, 1993.

——. *Gender Trouble: Feminism and the Subversion of Identity.* London: Routledge, 1990.

——. "Merely Cultural." *Social Text* 52/53 (fall/winter 1997): 265–77.

——. *The Psychic Life of Power*. Stanford, Calif.: Stanford University Press, 1997.

Cabreros-Sud, Veena. "Kicking Ass." In *To Be Real: Telling the Truth and Changing the Face of Feminism*. Edited by Rebecca Walker, 41–47. New York: Anchor Books, 1995.

Canguilhem, George. "Do Sciences of the Normal and the Pathological Exist?" In *On the Normal and Pathological*, 115–229. Boston: D. Reidel Publishing, 1978.

Carby, Hazel V. *Cultures in Babylon: Black Britain and African America*. London: Verso, 1999.

Caruth, Cathy. *Unclaimed Experience: Trauma, Narrative and History*. Baltimore: Johns Hopkins University Press, 1996.

——, ed. *Trauma: Explorations in Memory*. Baltimore: Johns Hopkins University Press, 1995.

Chambers, Veronica. "Lucy Liu: Embracing a New Definition of American Beauty." *USAweekend.com*, January 23, 2000, http://www.usaweekend.com/00_issues/000123/000123lucyliu.html (accessed November 14, 2006).

Chan, Anthony B. *Perpetually Cool: The Many Lives of Anna May Wong (1905–1961)*. Lanham, Md.: Scarecrow Press, 2003.

Chan, Sucheng. "The Exclusion of Chinese Women, 1870–1943." In *Entry Denied*, 94–146. Philadelphia: Temple University Press, 1991.

Chekhov, Michael. *On the Technique of Acting*. New York: HarperCollins, 1991.

Chen, Nancy N. "Speaking Nearby: A Conversation with Trinh T. Minh-ha." *Visual Anthropology Review* 8, no. 1 (spring 1992): 82–91.

Cheng, Anne Anlin. "Beauty and Ideal Citizenship: Inventing Asian America in Rodgers and Hammerstein's *Flower Drum Song* (1961)." In *The Melancholy of Race: Psychoanalysis, Assimilation, and Hidden Grief*, 31–63. New York: Oxford University Press, 2000.

Cheung, King-kok. "The Woman Warrior versus the Chinaman Pacific: Must a Chinese American Critic Choose Between Feminism and Heroism?" In *Conflicts in Feminism*. Edited by Marianne Hirsch and Evelyn Fox Keller, 234–51. New York: Routledge, 1990.

Chihara, Michelle. "There's Something about Lucy." *Boston Phoenix*, February 28, 2000.

Chong, Annabel. "Scat: Is It All Filth?" In *Inappropriate Behaviour: Prada Sucks and Other Demented Descants*, 109–15. Edited by Jessica Berens and Kerri Sharp. London: Serpent's Tail Press, 2002.

Chow, Rey. *Writing Diaspora: Tactics of Intervention in Contemporary Cultural Studies*. Bloomington: Indiana University Press, 1993.

Chrystos. *Not Vanishing*. Vancouver: Press Gang Publishers, 1988.

Chuh, Kandice. "Discomforting Knowledge." *Journal of Asian American Studies* 6, no. 1 (2003): 5–23.

——. "Race, Gender, and the Law: Asian American Women and Rape." In

Privileging Positions: The Sites of Asian American Studies. Edited by Gary Okihiro, 233–44. Pullman: Washington State University Press, 1995.

Chun, Kimberly. "*Sex: The Annabel Chong Story.*" *Asian Week* 21, no. 36 (May 4, 2000), 23.

Clinton, Paul. "Sex Sobers in Controversial Sundance Documentary." CNN.*com*, February 10, 1999, http://www.cnn.com/showbiz/movies/9902/10/annabel .chong (accessed November 14, 2006).

Cohen, Hart. "Brecht in Bangkok: An Account of Dennis O'Rourke's *Good Woman of Bangkok.*" In *The Filmmaker and the Prostitute.* Edited by Chris Berry, Annette Hamilton, and Laleen Jayamanne, 67–77. Sydney: Power Publications, 1997.

Collins, Patricia Hill. *Black Sexual Politics.* London: Routledge, 2004.

Constable, Nicole. *Romance on the Global Stage: Pen Pals, Virtual Ethnography and "Mail-Order" Marriages.* Berkeley: University of California Press, 2003.

Cowie, Elizabeth. "Pornography and Fantasy." In *Sex Exposed: Sexuality and the Pornography Debate.* Edited by Lynne Segal and Mary McIntosh, 132–52. New Brunswick, N.J.: Rutgers University Press, 1992.

Crary, Jonathan. *Techniques of the Observer: On Vision and Modernity in the 19th Century.* Cambridge: MIT Press, 1992.

Crenshaw, Kimberle Williams. "Mapping the Margins: Intersectionality, Identity Politics, and Violence against Women of Color." In *Critical Race Theory: The Key Writings That Formed the Movement.* Edited by Kimberle Creshaw, Neil Gotanda, Gary Peller, and Kendall Thomas, 357–83. New York: New Press, 1996.

Cvetokovich, Ann. *An Archive of Feelings: Trauma, Sexuality, and Lesbian Public Cultures.* Durham, N.C.: Duke University Press, 2003.

Dadyburjor, Farhad J. "A Thing for Ling." *Bangladesh Observer*, January 6, 2004, http://www.bangladeshobserveronline.com/new/2004/01/06/enter tainment.htm (accessed November 14, 2006).

Davis, Angela. *Woman, Culture, Politics.* New York: Vintage Books, 1990.

de Lauretis, Teresa. *Technologies of Gender.* Bloomington: Indiana University Press, 1989.

——. "The Stubborn Drive." *Critical Inquiry* 24, no. 4 (summer 1998): 851–77.

D'Emilio, John, and Estelle Freedman. *Intimate Matters: A History of Sexuality in America.* New York: Harper and Row, 1988.

Di Lauro, Al, and Gerald Rabkin. *Dirty Movies.* New York: Chelsea House, 1976.

Ding, Loni. "Strategies of an Asian American Filmmaker." In *Moving the Image: Independent Asian Pacific American Media Arts.* Edited by Russell Leong, 46–59. Los Angeles: UCLA Asian American Studies Center and Visual Communication, 1991.

Doherty, Thomas. *Pre-Code Hollywood.* New York: Columbia University Press, 1999.

duCille, Ann. "Othered Matters: Reconceptualizing Dominance and Difference in the History of Sexuality in America." *The Journal of the History of Sexuality* 1, no. 1 (1990): 102–27.

Dyer, Richard. *Stars*. London: British Film Institute, 1998.

Ehrenreich, Barbara, and Arlie Russell Hochschild. *Global Woman*. New York: Metropolitan Books, 2002.

Eng, David L. *Racial Castration: Managing Masculinity in Asian America*. Durham, N.C.: Duke University Press, 2001.

Enloe, Cynthia. *Bananas, Beaches and Bases: Making Feminist Sense of International Politics*. Berkeley: University of California Press, 1990.

Espiritu, Yen Le. *Asian American Women and Men*. Thousand Oaks, Calif.: Sage Publications, 1997.

Fanon, Frantz. *Black Skin, White Masks*. Translated by Charles Lam Marksmann. New York: Grove Press, 1967.

Feng, Peter X. "Recuperating Suzie Wong: A Fan's Nancy Kwan-dary." In *Countervisions: Asian American Film Criticism*. Edited by Darrell Hamamoto and Sandra Liu, 40–56. Philadelphia: Temple University Press, 2000.

Ford, Staci, and Gitanjili Singh Chanda. "Portrayals of Gender and Generation, East and West: Suzie Wong in the Noble House." In *Before and after Suzie*. Edited by Thomas Y. T. Luk and James P. Rice, 111–27. Hong Kong: New Age College, Chinese University of Hong Kong, 2002.

Foucault, Michel. *Discipline and Punish: The Birth of the Prison*. New York: Vintage, 1995.

——. *Ethics: Subjectivity and Truth (Essential Works of Michel Foucault)*. New York: New Press, 1997.

——. *The History of Sexuality*. Vol. 1. New York: Vintage, 1990.

——. *Power/Knowledge*. Edited by Colin Gordon. New York: Pantheon Books, 1980.

Fregoso, Rosa Linda. *The Bronze Screen*. Minneapolis: Minnesota University Press, 1993.

Freud, Sigmund. "Fetishism." In *Standard Edition of the Complete Psychological Works of Sigmund Freud*, translated and edited by James Strachey, vol. 21, 147–158. London: Hogarth Press, 1953–74.

——. "Formulations on the Two Principles of Mental Functioning (1911)." In *Standard Edition of the Complete Psychological Works of Sigmund Freud*, translated and edited by James Strachey, vol. 12, 213–26. London: Hogarth Press, 1953–74.

——. *Group Psychology and the Analysis of the Ego*. New York: Norton, 1959.

——. *The Interpretation of Dreams*. New York: Avon, 1980.

——. "Three Essays on the Theory of Sexuality." In *Freud on Women*. Edited by Elizabeth Young-Bruehl, 89–145. New York: Norton, 1992.

Fuchs, Cynthia. "A Picture about Lying." *Popmatters.com*, http://www.popmatters.com/film/reviews/s/sideways-2004-dvd.shtml (accessed September 29, 2006).

——. "This Epic Battle." *Popmatters.com*, http://www.popmatters.com/film/reviews/p/play-it-to-the-bone.shtml (accessed May 23, 2006).

Fung, Richard. "Center the Margins." In *Moving the Image: Independent Asian Pacific American Media Arts*. Edited by Russell Leong, 62–67. Los Angeles: UCLA Asian American Studies Center and Visual Communications, 1991.

——. "Looking for My Penis: The Eroticized Asian in Gay Video Porn." In *How Do I Look? Queer Film and Video*. Edited by Bad Object-Choices, 145–60. Seattle, Wash.: Bay Press, 1991.

Gaines, Jane. "White Privilege and Looking Relations: Race and Gender in Feminist Film Theory." In *Feminism and Film*. Edited by Ann Kaplan, 336–55. Oxford: Oxford University Press, 2000.

Gardner, Tracey A. "Racism in Pornography and the Women's Movement." In *Take Back the Night: Women in Pornography*. Edited by Laura Lederer, 105–14. New York: Morrow, 1980.

Gilman, Sander. *Difference and Pathology*. Ithaca, N.Y.: Cornell University Press, 1985.

——. *Making the Body Beautiful: A Cultural History of Aesthetic Surgery*. Princeton, N.J.: Princeton University Press, 2000.

Glenn, Evelyn Nakano. *Issei, Nisei, War Bride*. Philadelphia: Temple University Press, 1988.

Gong, Stephen. "A History in Progress: Asian American Media Arts Centers 1970–1990." In *Moving the Image: Independent Asian Pacific American Media Arts*. Edited by Russell Leong, 1–9. Los Angeles: UCLA Asian American Studies Center and Visual Communications, 1991.

Gonzalves, Theo. "Unashamed to Be So Beautiful: An Interview with Filmmaker Celine Salazar Parreñas." In *Countervisions: Asian American Film Criticism*. Edited by Darrell Hamamoto and Sandra Liu, 263–74. Philadelphia: Temple University Press, 2000.

Gopinath, Gayatri. *Impossible Desires: Queer Diasporas and South Asian Public Cultures*. Durham, N.C.: Duke University Press, 2005.

Gordon, Avery. *Ghostly Matters: Haunting and the Sociological Imagination*. Minneapolis: University of Minnesota Press, 1997.

Guerrero, Ed. *Framing Blackness*. Philadelphia: Temple University Press, 1993.

Hagedorn, Jessica. "Asian Women in Film: No Joy, No Luck." *Ms. Magazine* 4, no. 4 (January–February 1994), 74–79.

——. *Dogeaters*. New York: Pantheon Books, 1990.

Hahn, Kimoko. *Earshot*. Brooklyn: Hanging Loose Press, 1992.

Hall, Stuart. "Cultural Identity and Cinematic Representation." *Framework* 36 (1989): 68–81.

——. "New Ethnicities." In *Stuart Hall: Critical Dialogues in Cultural Studies*. Edited by David Morley and Kuan-Shing Chen, 441–49. London: Routledge, 1994.

——. *Representations*. London: Sage Publications, 1997.

Halley, Janet. "'Like Race' Arguments." In *What's Left of Theory? New Work on the Politics of Literary Theory*. Edited by Judith Butler, John Guillory, and Kendall Thomas, 40–74. New York: Routledge, 2000.

Hamamoto, Darrell. "The Joy Fuck Club: Prolegomenon to an Asian American Porno Practice." In *Countervisions: Asian American Film Criticism*. Edited by Darrell Hamamoto and Sandra Liu, 159–89. Philadelphia: Temple University Press, 2000.

Hamilton, Annette. "Mistaken Identities: Art, Truth and Dare in *The Good Woman of Bangkok*." In *The Filmmaker and the Prostitute*. Edited by Chris Berry, Annette Hamilton, and Laleen Jayamanne, 57–65. Sydney: Power Publications, 1997.

Hammonds, Evelyn. "Black (W)holes and Geometry of Black Female Sexuality." *Differences: A Journal of Feminist Cultural Studies* 6, nos. 2–3 (1994): 126–45.

——. "Race, Sex, AIDS: The Construction of 'Other.'" *Radical America* 20, no. 6 (1986): 28–36.

——. "Toward a Geneaology of Black Female Sexuality: The Problem of Silence." In *Feminist Theory and the Body: A Reader*. Edited by Janet Price and Margrit Shildrick, 93–104. New York: Routledge, 1999.

Harper, Philip Brian. *Are We Not Men?* London: Oxford University Press, 1998.

Harris, Larry. *The Stag Film Report*. San Diego: Socio Library Paper Back Books, 1971.

Hegel, G. W. F. "Independence and Dependence of Self-Consciousness: Lordship and Bondage." In *Phenomenology of Spirit*, 111–19. London: Oxford University Press, 1979.

Hershatter, Gail. *Dangerous Pleasures: Prostitution and Modernity in Twentieth-Century Shanghai*. Berkeley: University of California Press, 1997.

Heung, Marina. "The Family Romance of Orientalism: From *Madame Butterfly* to *Indochine*." In *Visions of the East: Orientalism in Film*. Edited by Matthew Bernstein and Gaylyn Studlar, 158–83. New Brunswick, N.J.: Rutgers University Press, 1997.

Higginbotham, Evelyn Brooks. *History and Theory: Feminist Research, Debates and Contestations*. Chicago: University of Chicago Press Journals, 1997.

Hine, Darlene Clark. *The African American Odyssey*. Upper Saddle River, N.J.: Prentice Hall, 2005.

——. *Dangerous Women*. New York: Routledge, 1997.

——. "Rape and the Inner Lives of Black Women in the Middle West: Preliminary Thoughts on the Culture of Dissemblance." *Signs* 14 (summer 1989): 912–20.

Hine, Darlene Clark, Elsa Barkley Brown, and Rosalyn Terborg-Penn, eds. *Black Women in America: An Historical Encyclopedia*. Brooklyn: Carlson Publications, 1993.

Hirata, Lucie Cheng. "Free, Indentured, Enslaved: Chinese Prostitutes in 19th C. America." *Signs* 5 (1979): 3–29.

Hoang, Nguyen Tan. "The Resurrection of Brandon Lee: The Making of a Gay Asian American Porn Star." In *Porn Studies*. Edited by Linda Williams, 223–70. Durham, N.C.: Duke University Press, 2004.

Hodges, Graham Russell Gao. *Anna May Wong: From Laundryman's Daughter to Hollywood Legend*. New York: Palgrave Macmillan, 2004.

Hoffman, Frank A. "Prolegomena to a Study of Traditional Elements in the Erotic Film." *Journal of American Folklore* 78, no. 308 (April–June 1965): 143–48.

Hwang, David Henry. *M. Butterfly*. New York: Penguin, 1994.

Jackson, Earl. "Graphic Specularity." In *Strategies of Deviance: Studies in Gay Male Representation*, 128–78. Bloomington: Indiana University Press, 1995.

Jacobs, Katrien. "Katrien Jacobs Fleshes out Maria Beatty." *Geekgirl.com.au*, http://www.bleuproductions.com/interview2htm (accessed May 23, 2006).

———. "The Lady of the Little Death." *Wide Angle* 19, no. 3 (1997): 13–40.

James, Joy. *Shadowboxing: Representations of Black Feminist Politics*. New York: St. Martin's Press, 1999.

JanMohamad, Abdul. "Sexuality on/of the Racial Border: Foucault, Wright, and the Articulation of 'Racialized Sexuality.'" In *Discourses of Sexuality from Aristotle to AIDS*. Edited by Domna Stanton, 94–116. Ann Arbor: University of Michigan Press, 1992.

Jay, Martin. *Downcast Eyes*. Berkeley: University of California Press, 1993.

Jayamanne, Laleen. "Reception, Genre, and the Knowing Critic: Dennis O'Rourke's *The Good Woman of Bangkok*." In *The Filmmaker and the Prostitute*. Edited by Chris Berry, Annette Hamilton, and Laleen Jayamanne, 25–33. Sydney: Power Publications, 1997.

Jordan, June. *Living Room: New Poems*. New York: Thunder's Mouth Press, 1985.

Julien, Isaac, and Kobena Mercer. "The Last Special Issue on Race." *Screen* 29, no. 4 (autumn 1988): 2–10.

Kang, Laura Hyun Yi. *Compositional Subjects*. Durham, N.C.: Duke University Press, 2002.

———. "Si(gh)ting the Asian/American Woman as Transnational Labor." In "New Formations, New Questions: Asian American Studies." Special issue, *Positions: East Asia Cultures Critique* 5, no. 2 (1995).

Kar, Law. "Suzie Wong and Her World." In *Before and after Suzie*. Edited by Thomas Y. T. Luk and James P. Rice, 67–72. Hong Kong: New Age College, Chinese University of Hong Kong, 2002.

Keller, Nora Okja. *Fox Girl*. New York: Viking Press, 2002.

Kelsky, Karen. *Women on the Verge: Japanese Women, Western Dreams*. Durham, N.C.: Duke University Press, 2001.

Kempadoo, Kamala. "Women of Color and the Global Sex Trade: Transnational

Feminist Perspectives." *Meridiens: Feminism, Race, Transnationalism* 1, no. 2 (spring 2001): 28–51.

Kempadoo, Kamala, and Jo Doezema. *Global Sex Workers*. New York: Routledge, 1998.

Kempadoo, Kamala, Jyoti Sanghera, and Bandana Pattanaik. *Trafficking and Prostitution Reconsidered: New Perspectives on Migration, Sex Work and Human Rights*. Boulder, Colo.: Paradigm Publishers, 2005.

Kendrick, Walter. *The Secret Museum: Pornography in Modern Culture*. Berkeley: University of California Press, 1996.

Kim, Elaine H. *Asian American Literature: Introduction to Writings in Social Context*. Philadelphia: Temple University Press, 1982.

——. "Dangerous Affinities: Korean Feminism (En)counter Gendered Korean and Racialized U.S. Nationalist Narratives." In "Korean American Cultural Production," edited by Elaine H. Kim, Eungie Joo, Jodi Kim, Susan K. Lee, and Eliza Hon. a special isse of *Hitting Critical Mass* 6, no. 1 (fall 1999): 1–12.

——. "Men's Talk: A Korean American View of South Korean Constructions of Women, Gender, and Masculinity." In *Dangerous Women: Gender and Korean Nationalism*. Edited by Elaine Kim and Chungmoo Choi, 67–117. New York: Routledge, 1997.

——. "Sex Tourism in Asia: A Reflection of Political and Economic Inequality." In *Korean Women in Transition: At Home and Abroad*. Edited by Evi-Young Yu and Earl H. Phillips, 121–44. Los Angeles: Center for Korean-American and Korean Studies, 1987.

Kim, Elaine H., Lilia V. Villaneuva, and Asian Women United of California, eds. *Making More Waves: New Writing by Asian American Women*. Boston: Beacon Press, 1997.

Kipnis, Laura. *Bound and Gagged*. New York: Grove Press, 1996.

——. "(Male) Desire and (Female) Disgust: Reading Hustler." In *Cultural Studies*. Edited by Lawrence Grossberg, Cary Nelson, and Paula Treichler, 373–91. London: Routledge, 1992.

Kleinhans, Chuck. "Teaching Sexual Images: Some Pragmatics." *Jump Cut* 40 (March 1996): 119.

Kojeve, Alexandre. *Introduction to the Reading of Hegel: Lectures on the Phenomenology of Spirit*. Ithaca, N.Y.: Cornell University Press, 1980.

Kondo, Dorinne. *About Face: Performing "Race" in Fashion and Theatre*. New York: Routledge, 1997.

Koshy, Susan. *Sexual Naturalization: Asian Americans and Miscegenation*. Stanford, Calif.: Stanford University Press, 2005.

Lacan, Jacques. "The Mirror Stage." In *Ecritis: A Selection*, 1–7. Translated by Alan Sheridan. New York: Norton, 1977.

La Capra, Dominick. *Writing History, Writing Trauma*. Baltimore: Johns Hopkins University Press, 2001.

Lane, Christopher, *The Psychoanalysis of Race*. New York: Columbia University Press, 1998.

Laplanche, Jean, and Jean-Bertrand Pontalis. *The Language of Psychoanalysis*. New York: Norton, 1974.

Laquer, Thomas. *Making Sex: Body and Gender from the Greeks to Freud*. Cambridge, Mass.: Harvard University Press, 1990.

La Salle, Mick. *Complicated Women: Sex and Power in Pre-Code Hollywood*. New York: St. Martin's Griffin, 2001.

———. *Dangerous Men: Pre-Code Hollywood and the Birth of Modern Man*. New York: Thomas Dunne Books, 2002.

Lau, Evelyn. *Runaway: Diary of a Streetkid*. Toronto: Coach House Press, 1995.

———. *In the House of Slaves*. Toronto: Coach House Press, 1994.

Lee, Helen. "Sex Acts: Two Meditations on Race and Sexuality." In "Film Feminisms." Special issue, *Signs: Journal of Women, Culture and Society* 30, no. 1 (autumn 2004): 1385–1402.

Lee, JoAnn Faung Jean. *Asian American Actors: Oral Histories from Stage, Screen, and Television*. Jefferson, N.C.: McFarland and Company, 2000.

Lee, Josephine. *Performing Asian America*. Philadelphia: Temple University Press, 1997.

Lee, Rachel. "Asian American Cultural Production in Asian-Pacific Perspective." *boundary 2* 26, no. 2 (summer 1999): 231–54.

———. "'Where's My Parade?' On Asian American Diva-Nation." In "Public Sentiments." Special issue, *Scholar and Feminist Online* 2, no. 1 (summer 2003), http://www.barnard.columbia.edu/sfonline/ps/lee.htm (accessed November 14, 2006).

Lee, Robert G. *Orientals: Asians in Popular Culture*. Philadelphia: Temple University Press, 1999.

Lee, Yuen Jee. "Why Suzie Wong Is Not a Lesbian: Asian and Asian American Lesbian and Bisexual Women and Femme/Butch/Gender Identities." In *Queer Studies: A Lesbian, Gay, Bisexual and Transgender Anthology*. Edited by Brett Beemyn and Mickey Eliason, 115–32. New York: New York University Press, 1996.

Leong, Karen. *The China Mystique*. Berkeley: University of California Press, 2005.

Leong, Russell. "To Open the Future." In *Moving the Image: Independent Asian Pacific American Media Arts*. Edited by Russell Leong, x–xxi. Los Angeles: UCLA Asian American Studies Center and Visual Communications, 1991.

Ling, L. H. M. "Sex Machine: Global Hypermasculinity and Images of the Asian Woman in Modernity." *positions: east asia cultures critique* 7, no. 2 (fall 1999): 277–306.

Liu, Cynthia. "When Dragon Ladies Die, Do They Become Butterflies?" In

Countervisions: Asian American Film Criticism. Edited by Darrell Hamamoto and Sandra Liu, 23–39. Philadelphia: Temple University Press, 2000.

Liu, Lucy. Interview with CBS News Entertainment. February 5, 1999.

Lorde, Audre. *Black Unicorn.* New York: Norton, 1978.

———. *Sister Outsider.* Freedom, Calif.: Crossing Press, 1984.

———. "Uses of Erotic: The Erotic as Power." In *Sister Outsider*, 53–59. Freedom, Calif.: Crossing Press, 1984.

Loti, Pierre. *Madame Chrysanthemum.* New York: Kegan Paul, 2002.

Louie, Miriam Ching. "Breaking the Cycle: Women Workers Confront Corporate Greed Globally." In *Dragon Ladies: Asian American Feminists Breathe Fire.* Edited by Sonia Shah, 121–31. Boston: South End Press, 1997.

Louie, Reagan. *Orientalia.* London: Powerhouse Press, 2003.

Lowe, Lisa. *Immigrant Acts: On Asian American Cultural Politics.* Durham, N.C.: Duke University Press, 1996.

Lu, Lynn. "Critical Visions: The Representation and Resistance of Asian Women." In *Dragon Ladies: Asian American Feminists Breathe Fire.* Edited by Sonia Shah, 17–28. Boston: South End Press, 1997.

Ma, Sheng Mei. *The Deathly Embrace.* Minneapolis: University of Minnesota Press, 2000.

MacKinnon, Catherine *Only Words.* Cambridge, Mass.: Harvard University Press, 1996.

MacKinnon, Catherine, and Andrea Dworkin, eds. *In Harm's Way: The Pornography Civil Rights Hearings.* Cambridge, Mass.: Harvard University Press, 1997.

Mahmood, Saba. "Feminist Theory, Embodiment, and the Docile Agent: Some Reflections on Egyptian Islamic Revival." *Cultural Anthropology* 16, no. 2 (May 2001): 202–36.

Maltby, Richard, Jr., and Alain Boublil. "Movie in My Mind." In *Miss Saigon*, music by Claude-Michel Schönberg; lyrics by Richard Maltby Jr. and Alain Boublil. Milwaukee, Wisc.: H. Leonard, 1987.

Manalansan, Martin. *Global Divas: Filipino Gay Men in the Diaspora.* Durham, N.C.: Duke University Press, 2002.

———. "Race, Violence and Neoliberal Spatial Politics in the Global City." *Social Text* 23, nos. 3–4 (fall/winter 2005): 141–56.

Mani, Lata. *Contentious Traditions: The Debate on Sati in Colonial India.* Berkeley: University of California Press, 1998.

Marchetti, Gina. *Romance and the "Yellow Peril": Race, Sex, and Discursive Strategies in Hollywood Fiction.* Berkeley: University of California Press, 1994.

Marks, Laura U. *The Skin of the Film.* Durham, N.C.: Duke University Press, 2000.

Marriott, David. *On Black Men.* New York: Columbia University Press, 2000.

Matsuda, Mari J. *Where Is Your Body? And Other Essays on Race, Gender and the Law.* Boston: Beacon Press, 1996.

Mayne, Judith. *Cinema and Spectatorship*. London: Routledge, 1993.

McClintock, Anne. *Imperial Leather: Race, Gender, and Sexuality in the Colonial Contest*. London: Routledge, 1995.

Medich, Rob. "Just Who Is Lucy Liu?" CBS News Entertainment, December 13, 1999, http://www.cbsnews.com/stories/1999/02/05/entertainment/main316 95.shtml (accessed November 14, 2006).

Mercer, Kobena. "Skin Head Sex Thing: Racial Difference and the Homoerotic Imaginary." In *How Do I Look?: Queer Film and Video*. Edited by Bad Object-Choices, 169–210. Seattle: Bay Press, 1991.

——. *Welcome to the Jungle*. London: Routledge, 1994.

Mimura, Glen. "Antidote for Collective Amnesia: Rea Tajri's Germinal Image." In *Countervisions: Asian American Film Criticism*. Edited by Darrell Hamamoto and Sandra Liu, 150–62. Philadelphia: Temple University Press, 2000.

Modleski, Tania. *Feminism without Women: Culture and Criticism in a Postfeminist Age*. New York: Routledge, 1991.

Mohanty, Chandra Talpade. "Cartographies of Struggle." In *Third World Women and the Politics of Feminism*. Edited by Chandra Talpade Mohanty, Ann Russo, and Lourdes Torres, 1–47. Bloomington: Indiana University Press, 1991.

Moon, Katherine. *Sex among Allies: Military Prostitution in U.S.-Korea Relations*. New York: Columbia University Press, 1997.

Moraga, Cherríe. *Loving in the War Years*. Cambridge, Mass.: South End Press, 2000.

Morgan, Robin. "Theory and Practice: Pornography and Rape." In *Take Back the Night*. Edited by Laura Lederer, 134–40. New York: Morrow, 1980.

Morris, Gary. "The Child Defiled. Sex: The Annabel Chong Story." *Bright Lights Film Journal* 29 (July 2000), http://www.brightlightsfilm.com/29/annabel chong.html (accessed September 29, 2006).

Moy, James. *Marginal Sights: Staging the Chinese in America*. Iowa City: University of Iowa Press, 1993.

Mumford, Kevin. *Interzones: Black/White Sex Districts in Chicago and New York in the Early Twentieth Century*. New York: Columbia University Press, 1997.

Muñoz, Jose Esteban. *Disidentifications: Queers of Color and the Performance of Politics*. Vol. 2 of *Cultural Studies of the Americas*. Minneapolis: University of Minnesota Press, 1999.

Nagle, Jill. *Whores and Other Feminists*. Boston: Routledge, 1997.

Nakamura, Eric. "Big Money Shot: Asia Carrera." *Giant Robot*, http://www.giantrobot.com/issues/issue14/asia/index.html (accessed May 23, 2006).

Negra, Diane. *Off-White Hollywood: American Culture and Ethnic Female Stardom*. London: Routledge, 2001.

Nguyen, Viet. *Race and Resistance: Literature and Politics in Asian America*. London: Oxford University Press, 2002.

Nichols, Bill. "Historical Consciousness and the Viewer: *Who Killed Vincent*

Chin?" In *Screening Asian Americans*. Edited by Peter X. Feng, 159–72. New Brunswick, N.J.: Rutgers University Press, 2002.

Ogunnaike, Lola. "The Perks and Pitfalls Of a Ruthless-Killer Role: Lucy Liu Boosts the Body Count in New Film." *New York Times*, October 13, 2003, E1.

Oh, Sandra. Interview in *Bitch*, April–May 2005, 46–52.

Oishi, Eve. "Bad Asians: New Film and Video by Queer Asian American Artists." In *Countervisions: Asian American Film Criticism*. Edited by Darrell Hamamoto and Sandra Liu, 221–41. Philadelphia: Temple University Press, 2000.

Olsen, Ralph. "How Those Stag Movies Are Made." *Modern Man* 5, no. 9 (March 1956): 32–37.

Omi, Michael, and Howard Winant. *Racial Formation in the United States*. New York: Routledge, 1994.

Ono, Kent. "Re/membering Spectators: Meditations on Japanese American Cinema." In *Countervisions: Asian American Film Criticism*. Edited by Darrell Hamamoto and Sandra Liu, 129–49. Philadelphia: Temple University Press, 2000.

Oren, Tasha. "Secret Asian Man." In *East Main Street*. New York: New York University Press, 2005.

Palumbo-Liu, David. *Asian/American: Historical Crossings of a Racial Frontier*. Stanford, Calif.: Stanford University Press, 1999.

Pao, Angela. "The Eyes of the Storm: Gender, Genre and Cross-Casting in Miss Saigon." *Text and Performance Quarterly* 12 (1992): 21–39.

Parmar, Pratibha. "That Moment of Emergence." In *Queer Looks: Perspectives on Lesbian and Gay Film and Video*. Edited by Martha Gever, Pratibha Parmar, and John Greyson, 3–11. New York: Routledge, 1993.

Parreñas, Rhacel. " 'White Trash' Meets the 'Little Brown Monkeys': The Taxi Dance Hall as a Site of Interracial and Gender Alliances Between White Working Class Women and Filipino Immigrant Men in the 1920s–30s." *Amerasia* 24, no. 2 (summer 1998): 115–34.

Peffer, George Anthony. *If They Don't Bring Their Women Here: Chinese Female Immigration before Exclusion*. Urbana: University of Illinois Press, 1999.

Penley, Constance. "Crackers and Whackers: The White Trashing of Porn." In *White Trash: Race and Class in America*. Edited by Matt Wray and Annalee Newitz, 89–112. New York: Routledge, 1996.

Penny, Mark. "One on One with Annabel Chong." *Offscreen*, October 15, 1999, http://www.horschamp.qc.ca/new_offscreen/annabel.html (accessed October 18, 2006).

Phelan, Peggy. *Unmarked: The Politics of Performance*. New York: Routledge, 1993.

Powers, John. "An Unreliable Memoir." In *The Filmmaker and the Prostitute*. Edited by Chris Berry, Annette Hamilton, and Laleen Jayamanne, 103–16. Sydney: Power Publications, 1997.

Projansky, Sarah. *Watching Rape: Film and Television in Profeminist Culture*. New York: New York University Press, 2001.

Quan, Tracy. *Diary of a Manhattan Call Girl*. New York: Three Rivers Press, 2001.

——. Foreword to *Orientalia: Sex in Asia* by Reagan Louie. New York: Powerhouse Books, 2003.

Queen, Carol. *Real Live Nude Girl: Chronicles of Sex-Positive Culture*. San Francisco: Cleis Press, 2002.

Read, Alan, ed. *The Fact of Blackness: Frantz Fanon and Visual Representation*. New York: Bay Press, 1996.

Realuyo, Bino. *The Umbrella Country*. New York: Ballantine, 1998.

Rivers, Tony. "Oriental Girls." GQ (British edition), October 1990, 160–62.

Rosca, Ninotchka. "Take *Miss Saigon* to Ho Chi Minh City." Paper published by Center for Concerned Artists, Philippines, November 2000.

Rosen, Ruth. *The Lost Sisterhood: Prostitution in America, 1900–1918*. Baltimore: Johns Hopkins University Press, 1982.

Rubin, Gayle. "Thinking Sex: Notes for a Radical Theory of the Politics of Sexuality." In *Pleasure and Danger: Exploring Female Sexuality*. Edited by Carol S. Vance, 267–319. London: Pandora Press, 1989.

——. "The Traffic in Women." In *Toward an Anthropology of Women*. Edited by Ranya R. Reiter, 157–210. New York: Monthly Review Press, 1975.

Russell, Catherine. *Experimental Ethnography: The Work of Film in the Age of Video*. Durham, N.C.: Duke University Press, 1999.

Said, Edward W. *Orientalism*. New York: Random House, 1979.

Sapphire. *Push*. New York: Random House, 1996.

Sartre, Jean Paul. "Concrete Relations with Others." In *Being and Nothingness*, 471–556. New York: Washington Square Press, 1993.

Scarry, Elaine. *The Body in Pain*. London: Oxford University Press, 1985.

Schlossman, David. *Actors and Activists*. New York: Routledge, 2002.

Seabrook, Jeremy. *Travels in the Skin Trade: Tourism and the Sex Industry*. Vancouver: University of British Columbia Press, 2001.

See, Lisa. "Anna May Speaks." In *Making More Waves: New Writing by Asian American Women*. Edited by Elaine H. Kim, Lilia V. Villanueva, and Asian Women United, 195–200. Boston: Beacon Press, 1997.

Segal, Lynne. "Sweet Sorrows, Painful Pleasures: Pornography and the Perils of Heterosexual Desire." In *Sex Exposed: Sexuality and the Pornography Debate*. Edited by Lynne Segal and Mary McIntosh, 65–91. New Brunswick, N.J.: Rutgers University Press, 1993.

Shah, Nayan. *Contagious Divides: Epidemic and Race in San Francisco's Chinatown*. Berkeley: University of California Press, 2001.

——. "Sexuality, Identity and the Uses of History." In *Q and A: Queer in Asian*

America. Edited by David Eng and Alice Hom, 141–56. Philadelphia: Temple University Press, 1999.

Shange, Ntozake. *For Colored Girls Who Have Considered Suicide When the Rainbow Is Enuf*. New York: Scribner Poetry, 1997.

Shimakawa, Karen. *National Abjection: The Asian American Body Onstage*. Durham, N.C.: Duke University Press, 2002.

Shimizu, Celine Parreñas. "Master-Slave Sex Acts: *Mandingo* and the Race/Sex Paradox." *Wide Angle* 21 (October 1999): 42–61.

———. "Theory in/of Practice: Filipina American Feminist Filmmaking." In *Pinay Power: Theorizing the Filipina/American Experience*. Edited by Melinda De Jesus, 329–35. New York: Routledge, 2005.

Shimizu, Celine Parreñas, and Helen Lee. "Sex Acts: Two Mediations on Race and Sexuality." In *Signs: Journal of Women, Culture and Society* 30, no. 1 (autumn 2004): 1385–1402.

Shocket, Dan. "Birth of the Blues." *Skin Flicks* 2, no. 2 (April 1981): 12–14, 26.

Silverman, Kaja. *Acoustic Mirror: The Female Voice in Psychoanalysis and Cinema (Theories of Representation and Difference)*. Bloomington: Indiana University Press, 1988.

———. *Male Subjectivity at the Margins*. London: Routledge, 1992.

———. *The Threshold of the Visible World*. New York: Routledge, 1996.

Simmel, Georg. "Sociability." In *On Individuality and Social Forms*. Edited by Donald N. Levine, 127–40. Chicago: University of Chicago Press, 1971.

Sobchack, Vivian. *The Address of the Eye*. Princeton, N.J.: Princeton University Press, 1991.

Somerville, Siobhan. *Queering the Color Line*. Durham, N.C.: Duke University Press, 2000.

Souter, Fanella. "The Bad Man of Bangkok?" In *The Filmmaker and the Prostitute*. Edited by Chris Berry, Annette Hamilton, and Laleen Jayamanne, 117–24. Sydney: Power Publications, 1997.

Spivak, Gayatri. "Can the Subaltern Speak?" In *Marxism and the Interpretation of Culture*. Edited by Cary Nelson and Lawrence Grossberg, 271–313. Urbana: University of Illinois Press, 1988.

Sprinkle, Annie. *Annie Sprinkle: Post-Porn Modernist; My 25 Years as a Multi-Media Whore*. San Francisco: Cleis Press, 1998.

Stacey, Judith. "Scents, Scholars and Stigma: The Revisionist Campaign for Family Values." *Social Text* 40 (fall 1994): 51–75.

Staiger, Janet. *Bad Women: Regulating Sexuality in Early American Cinema*. Minneapolis: Minnesota University Press, 1995.

Stanislavsky, Constantin. *Building a Character*. New York: Routledge, 1949.

———. *Creating a Role*. New York: Routledge, 1961.

Stedman, Raymond. *Shadows of the Indian*. Norman: Oklahoma University Press, 1982.

Stewart, Jacqueline. "Negroes Laughing at Themselves: Black Spectatorship and the Performance of Urban Modernity." *Critical Inquiry* (summer 2003): 650–77.

Stoler, Ann Laura. *Race and the Education of Desire*. Durham, N.C.: Duke University Press, 1995.

Strasberg, Lee. *At the Actors Studio*. New York: Theatre Communication Group, 1965.

Sturdevant, Saundra Pollock, and Brenda Stolzfus. *Let the Good Times Roll: Prostitution and the U.S. Military in Asia*. New York: New Press, 1993.

Sunder Rajan, Rajeswari. *Real and Imagined Women*. London: Routledge, 1993.

Tadiar, Neferti Xina M. "Filipinas 'Living in a Time of War.'" In *Pinay Power: Theorizing the Filipina/American Experience*. Edited by Melinda De Jesus, 373–85. New York: Routledge, 2005.

Tajima, Renee. "Lotus Blossoms Don't Bleed: Asian Women in Film." In *Making Waves: An Anthology of Writings by and about Asian American Women*. Edited by Asian Women United, 308–17. Boston: Beacon Press, 1989.

———. "Moving the Image: Asian American Independent Filmmaking 1970–1990." In *Moving the Image: Independent Asian Pacific American Media Arts*. Edited by Russell Leong, 10–33. Los Angeles: UCLA Asian American Studies Center and Visual Communication, 1991.

Tajima-Peña, Renee. "No Mo Pomo and Other Tales of the Road." In *Countervisions: Asian American Film Criticism*. Edited by Darrell Hamamoto and Sandra Liu, 245–62. Philadelphia: Temple University Press, 2000.

Takagi, D. Y. "Maiden Voyage: Excursion into Sexuality and Identity Politics in Asian America." In *Asian American Sexualities: Dimensions of the Gay and Lesbian Experience*. Edited by Russell Leong, 21–36. New York: Routledge, 1996.

Teish, Luisah. "A Quiet Subversion." In *Take Back the Night: Women on Pornography*. Edited by Laura Lederer, 115–18. New York: Morrow, 1980.

Thoma, Pamela. "Cultural Autobiography, Testimonial and Asian American Transnational Feminist Coalition in the 'Comfort Woman of World War II California' Conference." In *Asian American Women: The Frontiers Reader*. Edited by Linda Trinh Vo and Marian Sciachitano. Lincoln: University of Nebraska Press, 2004.

Ting, Jennifer P. "The Power of Sexuality." *Journal of Asian American Studies* 1, no. 1 (1998): 65–82.

Tolentino, Roland. "Bodies, Letters and Catalogs: Filipinas in Transnational Space." *Social Text* 48 (1996): 49–76.

———. "Identity and Difference in 'Filipino/a American' Media Arts." In *Screening Asian Americans*. Edited by Peter X. Feng, 111–32. New Brunswick, N.J.: Rutgers University Press, 2002.

"Top 50 in the Porn Industry." *Hustler Magazine*, December-January 1999.

Travers, Peter. "Review of *Sideways*." *Rolling Stone*, October 18, 2004, http://

www.rollingstone.com/reviews/movie/__/id/6562095?pageid=rs.Reviews
MovieArchive&pageregion=mainRegion&rnd=1124483812089&has-player=
false (accessed November 6, 2006).

Trinh T. Minh-ha. *Woman, Native, Other: Writing Postcoloniality and Feminism.*
Bloomington: Indiana University Press, 1989.

Truong, Thanh Dam. *Sex, Money and Morality*. London: Zed Books, 1990.

Urban, Andrew. "Dennis O'Rourke and *The Good Woman of Bangkok*." In *The
Filmmaker and the Prostitute*. Edited by Chris Berry, Annette Hamilton, and
Laleen Jayamanne, 145–58. Sydney: Power Publications, 1997.

Vance, Carol. "Negotiating Sex and Gender in the Attorney General's Commission on Pornography." In *Constructing Sexualities*. Edited by Suzanne LaFont,
346–57. New York: Prentice Hall, 2002.

Vo, Linda Trinh, and Marian Sciachitano. "Moving Beyond 'Exotics, Whores
and Nimble Fingers': Asian American Women in a New Era of Globalization
and Resistance." *Frontiers* 21, no. 1 (2000): 1.

Walker, Alice. "Coming Apart." In *You Can't Keep a Good Woman Down*, 41–53.
Orlando: Harvest Books, 1981.

——. "Porn." In *You Can't Keep a Good Woman Down*, 77–84. Orlando: Harvest
Books, 1981.

Walker, Janet. *Trauma Cinema*. Berkeley: University of California Press, 2005.

Wallace, Michele. *Invisibility Blues*. London: Verso, 1990.

Walsh, Joan. "Asian Women, Caucasian Men." *Image Magazine*, supplement to
San Francisco Examiner, December 2, 1990, 11–17.

Walters, Suzanna D. *All the Rage: The Story of Gay Visibility in America*. Chicago: University of Chicago Press, 2001.

Wang, Oliver. "Oh My! Oliver Wang Talks to *Double Happiness* Star Sandra Oh
about Her Character, Her Career and Her Role in Asian Canada/America."
Yolk Magazine, September 30, 1995, 15.

Warner, Michael. *The Trouble with Normal: Sex, Politics and the Ethics of Queer
Life*. Cambridge, Mass.: Harvard University Press, 2000.

Wartofsky, Alona. "The Trial of Dennis O'Rourke at Patpong." In *The Filmmaker and the Prostitute*. Edited by Chris Berry, Annette Hamilton, and
Laleen Jayamanne, 159–62. Sydney: Power Publications, 1997.

Waugh, Tom. "Good Clean Fung." In *Screening Asian Americans*. Edited by
Peter X. Feng, 243–52. New Brunswick, N.J.: Rutgers University Press, 2002.

——. *Hard to Imagine: Gay Male Eroticism in Photography and Film from Their
Beginnings to Stonewall*. New York: Columbia University Press, 1996.

Wiegman, Robyn. *American Anatomies: Theorizing Race and Gender*. Durham,
N.C.: Duke University Press, 1995.

Williams, Linda. "Corporealized Observers: Visual Pornographies." In *Fugitive
Images*. Edited by Patrice Petro, 3–41. Bloomington: Indiana University Press,
1995.

———. "The Ethics of Documentary Intervention: Dennis O'Rourke's *The Good Woman of Bangkok.*" In *The Filmmaker and the Prostitute.* Edited by Chris Berry, Annette Hamilton, and Laleen Jayamanne, 79–90. Sydney: Power Publications, 1997.

———. *Hard Core: Power, Pleasure, and the "Frenzy of the Visible."* Berkeley: University of California Press, 1989.

———. "Pornographies On/Scene, or Different Strokes for Different Folks." In *Sex Exposed: Sexuality and the Pornography Debate.* Edited by Lynne Segal and Mary McIntosh, 233–65. New Brunswick, N.J: Rutgers University Press, 1992.

———. "Porn Studies: Proliferating Pornographies On/Scene: An Introduction." In *Porn Studies.* Edited by Linda Williams, 1–23. Durham, N.C.: Duke University Press, 2004.

———, ed. *Porn Studies.* Durham, N.C.: Duke University Press, 2004.

———, ed. *Viewing Positions.* New Brunswick, N.J.: Rutgers University Press, 1994.

Williams, Linda Ruth. "Review of *Sex: The Annabel Chong Story.*" *Sight and Sound,* May 2000, http://www.bfi.org.uk/sightandsound/review/493 (accessed October 19, 2006).

Wolf, Naomi. "The Porn Myth." *New York Magazine,* October 20, 2003. http://nymag.com/nymetro/news/trends/n_9437/index.html (accessed October 19, 2006).

Wolf, Stacy. *Problem Like Maria.* Ann Arbor: University of Michigan Press, 2002.

Wong, Elizabeth. *China Doll.* Woodstock, Ill.: Dramatic Publishing, 1995.

Wong, Eugene Franklin. "The Early Years: Asians in the American Films Prior to World War II." In *Screening Asian Americans.* Edited by Peter X. Feng, 53–70. New Brunswick, N.J.: Rutgers University Press, 2002.

———. *On Visual Media Racism: Asians in the American Motion Pictures.* New York: Arno Press, 1978.

Yamamoto, Traise. "In/Visible Difference: Asian American Women and the Politics of the Spectacle." In *Race, Class and Gender* 7, no. 1 (January 2000): 43–56.

Yoshikawa, Yoko. "The Heat Is on *Miss Saigon* Coalition: Organizing Across Race and Sexuality." In *The State of Asian America: Activism and Resistance in the 1990s.* Edited by Karin Aguilar-San Juan, 275–94. Boston: South End Press, 1994.

Yu, Henry. *Thinking Orientals: Migration, Contact, and Eroticism in Modern America.* New York: Oxford University Press, 2002.

Yung, Judy. *Unbound Voices: A Documentary History of Chinese Women in San Francisco.* Berkeley: University of California Press, 1999.

Yung, Judy, and Peggy Pascoe. "Miscegenation Law, Court Cases, and Ideologies of 'Race' in Twentieth-Century America." In *Unequal Sisters.* 3rd ed. Edited by Vicki Ruiz and Ellen Carol Dubois, 161–82. New York: Routledge, 2000.

Zarco, Cyn. "My Worst Fear." In *Flippin': Filipinos on America*. Edited by Luis Francia and Eric Gamalinda, 258–59. New York: Asian American Writer's Workshop, 1996.

———. "Once Upon a Seesaw with Charlie Chan." In *Flippin': Filipinos on America*. Edited by Luis Francia and Eric Gamalinda, 260–61. New York: Asian American Writer's Workshop, 1996.

Zavella, Patricia. "Playing with Fire: The Gendered Construction of Chicana/Mexicana Sexuality." In *The Gender/Sexuality Reader: Culture, History, Political Economy*. Edited by Roger N. Lancaster and Micaela di Leonardo, 392–408. New York: Routledge, 1997.

———. "*Talk'n Sex*: Chicanas and Mexicanas Theorize about Silences and Sexual Pleasures." In *Chicana Feminisms: A Critical Reader*. Edited by Gabriela F. Arredondo, Aída Hurtado, Norma Klahn, Olga Nájera-Ramirez, and Patricia Zavella, 228–53. Durham, N.C.: Duke University Press, 2003.

Zelizer, Viviana. *The Purchase of Intimacy*. Princeton, N.J.: Princeton University Press, 2005.

Žižek, Slavoj. *For They Know Not What They Do: Enjoyment as a Political Factor*. London: Verso, 1991.

———. "From the Sublime to the Ridiculous: The Sexual Act in Cinema." In *The Plague of Fantasies*, 171–91. London: Verso, 1997.

Carrera, Asia, 28, 140, 159, 164, 183–84; *A Is for Asia,* 167–72; *Apassionata,* 165, 167, 171–73; beauty of, 165–66; commodification of personal history of, 171–74; Internet presence of, 173–74; *Last Little Whorehouse,* 165; money shots of, 166–67; *Phantasm,* 166–68

Casting Couch, 106

Chan, Anthony, 283–84n2

Chan, Jackie, 60

Chanda, Gitanjili Singh, 79

Chang, Christine, 296–97n8

Charlie's Angels series, 2, 27, 86, 275n4; Alex's disguises in, 60; Alex's sexuality in, 65, 84–85, 286–87n39

Cheang, Shu Lea, 227, 228, 296–97n8

Cheat, The, 138

Chekhov, Michael, 42–43

Chen, Joan, 271

Cheng, Anne Anlin, 78, 81, 82, 286n34

Cheung, King-kok, 15

"Child Defiled, The" (Morris), 175–76

Chin, Frank, 15

China, 27, 109, 127–33, 137

China Babe, 289n11

China De Sade, 154, 158–59

China Doll, 89

China Lust, 154, 156–58

China Mystique, The (Leong), 61–62, 283–84n2

Chinese Love Life, 27, 108–20, 132, 137

Cho, Margaret, 10; racialized sexuality portrayed by, 7–8, 16–17, 87, 189; stereotypes used by, 64

Chong, Annabel, 28, 140, 164, 191; contradictory double life of, 179–82; facial expressions of, 176, 178–80; Internet presence of, 164–65, 175, 181–82; performances of perversity

by, 177–84; prioritizing of sexuality of, 180–82; *Sex: The Annabel Chong Story,* 175, 179–82; *The World's Biggest Gang Bang,* 175–79, 181

Chrystos, 144–45

Chuh, Kandice, 145

Chun, Kimberly, 177, 179–80

Cimino, Michael, 68

Cinderella, 52

cinematic expression of hypersexuality, 25, 276nn17–18; historical contexts of, 136–37, 284n10; Hollywood productions of interracial love, 148–49, 153; homogenization of Asian ethnicities in, 13–15, 279n46; lotus blossom/dragon lady framework in, 3, 18–21; Oriental details in, 122–32; shaping imagined others of Asian/American women in, 13–15, 24, 277n24–25; stage performance vs., 26. *See also* pornography; sex tourist movies; stag films, 1920–34; stag films, post-1950s

Cleese, John, 86

College Coed 1 and *2,* 106

Collins, Patricia Hill, 285n16

colonial paradigms, 3; fears of sex and representation in, 277n21; hypersexual attributions to Asian/American women, 143; in *Miss Saigon,* 36, 39, 51; in sex tourist movies, 194–95; slavery contexts and, 142, 143; in *The World of Suzie Wong,* 79–80. *See also* Vietnam War

comedy performance, 80. *See also* Cho, Margaret

"Coming Apart" (Walker), 143

Compositional Subjects (Kang), 14, 277n25, 279n46

consumption. *See* spectatorship of hypersexuality

sexual vs. queer perspectives, 12–13, 276–77n19; moralism debates, 18–19, 276–77n19; pornography debates, 141–43, 291n11; on prostitution, 164–65; resistance assessments in, 225; sex-positive discourses in, 141–47, 175

femmes fatales. *See* racial stardom

Femme TV, 257

Feng, Peter, 78, 94, 231

film. *See* cinematic expression of hypersexuality

Filmmaker and the Prostitute, The (Berry, Hamilton, and Jayamanne), 191, 193–94, 198

filmmakers. *See* Asian/American feminist films

Flower Drum Song, 3, 27, 65, 78, 80–84; Hwang's remake of, 286n35; nontraditional gender roles in, 82–84; pleasure performed in, 81–82

Ford, Staci, 79

Forever Bottom!, 278n37

Foronda, Anthony, 50

Foucault, Michel, 9–10, 94; on pervasiveness of sexual knowledge, 21; on sexual identity, 19, 278n39

Fox Girl, 187

Freud, Sigmund, 297–98n9

Friendly, John, 293n44

Fuchs, Cynthia, 84, 270

Fung, Richard, 21, 227, 278n37

Gaine, Jane, 233

Gardner, Tracey A., 143, 178

Geisha, 28, 134

Geisha Girl, 28, 108, 134

gendered paradigms, 19; gender drag, 108, 124–25; marginalized groups and, 278–79n40. *See also* queer perspectives

Gibson, Mel, 86–87

Gilman, Sander, 279n44

globalized contexts. *See* sex tourist movies

Glover, Crispin, 2

golden-age pornography, 1940s–1990s, 183–94; Kristara Barrington's work, 153; classifications by race of, 140–41, 293n44; fantasy in, 163–64; genital shots in, 147–48, 150–52; historical contexts of, 147–48, 150, 152; interracial contexts of, 148–52; Mai Lin's work, 153, 159–62; money (face) shots in, 155; Oriental details in, 147–49, 152, 153, 157–60; production qualities of, 158; white ideals of beauty in, 159; Linda Wong's work, 153–59; yellowface representations in, 147–53

Gonzales, Mari Keiko, 227, 228

Good Woman of Bangkok, The, 2, 185–88, 194–200, 211, 223; agency and performance in, 212–22, 224; documentary fiction approach of, 189–93; interviews by O'Rourke in, 215–17; male anonymity in, 210; poverty in, 205–7

Gopinath, Gayatri, 276–77n19

Gordon, Avery, 99

Grace Lee Project, The, 11–12, 229, 254–56, 265, 298n23

Grass Sandwich, A, 106

Grey's Anatomy, 268

Hagedorn, Jessica, 11, 12, 68, 231

Hall, Stuart, 10, 53

Hard Core (Williams), 291n40

Harsanyi, Martha, 111–12, 290n23

Hartley, Nina, 165

Hart Schell und Schon, 257–58

Haunted, 293n44

marriage configurations: defense of marriage legislation, 277n22; notions of "proper," 13; queer marriage rights, 271–72, 280n50

Marriott, David, 11–12

M. Butterfly, 32, 79, 120

Menage Moderne du Madame Butterfly, 27, 109, 120–27, 137, 290n28

Mercer, Kobena, 53, 63

Mexican Honeymoon, 108

military tourism. *See* sex tourism

misidentification, 54–55, 283n55, 285n20

Miss Saigon, 1, 26; authorship of Asian/American actresses in, 41–51; bind of representation in, 30–31, 52–56; Broadway Theater production of, 40–41; critical response to, 34–38; crotch-grabbing acts in, 44–45, 47–48; embodiments of sexuality in, 44–51; Filipina cast members in, 41–42, 282n27, 282n34; Kim in yellowface in, 36; lotus blossom/dragon lady stereotypes in, 30–34, 37–38; Orientalist/colonial paradigms in, 36, 39, 51; productive perversity in, 56–57; protests against, 35; racialized portrayals of prostitution in, 32–39, 280n4; racist casting of, 36, 38–39, 43, 282n39; spectatorship of, 38–41, 49–51. See also *Making of Miss Saigon, The*

Miyagi, Mimi, 165, 272, 274, 293n44

Modleski, Tania, 232

Moffatt, Tracey, 296n46, 296–97n8

Mohanty, Chandra Talpade, 279n46

Moraga, Cherríe, 144–45

morality paradigms: assumed innocence/morality of white women, 32, 62, 65, 74–75, 280n6; feminist debates on, 18–19, 276–77n19; mor-

alistic scopophilia in pornography, 18, 104; in spectatorship of hypersexuality, 18–21, 104; in *The World of Suzie Wong*, 78–79. *See also* unreliability of representation

More Dirty Debutantes, 210

Morgan, Jonathan, 170, 172

Morgan, Robin, 141

Morris, Gary, 175–76, 180

movies. *See* cinematic expression of hypersexuality

Mumford, Kevin, 127

Muñoz, Jose Esteban, 276–77n19

My Niagara, 247, 298n19

Nagle, Jill, 276n13

Nakamura, Suzy, 252–54

Nalzaro, Edmund, 282n34

Natan, Bernard, 120

National Abjection (Shimakawa), 30, 281n20

national identity formations. *See* stereotypes

National Origins Act of 1924, 136–37

Negra, Diane, 62, 69–70

Negroes at Play, 108

Negron, Frances, 228

Nguyen, Viet, 273

Nice Colored Girls, 296n46, 296–97n8

Night in a Turkish Harem, 108

"Nine Inch Nails" (Berens), 189–90

normative sexuality, 29, 57; Asians' non-normative sexuality vs., 38, 138–39, 281n20; assumed innocence/morality of white women, 32, 62, 65, 74–75, 280n6; heterosexuality as, 18–21, 229, 278n37, 280n50; male/white male sexuality as, 31, 38–39; in marriage configurations, 271–72, 277n22, 280n50; redefined in Asian/American feminist films, 229;

standards of beauty in, 78, 159, 165–66; static nature of white femininity, 69; "third sex" alternatives to, 25; race-positive sexuality vs. (*see* race-positive sexuality; racialized sexuality); white sexuality as, 21, 26, 31, 38–39, 142, 279n44

Notorious C.H.O., 7–8

Ogunnaike, Lola, 60–61

Oh, Hyun Mi, 2, 3, 226–28, 296–97n8

Oh, Sandra, 45, 274, 279n46; in *Barrier Device,* 251–54; in *The Diary of Evelyn Lau,* 9–10; in *Double Happiness,* 249; in *Grey's Anatomy,* 268–69; in *Prey,* 237–43; in romantic comedy, 80; in *Sideways,* 269–70; on stereotypes, 64

Oishi, Eve, 273

On Black Men (Marriott), 11–12

101 Asian Debutantes series, 2, 185–86, 188–89, 201–25; agency and performance in, 212–22, 224; male anonymity in, 210; poverty in, 204–7; Roc's direction and narration in, 217–22; women's engagement of camera in, 207–9

One Night in Bangkok, 162

Ono, Kent, 20

Onodera, Midi, 227, 228

onscenity, 24, 280n51

On the Technique of Acting (Chekhov), 43

Oren, Tasha, 146

Oriental Babysitter, 154–55

Oriental details: in exotic dance, 129–30; in golden-age pornography, 147–49, 152, 153, 157–60; in *Miss Saigon,* 36, 39, 51; in stag films, 106, 122–32; in *The Thief of Bagdad,* 66–67; of white women in yellowface, 27–28, 102–6, 108, 127–29

Oriental Girlfriend, 28, 108, 151–52, 289n11

Orientalia, 8–9

Oriental Jade, 162

Orientals, 254

O'Rourke, Dennis, 185–200, 211–25. See also *Good Woman of Bangkok, The*

Page Law of 1870, 17–18

pain/trauma/violence in sexuality, 6, 23, 25–26, 273–74; Asian/American feminist portrayals of, 257–64; performativity of, 212–14; in pornography, 140–42, 144–45, 175–76, 178–79. *See also* pleasure in sexuality

Palumbo-Liu, David, 14, 116, 136, 155

Pao, Angela, 36, 282n39

Parfait, Ralph, 293n44

Parmar, Pratibha, 227, 228, 296–97n8

Parreñas, Celine. *See* Shimizu, Celine Parreñas

Passing Through, 298n17

passionate attachment process, 63, 97, 299n64

Payback, 2, 27, 60, 65, 86–88, 275n4

Penley, Constance, 104, 142

pen-pal brides, 18, 144

performance of hypersexuality, 4, 6, 13–15, 26; authorship of roles in *Miss Saigon,* 41–51; bind of representation in, 16, 31, 52–56, 77–78; Butler's theory of performance, 211–12; embodiments of strength in *Miss Saigon,* 44–51; encounters with audiences, 49–51; enjoyment of, 38–39; imago fantasies and, 91–92; passionate attachment process in, 63, 97, 299n64; perversity and, 6, 21–24, 26, 28, 56–57; pleasure and, 35–36, 81–82; race-positive sexuality and,

performance of hypersexuality, (*cont.*)
6, 25–26; in sex tourist movies, 211–
22; triangulation of self, actress, and
role in, 34–45, 51, 64, 91, 94–100,
153–64, 282n26. *See also* authorship
of hypersexuality; cinematic expression of hypersexuality; racial
stardom
Perpetually Cool (Chan), 283–84n2
perversity of hypersexuality, 1, 4–6, 13;
Annabel Chong and, 177–78; in
contemporary pornography, 174–
84; *Miss Saigon* and, 32–39, 41–51,
56–57; naked bodies and, 70–71;
political production of, 6, 21–24, 26,
28, 56–57; polymorphous legacies
of, 7–8; in portrayals of sexual
abuse, 261; in prostitution, 280n4;
in racial stardom, 64–77; in spectatorship, 34–35; in stag films, 138–
39; in *The Thief of Bagdad,* 67–72
Phantasm, 166–68
Philippino Couple, 108, 290n16
Picadilly, 89
picture brides, 17–18, 144
Pink Eye, 257
Plato, 289n8
Play It to the Bone, 65, 84
pleasure in sexuality, 2, 6, 19, 273–74;
in *Flower Drum Song,* 81–82; in
money (face) shots, 166; performativity of, 35–36, 86–87, 212–14,
217–22; in pornography, 140–42,
144–45, 175–76, 178–79; in spectatorship, 40, 282n23. *See also* pain/
trauma/violence in sexuality
political power paradigms, 2–3, 6, 14–
16, 278–79n40; in Asian/American
feminist films (*see* Asian/American
feminist films); bind of representation in, 16–17, 52–56; in Kwan's

roles, 77–78, 80–81; in Liu's roles,
84–88; passionate attachment process in, 63, 96–97, 299n64; in pornography, 3–4, 140–42, 144–45, 176,
178–79; in productions of perversity, 6, 21–24, 26, 28, 56–57; as protest, 53–55; in race-positive sexuality, 6, 25–26; in sex tourist
movies, 217–23, 296n46; in unknowability of subjective experience, 29, 98–99, 187–89
"Porn" (Walker), 143
pornography, 2, 3, 19, 27–28, 278n37;
black representations of, 142–46,
292n22; classification systems for,
111–13, 119–20, 140–41, 165, 293n44;
fantasy's role in, 146–47, 163–64,
182–83; feminist debates about, 141–
43, 291n11; historical contexts of,
136–37, 142–45, 147–48; Internet
commodification of, 28; money
(face) shots, 155–56, 166, 170; moralistic scopophilia in, 18, 104; "on
scene"/ "onscenity," 24, 280n51; paradigms in, 104, 141–43; phallus in,
209–10; pleasure, pain, power, and
politics, in, 140–42, 144–45, 176,
178–79, 212–14, 217–23, 221–23;
position of white male filmmakers
of, 187–89, 197, 224, 296n46; prostitution and, 107; queer versions of,
141; racial paradigms in, 28, 102–9,
141–47, 288n4, 289n6, 289n8, 291n11;
sex-positive discourses of, 141–47,
175; Vivid girls, 166–67; white male
viewers of, 102–3; white women in
yellowface and, 27–28, 102–6, 108,
127–29; women's experiences in,
104–5. *See also* contemporary pornography, 1990s; golden-age pornography, 1940s–1990s; sex tourist

movies; stag films, 1920–34; stag films, post-1950s

pornotopia, 133–39, 291n40

power. *See* political power paradigms

Powers, Ed, 177, 201, 210

Powers, John, 198

Premenstrual Spotting, 257–64

Prey, 230, 246–47, 249, 265; interracial sexuality in, 237–43; subjective transformations in, 242–43

Projansky, Sarah, 213

prostitute portraiture, 218–19

prostitution, 2–3; agency vs. victimization in, 9–10, 37, 276n13, 281n19; feminist discourse on, 164–65; girlhood desires of, 8–9; heart of gold stereotype of, 60, 78–80; lotus blossom/dragon lady stereotypes of, 30–34, 37–38; pleasure and perversity in, 8–9, 280n4; popular media portrayals of, 276n17; pornography and, 107; as stereotype for Asian female roles, 42, 282n28; as stereotype of immigrant Asian women, 17–18, 144. *See also* sex tourist movies

Quan, Tracy, 8–10, 17, 37, 45, 198, 281n19

Queen, Carol, 143

Queer Eye for the Straight Guy, 278–79n40

Queering the Color Line (Somerville), 277n21

queer perspectives: in Asian queer films, 227–28; on bottomhood, 278n37; lesbian sadomasochism, 19, 182; marriage rights struggles, 271–72, 277n22, 280n50; MIX NYC film festival, 263; on pornography, 141; queer of color perspectives, 228,

276–77n19, 278–79n40; on *Shanghai Express,* 72, 286n24; on stag films, 102, 124–25, 288n1, 289n8; valorization of sex in, 278–79n40; visibility concerns in, 12–13, 277n20

Quek, Grace. *See* Chong, Annabel

Rabkin, Gerald, 139

Race and the Education of Desire (Stoler), 277n21

"Race, Gender, and the Law" (Chuh), 145

race-positive sexuality, 6, 25–26, 29, 141, 267–74

racialized sexuality, 2–8, 25, 141, 147–48, 276n13; black representations of, 21–22, 107, 109, 129–30, 142–46, 285nn16–17, 289n10, 291n11, 292n22; bottomhood and gay Asian men, 278n37; in casting of Asian/American actresses, 36, 38–39, 43, 52–53; conundrum of Asian self-representations of hypersexuality, 11–13, 15, 276n18, 277n21; disease represented in, 134–35; essentialist debates on, 15; historical contexts for, 136–37, 142–45; homogenization of Asian ethnicities, 13–15, 279n46; in Internet contexts, 164–65; racial pornotopia vs., 133–39, 291n40; stag films' undermining of, 133–39; white women in yellowface, 27–28, 102–6, 108, 113–14, 127–29. *See also* feminist theories of racialized sexuality; interracial sexuality; racial stardom; stereotypes

racial stardom, 52, 285n15; bind of representation in, 62–63, 88–93; constructed in relation to white women, 62, 65; costumes and, 67, 70–71, 73, 286n23; dead-end careers racial stardom, (*cont.*)

and, 68–69; as embodiment of social categories, 92; essentialization of hypersexuality in, 62; in golden-era pornography, 153–64; Lucy Liu and, 84–88; lotus blossom/dragon lady dichotomy and, 18–21, 59; Nancy Kwan and, 77–84; passionate attachment process of, 63, 97, 299n64; perversity of hypersexuality in, 64–77; prostitute with heart of gold stereotype and, 60; self-representation in interviews and, 66; stars as agents of pleasure and power, 66, 285n16; stereotypic roles and, 59–64; struggles for recognition in, 63; triangulation of self, actress, and role, 34–45, 51, 64, 94–100, 153–64, 282n26; unreliability of representation and, 88–99; Anna May Wong and, 58–77. *See also* authorship of hypersexuality; performance of hypersexuality

Rated Sex, 161–62

"Recuperating Suzie Wong" (Feng), 231

representations of racialized sexuality, 11–13, 15. *See also* bind of representation; unreliability of representation

"Resurrection of Brandon Lee, The" (Hoang), 278n37

Revolution, 7–8

Riggs, Marlon, 228

Rivera, Rachel, 244

Roc, Jean Marc, 186–89, 201–25. See also *101 Asian Debutantes* series

Royalle, Candida, 165

Rubin, Gayle, 35, 105, 276n13, 281n9

Runaway: Diary of a Streetkid (Lau), 174

Russell, Catherine, 20

Saito, Machiko, 2, 3, 29, 227–28, 230, 265–66; distribution of films by, 263; *Femme TV*, 257; *Hart Schell und Schon*, 257–58; *Pink Eye*, 257; *Premenstrual Spotting*, 257–64

Sallie and Her Boyfriend, 129–30

Sally's Beauty Spot, 230–31, 246–47, 265; fetishism of racial sexuality in, 232–35; interracial sexuality in, 234–37

Salonga, Lea, 34, 37–38

Salt of the Earth, 108

Samurai Dick, 162

Sari Red, 296–97n8

sati/widow burning, 45–46

Saving Face, 271–72

Sayonara, 148, 153

Scarry, Elaine, 212

Scherezade and the Sultan, 108

Schlossman, David, 30, 36–38, 281n13, 282n39

scopophilia, moralistic, 18, 104

Seabrook, Jeremy, 197

Secret Museum, The (Kendrick), 146–47

See, Lisa, 89, 287n42, 287n46

Segal, Lynne, 141, 227, 297–98n9

self-authorship, 8

Señorita Lee, La, 2, 226–27

Señorita y la Criada, La, 109

Sexcapades, 160–61

Sex: The Annabel Chong Story, 175, 179–82

sex tourism, 3, 19, 28, 188–89, 294n3; in Asian/American feminist films, 229; "little brown fucking machine" slogan, 88, 185–87, 207, 287n41; in *Miss Saigon*, 44–45; myths of hedonism in, 187; in *The World of Suzie Wong*, 60

sex tourist movies: agency and performativity in, 211–22, 224; in Asian/American feminist film, 243–44; authorship in, 192–93, 200; commodification debates in, 188–89; documentary fiction approach in, 189–93; female sex tourism and, 244–45; film grammar of, 188; filmmaker participation in, 192–200; globalized contexts of, 188–89; gonzo approach in, 186, 201, 213, 218, 294n4; male anonymity in, 209–10; mutuality and victimization in, 197–98; narrations and interviews in, 215–22; political location of, 217–23; position of white male filmmakers of, 187–90, 197–99, 224, 296n46; post-colonial power relationships in, 193–200; poverty in, 204–7, 218; reality-based premise of, 187; role of phallus in, 209–10; unreliability of racial subjectivity in, 190, 192–200, 214–22; white male heroism in, 188, 190, 197–99; women's engagement of camera in, 187–88, 207–9. See also *Good Woman of Bangkok, The; 101 Asian Debutantes* series

sexual abuse, 257–64

"Sexual Act in the Cinema, The" (Žižek), 146

sexuality, 4; as analytic vector, 105, 289n8; definitions of, 267–68, 283n2

"Sexuality, Identity, and the Uses of History" (Shah), 276–77n19

sexual slavery, 37, 276n17. *See also* sex tourism

sex workers. *See* prostitution; sex tourism

Shah, Nayan, 134, 276–77n19, 278–79n40

Shanghai Express, 27, 52, 65; historical context for, 136; homoeroticism in, 72, 286n24; rape and murder in, 73–77; white woman saved in, 75

Shanghai Noon, 60

Shimakawa, Karen, 22, 30, 38, 281n20

Shimizu, Celine Parreñas, 248, 296n3

Shum, Mina, 249

Sideways, 268–70

Sin City Diary, 187, 244

Skydyking, 227

Slaying the Dragon, 285n19

Smith, Anna Nicole, 16

social class paradigms, 276n13

social experience of representation, 18–20. *See also* bind of representation; unreliability of representation

Somerville, Siobhan, 277n21

spectatorship of hypersexuality, 6, 13–15, 25–26; as act of violence on viewer, 21; bondage of hypersexuality in, 16, 31, 52–56; Feng's views of, 231; identification/disidentification, 39, 53–55, 281n21; imagined others of Asian/American women during, 13–14, 40, 53–54, 277n25; imago fantasies, 91–92; impact on actresses of, 49–51; of *Miss Saigon,* 38–41, 49–51; moralistic scopophilia in, 18–21, 104; onscenity/saturation of sexuality of, 24, 280n51; perversity in, 34–35; pleasure and pain in, 35–36, 40, 81–82, 86–87, 282n23; protest of, 53–54; as public and private act, 22; reception of, 98–99; visual paranoia in, 18–19; white male viewers of pornography, 102–3, 139, 290n21. *See also* unreliability of representation

Spelvin, Georgina, 156

Spivak, Gayatri, 188–89

Sprinkle, Annie, 143

Tarantino, Quentin, 60, 65
Teish, Luisah, 143, 178
Thief of Bagdad, The, 1, 27, 59, 65–66,
138, 286n24; costumes in, 67, 70–71,
73, 286n23; dragon lady's transfor-
mation in, 70–72; historical context
for, 136; perversity in, 67–72
third sex, 25
Thoma, Pamela, 279n46
Toll of the Sea, 26–27, 59, 286n24
Tom, Pam, 296–97n8
Travers, Peter, 270
Trinh T. Minh-ha, 142
Two Lies, 296–97n8
Two Nights and a Day, 109, 289n10
Tydings-McDuffie Act of 1934,
136–37

Under the Tuscan Sun, 268–69
unknowability of subjective experience. *See under* unreliability of
representation
unreliability of representation, 55, 88–
99; conundrums of self-
representations of hypersexuality,
11–13, 276n13; in Internet contexts,
164–65; political power and, 63, 96–
99; in pornography, 140–41, 175; in
sex tourist movies, 187–89, 214–22;
subjects-in-struggle and, 94–98; triangulation of self, actress, and role,
34–45, 51, 64, 94–100, 153–64,
282n26; unknowability of subjective
experience, 6, 20–21, 29, 49–51, 90,
98–99, 187–89, 214–24. *See also*
bind of representation
Uyehara, Denise, 64, 284n11

Very Bad Things, 286n37
Vietnam War contexts, 32, 44, 158–60,
162. See also *Miss Saigon*; sex tourist
movies

viewership. *See* spectatorship of
hypersexuality
violence. *See* pain/trauma/violence in
sexuality
Vivid girls, 166–67

Walker, Alice, 143, 178
Walk Like a Dragon, 148
Wallace, Michelle, 10, 283n55
Wang, Luoyang, 50
war brides, 17–18, 144, 150
Wartofsky, Alona, 194, 198
Watching Rape (Projansky), 213
Waugh, Tom, 108, 120–21, 124–25,
288n1, 289n8
websites. *See* Internet contexts
Wild at Heart, 292n29
Will and Grace, 278–79n40
Williams, Linda, 24, 104, 139, 280n51,
290n15, 291n40; on money shots,
166; on privileged position of white
male filmmakers, 197, 224; on stag
films, 135–36; on visualization of
women's sexuality, 142, 166
Wilson, Monique, 34
Wolf, Naomi, 142
Wolf, Stacy, 40, 52
Woman Outside, The, 187, 244
Wong, Anna May, 4, 26–27, 58–77,
286n24; as agent of pleasure and
power, 66, 285n16, 285n19; commentaries on roles of, 58, 66, 74,
88–90, 287n42, 287n46; critical
studies of, 61–62, 283–84n2; in-
fluence/iconicity of, 77, 84–85,
89, 288n61; later acting career of,
89; in *Shanghai Express*, 65, 72–
77; struggle for recognition by,
94–95; in *The Thief of Bagdad*,
65–72
Wong, Elizabeth, 89

❊ CELINE PARREÑAS SHIMIZU

is an associate professor of Asian American studies, film and media studies, and women's studies at the University of California, Santa Barbara. She is also the director of the films *Mahal Means Love and Expensive* (1993), *Her Uprooting Plants Her* (1995), *Super Flip* (1997), *The Fact of Asian Women* (2002), and *Birthright* (2007).